To Filip Bondy,

Thank you for y

being a great mentor!

Basketball Beyond Borders:
The Globalization
of the NBA

By
Chris Milholen

Cover Illustrator: Isaiah Batkay
Cover Image: Rick Bowmer via Associated Press

Basketball Beyond Borders: The Globalization of the NBA

By Chris Milholen

Amazon Kindle Direct Publishing
Copyright © 2019

Kindle Direct Publishing paperback edition December 2019

Manufactured in the United States

ISBN: 9781670469816
Imprint: Self Published

Dedicated to

Filip Bondy

My mentor, my guide, my professor

The Globalization of the NBA

Contents

Introduction

The 2018-19 NBA season was highlighted by Milwaukee Bucks Greek superstar Giannis Antetokounmpo being named the league's most valuable player. After winning the NBA's Most Valuable Player award, Antetokounmpo cemented his name as a new face of the NBA. A face that represents NBA Globalization.

He became the first foreign-born player to win the NBA honor since Dirk Nowitzki in 2007. In the history of the NBA, there have only been four players, including Antetokounmpo to win the NBA's Most Valuable Player award but that number is bound to rise just like the number of international players in the NBA is bound to rise. The international talent trend is reaching new heights as each year goes on but for the game of basketball, the narrative behind the globalization of the NBA has always been in the league's roots since its founding.

The game of basketball was born with international roots. Basketball was invented in 1891 by Dr. James Naismith, a Canadian physical education instructor, in Springfield, Massachusetts in 1891. The game of basketball started with local YMCA teams and handfuls of colleges.

As the game of basketball began to progress successfully, the National Basketball League was founded in 1898, becoming the first professional basketball league. The league lasted only until 1903, following a collapse due to teams departing the league but college basketball carried the game, gaining popularity across the United States.

Aside from becoming popular within the United States, the game did not begin to extend its international roots until 1946. The Basketball Association of America was founded on June 6, 1946. The BAA's first game was held in the famous Maple Leaf Gardens arena in Toronto, Canada, which featured a showdown between the New York Knickerbockers and the Toronto Huskies. Hank Biasatti, an Italian-Canadian, who is the first documented international basketball player, and Gino Sovran, a Canadian, were the founding pioneers of internationalization of basketball and were a part of the first wave of international players in the NBA. The NBA documents the history of the BAA, NBL, and ABA as their history. In addition to international talent participating in basketball, FIBA, the International Basketball Federation, grew the game of basketball in the founding international countries of Argentina, Czechoslovakia, Greece, Italy, Latvia, Portugal, Romania, and Switzerland. FIBA, founded in 1936 in Geneva, Switzerland, was sparked by the success of basketball on a global stage which dates to the game of basketball debuting as a demonstration sport in 1904 at the Summer Olympic Games, held in St. Louis, Missouri. Following the 1904 Summer Olympics, basketball vanished from the

Olympic Games until 1936, where it became an official medal event at the 1936 Summer Olympics, held in Berlin, Germany.

The National Basketball Association was founded on August 3, 1949, when the Basketball Association of America agreed to merge leagues with the National Basketball League. It was not until September 9, 1978, when the NBA decided to test global waters and play overseas. The NBA sent the Washington Bullets overseas to play in Israel against Maccabi Tel Aviv, a FIBA team, starting new beginnings for the league.

Throughout the history of the NBA, the league progressively gained international talent. It was not until 1984, where an international player received star notability. Hakeem Olajuwon became the first international born player drafted first overall in an NBA Draft, following a successful three-year run at the University of Houston.

Following Olajuwon, the number of international players in the NBA began to rise. From Patrick Ewing, Manute Bol, Drazen Petrovic, Dikembe Mutombo, Detlef Schrempf, Arvydas Sabonis, and many more, the NBA began to harvest some of the world best basketball talents.

As the game of basketball began to globalize each year, it was not until 1992 when the modern-NBA game was born. The 1992 United States men's basketball team, known as the "Dream Team," was made up of the NBA's greatest American-born talents such as Charles Barkley, Larry Bird, Magic Johnson, Michael Jordan, and six other players, which included Duke University's Christian Laettner. The "Dream Team" dominated and won gold. Their success spreads much farther than being crowned the best basketball nation in the world. Their dominance brought new fans across the world to the game of basketball and helped the NBA expand their notability across all borders of the world. Since the "Dream Team" dominated the global stage of basketball, their legacy will always be hovered around the global impact they made on basketball.

This book, *Basketball Beyond Borders: The Globalization of the NBA*, breaks down the history of the league globalizing. The book highlights international players, past and present, who not only helped spread the NBA and expand its borders across the world but their impact off the hardwood court and their legacy. On top of the long history of the greatest international players, this book breaks down historic events, teams, and themes that contributed to the NBA becoming one of the most popular global sport leagues in the world.

Chapter 1

Where Did Globalization Originate?

The term of *globalization* has many meanings and theories. Generally, globalization is the interaction among peoples and nations on a worldwide scale due to advances in communication and transportation. Globalization is not a recent development.

At this writing, the president of the United States is imposing another round of tariffs on products imported from the European Union, Canada, Mexico and China because all these areas responded to his first round of tariffs by putting tariffs on the American products they imported. It looks like a tariff war is under way. Imposing tariffs is, in a way, an attack on globalization that recent international phenomenon that gained new relevance in the 1980s and has mushroomed greatly ever since.[2]

Globalization is not new. Some scholars claim it was the great discovery of Christopher Columbus in 1492 that unleashed the era of great European exploration and the ultimate consequence of that era was worldwide trade. Columbus' discovery of the New World "effected the greatest commercial revolution in history before the coming of the airplane." [3] Europe gained new products from the Americas: the potato, tomato, artichoke, squash, and corn. The prices of gold and silver increased greatly because of their importation from the Americas; manufacturing increased as did trade between European nations.[2]

The term globalization was not generally in use until the early 1980s when Marshall McLuhan, the great Canadian communication theorist, popularized the term "the global village" as his definition of the world.[2]

No longer was the medieval motto of Gibraltar *ne plus ultra,* nothing further is out there, but it became *plus ultra,* more is out there.[2]

Globalization evolved around the 17th century as a private business phenomenon when chartered companies like British East India Company, founded in 1600, was often described as the first multinational corporation.[2]

The British East India Company, also known as the East India Company or John Company, was initially created to start trading with Southeast Asia, India, and East Asia. The main goal of the company was to expand British conquests, British control, and make money for the crown. The British East India Company wanted to compete with the Dutch and the Spanish who were very successful in international trading with nearby European countries at the time. The Queen of England, Queen Elizabeth I, wanted the company to succeed and be dominant. [3]

On December 31, 1600, Queen Elizabeth I gave the company a Royal Charter. A Royal Charter was a formal document issued by a monarch granting power or rights to a company or an individual person. The Royal Charter let the company technically become a nation without borders with the ability to issue royal orders, penalties, and to maintain its own army. It became a major factor in the development of international trade. [2]

For the next half of a century, the company ruled large areas of India and was very successful at trading. The company dominated the trading game until its downfall in 1857. The Indian Rebellion of 1857 battled against the British East India Company for a year and six months.[3] The rebellion ended with a downfall for the company and a transfer of rule to the British Crown due to the Government of India Act 1858.[2]

In 1874, The British East India Company eventually collapsed due to recurring financial problems. The financial problems were present due to the East India Stock Dividend Redemption Act which was passed in 1873. [2]

The British East India Company was instrumental in the initiation of globalization. The company not only was successful in trading goods, services, and making money but they passed their culture onto various countries.[2] Globalization is a key development which many businesses and corporations have hopped on.

The sports business industry is an industry that will never die and has its eyes on growth and development. The National Basketball Association, better known as the NBA is a professional basketball league in North America that has grown not just in popularity over the past couple of decades, but has it eyes on globalizing.

Chapter 2

The Game of Basketball is Born

Sports are created with two things in mind: passion and money. Primarily, a sport is invented with a focus on making a profit. Unlike most sports, the game of basketball was not focused on money at all at the time of its birth. Basketball was invented with one purpose, to have fun.

The game of basketball was invented in 1891 by James Naismith in Boston, Massachusetts. Dr. Naismith played four sports growing up. He played lacrosse, rugby, track, and soccer. While studying at Montreal's McGill University, Naismith participated in these sports making him a versatile college athlete. He was named McGill University's best all-around athlete twice. Naismith graduated from McGill University in 1887 advanced his studies at Presbyterian College in Montreal. He received his theology degree in 1890 but did not physically get the degree in his hands till 1915. [3]

Throughout his studies, Dr. Naismith stayed on the path of a physical instructor specializing in physical training. He wanted to use physical training as a motive to promote Christianity among young adult men.[3] Naismith planned on becoming a physical director and enrolled at YMCA Training School for the 1890-91 year. The course was new around the time Naismith enrolled at the YMCA Training School. The first course was offered in 1887 at the School for Christian Workers. After completing the course, Dr. Naismith was asked to stay on for the 1891-92 year but as an instructor.[3]

As an instructor in 1891, Dr. Naismith was teaching popular sports at the time: boxing, canoeing, swimming, and wrestling.[3]

Dr. Naismith was given an assignment to create a sporting game that was less injury-prone than football. Naismith played four sports growing up. He played lacrosse, rugby, track, and soccer.[3] His experiences with these sports helped generate ideas for his sport of basketball. At the time, football was the most popular sport in the United States. The game of football originated and grew from English rugby. Dr. Naismith played center on McGill University's football team. [3]

Dr. Naismith took over a class of eighteen prospective YMCA general secretaries. These eighteen people were all men who were required to take at least an hour of gym each day.[3] Due to the weather in Springfield, Massachusetts, outdoor play on fields was not always possible in the winter months. On top of the uneasy winter weather conditions, the class was boring and had the same regimen as the YMCA gymnasium programs.[3] When the position was handed to Naismith by the department's chairmen, Dr. Luther H.

Gulick, two instructors were confused and frustrated with the assignment, leaving Dr. Naismith to solve the problem.

> *"The trouble is not with the men but with the system we are using,"* Naismith told his workmates at faculty meetings. *"The kind of work for this particular class should be of a recreative nature, something that would appeal to their play instincts."* [3]

Dr. Naismith told Dr. Luther H. Gulick that it is possible to invent a new game and that the game should be easy to learn, intriguing, and accessible to play in the winter.

Dr. Gulick agreed with Dr. Naismith and gave him the green light to create a new game. Naismith would immediately trash the older system and instead focused his system around simple games. His class did not follow the new system leading to Dr. Naismith to try using the sports of lacrosse, rugby, and soccer but that did not work either. Dr. Naismith was discouraged and frustrated but that did not stop him from achieving his goal.[3]

Dr. Naismith would study popular sports breaking down each aspect of the sports. His goal was to create a simple sport that did not involve much equipment. The first thing he studied was the ball used in selective sports. Does the size of the ball matter? What size balls need equipment to use? Small balls would require more equipment. Examples of this are hockey, cricket, and lacrosse. Large balls did not need much or any equipment, soccer was an example. Naismith would decide to use a large ball so not much equipment was required, and simplicity would be accessible.[3]

Rugby, which evolved into the rising sport of American football, was the most popular sports at the time. The sport involved the use of a large ball. Dr. Naismith wanted his new sport to be played inside of a gymnasium. A game like rugby could not be played on a hardwood surface due to risk of serious injury. Dr. Naismith then realized what if they passed the ball and avoided tackling the problem would be solved; the answer was passing the ball.

Now that the fundamentals of the game were constructed, he only had to come up with the rules for the game; how would scoring work? Naismith focused the game around limited contact.[3] To have a game with limited contact, Naismith avoided the idea of ground scoring. Examples of sports that use ground scoring are football, hockey, and soccer. If Naismith was to lean towards ground scoring, the players would use excessive amounts of force to drive to the goal.

Dr. Naismith reflected on a childhood game called Duck on the Rock.[3] To achieve the best success in the game, the player had to throw the rock on an arcing angle. Dr. Naismith would incorporate that aspect of play into his new game and it would become the way to score the ball. He made the goal, in today's term, the basket, of his new game hang above the players heads which would avoid them to crowd around the goal to prevent a score.

The following day, Dr. Naismith asked the local janitor if he had any boxes to use as baskets for his new game. The janitor did not have boxes, but he gave Naismith two peach baskets. Once Dr. Naismith obtained the peach baskets, he climbed on a ladder and mounted the baskets on the lower railing of the gymnasium. Ironically, the distance between the floor and the baskets was ten feet which is the same distance today between the floor and the basketball hoops in the NBA and most leagues across the world. [3]

Dr. Naismith then created the thirteen rules of basketball on January 15, 1892. The thirteen rules state: [5]

1. The ball may be thrown in any direction with one or both hands.
2. The ball may be battered in any direction with one or both hands (never with the fist).
3. A player cannot run with the ball. The player must throw it from the spot on which he catches it, allowance to be made for a man who catches the ball when running at a good speed if he tries to stop it.
4. The ball must be held in or between both hands; the arms or body must not be used for holding it.
5. No shouldering, holding, pushing, tripping, or striking in any way the person of an opponent shall be permitted. The first infringement of this rule by any player shall count as a foul. The second shall result in disqualification until the next goal is made, or, if there was evident intent to injure the person, for the whole game, no substitute allowed.
6. A foul is striking at the ball with the fist, violation of Rules 3, 4, and such as described in Rule 5.
7. If either side (team) makes three consecutive fouls, it shall result in a goal for the opposing team.
8. A goal (now known as a basket) shall be made when the ball is thrown (shot) or battered from the grounds into the basket and stays there, providing those defending the goal do not touch or disturb the goal. If the ball rests on the edges, and the opponent moves the basket, it shall count as a goal.
9. When the ball goes out of bounds, it shall be thrown into the field of play by the person first touching it. In case of a dispute, the umpire (referee) shall throw it straight into the field. The thrower-in is allowed five second; if he hold it longer, it shall go to the opponent. If any side persists in delaying the game, the umpire shall call a foul on that side.

10. The umpire shall be judge of the men and shall not the fouls and notify the referee when three consecutive fouls have been made. He shall have the power to disqualify men according to Rule 5.

11. The umpire shall be the judge of the ball and shall decide when the ball is in play, in bounds, to which side it belongs, and shall keep the time. He shall decide when a goal has been made and keep account of the goals with any other duties that are usually performed by a referee.

12. The time shall be two 15- minute halves, with five minutes of rest in between.

13. The side making the most goals in that time shall be declared the winner. In case of a draw, the game may, by agreement of the captains, be continued until another goal is made.[5]

These original thirteen rules were published on January 15, 1891 in the Springfield College school newspaper, *The Triangle*. [3]

When the YMCA secretaries reported to class that morning, Dr. Naismith was ready to impress them with his new game. Naismith was so confident in his new game that if they were not impressed, he would not investigate other ideas of creating any other games.

During the exhibition game, many fouls were committed as expected but the game was a success. Within the following weeks, the game began to gain popularity with more than 200 people lining outside the gymnasium to get their shot at the new game. [3]

The first basketball game was held at the Springfield YMCA Training School in Massachusetts under Dr. Naismith's established rules on December 21, 1891. As small exhibition games continued for the next two years, in 1893, the game of basketball began to be played at handfuls of colleges.

Vanderbilt University is known to be the first college to form a basketball team. The Vanderbilt Basketball Team played its first game against a local YMCA team in Nashville, Tennessee on February 7, 1893.[12] Shortly after the establishment of the Vanderbilt Basketball Team, Geneva College was the second team to form a basketball team. Like Vanderbilt, Geneva College played their first game against New Brighton YMCA on April 8, 1893 in Beaver Falls, Pennsylvania. [3]

On February 9, 1895, the game of basketball started to evolve; the first collegiate basketball game was played. Hamline University faced Minnesota A&M. Minnesota A&M won the game nine-to-three. Individual games continued for the next couple of years but in 1898, the sports of basketball were formed into a professional league.[3]

Overall, the legacy of Dr. James Naismith will forever be hovered around his invention of the game of basketball. Today, Naismith is honored through several basketball awards in different divisions and leagues of basketball.

> *"Every season we celebrate the passion, tradition, and heritage of basketball that started with Dr. James Naismith's invention of this tremendous game,"* Eric Oberman, the Executive Director of the Atlanta Tipoff Club/ Naismith Awards said. *The presentation of the Naismith Trophy, basketball's most prestigious individual national award, is a way for our organization to honor his legacy and to reflect on his monumental contribution to sports."*

Chapter 3

The Early Evolution of Professional Basketball

The National Basketball League (1898-1904)

The first professional basketball league was founded in 1898. The league was named the National Basketball League (NBL). The league was the first basketball league in the world. The NBL was centered in Philadelphia, Pennsylvania but expanded north to the New York City and central New Jersey then towards Delaware. [7]

In its first season 1898-1899, the league had six teams. Three out of those six teams were based in the Philadelphia area: The Clover Wheelman, Germantown Nationals, and the Hancock Athletic Association.[7] The other three teams were based in the central New Jersey area: Millville Glass Blowers, Camden Electrics, and the Trenton Nationals.[7]

The National Basketball League had its debut game on December 1, 1898 at Textile Hall in Philadelphia. The Trenton Nationals played the Hancock Athletic Association in front of roughly 915 fans.[8] The first game was a competitive one displaying talent and excitement. The Nationals won the game 21 to 19.[8] Games continued throughout the season, but two teams collapsed in January 1899. Both of those teams were based in the Philadelphia area, but the other four teams competed throughout the rest of the season. The Trenton Nationals went on to win the first NBL Championship and finish the season with an 18-2-1 record. [8]

The NBL's second season was much more organized and stable. It was very important for the National Basketball League to establish a stable foundation entering its second season to gain popularity. The League established a new foundation by splitting into two sides. In post-modern terms, the NBL split into two conferences. One side contained the New York Wanderers, Camden Electrics, Pennsylvania Bicycle Club, Bristol Pile Drivers, Chester, PA, and the defending champions Trenton Nationals.[8] The team out of Chester, PA shortly dropped out but was replaced by the Millville team. Ironically, the Millville Glass Blowers initially decided not to participate in the second season of the league but decided to play after the departure of the Chester, PA team. [7]

Now that the teams were finalized, and the sides were decided, the National Basketball League began the 1900-1901 season with a total of seven teams. There were a couple of changes regarding teams but the finalized seven teams for the 1900-1901 season included the Trenton Nationals, Millville Glass Blowers, Bristol Pile Drivers, Camden Skeeters, Pennsylvania Bicycle Club, Burlington, and the New York Wanderers. [7]

With a stable league and popularity rising, the season schedule increased to a 32-game season.[8] This was a big increase for the league with many wonderings if teams would drop and the league would slowly collapse. The 1900-1901 season was a successful one with five of the seven total teams finishing with a winning record. Throughout the season, the NBL grew in popularity due to competitive play for most of the season. The New York Wanderers dominated the 1900-1901 season winning the League title. The NBL did not need a playoff campaign that season due to the Wanderers winning record. New York led by three games and won the league title. [7]

With the 1900-1901 season being a successful one of the NBL, there were high expectations for the new season. Due to the high expectations, the league once again extended their schedule to 40 total games and contained six teams; Bristol, Camden, Millville, Philadelphia, Trenton, and the defending champions New York.[8] Fans were familiar with the six teams from the previous season which boosted popularity and gave the NBL confidence to succeed.

With the new 40 game schedule, no teams would drop out in the NBL's third season and all the six teams were good. This gave the NBL a competitive appeal for fans and the six teams. Throughout the 1901-1902 season, all games were competitive and appealing to fans. In the end, the Bristol Pile Drivers took home the championship by three games and finished the season with a 28-12 winning record. [8]

The 1902-1903 season for the National Basketball League was a season in decline when the league started to fall apart. At first it looked like the National Basketball League was destined for another good season. The 1902-1903 season once again had two halfs. The first half contained The Bristol Pile Drivers, Burlington Shoe Pegs, Camden Electrics, Conshohocken, Philadelphia Phillies, New York Wanderers, and the Trenton Potters. The second half of the season had only six teams: Camden Electrics, Burlington Shoe Pegs, Wilmington Peaches, Trenton Potters, Conshohocken, and the New York Wanderers. [7]

Shortly into the second half of the season, disaster started to strike. Frank Reber, the head coach and owner of the Burlington Shoe Pegs decided to fire his whole team after poor performances.[8] In replacement to the Burlington team, Frank Reber brought the Bristol team and used their players to represent and play for Burlington. Shortly after the move, Phillies manager Frank Morgenweck fled from his team and purchased the Wilmington team. [8]

The Camden Electrics who was coached by Frank Morgenweck's brother Billy had a great season finishing with a 36-9 record and taking home the title.[7]

The off-season of 1903 is when the league started to fall apart. Only five teams decided to play the following season with the rest departing or failing to return. When the 1903-1904 season began, only five teams took part: the Camden Electrics, Trenton Potters, Conshohocken, Millville Glass Blowers, and the new St. Bridget's Biddies.[8] Shortly into the season, the Trenton Potters departed from the National Basketball League in December 1903. Camden would follow Trenton out of the National Basketball League five days after. This would lead to the collapse of the National Basketball League and on January 4, 1903 the league was abandoned. Billy Morgenweck was sued by the investors of the Camden Electrics shortly after but there was no other controversy behind the National Basketball League collapse. [8]

College Basketball (1893- 1938)

Shortly after the collapse of the first National Basketball League in 1903, college basketball across the United States began to grow tremendously. As mentioned before, college basketball began in 1893 when Vanderbilt University played against a local YMCA team in Nashville, Tennessee.

In 1900, the game of basketball spread throughout American colleges and universities. The first recorded college tournament in the United States was played in 1898: The Amateur Athletic Union's annual U.S. national championship tournament.[12] Today the Amateurs Athletic Union is best known as AAU. The tournament consisted of many colleges and universities spread across the United States which not only boosted the game of basketball to a whole new level but established college basketball. The main four college basketball teams were Butler, NYU, Utah, and Washburn.[10] All these teams won at least one title in the first two decades of the AAU national championship tournament. A bonus to these four team's successes is that they were spread across the country from New York to Utah.[8]

In 1904, the first documented tournament which exclusively featured college teams was the 1904 Summer Olympics held in St. Louis, Missouri.[16] This labeled basketball as a promoting sport, gaining popularity, also known as a demonstration sport. Basketball at the 1904 Summer Olympics included a collegiate championship tournament and was won by Hiram College, a private liberal arts college in Ohio. The 1904 Summer Olympics grew the popularity of college basketball which led to small nation-wide tournaments. [16]

In 1922, the first stand-alone post-season college tournament was established, the 1922 National Intercollegiate Basketball Tournament. The tournament was held in Indianapolis, Indiana and included the champions of the six major conferences across the United States. Initially, there were going to be eight conferences, but the Eastern Intercollegiate League and the Western Conference did not participate. [15]

The six conferences present in the 1922 National Intercollegiate Basketball Tournament were:

- Indiana Intercollegiate Athletic Association
- Illinois Intercollegiate Athletic Conference
- Michigan Intercollegiate Athletic Association
- Pacific Coast Conference
- Southern Intercollegiate Athletic Association
- Western Pennsylvania League [15]

In the end, Wabash College went on the win the tournament which led to the establishment of tournaments across the United States. The National Association of Intercollegiate Athletics Men's Basketball National Championship was held in 1937 but was outplayed by the National Invitation Tournament (NIT) which gained great amounts of popularity in 1938.[15] The NIT bought in six teams to compete for the championship in Madison Square Garden, New York. Temple went on to win the tournament beating Colorado to win the first NIT championship. [15]

After the first year of the NIT tournament, the National Collegiate Athletic Association (NCAA) tournament was established in 1939. [15] The NCAA tournament was a monumental tournament establishment which grew in popularity each year and is currently the biggest college basketball tournament across the United States and arguably the world.

Chapter 4

The Basketball Association of America

On June 6, 1946, the Basketball Association of America known as the BAA was founded in North America. With the establishment of the BAA, there were two other professional basketball leagues in the United States at the time: the American Basketball League and the National Basketball League. Both the ABL and the NBL played in small areas and in some cases small rooms across the United States limiting their popularity.

The BAA came to life after Maurice Podoloff, who was the president of the American Hockey League took on the idea of Walter Brown, owner of the Boston Garden, about empty hockey stadiums at night time should be a place for basketball. [19] Maurice Podoloff put this idea by Brown into action which established the BAA and he would eventually become the president of the BAA. After being appointed the president of the BAA, Podoloff was the first professional owner at the time to run two professional leagues in the United States while both leagues were running at the same time. [19]

The BAA was a well-organized league filled with owners who were experienced in business practices. Although the owners of the BAA were experienced in business, only very few of them had any experience when it came to sports management. To go along with the experienced business backgrounded owners, the BAA attempted to host their games in big market stadiums and arenas.[19] The league aimed to host games at Madison Square Garden and the Boston Garden, arguably the two most well-known arenas on the upper east coast of the United States.

The only downside to the BAA's establishment was the lack of talent in their league. The talent in the BBA was not quite equal to the other American basketball leagues at the time, which played a role in the BAA gaining popularity.

The BAA's Inaugural Season: 1946-1947

The Basketball Association of America had its inaugural season in 1946. The league consisted of 11 teams which were divided into two divisions; the Eastern Division and the Western Division. [18]

Each team in the BAA was given a schedule of 61 games but some teams only played in 60 of them due to their schedules. For a team to advance to the playoffs, it must finish in the top three of their division.[18] In other words, the top three teams of each BAA division advanced to the playoffs. The division's leading team by the end of the regular season was given a first-round bye and automatically advanced to the semifinal round.[19] The other two teams in each division would be obligated to compete in a best-of-three series and the winners of those series would advance to the semifinal round. Like the current NBA playoff format, the BAA final consisted of a best-of-seven series and the winner would be awarded the BAA championship.

The BAA's first game was a showdown between the Toronto Huskies and the New York Knickerbockers on November 1, 1946. The league's first game was held at the famous Maple Leaf Gardens arena in Toronto, Canada.[20] The game consisted of competitive play throughout the game thrilling the fans in attendance. In the end, the New York Knickerbockers went on to win the game 68-to-66.[17] Leo Gottlieb was the leading scorer in the win with 14 points.[17]

When playoffs came around, the Washington Capitols topped the Eastern Division with 49 wins and the Chicago Stags topped the Western Division.[18] In the end, the Philadelphia Warriors took home the BAA's first championship beating the Chicago Stags four games to one in the final series. [18]

The first season for the Basketball Association of America was a success but faced a couple of obstacles along the way. The biggest problem the BAA faced was their financial stability.[18] The league's teams struggled to profit throughout the season on each game. Despite its financial problems, the league was able to keep running due to the talent of the players keeping the league alive. A lot of the teams were made up of well-known college athletes who boosted the attendance.[18] The other big problem was within the facilities. Due to many of the stadiums and arenas sharing the facility with hockey teams, the basketball courts commonly faced trouble with water.[18] Owners of the facilities would place the wooden basketball court over the hockey ice resulting in wet surfaces and cancellation of games. This did not happen very often but occurred a couple times throughout the BAA's inaugural season. Another big obstacle the BAA faced was heating the facilities. Due to the hockey ice, owners would not heat the facilities resulting in a low number of fans.[18] The fans in attendance would often wear layers of clothing or leave early due to the cold. These were minor problems in the BAA's first season but let's get into the on-the-court problems.

In the inaugural season, the BAA did not establish a shot-clock rule. This gave teams the privilege of holding the ball for long periods of time which could go on for minutes. It was briefly discussed before the season was underway about making the game 60 minutes or have time periods. Holding the ball not only upset the opposing team but led to fans booing or losing interest in the game. The biggest loss regarding holding the ball was the other team. Not only did the game lose competitive action but would give the opposing teams limited time to take back the lead. [19]

Overall, the first season for the BAA was a successful one. Since the founding of the BAA, the league had its eyes on becoming not only a popular professional league but a major league sports in the United States. With their eyes on becoming a professional league, the BAA stood out from its basketball league rival, the National Basketball League. The BAA not only put on longer games than the NBL but had a higher foul limit per player. The BAA players were given a total of six fouls before being disqualified. The NBL went by the five foul limit which resulted in many disqualifications and lower intensity. [18] Following the inaugural season, there were a couple NBL players who took their talents to the BAA. With the BAA gaining professional basketball talent, the league grew in popularity and showed they could take over the professional basketball spotlight in the United States.

The 1947-1948 Season

With all eyes on how the Basketball Association of America would do in its second season, the league started with a disastrous twist. A couple of months before the start BAA's second season, four teams withdrew from the league. The four teams were the Cleveland Rebels, Detroit Falcons, Pittsburgh Ironmen, and the Toronto Huskies.[19] The four departures struck fear in the BAA leaving it with only seven teams but not for long. The Baltimore Bullets, an ABL league team joined the BAA giving the league stability. With the addition of the Baltimore Bullets, the BAA evenly divided both divisions by assigning the Baltimore Bullets and moving the Washington Capitols to the Western Division.[19]

On July 1, 1947, the BAA held its first college draft.[15] The draft would allow all teams to pick a couple of players to join their squad. The addition of the college draft drew in more fans and increased the popularity of the league. To go along with the boost in popularity, the league was gaining more talent and distributing it evenly.

For the BAA's second season, the league established a 48 regular game season. In its first season, the BAA had just about twenty more games. [18] The cutting of the schedule was a beneficial move for the league especially with its struggling financial situation. The 48-game season gave the league a bigger boost in finances and built up its financial situation.

The league did not change its playoff format entering its second season due to the competitive play and the popularity success. When playoffs came around the Philadelphia Warriors would win the Eastern Division while the Western Division was won by the St. Louis Bombers. [18] Both teams would have a successful playoff run and would eventually meet in the final round. The Warriors ended up winning the finals series 4-to-2 against the Bombers achieving back-to-back BAA champions.[18]

The off-season for the BAA was not as shaky as the previous off-season. The league only faced small financial problems but quickly turned itself around by adding four new teams to the league. Once again, the BAA stole talent from its rival league, the NBL, but this time the league was stealing teams. The BAA stole four teams that were a part of the NBL. The four teams which joined the BAA were the Fort Wayne Pistons, the Indianapolis Jets, the Minneapolis Lakers, and the Rochester Royals.[18] The four-team addition not only added come competition to each division but a massive gain in talent. Those four teams were arguably title contenders in the NBL and had big market players fans were very familiar with.

Due to the sudden addition of four teams to the BBA, the league had to adjust its divisions and change its playoff format. Both the Eastern Division and the Western Division contained six teams. The league also increased its schedule back to a 60-game schedule. Regarding the playoffs, there were now eight total teams from each conference that can make the playoffs: four from each division.

The regular season was very bright for the BBA. The season was filled with competitive play bringing in more fans to every game. In their third season, the BBA set league records for attendance and popularity. The Eastern Division was once again won by the Washington Capitols. The Capitols went on to win 38 regular season games.[19] The Western Division was more competitive during the regular season due to the BBA's two new teams: the Minneapolis Lakers and the Rochester Royals. Both teams went on to the final regular season game to crown a Western Division winner. In the end, the Royals would head to the playoffs on top of the Western Division with 45 total wins. The Lakers came up just short with 44 wins. [19]

When the playoffs came around, both divisions put on great playoff performances which thrilled the fans in attendance. The BAA set personal records for playoff attendance and eight teams put on great games. In the end, the Minneapolis Lakers advanced to the finals in the Western Division while the Washington Capitols won the Eastern Division punching their ticket to the final round. The Lakers would go on and win the finals defeating the Capitols four games to two. [19]

Chapter 5

The End of the BAA and the Founding of the National Basketball Association

On March 21, 1949, the BAA held their final college draft.[18] This was the second draft the BAA hosted, and it was a success. Many teams gained valuable talent needed in their rosters making the league more competitive.

Heading into the off-season, talks were constantly growing between the Basketball Association of America and the National Basketball League regarding a joining of leagues. The National Basketball League at the time was not doing as great as it once was, while the Basketball Association of America was growing each season. Over its past couple of years, the NBL lost talent from select players to teams to the BAA. [21]

On August 3, 1949, the Basketball Association of America agreed to merge leagues with the National Basketball League. [21] The move headlined through the United States sports media world. The joining of the two leagues created the National Basketball Association (NBA). The NBA, to this date, documents the BAA's history as their own and calls the move an expansion, not necessarily a merge.

The six NBL teams: Anderson, Denver, Sheboygan, Syracuse, Tri-Cities, and Waterloo joined forces with the ten BAA teams making the merge.[21] Shortly after the merge was announced, the Indianapolis Jets and the Providence Steamrollers dropped out. While the Jet and the Steamrollers dropped out, the Indianapolis Olympians joined the NBA. After the moves, the NBA had 17 total teams spread out across the United States. In addition to the spread of teams, all teams played in various well-known stadiums or arenas in great locations. [21]

With the NBA beginning its official first season in 1949, the new league recognizes the three prior BAA seasons as part of its own history (1946-47, 1947-48, and 1948-49). [21]

The NBA's first season was made up of 68 total games for their 17 teams. The regular season ran from October 29, 1949 till March 19, 1950. [21]

The Syracuse Nationals went on to win the Eastern Division with a record of 51 wins and 13 losses (.797). Out of their 68 total games, the Nationals played 44 games against Western Division teams, which were weaker compared to the Eastern Division teams. To go along with the struggles of the Western Division teams, none of their teams won more than half of their games against teams outside of their division. Five of the six Eastern Division teams went on to play 68 games that season; Syracuse played 64 games.[21]

In the Central Division, the Minneapolis Lakers would tie its division with a record of 51 wins and 17 losses (.750) with the Rochester Royals: also going 51-and-17 (.750). To determine placing in the division, the Minneapolis Lakers and the Rochester Royals played against one game against each other while the Chicago Stags and the Fort Wayne Pistons played prior to the 1950 NBA Playoffs. In the Central Division, five teams went on to play 68 games. [21]

In the Western Division, the Indianapolis Olympians came on top of the division with a record of 39 wins and 25 losses (.609) followed by the Anderson Packers, who recorded a record of 37 wins and 27 losses. [21]

When the 1950 NBA Playoffs came around, the Syracuse Nationals became the Eastern Champions, Minneapolis Lakers were the Central Champions, and Anderson Packers were the Western Champions. The New York Knicks were the Eastern runners-up, Fort Wayne Pistons were the Central Division runner-up, and the Indianapolis Olympians were the Western runners-up.[21] The 1950 NBA Playoffs ran from March 20, 1950 till April 6, 1950. The first official NBA Finals ran from April 8, 1950 till April 23, 1950. The Minneapolis Lakers would go on to in the NBA Championship beating the Syracuse Nationals four games to two crowing the Lakers as the first NBA Champions.

Chapter 6

The First Wave: International Players Take on the NBA

Hank Biasatti (Italian-Canadian, 1946)

After a successful first season for the National Basketball Association (NBA), the league was predominantly made up of North American players. The first documented international basketball player was Hank Biasatti in 1946.[27] Hank Biasatti was an Italian-Canadian player born in Beano, Italy. He grew up in Windsor, Ontario, where he became a star athlete in both basketball and baseball. Before he would pursue a professional career in athletics, Biasatti would serve in the Canadian Army in World War II. [28]

When he returned, Biasatti was a part of the Toronto Maple Leafs baseball team in International League. In addition to being a player with the Maple Leafs, he played for the 1943 London Army Team and during the war, Biasatti played for the London Majors in 1944 and 1945. [28]

While with the Majors in 1945, Hank Biasatti won the International Baseball League and the Ontario Baseball Association senior title. [28]

In 1946, Biasatti was invited to the inaugural training camp of the Toronto Huskies of the BAA. The Huskies were preparing for the first season of the BAA which led to becoming the National Basketball Association in 1949. Biasatti was one of six Canadians invited to the camp but was the only Canadian to make the team.[6] His Assumption College teammate Gino Sovran, who was a professional Canadian basketball player would join Biasatti and the Toronto Huskies a couple weeks after the beginning of the season. Gino Sovran and Hank Biasatti would go on to be the only Canadian players to play for the Huskies. [6]

Hank Biasatti played in the first game of the Basketball Association of America. Biasatti and the Toronto Huskies played the New York Knickerbockers on November 1, 1946.[17] He would go on to only play in six games for the Huskies and average 1.0 points and .400 percent from the field. Biasatti averaged less than field goal attempt in those six games but is known as the first professional international player to play in the NBA. His game-high points with the Huskies was two points. [25]

Biasatti left the Huskies after six games due to his passion to play the main sport he loved baseball. In December of 1946, Biasatti was handed an outright release from the Huskies. He told the Huskies we would be attending training camp for the Philadelphia Athletics, the professional baseball franchise which is today the Oakland Athletics. [28]

Despite being released by the Huskies, Biasatti was selected by the Boston Celtics in the 1947 Basketball Association of America's Draft. Biasatti never played a game for the Celtics and returned to baseball. [26]

Hank Biasatti would go on to have a successful professional baseball career following his departure from basketball. In 1947, Biasatti re-joined the Savannah Indians of the South Atlantic League. He would bat just under .300 for the Indians that season finishing second in home runs.[6]

In 1948, Biasatti re-joined the Toronto Maple Leafs and had another successful season hitting 21 home runs which was a team high.[6] The following season, 1949, Biasatti joined the Athletics professional team. He would play in 21 games for the team and started in four of them. In those 21 games, Biasatti was a pinch hitter 13 times for the team and played first base eight times. In the off-season, Biasatti joined the Buffalo Bisons, an International League team, but only lasted with the team through 1951. Biasatti took a job as a player-manager for another International League team, the Waterloo Tigers playing first base and roles as a pitcher in 1953. [6]

The following season, Biasatti ended his playing career and pursued a managerial role with the Drummondville A's, a team in the Quebec Provincial League in 1954. In 1955, he managed the Lancaster Red Roses, a Class B team in the Piedmont League. The Piedmont League played from 1920 until 1955. [6]

With the Piedmont League ending, Biasatti went back to his basketball roots. In 1956, he was named the head basketball coach of Assumption University, formerly known as Assumption College, where he played basketball before entering the Canadian Army during the Early Cold War.

In his first season as head coach, Biasatti led the team to the Ontario-Quebec Senior Intercollegiate Basketball League Championship. He would go on to be the head coach of Assumption University for six seasons before retiring from all professional athletic duties. [26]

In 1982, Hank Biasatti was inducted into the Windsor/Essex County Sports Hall of Fame. He was also inducted into the University of Windsor Alumni Sports Hall of Fame in 1986 and the Canadian Basketball Hall of Fame in 2001. Hank Biasatti died at the age of 74 but his legacy lives on forever.

Gino Sovran (Canadian, 1946)

As noted before, the other Canadian to join the Toronto Huskies, Gino Sovran. Gino Sovran, who was one of the NBA's first international players, began his basketball career with Hank Biasatti at Assumption College from 1942 till 1946.[29] While at Assumption with Biasatti, Sovran capped more than one thousand career points and was the team captain for his final two seasons at the College. Gino Sovran averaged 17.1 points as a junior at the college. [29]

Gino Sovran played for the University of Detroit as a member of the Detroit Mercy. He excelled at Detroit Mercy and was the team's leading scorer in the one season he was there (1945-1946). Later, Sovran rejoined Hank Biasatti at Assumption College helping the team win the Ontario and Eastern Canada senior basketball championships in 1946.

> *"It was from a man in Toronto whose name I recognized because he had been the sports editor of the Windsor newspaper,"* Gino Sovran told the NBPA in 2016. *"He told me there's going to be a new professional basketball league, and Toronto is going to have a team in it. Are you interested in trying out for it? Since I was in a work semester of an engineering program at Detroit, I said, 'Well, why not?'"*[29]

Sovran joined Biasatti in Toronto and signed with the Huskies two weeks into the season. He made his debut with the Huskies on November 22, 1946 against the Boston Celtics.[30] Like Biasatti, Sovran would not last long with the Huskies playing in only six games with the team. He was waived by the Huskies on December 29, 1946. In those six games, Sovran averaged 1.8 points and 0.2 assists closing his professional basketball career. [30]

In 1997, Sovran was inducted into the University of Windsor Alumni Sports Hall of Fame. He was later inducted into the Canadian Basketball Hall of Fame in 2002. He was also honored and recognized at several Toronto Raptors games, including the 50th anniversary of the Huskies first game with the surviving members of that Huskies team and the Knicks team at center court. Gino Sovran was the last surviving member of those two teams before his passing in 2016.[29]

In addition to his professional basketball career, Sovran was a track and field athlete in high school setting records in the events high jump and triple jump during his days as a student.

Sovran earned his doctoral degree from the University of Minnesota and worked for General Motors as a research engineer for 40 years before retiring at the age of 70.[29]

Bob Houbregs (Canadian, 1953)

Bob Houbregs, a Canadian basketball player, entered the NBA in 1953. He was selected as the second overall pick in the 1953 NBA Draft by the Milwaukee Hawks.[31]

Prior to entering the NBA, Bob Houbregs was a student athlete and played college basketball at the University of Washington from 1950-1953. The 6-foot-7 Canadian led Washington to its only Final Four appearance in his final year at the University and averaged 34.8 points per game in the postseason. He was Washington's leading scorer until the 1980s. Houbregs currently ranks fifth on that list with 1774 career points. [31]

Houbregs' number 25 was retired by the University and won many honors and awards during his college playing days.

- Three time First-team All-PCC (1951-1953)
- Consensus second-team All-American (1952)
- Consensus first-team All-American (1953)
- Helms Foundation Player of the Year (1953) [32]

Coming into the NBA, Bob Houbregs was viewed as a great center/power forward who could change an NBA franchise. Houbregs was a star at Washington and showed serious potential to be a great future NBA player.

Houbregs played the 1953-1954 season with two teams; the Milwaukee Hawks and the Baltimore Bullets. In 1954, Houbregs played for the Boston Celtics and played with the Fort Wayne Pistons in 1954 as well until the end of his five-year career in 1958. He wore five numbers during his five-year career; 10, 14, 20, 8, and 17. [32]

In his five-year career, Houbregs averaged 9.3 points, 5.5 rebounds, and 1.8 assists per game. His career totals were 2,611 points, 1,522, and 500 assists. [32]

During his post professional basketball career, Houbregs served as the general manager for the Seattle SuperSonics for three years (1970-1973).

He was elected to the Naismith Basketball Hall of Fame in 1987 and was inducted into the Canadian Basketball Hall of Fame in 2000. He died on May 28, 2014. [33]

Scott Woodward, University of Washington's athletic director has high praise for Houbregs following the news of his passing.

"Bob was an icon in our community. His efforts on the court helped put Washington basketball on the map, but what made him remarkable was his character beyond the game of basketball. He had a way of connecting with people in a very genuine manner, and his presence will be truly missed here." [33]

Chris Harris (British, 1955)

With the first two notable NBA international players coming from Canada, Chris Harris took a different journey to get to the NBA. Christopher R. Harris, better known as Chris Harris, moved from Southampton England to New York City when he was a young kid. [40]

Chris Harris, who is best known for his time as a British sports broadcaster, was the first player from England to compete in the NBA. The British ball player is also the first foreign born player to go undrafted in the NBA's history. [40]

When Chris Harris moved to New York City, his family had strong ties to their new country. His family, for generations, was involved in Atlantic shipping trades on both sides of his family. [40]

Harris played his high school basketball at Sewanhaka High School in Floral Park, New York. [40] The name of the high school translates to "Island of Shells" in English and is located on Long Island.

While at Sewanhaka, Harris excelled at basketball leading to the University of Dayton rewarding him with an athletic scholarship at 18 years old. Harris began his college ball career in 1951 during the Korean War which began in 1950. During the Korean War, freshman college athletes were able to be a part of varsity level teams giving Harris the opportunity to join the varsity team. [40]

During his freshman season with Dayton, Harris was a big contributor to their success. Don Meineke, who was Harris' teammate at Dayton and was selected with the 12th overall pick in the 1952 NBA Draft, led the Flyers during Harris' rookie season. The Flyers went 28-5 in Harris' first season but would lose in the National Invitational Tournament (NIT) final game to La Salle 75-64 on March 15, 1952 at Madison Square Garden in New York City. [40] The National Invitational Tournament (NIT) final game is now considered the National Championship game.

Chris Harris' sophomore season was not nearly as successful as his rookie season. With Meinke now in the NBA, the Flyers had a disappointing season going 16-13 and did not advance to the National Invitational Tournament (NIT). [39]

A notable highlight of Harris' sophomore season with the Flyers was when he played a full game and took down top ranked Seton Hall University on March 1, 1953, the second-to-last game of the season. The win handed Seton Hall their first loss in 28 games. [6]

Harris' junior year was a successful season with the Flyers having a talented roster. The Flyers went 25-7 behind Harris, Bill Uhl, who was an All-American, Jack Sallee, and Don Donoher, who became the Flyers head coach a decade later (1964-1989). Despite going 25-7, the Flyers lost in the National

Invitational Tournament (NIT) Quarterfinals to Niagara 77-74 on March 8, 1954 ending their season. [40]

Now in his senior season, Chris Harris had his eyes on making it to the NBA. His skill set matched up with his potential to be an NBA player specializing in defense. Harris and the Flyers punched their ticket to the National Invitational Tournament going 21-3. Dayton cruised past the first round beating St. Louis. In that game, Harris set a Madison Square Garden record with 13 total assists.[39] The Flyers did not stop there, they beat Maurice Stokes and St. Francis in overtime winning 79-73. Harris and the Flyers had once again made it to the National Invitational Tournament final to take on Duquesne University, which were ranked number four. Well just like his freshman season, Harris and the Flyers would lose in the finals to a final score of 70-58 on March 19, 1955. [40]

As noted before, Chris Harris was not drafted in the 1955 NBA Draft. He signed with the St. Louis Hawks, now known as the Atlanta Hawks, but was traded only 15 games into his rookie season to the Rochester Royals for Jack Coleman and Jack McMahon. Harris played a total of 41 games during his rookie season and averaged 2.5 points. [38]

Harris decided to end his NBA career after his rookie season to pursue a new business while his wife was pregnant with his first child. Despite stepping away from professional basketball after one season, Hawks coach Alex Hannum asked Harris to rejoin the team to bring guard depth, but he declined the offer.[40] Ironically, the Hawks won the NBA Championship that same year.

This would not be the end of Harris' involvement in basketball. The former British basketball player became a sports broadcaster for his alma mater, the University of Dayton. Chris Harris was a play-by-play basketball announcer for WHIO Radio on CBS from 1965 till 1981 and was known as "the Voice of the Flyers." Harris additionally served as the stations' sports director. [41]

In 2013, Harris was inducted into the University of Dayton Athletic Hall of Fame for his play on the court and his broadcasting off the court.

At the time of this writing, Chris Harris, who is 85 years old, is active in the National Basketball Retired Players Association.[40]

In an interview with MVP Ultimate Basketball, Chris Harris said he would be open to work at an NBA office in the United Kingdom. Unfortunately, the offer never came his way.

> *"No. I couldn't have even imagined that. I ran into a guy from the NBA at a Retired Players Association event and he told me they were opening a UK office. I told them I'd be happy to go over and see my old country." [41]*

Despite not getting the call, Chris Harris is forever known as the first international basketball player to play in the NBA from England.

Mike D'Antoni (Italian-American, 1973)

Mike D'Antoni, current Houston Rockets head coach at the time of this writing, is known today as one of the best coaches since the late 1990s for his fast-paced offensive system. Before Mike D'Antoni became one of the most well-known coaches of the 21st century, he was one of the first successful international players in the National Basketball Association.

Mike D'Antoni, who holds dual American and Italian citizenship, was born in West Virginia in 1951. He played his high school basketball at Mullens High School in Mullens, West Virginia. Mullen High School has produced many professional athletes including one other NBA player, Scott Wedman, who played 12 years in the league with the Kansas City-Omaha/Kings, Cleveland Cavaliers, and Boston Celtics. Mullens also produced Brendan Winters, son of former NBA coach Brian Winters. Brendan went on to play five seasons overseas with Nantes of the Pro B league in France, Bayer Giants Leverkusen of the Pro B league in Germany, Atomeromu SE of the Nemzeti Bajnoksag league in Hungary, and Aris in the Greek league in Greece.[47]

Mike D'Antoni played his college basketball at Marshall University for three seasons before declaring for the 1973 NBA Draft. He was selected by the Kansas City-Omaha Kings with the 20th pick of the second round. D'Antoni played three seasons for the Kings from 1973-1975 and averaged 3.4 points, 1.9 assists, and 1.2 steals. After his three seasons with the Kings, D'Antoni played for the Spirits of St. Louis in the American Basketball Association (ABA). He played with St. Louis for only one season (1975-1976) before returning to the National Basketball Association as a member of the San Antonio Spurs. Despite returning to the NBA as a member of the Spurs, his time there was limited to two games before jumping on an opportunity to play overseas. [47]

As said before, D'Antoni who has Italian citizenship and took his skills overseas to play for Olimpia Milano of the Italian LBA league. [48] His playing career overseas was nothing like his play in the United States. D'Antoni played from 1977-1990 with Milano ending his playing career with a decorative resume.

- His number 8 retired by Olimpia Milano
- Two times EuroLeague Champion (1987, 1988)
- Five times LBA Champion (1982, 1985, 1986, 1987, 1989)

- Two times Italian Cup Winner (1986, 1987)
- FIBA International Cup Champion (1987)
- Korac Cup Champion (1985)
- 50 Greatest Contributors in EuroLeague History (2008 Honoree)
- Voted Italian LBA league's top point guard of all-time (1990) [48]

Mike D'Antoni was selected to play on the senior men's Italian national team for the
1989 EuroBasket Tournament. [46]

Today, Mike D'Antoni, also known as "Il Baffo" which is Italian for "The Mustache," is Olimpio Milano's all-time leading scorer and is known as one of the best defensive guards in Italian LBA league's history. [48]

Despite putting his playing shoes away and calling a celebrated playing career, D'Antoni jumped right into coaching for Olimpio Milano. He coached the club from 1990 to 1994. In those four years, he led his team to the 1992 FIBA EuroLeague Final Four appearance and a 1992-93 Fiba Korac Cup title. After D'Antoni and Olimpio Milano parted ways, he took his coaching talents to Benetton Treviso, another Italian basketball club.[48]

Mike D'Antoni was the head coach of Benetton Treviso from 1994-1997 leading his new team to a FIBA European Cup and Italian Cup in 1995 and won the Italian National Domestic league title in his last season (1996-97). [47]

Following his coaching at Benetton Treviso, D'Antoni got the call to coach in the National Basketball Association for the 1997-98 season. He was named the Nuggets Director of Player Personnel and did some broadcasting work for TNT covering the NBA. The following year, D'Antoni was named the head coach of the Nuggets but was relieved of his duties after an unsuccessful tenure during the lockout season 1998-99.[46]

Mike D'Antoni was then be hired by the San Antonio Spurs as a scout for the 1999-2000 season followed by an assistant coaching position with the Portland Trail Blazers for the 2000-01 season.

After two quick jobs with the Spurs and Trailblazers, D'Antoni was hired by the Phoenix Suns as an assistant head coach in 2002. In 2003, he was promoted to head coach of the Suns.

D'Antoni was the head coach of the Suns from 2003 to 2008 and was a successful head coach during that tenure. He did a great job developing NBA Hall of Fame guard Steve Nash in his fast-paced offense. While under D'Antoni, Nash was a two-time Most Valuable Player (2005, 2006) and a six-time All-Star (2002, 2003, 2005, 2006, 2007, 2008).

Due to his success with the Suns, D'Antoni was selected to the Team USA coaching staff for the 2006 FIBA World Championship. [46] He was an assistant coach under current Duke University head coach Mike Krzyzewski. Team USA took home Bronze Medals for the 2006 FIBA World Championship.

D'Antoni's success as head coach got him promoted to Suns general manager in 2007 but have the position to current Golden State Warriors head coach Steve Kerr on June 2, 2007. Kerr would retire from his Suns general manager duties in June 2010. [46]

After the Suns were eliminated in the 2008 playoffs, D'Antoni decided it was time for a change. Steve Kerr wanted him to stay with the team but allowed him to listen to head coaching offers and speak to teams interested in him. When all things were said and done, D'Antoni departed Phoenix for the big apple, New York City to coach under the Madison Square Garden lights.

D'Antoni agreed to a four-year contract with the New York Knicks to become their head coach. [47]

His first two seasons as the Knicks head coach were not successful. Amar'e Stoudemire, who played for D'Antoni with the Suns left Phoenix reunited with his former coach in New York in 2010. On February 22, 2011, the Knicks brought in Chauncey Billups and Carmelo Anthony in a blockbuster three team trade. [47]

Despite forming a big three in Chauncey Billups, Amar'e Stoudemire, and Carmelo Anthony, D'Antoni and the New York Knicks were swept in the first round of the Eastern Conference playoffs.

Less than a year later, D'Antoni resigned as the head coach of the New York Knicks on March 12, 2012. [46]

After resigning from the Knicks, D'Antoni returned for Team USA for the 2012 London Olympics under Mike Krzyzewski and reunited with two of his Knicks Carmelo Anthony and Tyson Chandler. Team USA would go on to win gold at the 2012 Summer Olympics in London successfully defending their gold medals they won in the 2008 Olympics. [46]

D'Antoni agreed to a three-year contract with the Los Angeles Lakers to become their new head coach on November 12, 2012 replacing Mike Brown, who was fired five games into the 2012-13 season. Now the Lakers head coach, D'Antoni reunited with his most successful guard Steve Nash, who was traded to the Lakers the previous summer. [47]

Kobe Bryant was thrilled with the addition of Mike D'Antoni. As a young kid, Bryant grew up watching D'Antoni play in Italy for Olimpia Milano battling against his father in the Italian league.[48] The connection between Kobe Bryant and Mike D'Antoni grew during their time with Team USA especially in the previous summer during the 2012 Summer Olympics in London.

D'Antoni did not make his Lakers head coaching debut until November 20, 2012 due to him recovering from a knee replacement.

He coached the Los Angeles Lakers from 2012-14 and led the team to two playoff appearances (2011 and 2012) but were eliminated in the first round both seasons. [47]

D'Antoni resigned as the head coach of the Los Angeles Lakers on April 30, 2014 after the Lakers declined to pick up his team option for the 2015-16 season. The Lakers paid D'Antoni four million dollars for the 2014-15 season following the decline of his option.[47]

On December 18, 2015, D'Antoni joined the Philadelphia 76ers as an associate head coach under head coach Brett Brown. Less than a year later, on June 1, 2016, the Houston Rockets and D'Antoni agreed on a three-year contract for him to become the head coach. D'Antoni would win the 2017 NBA Coach of the Year while one of his player, Rockets guard Eric Gordon, won Sixth Man of the Year that same year (2017).[47] At the time of this writing, D'Antoni is still the head coach of the Houston Rockets.

Swen Nater (Dutch, 1973)

Swen Nater was born in Den Helder, North Holland, Netherlands on January 14, 1950.[43] In his early childhood years, Nater was moved to an orphanage with his sister from when he was three. While in an orphanage with his sister, his mom and her second husband moved to the United States. Three years later, Swen Nater and his sister reunited with their family in the United States due to a television series called *It Could Be You*. The show discovered the situation the family was in: Swen Nater and his sister being separated from their family and living with a new family in a new home. The family reunited on television screens. The show, *It Could Be You*, was a gameshow produced by Ralph Edward Productions in the late 1950s and was broadcasted daily. The show aired six daytime seasons and one primetime season under the NBC network.[53] Swen and his sister were reunited with their mother.

In his teen years, Swen Nater attended Woodrow Wilson Classical High School, which is in Long Beach, Los Angeles County, California.[43] Other notable athlete alumni from the high school are Bob Bailey, who played in the MLB from 1962-78 being a part of five teams winning a championship with the Cincinnati Reds in 1976; Bruce Fraser, who is currently an assistant for the Golden State Warriors, and John Merrick, who is a former professional golfer winning one PGA Tour and one Web.com Tour.

After Nater graduated from high school, he attended Cypress College in Cypress, California. While at Cypress College, Nater played two seasons of college basketball at the community college.[53] Nater did not get much time on the court as a freshman but big things were to come in his sophomore year. As a sophomore, Nater received a major increase in his playing time. He excelled on the court as a center and was named a Community College All-American.

His play and being named an All-American earned him a scholarship to continue his education and basketball dreams at the University of California, Los Angeles (UCLA). [53]

UCLA had a rising yet decorative college basketball program during Swen Nater's arrival. John Wooden, who is a ten-time NCAA Division I Championship head coach, was the head coach of the Bruins. Nater did not begin playing right away for his new college team. He redshirted his first year at UCLA but gained knowledge and watched the team play. While redshirting, UCLA won its fifth straight NCAA Division I Championship and John Wooden's seventh. Despite the successful season, the 1972 Championship game was a scare for the program. It was the smallest win margin, five points, in any championship game Wooden coached defeating Florida State. Despite not playing Nater, who played center, got the mentorship from one of the best centers in NCAA Division I history, Bill Walton. Nater told the *Los Angeles Times* in 1988 that the redshirting and getting mentoring from Walton were an investment.

> *"It was like an investment,"* Swen Nater said. *"I could of had more publicity if I had gone somewhere else. I thought if I stayed with it, all those fundamentals, all that (John) Wooden coaching and all the playing against Bill Walton would pay off."* [53]

When it was Nater's time to take the court, it was the 1972-73 season. That 1972-73 season was one of the most memorable seasons not just in UCLA's history but in NCAA Division I history. The Bruins went a perfect 30-0 sweeping through the NCAA Tournament and winning the Championship in blowout fashion defeating Memphis State by 21 points. [54] Walton won the Player of the Year while Wooden won the Coach of the Year that season.

Nater did not start a game for the Bruins, due to Walton, but ended his career at UCLA with two championships and being a proud member of arguably the best team in NCAA Division I Men's Basketball.

In 1973, Nater was eligible for the 1973 NBA Draft and declared. He was selected with the 16th overall pick in the first round by the Milwaukee Bucks. This was not the first time Nater was drafted by the Bucks. [43]

In the 1972 ABA Draft, Nater being selected with the 16th pick by the Bucks, he became the first college player to be selected without starting a single game in college. [53] Despite being drafted by Milwaukee, Nater signed with the team that drafted him in the dispersal draft, the Virginia Squires. Only three months later, Nater was traded to the San Antonio Spurs. The Squires received a draft pick and $300,000 for the rookie in the deal. [53] He played 13 games for the Squires showing signs of good potential. Nater averaged 22.0

minutes, 12.6 points, 9.1 rebounds, and 0.9 blocks. Like his collegiate days, Nater did not start one of those 13 games. [43]

Now a Spur, Nater played 62 games with the team for the rest of the 1973-74 season. Nater saw his minutes go up and his role advance. He averaged 32.3 minutes, 14.5 points, 13.6 rebounds, and 0.8 blocks per game with San Antonio.[43] His .551 field goal percentage led the ABA as well. Nater was awarded the Rookie of the Year and was named to the All-ABA Second Team. In addition, Nater participated in the ABA All-Star Game. [43]

Nater played two more seasons in the ABA following his accomplished rookie season. He played for the San Antonio Spurs for the 1974-75 season. Nater proved that he was not a 'one season fluke.'[53] The Dutch player saw another role boost with the team. He played in 78 games for the Spurs in his second season averaging 34.8 minutes, 15.1 points, a career-high 16.4 rebounds, and 1.1 blocks.[43] Nater played for the New York Nets. He played alongside ABA-NBA Hall of Famer Julius Erving. With his third team, Nater saw his minutes and role go down. Despite the drop, Nater produced good numbers. He played in 43 games with the Nets averaging 23.6 minutes, 8.7 points, 10.3 rebounds, and 0.7 blocks: Good play for a second option player.[53]

Nater then rejoined the Virginia Squires to cap off the 1975-76 ABA season. He played the remaining 33 games and averaged similar numbers: 23.5 minutes, 11.3 points, 9.8 rebounds, and 0.8 blocks. [53]

As discussed before, on September 15, 1976, the ABA completed its merge with the NBA. With the merge, Nater took his basketball talents to the NBA.

His NBA career began with the team that drafted him in the 1973 NBA Draft, the Milwaukee Bucks. He played only one season with the Bucks. Nater played in 72 games with Milwaukee averaging 27.2 minutes, 13.0 points, 12.0 rebounds, and 0.7 blocks.[43] He finished the season with Milwaukee as their number two center. Kareem Abdul-Jabbar was the starting center.

After his first NBA season with the Bucks, he was traded to the Buffalo Braves. The 1977-78 season was the last season the Braves played in Buffalo. The franchise relocated to San Diego the following season. He played in 78 games averaging a career-high 35.6 minutes, 15.5 points, 13.2 rebounds, and 0.6 blocks. [43]

Now a San Diego Clipper, Nater played five seasons with the Clippers. His numbers with the Braves/Clippers were the best of his career. He played in a combine 348 games averaging 31.8 minutes, 13.5 points, 12.0 rebounds, and 0.5 blocks.[43] During his time in San Diego, Swen Nater was the face of the team. The fans adored the Dutch player. In 1980, Nater was the NBA's rebound leader. [53]

Prior to the 1983-84 season, Nater was once again traded. He was traded to the Los Angeles Lakers in a four-player deal which included a draft pick. The deal sent Nater and just out of college Byron Scott to the Lakers in exchange for Eddie Jordan, Norm Nixon, and a 1986 second-round draft pick. That 1986 second-round pick eventually became Jeff Hornacek.[53]

The addition of Nater and Scott to Los Angeles benefited the franchise and turned the franchise into a title contending team. Nater played in 69 games for the Lakers and averaged 12.0 minutes, 4.5 points, 3.8 rebounds, and 0.1 blocks.[43] His numbers dropped tremendously due to coming off the bench and not having a big role. Nater was the backup and sometimes third string center option for the Lakers. Hall of Famer and arguably the greatest NBA center Kareem Abdul-Jabbar was the starting center for the Lakers. That Lakers team included the great names of Magic Johnson, James Worthy, Bob McAdoo, Mitch Kupchak, Kurt Rambus, and Michael Cooper. The head coach of the Lakers was Pat Riley and the Executive was NBA great Jerry West.

The Lakers went on to finish first in the Pacific Division with a record of 54-28.[43] Despite the regular season success, the Boston Celtics, who had Larry Bird, Kevin McHale, Danny Ainge, and Robert Parish, defeated the Lakers in game seven of the NBA Finals to win their fifteenth championship.

The following offseason, the Lakers decided not to offer Swen Nater a new guaranteed contract.[53] This would be the end of Swen Nater's NBA career.

Now out of the NBA, Nater decided to take his basketball talents overseas and play for the Australian Udine, a team in the Italian League. He thrived with his new team becoming one of the best players throughout the league. The Udies ended up being relegated, leading Nater to join a new team. He joined Barcelona in the Spanish League but decided to retire shortly after signing the contract. [53]

Swen Nater's career started to decline due to a knee injury. A knee injury was a common injury amongst big men in the league.

During his retirement, Nater co-authored books with his former UCLA Bruins head coach John Wooden and Pete Newell.

Ernie "Kiki" VanDeWeghe (West German, 1980)

In 1980, Ernie Maurice "Kiki" VanDeWeghe III entered the NBA joining the small group of international born players to take their talents to the top basketball league in the world. Kiki VanDeWeghe was born in Wiesbaden, West Germany on August 1, 1958. [58]

Before we dive into his career as one of the first international born NBA players, in 2013, Kiki changed the spelling of his last name, initially Vandeweghe, to VanDeWeghe. The reasoning behind the last name spelling change was to honor his grandfather. His parents did not change their last name and stuck with Vandeweghe. [58]

Kiki is the son of former NBA player Ernie Vandeweghe, who ran a short eight year run in the NBA with the New York Knicks. Following his retirement from professional basketball, Ernie Vandeweghe served in the Air Force overseas in Germany as a physician during the time of Kiki's birth. His mother, Colleen Kay Hutchins, was the 1952 Miss America pageant winner.[58]

Despite being born in West Germany, Kiki was raised in the United States and attended Palisades Charter High School, in Los Angeles California. Palisades Charter High School has produced notable NBA alumni.

- Jeanie Buss, who graduated in 1979, and currently serves as the president and co-owner of the Los Angeles Lakers and serves on the NBA's board of governors.
- Steve Kerr, who graduated in 1983, and is an eight-time NBA Champion and the Head coach of the Golden State Warriors [58]

Kiki VanDeWeghe played basketball at Palisades Charter High School excelling in the sport. His athleticism and talent earned himself a spot at UCLA as a freshman for the 1976-77 season. At the time, UCLA was in the Pac-8 conference. In his freshman season, VanDeWeghe did not see many minutes for the Bruins. He averaged 10 minutes a game coming off the bench under head coach Gene Bartow, who was in his second season with the Bruins.[62] With VanDeWeghe averaging just 10 minutes per game, he made the most of each minute. He averaged 3.6 points, 1.8 rebounds, and 1.0 assists. VanDeWeghe played in 23 games for the Bruins that season. [62]

Marques Johnson, who was in his senior season, was the captain of the Bruins, and started over VanDeWeghe.

The Bruins finished that season with a 23-4 record punching their ticket to the NCAA Tournament as a two seed. UCLA was upset by the Idaho State, who were not ranked, in the Sweet Sixteen. [62]

In his sophomore season, VanDeWeghe came off the bench to forwards David Greenwood, who was a junior, and James Wilkes, who was also a sophomore. The Bruins hired a new head coach for VanDeWeghe's sophomore season. Gary Cunningham, who was a Bruins assistant coach for the decade prior, took over for Bartow. Cunningham played for UCLA from 1960-1962 before declaring for the 1962 NBA Draft selected with the 58th pick by the Cincinnati Royals. [58]

Despite coming off the bench for the second consecutive season, VanDeWeghe received a bigger role with the Bruins. His minutes increased from 10 a game as a freshman to 21.1 minutes per game as a sophomore. He averaged 8.9 points, 4.4 rebounds, and 1.5 assists in 28 games for the Bruins. [62]

The Bruins finished the regular season on top of the Pac-8 conference with an overall record of 25-3 and a conference record of 14-0. Despite a successful season, UCLA was once again bounced out of the NCAA Tournament by Arkansas. [62]

Heading into his junior season, the Pac-8 Conference was now the Pac-10 Conference. UCLA entered the season ranked number two in the country with big expectations. VanDeWeghe received a starting job as a forward on the Bruins alongside senior David Greenwood, junior Greg Sims, senior Roy Hamilton, and senior Brad Holland.

VanDeWeghe played in 30 games for UCLA his junior season averaging career-highs across the board. He averaged 14.2 points, 6.3 rebounds, and 1.5 assists. Kiki shot a college career-high .662 from the field and .812 from the foul line. [62]

The Bruins, once again, finished on top of the Pac-10 Conference with an overall record of 25-5 and a conference record of 15-3 followed by USC. UCLA thrived early in the NCAA Tournament but lost to DePaul in the Regional Final. The Bruins beat DePaul in the second game of the regular season. [62]

Following his junior season, three of the Bruins starting five declared for the 1979 NBA Draft: David Greenwood, Roy Hamilton, and Brad Holland. All three players were draft lottery players. Greenwood was selected with the second overall pick by the Chicago Bulls, Hamilton went 10th to the Detroit Pistons, and Holland went 14th to the local Los Angeles Lakers. [58]

Now a senior, VanDeWeghe and the Bruins' expectation were not as high anymore. After losing three seniors, who were starters last season, the roster was filled with new players out of high school. VanDeWeghe and Wilkes, the remaining starters from last season, were the only seniors on the team. On top of the departure of talented seniors to the NBA, the Bruins decided to once again change head coaches. This time, UCLA went with a well-known coach to take the throne.

UCLA hired Larry Brown as their head coach prior to the 1979-80 season. Brown was an experienced coach, who coached on both the college level and the professional level. From 1965-67, Brown was an assistant for the University of North Carolina Tarheels, was the head coach of the Carolina Cougars in the former American Basketball Association from 1972-74 and was the head coach of the Denver Nuggets from 1974-79. This was the first time, Brown coached a collegiate team.

Kiki VanDeWeghe for the first time was the leader of UCLA during his senior year. He played in 32 games for the Bruins averaging 33.8 minutes, 19.5 points, 6.8 rebounds, and 1.7 assists: all career-highs. He also took almost double the amount of field goals per game compared to last season: 8.9 during his junior year and 13.1 his senior year. [62]

The Bruins finished third in the Pac-10 Conference behind Oregon State and Arizona, who were both ranked throughout the season. The Bruins finished the regular season with a 17-9 record and a conference record of 12-6. [62]

Despite a rough season, compared to his previous three years at UCLA, the Bruins slipped into the NCAA Tournament. After just slipping into the NCAA Tournament, VanDeWeghe and the Bruins thrived and punched a ticket to the final. The Bruins upset number one DePaul, the team that took them out the previous year. Despite upsetting DePaul, the Bruins lost in the final to the University of Louisville ending Kiki VanDeWeghe's college career. Kiki finished eighth all time in career points in UCLA Bruins Men's Basketball with 1,380 points. VanDeWeghe declared for the 1980 NBA Draft following the end of his senior season.[62]

VanDeWeghe had an NBA Draft experience that not too many players have had. After being selected with the 11th overall pick in the 1980 NBA Draft by the Dallas Mavericks, Kiki immediately requested a trade.[58] Kiki publicly said he did not want to play for the Mavericks. With VanDeWeghe wanting out without even trying on the uniform, Dallas was forced to trade their first-ever draft pick. The Mavericks received first-round picks in 1981 and 1985 while the Nuggets received the rights to VanDeWeghe and a 1986 first-round pick. The trade became official on December 3, 1980.[58]

VanDeWeghe told the *Spokesman Review,* his thoughts on the trade and his displeasure if he was not traded by the Mavericks.

> *"I prepared myself for the worst, which was not playing this season,"* VanDeWeghe said. *"I'm grateful to the Nuggets for expressing an interest in me. Otherwise, I might have sat out all year, and that's not a happy thought. I'm glad to be playing here. This is a beautiful city, and these are good people here."* [57]

VanDeWeghe also talked about his former UCLA coach, Larry Brown, who was the head coach for the Nuggets prior to joining the Bruins, how his influence and praise for Denver was one of the main reasons he wanted to join that team.

> *"Larry Brown loves Denver and this team, and he was one of the main reasons I was so excited to come here."* [57]

Ironically, the trade worked out in the Mavericks favor down the line. The first draft pick the Mavericks obtained from the trade turned out to be Rolando Blackman, who became one of the greatest Mavericks of all-time and was a three time All-Star and is second in total points scored in Dallas' franchise history.[58]

Carl Scheer, who was the Nuggets President and General Manager when Denver traded for Kiki VanDeWeghe, talked about how trading for VanDeWeghe was like getting their 1981 Draft choice a year early.

> *"We're tremendously pleased to have Kiki VanDeWeghe join our organization. He's an outstanding player who comes from a winning program. Signing him now is like getting our 1981 draft choice a year early. We'll have the benefit of working with him for the remainder of this season, and that gives us a big head start over any rookie we could have drafted next year."* [56]

Donnie Walsh, who was the Nuggets head coach at the time, was not more pleased with the acquisition of VanDeWeghe to his team and how he fits into their system perfectly.

> *"Kiki's style of play will fit into our style immediately, and although he'll have some things to learn about the NBA, we think he's good enough to help us significantly in a matter of weeks. We know he'll give us scoring off the bench right now."* [56]

VanDeWeghe played four seasons with the Nuggets becoming an All-Star in back-to-back seasons in 1983 and 1984. In those two years when VanDeWeghe was an All-Star, were the best seasons of his career. [55]

During the 1982-83 season, VanDeWeghe averaged 26.7 points, 5.3 rebounds, and 2.5 assists leading the Nuggets to a 45-37 regular season record, a second-place finish in the NBA Midwest Division, and made the 1983 NBA Playoffs.[55] In the playoffs, VanDeWeghe and the Nuggets beat the Phoenix Suns in the NBA Western Conference First Round 2-to-1 in the series to advance to the NBA Western Coference Semifinals. In the Semifinals, they fell to the San Antonio Spurs 4-to-1 in the series. [59]

During the 1983-84 season, which was the last season VanDeWeghe was selected as an All-Star, he averaged a career-high 29.4 points, 4.8 rebounds, and 3.1 assists leading the Nuggets to a slightly worse record of 38-44 finishing third in the NBA Midwest Division and to the playoffs.[55] In the playoffs, the Nuggets struggled in the Western Conference first-round falling to the Utah Jazz 2-to-3 in the series. [59]

VanDeWeghe played 293 games for the Mile-High City averaging 33.4 minutes, 23.3 points, 5.3 rebounds, and 2.7 assists during his time as a Nugget. [55]

Following the best seasons of his career, VanDeWeghe was traded in the offseason to the Portland Trail Blazers joining Clyde Drexler.[58] Denver received three players and two draft picks in return for VanDeWeghe. Portland believed bringing in the Nuggets sharpshooter would give Portland a dynamic duo in Kiki VanDeWeghe and Clyde Drexler. What Portland was hoping for did come true.

Clyde Drexler and VanDeWeghe were one of the best shooting duos in the NBA during the 1984-85 season leading Portland to a 42-40 regular season record finishing second in the NBA Pacific Division. [60] The Trail Blazers blew past the team that initially drafted VanDeWeghe, the Dallas Mavericks, in the first-round of the Western Conference Playoffs winning the series 3-1.[60] Despite cruising to the Western Conference Semifinals, Portland was crushed by the Los Angeles Lakers 1-4. In his first season with Portland, VanDeWeghe averaged 22.4 points, 3.2 rebounds, and 1.5 assists. [55]

VanDeWeghe spent a total of five seasons with the Trail Blazers.[60] During the 1986-87 season, he shot a career-best .481 from behind the arc making him one of the most consistent three-point shooters in the league that season. As a Trail Blazer, VanDeWeghe played 285 games averaging 23.5 points, 2.9 rebounds, and 2.2 assists. [55]

For the third time in his career, VanDeWeghe was traded. This time he was traded to the Mecca of Basketball joining the New York Knicks. As mentioned before, his father spent his entire NBA career with the New York Knicks. [58]

Kiki VanDeWeghe played four seasons with the Knicks alongside Patrick Ewing. In his final two seasons with the Knicks, VanDeWeghe came off the bench for New York as a sharpshooter off the bench. In those four seasons, Kiki played 191 games averaging 11.5 points, 1.9 rebounds, and 1.3 assists. [55]

VanDeWeghe played one more season in the NBA with the Los Angeles Clippers. He started only three of the 41 games that season averaging a career-low 6.2 points, 1.2 rebounds, and 0.6 assists. [55]

After retiring from the NBA, VanDeWeghe ironically joined the Dallas Mavericks in 1999 as an assistant.[58] He worked with NBA international Germany superstar Dirk Nowitzki developing his shooting and overall development. Kiki did spend some time as an assistant coach with Dallas as well.

After a short run with Dallas, VanDeWeghe got another job with one of his former teams: the Denver Nuggets. He was hired as the Nuggets general manager. [58] While in office, VanDeWeghe drafted Carmelo Anthony in the 2003 NBA Draft. Carmelo Anthony was coming off a historic National Championship season with Syracuse and was a top prospect in the NBA Draft. Carmelo Anthony was selected with the third overall pick.

Despite selecting Carmelo Anthony, who turned out to be what most expected the Orange player to be, VanDeWeghe did have some bad decision as general manager. The Nuggets traded for New Jersey Nets center Kenyon Martin. Martin was one of the best power forwards in the NBA boosting the Nets to back-to-back Finals appearances but what he traded away to get Kenyon Martin was too much. The Nuggets sent their future three first-round picks to New Jersey in the deal which backfired.

VanDeWeghe was let go by Denver following the 2006 playoffs. [58] The Nuggets were eliminated in the first-round. Following his departure from the Nuggets, VanDeWeghe served as an ESPN NBA analyst for the 2006-07 season.[58] His gig with ESPN did not last long because he had another NBA offer coming his way.

VanDeWeghe would join as a special assistant to New Jersey's team president and general manager Rod Thorn, the team that he traded three-first round picks to, the Nets. [58] Rod Thorn replaced Ed Stefanski with VanDeWeghe. Ed Stefanski, who did spend time as the general manager of the Nets, was heading to the Philadelphia 76ers as general manager, the team that drafted him as a player in 1976.

With the Nets, VanDeWeghe took the role of interim head coach of the Nets in 2009. He replaced Lawrence Frank, who was the head coach of the Nets since 2004. VanDeWeghe would only coach that season for the Nets. When Mikhail Prokhorov brought the Nets in 2010, VanDeWeghe was not offered to return to the Nets. [58]

In 2013, VanDeWeghe was back in the NBA front office scenery but not with one team. He joined the NBA leadership team as the Executive Vice President of Basketball Operations of the NBA. Later that year, he was promoted to Senior Vice President of Basketball Operations.[61]

As NBA Careers notes, Kiki VanDeWeghe is involved in a broad range of basketball matters including the development of playing rules and interpretations, game analytics, disciplinary matters, and policies and procedures relating to the operation of NBA games. He also serves as a key liaison between the league office and its teams, drawing upon his years of experience as a general manager, coach and player. Additionally, Kiki VanDeWeghe serves as a board member for both the NCAA's Competition Committee and FIBA. Kiki VanDeWeghe spent some time prior to his role with the NBA as a FOX Sports West writer and analyst covering the Los Angeles Clippers.[61]

The Globalization of the NBA

Chapter 7

Basketball Debuts at the Summer Olympics

The 1904 Summer Olympics

The Olympics are prestigiously known as the leading international sporting event in the world. Basketball, as discussed before, was invented by Dr. James Naismith in Springfield, Massachusetts in 1891. The game of basketball became popular throughout the United States in the following decades and was one of the most popular indoor sporting events at the time.

Only 13 years later, the game of basketball was introduced in the 1904 Summer Olympics. The 1904 Summer Olympics, which is officially known as the Games of the III Olympiad, was held in St. Louis, Missouri.[63] This was the first time in Olympics history the event was held outside of Europe. The main advertisement for the Olympics headlined the famous World's Fair Louisiana Purchase Exposition. The Olympic Games opened on July 1, 1904 and closed on November 23, 1904. There were 95 total events in 16 sports and 17 disciplines. [63] The current three-medal system was introduced at the 1904 Olympic Games: gold, silver, and bronze.

The Olympics included 12 nations and a total of 651 athletes. Out of those 651 athletes, only six were women.[63] The 1904 Olympic Games did not showcase some of the top athletes outside of the United States and Canada. The Russo-Japanese War, which occurred at the time of the Olympics, February 1904 to September 1905, forced many international athletes to not participate in the Games. Out of the 651 athletes who competed in the 1904 Olympic Games, only 62 of them were international athletes from other countries other than Canada.[63]

The Olympics was made up of sports and demonstration events. The sports that took part in the Olympics were Archery, Athletics, which was running events, Boxing, Cycling, Fencing, Football, Golf, Gymnastics, Lacrosse, Roque, Rowing, Tennis, Tug of war, Weightlifting, and Wrestling. There were also two aquatic events played at the Olympics: Diving and Swimming. [63]

The demonstration sports at the 1904 Summer Olympics were American Football, Baseball, Gaelic Football, and Hurling. The other demonstration sport was the game of basketball. This was the first time in the history of the sport that it was included in the Olympics as a demonstration sport. [63]

There was a total of four different basketball events in St. Louis. Two YMCA basketball teams participated in the Summer Olympics in Amateur Championships: Buffalo German YMCA and Chicago Central YMCA. The other teams that competed in the Amateur Championships at the Games were Missouri AC, Sawyer AB, Turner Tigers, and Xavier AA. Buffalo German YMCA won the Amateur Athletic Union (AAU) national basketball tournament at the Olympics that year.[63]

Basketball at the 1904 Summer Olympic Games included other levels of basketball such as college, high school, and elementary basketball. Only three colleges took part in the demonstration sport: Hiram College in Ohio, Wheaton College in Illinois, and Latter-Day Saints' University in Salt Lake City, which is now Brigham Young University. All teams played only two games in the Olympics. Hiram finished with a perfect 2-0 while Wheaton finished with a record of 1-1 followed by Latter-Day, which did not win going 0-2. [66]

Hiram, to this day, is the only college team in the country with a team Olympic gold medal.[64] Their Olympic win is referred to as the Olympic Intercollegiate World Championship. [64] The college was selected to compete in the Olympic Games because of their well-known reputation as one of the top collegiate teams in Ohio. Their accomplishment was selected as one of Sports Illustrated's Most Intriguing Events of the 20th Century.

High school basketball in the Olympics included four teams: New York, Chicago, Saint Louis, and San Francisco. New York dominated in the Olympics finishing with a perfect 3-0 record and winning. Chicago finished second with an overall record of 2-1 followed by Saint Louis at 1-2. San Francisco did not have a good tournament going winless, 0-3. [63]

Following the 1904 Summer Olympics, basketball vanished from the Olympics until 1936. There were four Summer Olympics when basketball was not a part of the Olympics: 1908, 1912, 1920, 1924, 1928, and 1934.

The 1936 Summer Olympics was a historic event that changed basketball forever. The Summer Olympics was held in Berlin, Germany.[68] For the first time, basketball was an official medal event in the Olympics. The basketball tournament ran from August 7, 1936 until August 14, 1936. There was a total of 21 nations that participated in the basketball tournament: Belgium, Brazil, Canada, Chile, Republic of China, Czechoslovakia, Egypt, Estonia, France, Germany, Italy, Japan, Latvia, Mexico, Peru, Philippines, Poland, Switzerland, Turkey, United States, and Uruguay. Heading into the Olympics, there were 23 nations, but two nations withdrew prior to the competition. The two nations that withdrew were Hungary and Spain. The tournament, at the time, was the largest tournament of team sports in the Olympics. [68]

During the Olympics, the International Basketball Federation, best known as FIBA, and the International Olympic Committee, the IOC, tested to see if the sport of basketball could be both an indoor and outdoor sport.[68] Basketball outdoors was played on grass tennis courts, which gave teams some difficulty in all weather conditions.

The United States cruised through the tournament and faced Canada in the Olympic finals, beating the Philippines and Mexico. In the finals, the United States won gold defeating Canada 19-8. With the loss, Canada finished with silver medals, followed by Mexico, which won bronze. [68]

The United States gold medal team was made up of current or former college players led by captain Frank Lubrin, who played for UCLA. Along with Frank Lubrin, there were four other Bruins on the team: Sam Balter, Carl Knowles, Donald Piper, and Carl Shy. Below are the other players on the championship team.

- Ralph Bishop
- Joe Fortenberry
- Terry Gibbons
- Francis Johnson
- Art Mollner
- Jack Ragland
- Willard Schmidt
- Dwayne Swanson
- Bill Wheatley [68]

Following the 1936 Summer Olympics in Berlin, Germany, the sport of basketball was established as a traditional Olympic sport. The United States dominated the Summer Olympics, winning the tournament in six straight Olympics.

The 1972 Summer Olympics Controversy

The 1972 Summer Olympics were held in Munich, West Germany.[69] More countries wanted to participate in the Olympic basketball tournament but there were qualifications held to determine what countries were in and which were left out. There were countries that received automatic qualifications. West Germany was granted as one of those countries due to the country being the host nation of the 1972 Summer Olympics.[69] The other countries which received automatic qualifications were the four teams that placed in the top four during the 1968 Summer Olympics, in Mexico City, Mexico. Those four teams were the United States, which won gold, Yugoslavia which won silver, the Soviet Union, which won bronze, and Brazil. FIBA held continental tournaments and a pre-Olympic tournament to determine the other teams. The pre-Olympic tournament alone granted two countries spots in the 1972 Summer Olympics basketball tournament. [69]

When it was time for the 1972 Summer Olympics, the tournament consisted of 16 nations. The other 11 teams in the tournament were Australia, Cuba, Czechoslovakia, Egypt, Italy, Japan, Philippines, Poland, Puerto Rico, Spain, and Senegal. [69] Despite qualifying, Egypt withdrew from the tournament mainly due to the Munich massacre, which affected their country. Despite withdrawing, Egypt went 0-7 in their group. [69]

The tournament was broken up into two groups: Group A and Group B. Both groups were made up of eight teams. Australia, Brazil, Cuba, Czechoslovakia, Egypt, Japan, Spain, and the defending gold medalists, the United States. The teams in Group B were Italy, Philippines, Puerto Rico, Poland, Senegal, the Soviet Union, West Germany, and Yugoslavia. [69]

In Group A, the United States went 7-0, finishing first, followed by Cuba, which finished with a 6-1 record. In Group B, the Soviet Union went 7-0, taking first, followed by Italy, which went 5-2. [69] Those four teams advanced to the knockout round to compete for medals. The top teams in both groups faced off against the second-place teams in the groups so the United States faced Italy while the Soviet Union faced Cuba in the medal bracket. The United States easily defeated Italy advancing to the gold medal game while the Soviet Union just slipped by Cuba to advance.

The 1972 Summer Olympic men's basketball final between the United States and the Soviet Union was one of the most controversial events in Olympic Games history. The United States, due to winning the past seven Summer Olympic basketball tournaments, was favored to win their eighth straight gold medal. Entering the game, the United States had a perfect 63-0 record in Olympic basketball tournament competition. On the other hand, the Soviet Union won silver medals during the 1952, 1956, 1960, and 1964 Summer Olympics, in 1968, the Soviets won bronze. [69]

The finals were much more than a basketball game for these two nations. During the time of the 1972 Summer Olympic men's basketball final, the Cold War was active. This meant that the gold medal game was heavily revolving around politics. There were rumors that the Communist Party of the Soviet Union, CPSU, bribed Olympic officials to win 50 gold medals at the 1972 Summer Olympics.[69] At the time of the Olympics, the Soviet Union was celebrating its 50-year anniversary, so winning 50 gold medals would reflect well with their anniversary. While the Olympics were aired, many viewers, primarily American viewers, believed the United States was not a liked nation and that the games were anti-American.

When comparing the two teams, the United States had the youngest team in their Olympic men's basketball history. It was common for the top college players to participate in the Olympics as part of the United States team before taking their talents to the professional leagues. Doug Collins, best known for his NBA coaching career, and North Carolina State center, Tommy Burleson, were the notable players on the United States team. The United States heavily pursed Bill Walton, who was clearly the best college player at the time, but Walton declined to participate. The team was also made up of new players. The United States never kept the same players from the previous Summer Olympics. On the other hand, the Soviets were a very experienced team. Most of their players played in at least one Summer Olympics tournament prior to the 1972 Summer Olympics.

The game, as noted before, was filled with controversy. The controversy occurred on three different inbound plays but most notably in the final three seconds of the game. The United States thought they won the game. After two foul shots by Collins and the United States up by one point, the Soviet Union's inbound pass was deflected, and the time ran out. Following the play, Renato William Jones, the secretary-general and co-founder of FIBA, stormed onto the court and ordered the officials to tack on three more seconds on the game clock. With an additional three seconds on the game clock, the Soviet's connected on a full court inbound pass leading to Aleksandr Belov's game winning layup. [69]

Following the Soviet's corrupt win, the United States immediately filed a formal protest. Neil Amdur of the *New York Times* was reporting on the game and described his personal experience of what went on following the protest.

> *"The game ended at 1:14 a.m,"* Amdur noted in his 2012 *New York Times* story. *"The Americans filed a formal protest, and a five-member FIBA jury was convened. As late as 3 a.m., while I was filing my article and phoning inserts, players, fans and officials lingered outside the locker rooms awaiting a decision that would not be overturned."* [70]

Herbert Mols, the resident manager of the United States team, had an argument with Ferenc Hepp, the jury's chairman from Hungary. Ferenc Hepp, when announcing the verdict, did not provide the exact vote count but did say the decision was not unanimous. [70] The jury did not favor the Americans. It was made up of five members and three of those five members were from Soviet-allied nations.[70] Telling by the verdict, it was clear the Cold War and politics played a big role. According to multiple sources, the verdict was 3-to-2. Rafael Lopez, who was from Puerto Rico, and Claudio Coccia, who was from Italy, confirmed they both voted for the United States. Puerto Rico and Italy were both US-allied nations. The three votes, which outnumbered the two US votes were from Ferenc Hepp, Adam Baglajewski and Adres Keiser. All three jury members were all from Soviet-allied nations. As mentioned before, Ferenc Happ was from Hungary. Adam Baglajewski was from Poland while Adres Keiser was from Cuba. Ferenc Hepp was the only jury member to see all five votes on the ballot.

Ivan Edeshko, the Soviet Union player who threw the game-winning pass for his team, strongly believed the United States did not act right following the loss.

> *"The American team was offended, and it wasn't right,"* said Ivan Edeshko, *the player who threw the game-winning pass for the Soviets. "It was the cold war. Americans, out of their own natural pride and love of country, didn't want to lose and admit loss. They didn't want to lose in anything, especially basketball."* [71]

Following the 1972 Olympic Games, the United States Olympic Committee filed another appeal. The appeal was directed this time to the International Olympic Committee, which is a non-government sports organization based in Switzerland. Renato Righetto, who was a Brazilian referee and officiated the United States-Soviet Union gold medal game, supported the appeal strongly. In addition to Renato Righetto's strong support, Andre Chopard supported the appeal as well. Andre Chopard, who was a 12-year veteran timekeeper and was the timekeeper during the game, added three extra seconds on the clock, leading to the Soviet's game winning basket, bizarre. [69]

As expected by many, the second appeal was unsuccessful. Although the second appeal was turned down, the International Olympic Committee ruled that the appeal was under FIBA's jurisdiction in 1973. [71]

Following the two unsuccessful appeals, the United States commonly urged their players to accept their silver medals. Initially, the United States team heavily denied accepting the silver medals following the unprecedented ruling in the gold medal game. [69]

Most of the team members refused to accept the silver medals, even if it was awarded to them in an official ceremony. The International Olympic Committee stated that if the medals were awarded to the United States team members, all members must accept the medals. To this day, the silver medals sit in a vault in Lausanne Switzerland. [69]

Michael Bantom, who was one of the United States best players in the gold medal game, explained his reasoning why he was not going to accept his silver medal.

> *"If we had gotten beat, I would be proud to display my silver medal today,"* Bantam said. *"But, we didn't get beat, we got cheated."* [70]

His teammates, Doug Collins, expressed the reasoning in an emotional way.

> *"It was sort of like being on top of the Sears tower in Chicago celebrating and then being thrown off and falling 100 floors to the ground,"* said Collins. *"That's the kind of emptiness and sick feeling I felt."* [70]

ESPN produced a *30 for 30* short documentary, *Silver Reunion*, on the 1972 United States Men's Olympic basketball team, which included 12 members of that team in 2012. The film displayed the anger and disappointment of the 12 members on the ruling and the appeal.

As for the gold medal Soviets, they celebrated the win proudly. The controversy was clearly hidden in the celebrations and the members were viewed as heroes. To this day, the controversy behind the 1972 Olympic Men's basketball finals is considered as one of the most corrupt events in basketball history.

The 1976 Summer Olympics

The 1976 Summer Olympics Basketball Tournament was held in Montreal, Canada, and ran from July 18th to July 27th.[72] Looking for revenge, the United States basketball team had a big chip on its shoulder. They wanted to prove that not only they deserved to win four years ago but put their country back on top with gold medals around their necks.

In addition to the United States men's team, the 1976 Summer Olympics was monumental to the game of basketball. Women's basketball was introduced to the Olympic Games. The Women's tournament consisted of only six teams. In the end, the Soviet Union Women's team won gold followed by the United States winning silver. Bulgaria won bronze in the women's tournament. [72]

The men' Olympic tournament initially consisted of 13 teams. The 13 teams in the men's tournament were Australia, Canada, China, Cuba, Czechoslovakia, Egypt, Italy, Japan, Mexico, Puerto Rico, the United States, the Soviet Union, and Yugoslavia. [72] Like the 1972 Summer Olympics, Egypt withdrew from the tournament. The country withdrew due to the boycott of several African countries against New Zealand. Egypt did play five games in the group stage of the tournament but all games involving the country were forfeited. [72]

The format of the tournament was identical to the 1972 Summer Olympics: two groups, Group A and Group B, and the top two teams of each group advance to the semifinal round. Both groups had six teams.

Group A consisted of Australia, Canada, Cuba, Japan, Mexico, and the Soviet Union. Group B consisted of Czechoslovakia, Egypt, Italy, Puerto Rico, the United States, and Yugoslavia. [72]

In Group A, the Soviet Union finished first with a perfect record of 5-0 followed by the host nation Canada, who went 4-1. In Group B, the United States finished first with a perfect record with 5-0 followed by Yugoslavia, who went 4-1. [72]

In the Championship bracket, the United States won in blowout fashion against Canada, 95-77, returning to the gold medal game. The Soviet Union faced off in the semifinals against Yugoslavia. The Soviet's would fall short of advancing to the gold medal game, falling to Yugoslavia, 89-84. The Soviet Union would win bronze in the tournament defeating the host nation, Canada, 100-72. [72]

In the gold medal game, the United States won gold, once again in blowout fashion, defeating Yugoslavia, 95-74. The United States team did not have one player from the 1972 Summer Olympics on their team. [72]

For the Women's Olympic Tournament, it was a single-round tournament, due to the low number of teams. The Soviet Union Women's team won gold finishing with a perfect record of 5-0. The United States followed, winning silver medals, finishing with a record of 3-2. Bulgaria won bronze finishing with a 3-2 record. [72] The United States won silver due to a victory over Bulgaria in the tournament, breaking the tie.

Chapter 8

The NBA Takes its Games Global

It was only a matter of time until the National Basketball Association experimented overseas. The game of basketball in general was gaining tremendous popularity around the world, mainly due to the game becoming an Olympic sport. Many countries participated in the Olympic games, as discussed before, engaging their fans and giving the game of basketball a worldwide perspective.

On September 9, 1978, the first-ever game between an NBA team and an International Basketball Federation (FIBA) team took place in Tel Aviv, Israel. The Washington Bullets faced off against Maccabi Tel Aviv at the Yad Eliyahu Arena. The game was an NBA exhibition game, so the result did not affect either teams season record. [73]

The Bullets were one of the top teams in the NBA heading into the 1978-79 season. In the previous season, Washington won the 1978 NBA Finals, defeating the Seattle Supersonics in Game 7. [75] At the time of this writing, the 1978 NBA Championship is the only championship title the franchise has won. In the regular season, the Bullets finished the season with a 44-38 record landing them second in their division, the NBA Central Division.[75] The Bullets had two future NBA Hall of Famers on that championship team: Elvin Haynes and Wes Unseld.

Maccabi Tel Aviv was coming off a historic season prior to facing the Bullets. The Cold War was at its peak in 1977 and the FIBA European Champions Cup of the EuroLeague was worried regarding how the war would affect the tournament. CSKA Moscow, referred to as the Soviet Army or Red Army team, were heavy favorites to win the championship. In fact, CSKA Moscow had six players from the 1972 Summer Olympic team who beat the United States in the controversial finals.

The two teams did not like each other due to politics between Israel and the Soviet Union. CSKA Moscow not only did not want to play Tel Aviv but the Soviets refused to grant visas to the players to play them in Moscow. This led to the game being played in Virton, Belgium in a semifinals matchup. The game was bigger than a basketball game for both teams. Many of the viewers of the game were not into basketball. In fact, most of Israel tuned into the game, drawing more attention to the game of basketball and attracting new fans to the sport. In the end, Tel Aviv defeated Moscow, 91-77 which is one of the biggest EuroLeague upsets in history. [76]

Maccabi went on to defeat Mobilgirgi Varese in the FIBA European Champions Cup Finals, which was one of the teams six EuroLeague Championships. [76]

Heading into the NBA's first-ever international game, the Bullets were expected to dominate the game and a blowout was expected. Maccabi, in front of their fans, went on to upset the Bullets, winning 98-97. [73] The Yad Eliyahu Arena sold out three weeks prior to the game.

For the Bullets, the game was not the biggest takeaway from their trip to Israel. According to William Claiborne of *The Washington Post*, the players valued the experience to travel to Israel and experience the culture. In other words, they enjoyed the experience like tourists.

> *"It was very humbling. It's age. It's power. It's thousands of years. It's really something,"* said general manager Bob Ferry as he watched his players gape at the Old City with uncharacteristic solemnity. [73]

For Haynes, visiting the birthplace of Christ was his biggest takeaway.

> *"What can you say? It's the birthplace of Christ,"* Haynes said. *"It holds so many things close to you."* [73]

The game between the Washington Bullets and Maccabi Tel Aviv was the only NBA game played on international soil in 1978. The NBA, after acknowledging the success of their first NBA international game, decided to schedule three more international games featuring the Bullets in 1979. [1]

All three games were played prior to the start of the 1979-80 NBA season. The first NBA international game took place in Beijing, China. The game featured the Bullets matchup against the Chinese National Team. [74]

This was another historic event in NBA history. Washington became the first United States professional sports team to be invited to China. Deng Xiaoping, who was the chairman of the Chinese People's Political Consultative Conference, invited the team to China and play. [74] Months prior to the first game in China, United States President Jimmy Carter soothed relations with China. An invitation was extended following the relations of the two countries and forgoing any diplomatic ties for the game. Due to Washington's well-known success, highlighted by their 1978 NBA Championship, and last year's international game in Israel, the team was an easy pick to represent the NBA in China. The Bullets proudly accepted the offer to play in China. [74]

The Bullets, who flew coach across the Pacific Ocean, were very popular once they arrived in China. The team was swarmed by crowds in

Tiananmen Square. The players were not quite use to the hospitality the country had to offer. The team stayed in a hotel with no air conditioning.

In the Bullets first international matchup against Chinese National Team, Washington slipped by, winning 96-85. With the win, the Bullets picked up their first win as a franchise outside of the United States. The win was also the first win for any United States professional sports team in China. [77]

Five days later, Washington had their second and final game in China that year. The Bullets faced the Shanghai Team in Shanghai, China. Today, the Shanghai team is named the Bayi Rockets Shuanglu Dianchi Rockets. Shanghai was led by Yao Zhiyuan, a 6-foot 10-inch center. Yao Zhiyuan is best known as the father of NBA Hall of Fame and the sixth and current President of the Chinese Basketball Association, Yao Ming. Like the National Team, Shanghai did not put up a fight against the Bullets. Washington won the game easily, 113-80. [74]

The two games in China was not only monumental for the Bullets and the NBA but for the country of China. Following the Bullets exhibition games, basketball rapidly increased in popularity. Today, basketball ranks as the top team sport in China and is played by more than 300 people in the country. As for NBA viewership in China, more than 700 million people tune in and watch NBA programming's. [1]

Jerry Sachs, the vice president of the Bullets, told *The Washington Post* that it was Abe Pollin's dream to spread the game of basketball internationally. Abe Pollin was the team's owner during the China visit.

> *"It was all Abe's desire to take that team and go to China,"* said Sachs. [74]

Following the visit to China, Washington had one more stop on their international tour. The Bullets traveled to the Philippines to take on the Philippine Basketball Association All-Stars (PBA). This was the first time an NBA team played in the country. The PBA team was made of up of superstars imported from other clubs in the country. Ramon Fernandez highlighted the PBA team. Fernandez is regarded as the greatest Filipino player of all time and is the PBA's all-time leader in points, rebounds, and blocks. He also ranked second in assists and steals. [1]

The game was played in front of a sold out Araneta Coliseum crowd. In that sold out crowd, Imelda Marcos, who was the Philippines First Lady, was in attendance for the game. This was arguably the biggest competition the Bullets faced during their preseason international tour. Despite the competition, Washington won the game, beating the PBA, 133-123. [1] There was a small scuffle during the game. Like China, the game of basketball grew in popularity rapidly following the game. That was the last NBA international game played until 1984. [1]

Larry O'Brien, the NBA Commissioner, was succeeded by David Stern. Stern, whose first affiliation with the NBA came in 1966, became the NBA Commissioner on February 1, 1984. The new commissioner quickly jumped on globalizing the NBA like O'Brien did in 1978-79. Stern orchestrated the New Jersey Nets and the Phoenix Suns to travel back to Israel in August of 1984. On top of returning to Israel to play four games, Stern set up the Seattle SuperSonics to head to Italy and West Germany to play six games around the same time. [1]

Maccabi Tel Aviv, which was the only international team to win a game over an NBA team back in 1978, was set to face both the Nets and the Suns that summer. [1] Hapoel Tel Aviv, another successful basketball club from Israel, were also set to play the two NBA teams that summer. In total, four games were lined up.

On August 28, 1984, Phoenix played Hapoel Tel Aviv while the Nets played Maccabi Tel Aviv. The Suns won their first game in Israel, cruising to a 111-91 victory. For the Nets, who were expected to win, lost to Maccabi Tel Aviv in a nail biter, 104-97. [1]

The next two games were played two days later, August 30, 1984. The Suns faced off against Maccabi Tel Aviv while the Nets looked for their first international win against Hapoel Tel Aviv. New Jersey played first and ended up blowing out Hapoel Tel Aviv, 101-82, picking up the win. As for the Suns, they did not play well. Maccabi Tel Aviv continued their dominance over NBA teams defeating Phoenix, 113-97. Macabbi Tel Aviv picked up two wins, tallying their total to three wins over NBA teams. The four games were a success for all teams and both leagues. [1]

For the SuperSonics, who did not qualify for the NBA playoffs the previous season, were looking to begin their preseason international tour on a winning note. On August 24, 1984, Seattle took on SSV Hagen, who are known today as BBV Hagen of the Regionalliga League in Germany. The game was played in Hagen, West Germany in front of yet another sold out crowd. As expected, the SuperSonics defeated SSV Hagen, 94-87. [1] The following day, August 25, 1984, Seattle traveled to Langen, West Germany, to face ASC 46 Göttingen, who are still a basketball club today. Seattle dominated the game winning in blowout fashion, 119-95. [1]

After back-to-back games in Germany for the SuperSonics, Italy was the next stop on their international tour. Seattle faced Benetton Treviso in Treviso, Italy on August 29, 1984. Treviso was viewed as one of the best basketball clubs in Italy and could give Seattle a run for their money. Well, the SuperSonics were not too fazed and won the game 124-101. [1]

The SuperSonics, after one exhibition game in Italy, headed to Vevey, Switzerland for their fourth international game. The game was the first time in NBA history that an NBA team played in the country of Switzerland. On August 31, 1984, Seattle faced Vevey Basket, who are known today as Vevey Riviera Basket or Riviera Lakers of the Swiss Basketball League. Vevey Basket was one of the best teams in their league at the time and were expected to have a good show out against the SuperSonics. As expected, Seattle got a run for their money but escaped, winning 111-110, to stay undefeated on their international tour.[1]

Seattle had two games remaining on their international tour. Both games were in West Germany. On September 5, 1984, the SuperSonics faced ASC 46 Göttingen. The two teams faced off weeks prior to the rematch and the SuperSonics easily won. This time was no different. Seattle won in blow out fashion once again, winning 106-76. [1]

The following day, September 6, 1984, Seattle faced TSV Bayer 04 Leverkusen in Leverkusen, West Germany to wrap up their international tour. TSV Bayer 04 Leverkusen is known today as the Bayer Giants Leverkusen of the ProB League in Germany. At the time of the game, they were one of the top teams in their league but were not expected to win against Seattle. As expected, the SuperSonics easily defeated TSV Bayer 04 Leverkusen, 109-86, capping their undefeated international tour. [1]

While Seattle was midway through their international exhibition games, the New Jersey Nets and the Phoenix Suns participated in the 1984 Italian Open. The 1984 Italian Open included a total of nine games in which either the Nets or the Suns faced international competition.

On September 2, 1984, New Jersey faced the Australian Udine in Udine, Italy.[1] Australian Udine were founded in 1944 but dissolved in 2011. The team started to dissolve in 2009 after falling to the second division of the Serie A League in Italy. After playing two seasons in the second division, the team pulled out of the league and shortly after, professional basketball.

In 1984, Australian Udine were a rising team with good talent gaining notability in Italy. Although the team was starting to put it all together, they did not stand a good chance against the Nets. New Jersey defeated Udine, winning 113-95. [1]

The following day, September 3, 1984, the Phoenix faced off against Ciao Crem Varese in Varese, Italy. The club which is also known as Pallacanestro Varese is a historically decorated basketball team. In their history, the club has won a total of 10 Italian League Championships, four Italian Cups, one Italian Supercup, three Intercontinental Cups, five EuroLeagues, and two Saporta Cups. At the time of the game against Phoenix, the club dominated the 1970s in the Italian first-tier level LBA but were not so bright in the early 1980s. [78]

When the club faced Phoenix, the Suns were expected to easily handle Ciao Crem Varese. As expected, the Suns defeated the Italian club by a big margin, winning 103-80, in front of a sold-out crowd. [78]

New Jersey played Simac Milan in their second game of the 1984 Italian Open. The game was played in Milan, Italy and in front of a sold-out crowd. Simac Milan, known today as Pallacanestro Olimpia Milan, which has produced current NBA players such as Danilo Gallinari and as mentioned before, Mike D'Antoni, are one of the most decorated Italian clubs in history. The club dominated the 1980s, winning five Serie A Championships, one European Championship Cup, one Italian Cup, and the 1987 FIBA Club World Cup. Despite being successful, Milan did not stand much of a chance against the Nets, losing 127-80. [78]

On August 6, 1984, the Suns faced the Australian Udine, who were looking to avenge their loss against the Nets, in Udine, Italy. The Suns had full control throughout the game and won, 118-83. The following day, August 7,1984, Phoenix was back in action to face Simac Milan, who like the Australian Udine, dropped their first game to New Jersey. Simac Milan would drop their second game also, losing to Phoenix, 118-93. [78]

On August 7, 1984, the Nets played Granarolo Bologna, in Rome, Italy. Granarolo Bologna was one of the top European clubs throughout the 1980s. The club has won 15 Italian Championships, eight Italian Cups, two EuroLeagues, one Saporta Cup, one Champions League, one EuroChallenge, one Italian SuperCup, one Italian LNP Cup, and one Serie A2 Basket Championship. Granarolo Bologna was not expected to win against New Jersey heading into this game. As expected, the Nets steam rolled Granarolo Bologna, winning 142-106. [78]

Two days later, on August 9, 1984, the Nets played Ciao Crem Varese in Rome, Italy. Ciao Crem Varese were looking to rebound from their blowout loss against Phoenix. They played better against New Jersey but ended up losing, 123-111. [78]

For Phoenix, they had two games remaining in the 1984 Italian Open. On August 9, 1984, they faced Granarolo Bologna in Rome, Italy. This was Granarolo Bologna's last chance to get a win over an NBA team. Things did not go as planned for them in the game against Phoenix. The Suns won in blowout fashion, 121-87. [79]

In the final game of the 1984 Italian Open, the Suns and the Nets faced off in Milan, Italy on August 11, 1984. Both teams put on a show in front of a sold-out crowd and in the end, Phoenix came out on top, winning 148-121. [1]

After the 1984 Italian Open, David Stern and the NBA took a four-year break from international competition. In 1988, Stern pulled together another monumental milestone in NBA history. The Atlanta Hawks were heading to the Soviet Union in the July of 1988 to play the Soviet Union National Team. [1]

This was the first time in NBA history that an NBA team played in the Soviet Union. The Hawks were coming off a successful 1987-88 season, led by Dominique Wilkins, who will be headlined later in this book. Atlanta finished third in the NBA Central Division and was the fourth seed in the Eastern Conference come playoffs. In the playoffs, the Hawks were eliminated in the Eastern Conference Semifinals to Hall of Famer Larry Bird and the Boston Celtics.

Dominique Wilkins made the All-NBA Second Team and was named the Eastern Conference All-Star Team. Wilkins teammate, Doc Rivers, who at the time of this writing is the Los Angeles Clippers head coach, also made the 1988 NBA All-Star Game. Mike Fratello, who was the Hawks head coach that season, was also the NBA All-Star Game head coach. [1]

Atlanta played three games against the Soviet Union National Team.[80] Prior to playing the Soviet Union National Team, the three-game series was formed due to the negotiations between TBS, the NBA, and Goskomsport. Goskomsport was the Soviet Union's home of sports. The three games series is known as the Atlanta Hawks Tour of the Soviet Union. David Stern joined the Hawks on the tour as well. [80]

Stan Kasten, the Hawks president and then the team's general manager, talked about how the trip was a huge culture shock and how difficult it was sometimes.

> *"It was such a culture change for all of us. It was still very much Cold War and Iron Curtain-type Soviet Union, "* said Hawks President Stan Kasten. *"So it was difficult for many of us. But for players, who are used to first class this and first class that, it really was quite a culture shock. "* [80]

On July 25, 1988, Atlanta played game one of their three games series against the Soviet Union National Team in Tbilisi, Soviet Rep. of Georgia. Game one was full of lead changes throughout the game and excitement. In the closing seconds, John Battle of the Hawks hit a buzzer-beater to give his team the win. Dominique Wilkins did not play in game. The Russians failed to book a connecting flight from Moscow and the sports official did not wait for him. This left Wilkins abandoned at the Moscow Sheremetyevo Airport. On top of being abandoned at the airport, the Hawks star and one of the NBA's top players did not have any Russian money, leaving him without any options to get food or get a beverage. For Wilkins, it was a serious issue, but he joked around about it afterwards.

"12-hours with no basketball representatives or anybody I knew at the airport. So I sat there for 12 hours by myself, but it was fine. Looking at machine guns, guys 12 years old looking at your ID, and all that stuff. It was fun," Wilkins said facetiously. [80]

Two days later, on July 27, 1988, the two teams faced off in Vilnius, Lithuania. Dominique Wilkins, after a rough experience and missing game one, joined his team for game two. Like game one, the second matchup between the two teams was very similar. This time, the game went into overtime but there was some confusion at the final buzzer with the score tied up at 92. One Soviet official initially called the game to end in a tie and the Soviet Union National Team players left the court. Mike Fratello argued that the game must continue, and the game could not end in a tie. Mike Fratello and the Hawks were correct to argue for overtime due to the international rules which forbid any game ending in a tie.[80]

The game went into overtime and the Hawks ended up winning game two, 110-105. Wilkins led his team to the win scoring 29 points. [80]

After the game, Mike Fratello told reporters why his team argued to keep playing rather than end in a tie.

"Let me get this straight. We fly halfway around the world, go from Moscow to Sukumi to Tbilisi to Moscow for a connecting flight to Vilnius, and we're going to tie?" [80]

Scott Cunningham, who was the Atlanta Hawks team photographer, said the Lithuanian crowd for game two was the best crowd they experienced on the trip.

"That was by far the best crowd that we had," recalled Cunningham. *"They were loud and appreciate for both sides."* [80]

With the Hawks winning the first two games and looking for a clean sweep of the Soviet Union National Team, both teams headed to Moscow, Russia for game three. The Soviets avoided a clean sweep in the series and defeated Atlanta 132-123. Aleksandr Volkov and Šarūnas Marčiulionis led the Soviets combining for 55 of the teams 132 points. [80]

The three-game series against the Soviet Union National Team was quite a whirlwind for the Hawks. Dominique Wilkins, who had the roughest trip out of any of the players, appreciated the trip and gained respect and appreciation for the country.

"It was just a hard trip. It was a nice experience. It made me appreciate this country," Wilkins said. *"It was a fun experience, because you had all your teammates with you. But it was a rough trip as far as the food and the travel."* [80]

As Dominique Wilkins noted the food was a rough patch in the trip. In fact, the Hawks radio play-by-play announcer Steve Holman described what the kind of food they ate.

"Cucumbers and tomatoes," said Hawks radio play-by-play man Steve Holman. *"That's what we ate for 15 days. It was pretty rough as far as the food goes. It was the best they had, but the milk had lumps in it, for example."* [80]

"At the end of the trip, they knew that the players weren't eating right," Holman said. *"So they had spaghetti and real marinara sauce sent into Moscow. Mike Fratello and David Stern did the cooking for the whole group."* [80]

Dominique Wilkins, who was entering the prime of his career, thought even less of the Russian food.

"It was terrible, like it had radiation in it." [80]

Besides from the terrible food, the Hawks enjoyed the playing aspect against the Soviet Union National Team.

"That Soviet team was very solid with (Alexandr) Volkov and (Sarunas) Marciulionis. They were tough," Wilkins said. *"The games were fun."* [80]

"Looking back at it now, it was a tremendous experience for my wife and I," Holman said." [80]

As for Alexandr Volkov and Šarūnas Marčiulionis, they would join the NBA later in their careers. Volkov played two seasons with the Hawks in 1989-90 and 1991-92 while Šarūnas Marčiulionis played several NBA seasons splitting time with the Golden State Warriors, the Seattle SuperSonics, the Sacramento Kings, and the Denver Nuggets and played six seasons. In those six seasons, he finished as Sixth Man of the Year twice and at the time of his playing career, played the most minutes as an international player.

For Alexandr Volkov, playing against the Hawks was a huge catalyst for his pursuit to play in the NBA. In fact, Alexandr Volkov was drafted with the Hawks sixth round pick in the 1986 NBA Draft. Despite being drafted in 1986, he did not play with the Hawks till 1989.

> *"I remember every detail. It was a great memory,"* Volkov said. *"It was great for my basketball career and Soviet basketball."* [80]

> *"I idolized the NBA,"* Volkov said, *"I was the happiest guy in the world that moment when I put on a Hawks uniform and put on my shoes on the floor for the first game. It was a dream come true."* [80]

Steve Kasten talked about drafting international players and said that he believed when he watched the Soviets play that a good amount of them could make the NBA if they were given the opportunity.

> *"We thought they could make the NBA if they were given the opportunity,"* Kasten explained. *"Remember, back then and even today, if you're not a first-round pick, your chances of making the league are virtually nil. So we spent all this time drafting neighbor's kids, and friend of other people in the seven, eighth, ninth round. What was the point of that."* [80]

> *"So we decided to draft world-class players. All of whom were on their national teams and represented the best of all these countries. They had played successfully in international competition. So we had a much better chance with any of them than what we were doing here."* [80]

Atlanta also drafted Arvydas Sabonis, who was recovering from his second torn Achilles. Sabonis was a 7-foot 4-inch center who was selected with a fourth-round pick in 1986 and will be highlighted later in this book.

Chapter 9

The Human Highlight Film

Dominique Wilkins was born on January 12, 1960 in Paris, France. Dominique Wilkins' father, John Wilkins was a sergeant in the U.S Air Force stationed in France. The future NBA star had seven siblings. One of his siblings, Gerald Wilkins, who is four years younger than Dominique, went on to have a 14-year career in the NBA, playing for four teams. [83]

Dominique Wilkins lived in a total of 10 cities in three different countries by the time he turned 15 years old. His family settled back in the United States, first moving to Dallas, Texas. After a short stint in Dallas, Dominique Wilkins and his family moved to Baltimore, Maryland, where he played his freshman season of high school basketball. In his sophomore season, the Wilkins family moved to Washington, North Carolina, where he played high school basketball for Washington High School. The high school also produced Washington Nationals longtime third baseman, Ryan Zimmerman.[83]

Dominique Wilkins dominated high school basketball, leading his team to consecutive Class 3-A State Championships in 1978-79. In those championship seasons, Wilkins won back-to-back Most Valuable Player honors. Wilkins also won state MVP in 1978 and 1979. His high school play was heavily covered by media outlets across the United States. The talented teenage basketball player was named to the 1979 McDonald's All-American Game in Charlotte, North
Carolina as a 6-foot 7-inch small forward. [81]

Other players who were named to the 1979 McDonald's All-American game were Clark Kellogg, Ralph Sampson, Isiah Thomas, and James Worthy. The class of 1979 is famously known as one of the best McDonald's All-American classes in the program's history.

Dominique Wilkins played well in the game recording a double-double with 16 points and 12 rebounds. Isiah Thomas and John Paxton led the East to nail biter 106-105 overtime victory. Thomas scored 19 points followed by Paxton with 14 points.

In 2012, Douglas Freeland, who is the director of the McDonald's All-American Games, named Dominique Wilkins as one of the 35 greatest McDonald's All Americans prior to the 35th annual McDonald's All-American Game.

"This list of great McDonald's All Americans recognizes 35 years of basketball excellence," said Douglas Freeland, director of the

McDonald's All-American Games. *"These players are a veritable 'who's who' of basketball's modern era."* [81]

"For 35 years, the McDonald's All-American Games have showcased the top high school basketball players nationwide," said Morgan Wooten, McDonald's All-American Games Selection Committee Chairman. *"These 35 players are representatives of all the great players that have played in the McDonald's All-American Games over the years."* [81]

Dominique Wilkins also ran and jumped for the track team at Washington High School. Dominique excelled at track as well being named to multiple All-American teams. For basketball and track, Wilkins was named to a total of seven All-American teams. [83]

In 2012, *ESPN Films* produced a documentary on Wilkins' upbringing and early life, *"Dominique Belongs to Us."* The film highlights Wilkins leading his small school to multiple championships while documenting his roots, growth as a teenager, life as a college star, and an NBA superstar. [82]

After receiving multiple scholarships from NCAA Division 1 programs to play basketball and run track, Wilkins declared for the University of Georgia. The talented teenager came to Georgia with the reputation of being a game changing player with serious NBA potential.

Wilkins went on to spend three years at the University of Georgia and dominated on the college level. While a Georgia Bulldog, Wilkins' famous nickname was established: "The Human Highlight Film."

During his freshman season, Wilkins only played in 16 total games but still produced consistently throughout the season. He averaged 31.8 minutes, 18.6 points, 6.5 rebounds, 1.7 steals, 1.4 assists, and 1.3 blocks. [85] In his sophomore season, Dominique Wilkins had the best season of his Bulldog career. He received a bigger role on the team and was one of the main offensive options. On top of being one of the top offensive options, Wilkins was stellar on the defensive end. He played 31 games for Georgia averaging 37.3 minutes, 23.6 points, 7.5 rebounds, 2.4 blocks, 1.7 assists, and 1.3 steals in his sophomore season.[85] Wilkins won the 1981 SEC Men's Basketball Player of the Year. In his junior season, Wilkins started 27 of the 31 games he played in and averaged 34.9 minutes, 21.3 points, 8.1 rebounds, 1.4 blocks, 1.2 assists, and 1.0 blocks.[85] His junior season play earned him multiple honors and awards including Associated Press (AP) Third-team All-American and National Association of Basketball Coaches (NABC) and United Press International (UPI). Following the end of his junior season, "The Human Highlight Film" decided to forgo his senior season and declare for the 1982 NBA Draft. [83]

Dominique Wilkins was drafted by the Utah Jazz with the third overall pick. Only James Worthy, who was selected first overall by the Los Angeles Lakers, and Terry Cummings, who was selected second by the San Diego Clippers, went before Wilkins in the 1982 NBA Draft. [92] Despite being drafted by the Jazz, Utah faced severe cash problems leading to their third overall pick being traded to the Atlanta Hawks a couple months following the draft. The Jazz traded him for one million dollars cash, Freeman Williams, and John Drew.[83] To this day, that trade has been highlighted as one of the worst trades in NBA history, with Utah on the negative side. Freeman Williams and John Drew never lived up to expectations and lasted only a few seasons in the NBA while Dominique Wilkins went on to build a Hall of Fame career.

Wilkins had a great rookie season, earning NBA All-Rookie First Team and played all 82 games. The talented rookie started in all 82 games for Atlanta and averaged 32.9 minutes, 17.5 points, 5.8 rebounds, and 1.6 assists.[82] Terry Cummings, Clark Kellogg, James Worthy, and Quintin Dailey were the other four players on the 1982-83 NBA All-Rookie First Team. The NBA did not introduce an NBA All-Rookie Second Team until the 1988-89 season.[82]

Wilkins' third season in the NBA with Atlanta was the catalyst for his image of being one of the top dunkers in the league's history. "The Human Highlight Film" participated in his second NBA Slam Dunk Contest, the 1985 NBA Slam Dunk Contest. The 1985 NBA Slam Dunk Contest, to this day, is known as one of the best dunk contests in the league's history. The contestants in the 1985 NBA Slam Dunk Contest, which was held in Indianapolis, Indiana included Wilkins, Michael Jordan, Clyde Drexler, Julius Erving, Darrell Griffith, Larry Nance Sr, Terence Stansbury, and Orlando Woolridge. In the first round, Wilkins totaled 145, which was the highest first round in the contest, and advanced to the semi-final round. Michael Jordan and Terence Stansbury both recorded 130, joining Wilkins in the semi-final round. Julius Erving also advanced to the semi-final round, beating out Clyde Drexler, Darrell Griffith, and Orlando Woolridge, who were all eliminated. [87]

In the semi-final round, Michael Jordan performed the most iconic dunk of his career by leaping from the free throw line and slamming it with one hand, scoring him a perfect 50. His 50 was the only perfect scored dunk during the semi-final round. Wilkins continued to put on a show, scoring 140 in the semi-final round, advancing to the finals. For Michael Jordan, he topped the semi-final round, scoring 142, clinching a finals appearance. Julius Erving, who scored 132, Larry Nance Sr, who scored 131, and Terence Stansbury, who scored 136, were eliminated. [87]

In the finals, Wilkins put on a show in front of the Indianapolis crowd. "The Human Highlight Film" saved his best dunks for the finals and scored perfect 50s. Wilkins first dunk was a stellar off the backboard reverse thunderous slam with both hands. His second dunk was an acrobatic two-handed windmill dunk securing the contest and winning his first NBA Slam Dunk trophy. [87]

In 1990, Wilkins won his second and final NBA Slam Dunk Contest of his historic career. "The Human Highlight Film" participated in the 1988 NBA Slam Dunk Contest but lost to Michael Jordan, the player who he defeated in his first NBA Slam Dunk Contest win. To this very day, Wilkins strongly believes he should have won over Michael Jordan.

> *"I don't care what anybody says - I believe I won,"* Wilkins said. *"Everywhere I go people tell me I was robbed. In a way, I'm tired of talking about because there isn't a day that goes by I don't hear about it. Look, I'll say it like this. MJ (Michael Jordan) was the man back then. It was his city, they weren't going to let him lose."* [88]

The following year, in 1989, Dominique Wilkins decided to sit out and not participate. In 1990, Wilkins did not have the chance to battle Michael Jordan for a third time and get revenge in the NBA Slam Dunk Contest. Michael Jordan decided to retire from dunk competition but that did not mean Wilkins did not have any tough competition in 1990. Billy Thompson, Kenny Smith, Scottie Pippen, Shawn Kemp, Rex Chapman, Kenny "Sky" Walker, and Kenny Battle were the seven other contestants in the competition.

In the first round, Wilkins scored a total of 96.3 in the two dunks he recorded, which placed second. Shawn Kemp dominated the first round, recording a first round high 98.2. Kenny "Sky" Walker recorded 95.2 followed by Kenny Smith, who recorded 93.0. All four advanced to the semifinals of the 1990 NBA Slam Dunk Contest. Scottie Pippen, Rex Chapman, Billy Thompson, and Kenny Battle all fell short and were eliminated. [83]

In the semifinals, all four contestants put on a show. Kenny Smith dominated the first round and placed first with a total score of 98.3 followed by Wilkins with 97.7. Both Kenny Smith and Wilkins advanced to the finals. Kenny Walker, who scored 97.4 and Shawn Kemp, who recorded 96.4, were eliminated.[83]

In the finals, Wilkins outscored Kenny Smith by a final scorecard of 146.8 to 145.1, crowning his second NBA Slam Dunk Contest title. The 1990 NBA Slam Dunk Contest was the last NBA Slam Dunk Contest "The Human Highlight Film" participated in. [83]

During the years Dominique Wilkins, participated in the NBA Slam Dunk Contest, the top stars of the league participated as well. That was a big takeaway for "The Human Highlight Film."

> *"We had all the big-name players,"* Wilkins said. *"I went up against Doctor J (Julius Erving), MJ, Larry Nance (Sr), Tom Chambers, and*

Spud Webb. If you were a star, you did the dunk contest. And if you weren't a star player, you wanted to match up with the big dogs. It mattered." [88]

Another huge takeaway from participating in the NBA Slam Dunk Contests were the cash money prize if crowned the winner.

"We obviously weren't making as much money as these guys now," Wilkins said. *"So yeah, that dunk contest money helped a lot. They should consider upping the prize. Maybe it'll convince some of these stars to get in it. To us 25 stacks was a big deal. To these guys it's pocket change."* [88]

During his time competing in the NBA Slam Dunk Contests, Wilkins was a member of the Atlanta Hawks. He spent the first 12 seasons of his career as a Hawk, leading Atlanta to the playoffs in eight of those 12 seasons. He played a total of 882 games as a Hawks and averaged 36.9 minutes, 26.4 points, 6.9 rebounds, 2.6 assists, and 1.4 steals per game.[92]

Wilkins did not deliver a championship to the city of Atlanta but will be remembered as one of the best players to ever wear a Hawks uniform and has quite the resume. He is also one of only four players to have their jersey number retired by the Atlanta Hawks.

- NBA All-Rookie First Team (1983)
- Two-time NBA Slam Dunk Contest champion (1985, 1990)
- Nine-time NBA All-Star (1986-1994)
- All-NBA First Team (1986)
- NBA scoring champion (1986)
- Four-time All-NBA Second Team (1987, 1988, 1991, 1993)
- Two-time All-NBA Third Team (1989, 1994)
- No. 21 retired by the Atlanta Hawks [92]

Following his twelfth season with Atlanta, Wilkins was traded to the Los Angeles Clippers for Danny Manning. The trade stunned the NBA universe leaving everyone wondering why the Hawks, who were in first place in the Eastern Conference trade away a consistent franchise player. He was averaging 24.4 points and 6.2 rebounds for the Hawks before the trade was made official.[92] The main reason many believe Wilkins was dealt to Atlanta was a reason he once experienced: money issues. The Hawks were wary about offering a long-term contract to Wilkins, who was 35 years old at the time and already had an Achilles injury and a couple small injuries in the past.

A month later, on March 25, 1994, Dominique Wilkins made his return to Atlanta as a Clipper and recorded 36 points and 10 rebounds against his former team. As a Clipper, Wilkins started and played in 25 games and averaged 37.9 minutes, 29.1 points, 7.0 rebounds, and 2.2 assists. [92]

Following his short stint with Los Angeles, Wilkins signed with the Boston Celtics as a free agent in the summer of 1994. He played a total of 77 games, starting in 64 games, for the Celtics in the 1994-95 season and averaged 31.5 minutes, 17.8 points, 5.2 rebounds, and 2.2 assists.[92] It was clear his numbers started to dissolve, and it was highly due to his role with Boston. Wilkins was not pleased with the role he had with the Celtics and in August of 1999, "The Human Highlight Film" made a big decision to take his basketball talents overseas.

At 35 years old, Wilkins agreed to a two-year contract worth around $7 million with Panathinaikos of the Greek League. The club was really invested in signing the talented NBA All-Star and even went the extra mile to lure him to Greece. Wilkins was offered custom housing, multiple cars, a house maid, and the team paid his taxes in Greece. [89]

Panathinaikos, with the help of Wilkins, won the EuroLeague Final Four of 1996, which was played in Paris, France, his birthplace. Wilkins was named the Final Four MVP and won the Greek Cup with Panathinaikos, but his team fell short of the Greek League national championship. Panathinaikos lost to Olympiacos three games to two in a best of five series in the Greek League Finals. Wilkins played a total of 30 games in Greece and averaged 32.0 minutes, 21.0 points, and 8.0 rebounds.[92] Despite having success in Greece, Wilkins was not happy.

In January of 1996, Wilkins complained about how he was being treated. He was eventually fined $40,000 and was told by the club to keep his mouth shut.

> "I had reached my frustration point," Wilkins said. "I said, 'I'm tired of being treated like crap, I'm not going to be treated like that anymore.'" [89]

Dominique Wilkins then expressed his frustration for his coaches wanting him to play better on the defensive end and not making all his shots.

> "That was the kind of psychology they used, to try to make me play better," Wilkins said sarcastically. "I would tell them, look, I've played some of the best basketball that's ever been played, against the best who've ever played - but they don't want to hear what you have to say. They don't listen to the players." [89]

Paul Giannakopoulos, the club president, expressed his opinion on the egos of NBA stars like Dominique Wilkins.

> *"I find now that the stars of the NBA are like the stars of Hollywood,"* said the club president, Paul Giannakopoulos. There are reports that he was paying around $3.5 million of his salary. [89]

At the time of his move to Greece, other NBA stars respected his decision and said that he was making the right choice during that point of his career.

> *"Julius Erving, Charles Barkley, Joe Dumars - they all told me I was doing the right thing,"* Wilkins said. *"There must have been 20 or 30 players at the Mike Tyson fight in August, and not one guy questioned why I was doing it."* [89]

Wilkins was even fined up to $50,000 by his club for making frequent trips back to the United States during their season on top of complaining. Despite all the controversy behind him in a Panathinaikos uniform, his one season overseas was memorable. He left Greece with quite some hardware and league honors: EuroLeague champion, EuroLeague Final Four MVP, Greek Cup winner, Greek Cup Finals Top Scorer, and the Greek Cup Finals MVP. [89]

After just one season in Greece, Dominique Wilkins returned to the NBA as a member of the San Antonio Spurs. With the Spurs, his main role was to come off the bench and provide a boost on both ends of the floor. David Robinson, who was the Spurs biggest star, missed a majority of the 1996-97 season due to injuries, leaving Wilkins to shine. Despite coming off the bench, Wilkins led the team in scoring, starting 26 of the 63 games he played, averaging 18.2 points, 6.4 rebounds, and 1.9 assists per game. [92]

Ironically, following his one season stint with San Antonio, Wilkins decided to once again play basketball overseas. He signed a deal with Bologna of the Italian League for the 1997-98 season. Wilkins played a total of 34 games in the Italian League and averaged 33.5 minutes, 17.8 points, 7.3 rebounds, and 1.7 assists.[92] "The Human Highlight Film" would only spend that season in Italy before returning to the NBA for one last ride.

Wilkins signed with the Orlando Magic and played alongside his brother Gerald Wilkins. He only played 27 games and started in two games for Orlando and averaged 9.3 minutes, 5.0 points, 2.6 rebounds, and 0.6 assists before retiring. [92]

"Father Time don't wait for no one, man," Wilkins told *The Undefeated. "We try to fight it, but you just can't fight it. The competitiveness kind of kicks in and keeps your mind thinking you can do it on that level. And that's a great thing about being a great competitor. You're not able to do it like you once were, but you can still be effective in other ways."* [90]

Since 2004, Wilkins has served as the Hawks Vice President of Basketball. His role includes working with management and business operations within the Hawks organization. His main role with the Hawks is advising the senior management team when it comes to basketball. On top of his front office role, Wilkins also appears as a color commentator at Atlanta's game. His partner is Bob Rathbun, who has been the Hawks' play-by-play announcer for many years. [86]

In March of 2015, the Hawks honored Wilkins by unveiling a statue of him outside their arena: Phillips Arena in Atlanta.

On September 8, 2006, Wilkins was inducted into the Naismith Memorial Hall of Fame. Along with Wilkins, Joe Dumars and Charles Barkley were in the same Hall of Fame class. [86]

Dominique Wilkins will forever be remembered as one of the best highlight dunkers in NBA history and one of the best players to play for the Hawks. He is also one of the best NBA players to be born in France.

Chapter 10

Hakeem 'The Dream' Olajuwon

Hakeem "The Dream" Olajuwon is viewed as one of the NBA's pioneers when it comes to the league globalizing.

Hakeem Olajuwon was born in Lagos, Nigeria on January 21, 1963 to two parents who worked in the Yoruba cement business. He had a total of seven siblings and his parents valued and taught all their kids to be hardworking and not take anything for granted. [99]

Growing up, Hakeem Olajuwon thrived in the sport of soccer. Soccer was and is still one of the most popular sports in Nigeria. He was a goalkeeper due to his size at a young age and played soccer up to his late teen years in Nigeria. [99]

"Soccer in Nigeria is like basketball in America," Olajuwon said. *"In Nigeria, playing soccer is natural."* [100]

"The Dream" discovered the game of basketball in a unique way. A Nigerian coach saw potential in the tall teenager and asked him if he can dunk a basketball. At first, he could not dunk but this was just the beginning of his journey. The Nigerian teenager played for the Nigerian junior national team in the All-African Games in 1979. "The Dream" showed great potential as a big man and has stellar footwork and versatility for a man his size. His talent and uniqueness for a near seven-footer caught the eye of an opposing basketball coach in Nigeria at an international tournament in Angola, who told him he should look into attending a college in the United States and keep his eyes peeled for a basketball scholarship. [99]

"I responded to him that I didn't know anybody in America," Olajuwon said. [100]

The same coach helped Hakeem Olajuwon get in touch with Guy Lewis, who was the head basketball coach at the University of Houston. After talking with Guy Lewis, Olajuwon was granted a tryout in America to be a part of the team. "The Dream" had a successful tryout, stunning viewers and landing him a scholarship with the University of Houston. Olajuwon instantly felt at home at the University of Houston. He declared as a physical education student in the College of Education and valued education. The value of education was highly due to his upbringing and what his parents stressed to all their kids: hard work and the value of education. [99]

His first year at the University of Houston was not a breeze for the Nigerian teenager. Olajuwon had to redshirt his freshman year at the University of Houston due to the NCAA's rule of clearance. Although he had to redshirt, he did manage to play occasionally his freshman season. The Nigerian teenager asked his coaches if he can receive more playing time for the Cougars.[93] In return, former University of Houston Alum and NBA All-Star Moses Malone, who was a Houston Rocket at the time, started to work with Hakeem Olajuwon. Moses Malone helped Hakeem Olajuwon develop his skills and adjust to the college level. It did not take long for Hakeem Olajuwon to begin to show some serious potential, not just on the college level but bright signs of a professional basketball career. In his freshman season, Olajuwon averaged 18.2 minutes, 8.3 points, 6.2 rebounds, and 2.5 blocks per game.[93] He played a total of 25 games, starting in six of them. The Cougars placed second in the Southwest Conference and had a conference record of 11-5 with an overall record of 28-5. Houston, despite a successful regular season, fell to the University of North Carolina in the Final Four of the NCAA Tournament, ending their season. [93]

In his sophomore season, 1982-83, at the University of Houston, Olajuwon was a member of the "Phi Slama Jama" fraternity. The "Phi Slama Jama" fraternity is also known as the "college dunking fraternity" and was made up by Olajuwon, Clyde Drexler, Famers Clyde, Michael Young, and Larry Micheaux. The same season, Olajuwon was nicknamed "The Dream." A catalyst to being nicknamed "The Dream" was his famous go-to post move called "The Dream Shake," where we would spin and pivot his foot confusing the defender and him finishing with an easy layup or dunk. [94]

Hakeem Olajuwon received a much bigger role with the Cougars. His minutes nearly doubled but still came off the bench quite often for Houston. The Cougars, once again had great success in the regular season, breezing through the Southwest Conference, finishing first with a conference record of 16-0 and an overall record of 31-3. [93] Houston was ranked as the number one team in the country for a majority of the second half of the season, leading into the NCAA Tournament. The Cougar even rode a 26-game winning streak heading into the NCAA Tournament. [99] Hakeem Olajuwon excelled in the regular season and boosted the Cougars all the way to the 1983 National Championship Game to face Jim Valvano's famous North Carolina State Wolfpack team. The Championship Game is known as one of the most famous championship games in NCAA history due to the ending. Olajuwon checked out of the game multiple times to receive oxygen, leaving NC State to remain close throughout the game. In the final seconds, Dereck Whittenberg of NC State shot the ball from nearly half-court allowing his teammate, Lorenzo Charles, to catch the airball and dunk it at the buzzer to give Jim Valvano and

NC State to win the 1983 National Championship. Despite losing, Olajuwon was unanimously awarded the Most Valuable Player of the 1983 NCAA Tournament. At the time of this writing, Olajuwon is still the only player to be awarded the NCAA Tournament Most Valuable Player as a player on the losing team. Olajuwon played in a total of 34 regular season games for the Cougars in the 1982-83 season and averaged 27.4 minutes, 13.9 points, 11.4 rebounds, 5.1 blocks, and 1.4 steals per game.[93] Following his sophomore season, the hype behind Hakeem Olajuwon started to swirl on the professional level.

Hakeem Olajuwon's junior season at the University of Houston was very special. Houston lost a good amount of talent following the 1982-83 season. Two players of the "Phi Slama Jama" decided to declare for the 1983 NBA Draft. Clyde Drexler was drafted with the 14th overall pick in the 1983 NBA Draft by the Portland Trail Blazers and Larry Micheaux went 29th overall to the Chicago Bulls. This left Olajuwon as the main player for the Houston Cougars. Michael Young and Alvin Franklin were still at Houston with Olajuwon. Olajuwon's junior season was yet another successful season not just for him but for Houston as well. [94]

Houston went 32-5 in the regular season, finishing with a conference record of 15-1. The team bounced around the top ten in national rankings throughout the season, with their lowest ranking coming in Week 1 at number 8. The Cougars finished the regular season and entered the NCAA Tournament as a five seed. Houston battled their way into the 1984 National Championship game to face Patrick Ewing and Georgetown. In the championship game, Hakeem Olajuwon and Houston fell short, losing to Georgetown 84-75. [93]

Despite losing out on another National Championship, Olajuwon had a career-high junior season. "The Dream" played in 37 regular season games and averaged 34.1 minutes, 16.8 points, 13.5 rebounds, and 5.6 blocks per game.[93] Olajuwon was awarded two NCAA awards: Southwest Conference Player of the Year and Consensus first-team All-American.

Following his junior season, Olajuwon was torn regarding his decision to forgo his senior year and enter the 1984 NBA Draft or remain at The University of Houston, receive his degree, and enter the 1985 NBA Draft. At the time of his draft decision, there was not an NBA Draft Lottery system. The number one overall pick in the NBA Draft was awarded to a team that won a coin flip. The coin flip was between the Houston Rockets and the Portland Trail Blazers. Olajuwon was hoping that the Rockets were awarded the first overall pick and he would be drafted with the pick. At the time, Hakeem Olajuwon was viewed as the unanimous number one pick, ahead of college talents like Charles Barkley, Michael Jordan, and John Stockton.

On the other hand, there were many reports that if Houston were awarded the second overall pick, they were going to package the pick and Olajuwon's former college teammate Clyde Drexler to Portland for Ralph

Sampson. In Olajuwon's autobiography, *Living the Dream*, he states that if that trade did happen, Michael Jordan was set to be selected with the second overall pick and play alongside him and Clyde Drexler. Despite the rumors, the coin flip awarded the Rockets the first overall pick in the 1984 NBA Draft. With that first overall pick, the Rockets selected Olajuwon. Olajuwon was the first-ever international born player to be selected with the first overall pick in the NBA Draft. [95]

Olajuwon was expected to take the Rockets from one of the worst teams in the league to at least a playoff contender. In his rookie year, he certainly did make quite an impact. The Rockets had 19 more wins than last season and averaged 20.6 points and 11.9 rebounds, shooting .538 from the field.[98] Michael Jordan, who was selected third in the 1984 NBA Draft, behind Olajuwon, won the 1985 NBA Rookie of the Year Award. Olajuwon finished second behind Michael Jordan for the award. As a rookie, "The Dream" ranked second in the league in blocked shots, averaging 2.68 a game, and fourth in rebounding, averaging 11.9 a game.[98] In just his first season, he was voted into the 1985 NBA All-Star Game and at the end of the season was named to both the NBA All-Rookie Team and the NBA All-Defensive Team. His teammate, Ralph Sampson was also named to the NBA All-Defensive Team, becoming the first teammates since Elgin Baylor and Wilt Chamberlain in 1970.

Hakeem Olajuwon helped the Rockets make the 1985 NBA Playoffs. Despite making the playoffs, the Rockets faced a first-round exit, losing to the Utah Jazz in five games. Despite an early playoff exit, Olajuwon's rookie season cannot be overlooked. He played and started in all 82 games for Houston and averaged 20.6 points, 11.9 rebounds, and 2.7 blocks. [98]

"The Dream" went on to play a total of 17 seasons with the Rockets. At the time of this writing, Olajuwon is the only player in NBA history to spend 17 years with one franchise but not play their entire career with the team. "The Dream" ranked sixth behind Reggie Miller, who played 18 seasons with the Indiana Pacers, to spend that many seasons with one team.

In the 1993-94 season, Olajuwon won his first-ever professional basketball championship. "The Dream" led the Rockets to the 1994 NBA Finals. His teammate Kenny Smith was a big contributor to the Rockets that season and often hit big shots in clutch moments. Sam Cassell, Robert Horry, and Vernon Maxwell were also members of the Rockets that season.

The Rockets faced off against Pat Riley and the New York Knicks. The Knicks were led by Patrick Ewing, another pioneer to NBA Globalization, who will be mentioned later in this book. Along with Patrick Ewing, the Knicks had Charles Oakley and John Starks as the main leaders of the team. The 1991 NBA Finals came down to Game 7 and was the second time the NBA Finals were decided in a Game 7 since the 2-3-2 format came into play in 1985. Hakeem Olajuwon had a tremendous amount of pressure to win Houston their first-ever NBA Championship. The Rockets fell to Larry Bird and the Boston Celtics, who won titles in 1981 and 1984, in the 1986 NBA Championship, which was Hakeem Olajuwon's second season in the league. [99]

"The Dream" dominated in the 1994 NBA Finals, scoring at least 21 points in each game. His scoring high in the 1994 NBA Finals was 32 points in Game 4 in front of a sold-out Madison Square Garden Crowd. When it came down to Game 7, Hakeem Olajuwon stepped up, scoring 25 points to go along with 10 rebounds and seven assists to crown Houston as the 1994 NBA Champions. His final numbers to covet the Rockets first-ever championship were 26.9 points, 9.1 rebounds, 3.9 blocks, and 3.6 assists.

> *"If you write a book, you can't write it any better,"* Olajuwon said after Game 7. *"It has been a great season for us, and I'm just so happy to bring a championship to this city, Houston. It means a lot."* [101]

> *"In college, we went to the Final Four three times, and played in the finals twice. We had been close so many times,"* Olajuwon said. *"When you finally win your first championship, it has so much value, because you have been there so many times."* [101]

"The Dream" became the first player in NBA history to win MVP, Defensive Player of the Year, and Finals MVP honors in the same season, 1993-94. [95] That was the only season Olajuwon won MVP for his regular season play. A main reason that always hovers above his MVP season was that Michael Jordan was not in the league that season. The Chicago Bull decided to retire from the game of basketball, following Chicago's three-peat championship run. The sudden and shocking retirement has many speculations with gambling being the main catalyst to the decision. Michael Jordan, that season, played for the Chicago White Soxs of the Major League Baseball but returned to the Bulls the following season.

The following season, 1994-95, Hakeem Olajuwon's college teammates and one member of his famous "Phi Slama Jama" dunk fraternity, Clyde Drexler, joined the Rockets, instantly putting Houston as serious contenders to win back-to-back NBA Championships. "The Dream" commented following Clyde Drexler's arrival to Houston, saying it was a dream that became a reality.

> *"It was a dream, and then it was a reality. We had to make it happen,"* Olajuwon said. *"That year was very special."* [94]

As expected, Olajuwon and the Rockets advanced to the 1995 NBA Finals, in search to win back-to-back titles. Houston faced the Orlando Magic, who had a rising center in Shaquille O'Neal and Penny Hardaway. The Magic team also included sharpshooter Dennis Scott and Horace Grant.

In Game 1, Kenny Smith hit a then NBA Finals record, seven three-pointers. The last three he hit in that game tied the score up at 110 with 1.6 second remaining in regulation. The game was sent into overtime. In the final seconds of overtime, Olajuwon tipped in a missed layup by Clyde Drexler with 0.3 seconds left to secure the Game 1 win and take a 1-0 lead in the NBA Finals. "The Dream" finished with 31 points, which was the game-high. The rest of the series was all Hakeem Olajuwon and the Rockets. Houston swept Shaquille O'Neal and the Magic to crown Houston the 1995 NBA Champions, winning back-to-back titles for the first time in franchise history. [99]

Olajuwon won the battle against a young Shaquille O'Neal. "The Dream" averaged 32.8 points per game in the 1995 NBA Finals while Shaquille O'Neal averaged 28.0 points per game. In all four game, Olajuwon outscored the Magic's big man. In Game 2, Olajuwon scored 34 followed By Shaquille O'Neal with 33 points, which was the closest O'Neal got to "The Dream." [99]

Hakeem Olajuwon's stellar NBA Finals performance won him his second straight NBA Finals MVP award, becoming the sixth player in NBA history to win back-to-back Finals MVP, joining Larry Bird, Magic Johnson, Michael Jordan, Kareem Abdul-Jabbar, and Willis Reed. Although becoming the sixth player to do so, Hakeem Olajuwon and Michael Jordan were the only players to accomplish the honor consecutively. The 1995 NBA Finals win was the last time "The Dream" won an NBA Championship and the last time the Houston Rockets won a title. It was also the last year of Houston's league dominance in the Western Conference.

With the Rockets, Olajuwon spent a total of 17 seasons with the team. His 17-year run, at the time of this writing, was the longest tenure for any Rockets player in their franchise history. In those 17 seasons, "The Dream" played a total of 1,177 games and averaged 35.7 minutes, 21.8 minutes, 11.8 rebounds, 3.1 steals, 3.0 blocks, and 1.7 assists. [98]

As a Rocket, Olajuwon won multiple NBA awards and league honors:

- NBA All-Rookie First Team (1985)
- Four-time NBA All-Defensive Second Team (1985, 1991, 1996, 1997)
- Twelve-time NBA All-Star (1985-1990, 1992-1997)
- Three time All-NBA Second Team (1986, 1990, 1996)

- Five-time NBA All-Defensive First Team (1987, 1988, 1990, 1993, 1994)
- Six time All-NBA First Team (1987-1989, 1993, 1994, 1997)
- Two-time NBA Rebounding Leader (1989, 1990)
- Three-time NBA Blocks Leader (1990, 1991, 1993)
- Three time All-NBA Third Team (1991, 1995, 1999)
- Two-time NBA Defensive Player of the Year (1993, 1994)
- NBA Most Valuable Player (1994)
- Two-time NBA Champion (1994, 1995)
- Two-time NBA Finals MVP (1994, 1995) [98]

On October 29, 1996, NBA Commissioner David Stern announced the 50 Greatest Players in National Basketball Association History at the Grand Hyatt Hotel in New York. The Grand Hyatt Hotel was the same place where the original NBA charter was signed back on June 6, 1946. At the time of the NBA charter signing, the hotel was named the Commodore Hotel.

The 50 players honored were selected by a voting panel of former players, former coaches, and media members. The top ten head coaches and top ten single-season teams were also selected by media members. [99]

For the players that were able to vote, they were not allowed to vote for themselves. Out of the players who voted, only three of them were not included on the team: Bill Bradley, Johnny Kerr, and Bob Lanier.

Hakeem Olajuwon was voted as one of the 50 Greatest Players. At the time, "The Dream" was easily one of the top NBA big men in their history and there was no question he would make the cut. Despite making the list, none of his Houston Rockets team made the cut for top 10 season-long teams. Out of the teams that made the honor, no team was selected during the two years Olajuwon's Rockets won the NBA Finals: 1994 and 1995.

Following Hakeem Olajuwon's 17th season with the Rockets, he decided to turn down a $13 million-dollar deal with Houston. At the time of the offer, Houston was in the process of rebuilding and dealing the rest of their players from the 1990s. [99]

On August 2, 2001, "The Dream" was traded to the Toronto Raptors in exchange for multiple draft picks. At the time of the trade to Toronto, Hakeem Olajuwon was 39 years old and "father time" was knocking at his door.

"The Dream" played a total of 61 games for the Raptors, starting in 37 of them, and averaged 22.6 minutes, 7.1 points, 6.0 rebounds, and 1.5 blocks per game.[98] Following the 2001-02 season, Olajuwon retired from the NBA. At the time of his retirement, "The Dream" was the league's all-time leading shot blocker with 3,830 blocks. His NBA career consisted of 1238 games and he averaged 21.8 points, 11.1 rebounds, 3.1 blocks, and 2.5 assists. [98]

Besides from his historic NBA career, Olajuwon was a member of the 1996 United States Olympic Men's Basketball Team and won gold in Atlanta. He wanted to play for the original 1992 United States Olympic Men's Basketball Team, famously known as "The Dream Team," which will be noted later in this book, but he was not a United States citizen at the time. Hakeem Olajuwon became a United States citizen on April 2, 1993.[99]

In 2008, Hakeem Olajuwon was voted into the Naismith Memorial Basketball Hall of Fame. Following his induction, the Rockets unveiled a statue of him outside their Toyota Center in Houston. [99]

During the 2013 NBA Draft, Hakeem Olajuwon made an appearance during the final selection. The 2013 NBA Draft was the final time David Stern partook in the draft following his resignation as NBA Commissioner. David Stern's first NBA Draft pick he ever called was Hakeem Olajuwon back in 1984 so it was well deserved for "The Dream" himself to be alongside of David Stern as he called his final selection.

In 2016, Olajuwon became a member of the FIBA Hall of Fame. During retirement, Hakeem Olajuwon has worked with various NBA stars and legends such as Kobe Bryant on ways to improve their footwork and post moves.

Hakeem Olajuwon's NBA career made him famous and is why he is one of the best basketball players to ever play in the NBA. To him, he looks at himself as more than a basketball player and is blessed to come from Africa.

> *"When I look at the system here and look at my position - not just as a basketball player, but when I look around me at the values of the people and the culture and compare them with the values of where I came from - I feel so blessed to be from Africa."* [96]

Chapter 11

Patrick Ewing and the 1985 NBA Draft Lottery

Patrick Aloysius Ewing was born on August 5, 1962, in Kingston, Jamaica to his parents Carl and Dorothy. His father was a mechanic while his mother was a homemaker. Patrick Ewing grew up with five sisters and one brother. [108]

Growing up in Jamaica, Patrick Ewing played cricket and soccer, which were two of the most popular sports in the country. He played both cricket and soccer at high level. Patrick Ewing lived in Jamaica until he was 12 years old. [108]

When he was 12, Ewing moved to the United States, joining the rest of his family. His mother and four of his siblings moved to the United States before him.[108] He moved to Cambridge, Massachusetts and shortly after the move, he discovered the game of basketball. Ewing attended Cambridge Rindge and Latin School, known as CRLS, and played basketball under coach Mike Jarvis. He quickly became a very talented basketball player, gaining notability in the state. Despite quickly making a name for himself on the basketball court, not everything was a breeze for the talented Jamaican teen. Ewing was racially taunted quite often by opposing fans and in public. Coach Mike Jarvis remembers when he first heard the racial taunts. For him, it hit home and brought back memories when he was racially taunted due to him being an African American. [103]

> *"You have to understand how it hits you,"* Jarvis told Jackie MacMullan in the *Boston Globe*. *"I can still remember the first time someone called me that. I was riding my bicycle, and I heard it. ...You don't ever forget that. But if you are Patrick, you start to realize very early in life it's part of the territory."* [103]

Despite the chants and the rowdy racial taunts, Ewing still excelled on the court and was showing great college basketball potential. It even made Ewing mentally stronger and he gained a thick skin.

> *"Everyone looked at me like some kind of freak. The older guys taunted me. They told me I would never be anything. They said I would never learn the game. At first, I couldn't understand why they*

said those things. But I got used to it. And I learned not to let what anyone said affect me." [103]

With college on the horizon for Ewing, he enrolled in the MIT-Wellesley Upward Bound Program: a federally funded educational program, founded in 1965.[105] During his senior year, he was ready to announce where he would be playing college basketball. He made the announcement in Boston, where locals were hoping he would declare to Boston College or Boston University and continue watching him proudly represent the Boston area. The Jamaican teenager was highly expected to sign with the University of North Carolina and play for Dean Smith. When it was time for the announcement, Patrick Ewing signed a letter of intent to play basketball at Georgetown University under Coach John Thompson. This left the locals stunned and speechless. Some even left the room with faces of disappointment and hate. There was some negative speculation regarding Ewing going to Georgetown. His academics did not quite match the standard student's grades to the university which brought up the speculation that Georgetown only went after him for his basketball talent. John Thompson and Georgetown dismissed the speculation and shortly after it was no longer a conversation or debate to be made. [105]

With Patrick Ewing on his way to Georgetown, the university made a big change to benefit fans. They moved their home court from the McDonough Gymnasium to the Capital Centre for its home games. The Capital Centre held more seats for fans. The result of the relocation, following Ewing's freshman season, was expected. The attendance for home games doubled.

In his freshman season, Ewing lived up to the expectations. He started on the varsity team and was one of the team's best players on both ends of the floor. He came off the bench in Georgetown's first game but following his first game, he became a starter.

Patrick Ewing was not the captain of the team his freshman season. The captain title went to Eddie Meyers, who was a sophomore. The Georgetown Hoyas went 30-7 in the regular season, 10-4 in Big East competition, and ironically, Ewing's breakout game as a member of the Hoyas came at Madison Square Garden in New York City. The Hoyas played St. John's for their Big East season opener. Ewing and Georgetown blew out St. John's 72-42. Following the win, Ewing immediately became the talk of college basketball as one of the best big men in the game. [106]

In the 1982 NCAA Tournament, Georgetown was ranked as a number one seed, receiving a first-round bye in the tournament. The Hoyas blew through the tournament, advancing to the 1982 NCAA Tournament Final to face North Carolina, the team Ewing considered joining as a senior in high school. The game came down to the final seconds. The Hoyas threw up a half court heave to win the championship, but it did not go in, crowning North Carolina the 1982 NCAA Champions, winning 63-62 in front of an NCAA record 61,612 fans in attendance. Following the championship loss, the Hoyas were ranked number six in the season's final Associated Press Poll. Five seniors on the Hoyas graduated and were no longer on the team. Ewing capped off his freshman season playing a total of 37 games, starting in 36 of them, and averaging 28.8 minutes, 12.7 points, 7.5 rebounds, and 3.2 blocks per game.[106]

In Ewing's sophomore season, Georgetown returned to the NCAA Tournament after another successful season. The Hoyas finished fourth in the Big East with a conference record of 11-5 and an overall record of 22-10.[106] Prior to the 1983 NCAA Tournament, in the Big East Tournament, Georgetown lost to Syracuse in the quarterfinals. By placing fourth in the Big East, the Hoyas were awarded another first round bye in the 1983 NCAA Tournament and were listed as the five seed in the Midwest Region bracket. Surprisingly, Georgetown lost to Memphis State in the second round of the 1983 NCAA Tournament ending their season. Ewing played and started a total of 32 games for the Hoyas his sophomore season and averaged 32.0 minutes, 17.7 points, 10.2 rebounds, and 3.3 blocks per game.[106] The Hoyas big man was named to his first Consensus first-team All-American that season.

Patrick Ewing had quite the junior season for Georgetown. The Hoyas finished with a regular season record of 34-3 and a conference record of 14-2. Georgetown won the Big East regular season championship and the 1984 Big East Tournament championship. The Hoyas leter defeated Providence in the quarterfinals and their Big East rival St. John's in the semifinals, Ewing and the Hoyas were due for a 1984 Big East Finals matchup against their main rival, Syracuse. In the 1984 Big East Championship game, Ewing recorded a double-double with 27 points and 16 rebounds, leading the Hoyas to a 81-72 win to win their Big East Tournament Championship and Ewing's first title. [106]

When it was time for the 1984 NCAA Tournament, Georgetown was the number one seed in the West Region and was awarded a first-round bye. In the second round, Ewing and the Hoyas just escaped an early exit. South Methodist University, best known as SMU, led the game up until the Hoyas came back and tied it up at 34 with just under three minutes remaining. Georgetown went on to advance, winning 37-36.[106]

The Hoyas cruised to the Final Four to face Kentucky. Kentucky, at the time of the matchup, never lost a semifinal game until Ewing and Georgetown broke that streak. The Hoyas cruised to the NCAA Tournament Final with the win, beating Kentucky, 53-40. [106]

In the 1984 NCAA Tournament Final, Ewing and the Hoyas faced Houston. Georgetown played very well against Houston and had control throughout the final. Coach John Thompson, in the final minutes of the game, began to sub out the Hoyas starters to let some bench players feel the moment of winning the NCAA Tournament Championship. Georgetown won the 1984 NCAA Tournament Championship 84-75. [106]

As noted before, Ewing had quite the junior season for Georgetown. The Hoyas' big man played in a total of 37 games, starting in 33, and averaged 31.9 minutes, 17.7 points, 10.2 rebounds, and 3.3 blocks per game.[106] His impressive junior season was not just highlighted by a Big East title and a National Championship. Ewing was named to his second consecutive Consensus first-team All-American but was also awarded the 1984 Big East Player of the Year, NCAA Final Four Most Outstanding Player. [106]

Following his junior season, there was speculation that Ewing should declare for the 1984 NBA Draft and forgo his senior season. He was a decorated college champion with the Hoyas and won multiple individual awards and honors. With the NBA Draft on his mind, Ewing decided to return for his senior season with the Hoyas due to one main reason: his mother.

Patrick Ewing's mother passed away in 1983 and was never able to see her son win a college title or his historic NBA career. But at the time of his decision, Ewing remembered what his mother stressed and valued. She strongly believed that the key of opportunities in the United States was a college degree. At the time of his decision, Patrick Ewing said *"Money's never been the most important thing in my life."* [108]

In addition to his decorated junior season with the Hoyas, Ewing played for the U.S Men's basketball team in the 1984 Olympics. The 1984 Olympics took place in Los Angeles, California and the United States won gold. Earlier in the year, on May 20, 1984, Ewing's first son was born to his girlfriend, Sharon Stanford. His son, Patrick Ewing, Jr., went on to have a productive basketball career as well, splitting time in the NBA Development League and overseas.

In Ewing's senior season, it was clear the Hoyas' big man would leave Georgetown not just with a B.A degree but declare for the 1985 NBA Draft. Patrick Ewing was named the captain of the Hoyas for the first time. He led Georgetown to another great regular season, finishing with an overall record of 35-3 and a Big East Conference record of 14-2. [106]

Georgetown were considered the favorites to win the 1985 Big East Tournament. Despite being the favorites, Chris Mullin and St. John's were right up there. The Hoyas defeated Connecticut in the quarterfinals and their rival, Syracuse, in the semifinal to advance to the final. The Hoyas faced St. John's in the Big East Final. Georgetown defeated St. John's to win their second straight Big East Tournament and giving Patrick Ewing another piece of hardware to add to his college basketball resume. [106]

Entering the 1985 NCAA Tournament, Ewing and Georgetown were ranked as the number one seed in the East Region. In the tournament, Georgetown breezed to the Final Four. In the Final Four, Ewing and

Georgetown faced off, once again, with Chris Mullin and St. John's. Chris Mullin struggled against Georgetown and only scored eight points in the game. The Hoyas went on to blow out St. John's, 77-58.[106]

Then came the chance to send Ewing off to the 1985 NBA Draft the best way a college player could: capping the season off with a National Championship. Georgetown faced Villanova and were considered the heavy favorites to win. Villanova was the cinderella team of the 1985 NCAA Tournament. They were an eight seed and upset Michigan, then Maryland, and North Carolina to get to the 1985 NCAA Tournament Final.[105]

In the Final, Villanova set an NCAA record, which at the time of this writing, still stands. The Wildcats shot 22-of-28 from the field and 22-of-27 from the foul line.[105] In the second half, the Wildcats only missed one shot. Georgetown shot good as well but not as great as the Wildcats. Due to Villanova's very consistent shooting and record-breaking Finals performance, the Wildcats shockingly upset Ewing and Georgetown, 66-64. To this day, this upset is in the conversation for the greatest upset in NCAA and basketball history. [105]

Following the loss and the chance to win back-to-back NCAA Tournaments, Patrick Ewing finished his senior year and graduated from Georgetown, receiving his B.A.

Ewing left Georgetown holding several Georgetown records. He is the all-time leading rebounder, all-time shot blocker, second all-time leading scorer, fifth in steals, and most games played in a college career. Following the end of his senior season, Patrick Ewing was awarded his third Consensus first-team All-American, and his second Big East Player of the Year. [106]

Since Ewing leading Georgetown to the NCAA Tournament Finals in 1985, the Hoyas, at the time of this writing, have yet to reach the National Championship game since.

Ewing was highly expected to be selected with the first overall pick in the 1985 NBA Draft. The 1985 NBA Draft was very different from the league's previous drafts. Instead of deciding which team gets the first overall pick by coin flip, David Stern announced that the number one pick will be selected in lottery style. All NBA teams that did not make the playoffs in the previous season were placed in the NBA Draft lottery, which meant seven teams would have an equal opportunity to get the first overall pick in the 1985 NBA Draft.

Each of those seven teams had an envelope with their logo and team name inside of their envelope and all seven envelopes were placed in a large clear ball, called a hopper. David Stern then shuffled the hopper and the one envelope he picked out of the hopper was awarded the first overall pick in the 1985 NBA Draft. The team that was inside the envelope David Stern picked out of the hopper was the New York Knicks, who had their eyes on drafting the

Hoyas big man. Ewing had several stellar performances under the Madison Square Garden lights in his four years at Georgetown and once David Stern unveiled the Knicks have won the first pick, there was no question Patrick Ewing was going to become a New York Knick. In 1985, the league's best players were commonly determined by height and size, rather than skill. [104]

The 1985 NBA Draft Lottery was full of speculation that David Stern rigged the selection. The years prior, 1980-1984, were not the best years for the NBA. The league was not making a whole lot of money and the competition was not spread past four to five teams, there was a drug problem, with an estimated 75% of players on drugs, and in 1982, the league was leaning towards removing six teams due to money problems. In addition, the NBA's $90 million plus television deal with CBS was nearing its end. [105]

There were also many NBA teams losing on purpose, in other words *tanking,* to get the first pick in the 1985 NBA Draft. San Diego Clippers owner Donald Sterling publicly said his team can win by losing.

> *"We've got to bit the bullet,"* Sterling said. *"We can win by losing."* [104]

Donald Sterling was not wrong at the time. The draft order, prior to the lottery system, was determined by inverse order of finish. The two worst teams of each conference had the chance of earning the first overall pick by a flip of a coin.

The team that was awarded the first overall pick in the 1985 NBA Draft, in other words, draft Patrick Ewing, would have their franchise changed forever. Patrick Ewing's impact was much more than what he could do on the court in an NBA uniform. The Hoyas big man could easily boost a franchise's ticket sales and overall revenue. In the 1983-84 season, Madison Square Garden was rarely sold out and often only half filled with fans. It was also clear that New York was the league's biggest marketplace.

As the *New York Times* noted prior to the 1985 NBA Draft Lottery, the league will benefit most if Ewing is a New York Knick.

> *"There is a strong feeling among league officials and television advertising executives that the NBA will benefit most if [Ewing] winds up in a Knicks uniform."* [104]

Stan Kasten, the general manager of the Atlanta Hawks at the time of the 1985 NBA Draft Lottery, strongly believed that David Stern would pull the New York Knicks envelope out of the hopper at a college tournament in Hawaii.

"I was sitting with a couple of NBA guys," Kasten said. *"And I remember one high-ranking-team executive, who I will not name, was a million percent convinced of what was going to happen. 'He's (Patrick Ewing) going to the Knicks,' he kept saying. 'He's going to the Knicks. It's all arranged. I didn't believe him at the time."* [104]

The 1985 NBA Draft Lottery was filled with over 100 credentialed media members and invited more than 100 additional guests. In addition, multiple television outlets broadcasted the lottery live so there was a lot of eyes and pressure to see which team gets the first pick, in other words, get Ewing.

Then came the moment everyone was waiting for. David Stern walking up the podium and dropping all the envelopes into the hopper. Jack Joyce, the league's head of security, spun the hopper five times, shuffling the envelopes. Then, David Stern started to touch and feel all seven envelopes while looking the other way before finally grabbing one.

After picking five envelopes, David Stern was left with two remaining envelopes. The two teams were the Indiana Pacers and the New York Knicks. He announced that the New York Knicks will have the first pick in the 1985 NBA Draft, the speculation and fraud talks began a media circus. Ironically, the Knicks envelope had a creased corner. The biggest speculation to the New York Knicks getting the first pick was that their envelope was frozen and put in a fridge, so it was easy for David Stern to feel which envelope contained the New York Knicks. Following the Knicks announcement, Patrick Ewing was pictured smiling and full of joy. David Stern was filled with excitement and joy.

"We were very pleased with the lottery," Stern told the press. *"The interest was great. People are talking about the lottery instead of drugs, unauthorized franchise moves or anything else negative."* [104]

When David Stern was asked about the speculation of the 1985 NBA Draft Lottery being fixed for the New York Knicks, the NBA Commissioner shrugged off those questions and did not care what people thought if they did think it was fixed.

"If people want to say that [the lottery was fixed], fine," Stern said. *"As long as they spell out name right. That means they're interested in us. That's terrific."* [104]

Only a few hours following the 1985 NBA Draft Lottery, the Madison Square Garden ticket office received more than 1,200 calls. Ewing, who was surprisingly shy, was granted two interviews: CBS and Sports

Illustrated. Following the interviews, Ewing grabbed a New York Knicks jersey and the infamous cover portrait was made. [104]

In his rookie season, Ewing faced the injury bug often but was still awarded the 1986 NBA Rookie of the Year award and was named to the NBA All-Rookie First Team. The Knicks center was also named an NBA All-Star in his rookie season. The Knicks center played a total of 50 games his rookie season, starting in all 50, and averaged 35.4 minutes, 20.0 points, 9.0 rebounds, and 2.1 blocks per game. [107] As for New York, the franchise did not get better record-wise at all. In fact, they lost one more game. The team went from 24-58 before drafting Ewing and then following Ewing's rookie season, the Knicks went 23-59. [107]

Ewing went on to play 15 seasons with the New York Knicks, playing in a total of 1,039 career games. In those 15 seasons, Ewing lived up to just about every NBA player expectation.

- NBA Rookie of the Year (1986)
- Eleven-time NBA All Star (1986, 1988-1997)
- Three-time NBA All-Defensive Second Team (1988, 1989, 1992)
- Six-time All-NBA Second Team (1988, 1989, 1991-1993, 1997) [107]

Patrick Ewing averaged 36.2 minutes, 22.8 points, 10.4 rebounds, and 3.2 blocks per game. His 1,039 games played in a New York Knicks uniform is the most all-time in the franchise's history and he is, at the time of this writing, the only Knick to play more than 1,000 games with the team. [107]

In 2000, following his 15th and final season in New York, Ewing was traded to the Seattle SuperSonics. The Knicks center was part of a three-team trade which send him to Seattle, Chris Dudley to the Phoenix Suns, and New York received Glen Rice, Luc Longley, Travis Knight, Vladimir Stepania, Lazaro Borrell, Vernon Maxwell and two second-round picks. The two second-round picks belonged to the SuperSonics. [105]

Ewing played 79 games for the SuperSonics in 2000-01, starting in all 79, and averaged 26.7 minutes, 9.6 points, 7.4 rebounds, and 1.2 blocks per game.[107] Following one season in Seattle, Ewing played his next and final season with the Orlando Magic, coming off the bench. Ewing played 65 games, starting in four games, and averaged 13.9 minutes, 6.0 points, 4.0 rebounds, and 0.7 blocks per game.[107] On September 18, 2002, Ewing announced his retirement from the NBA but only as a player.

In addition to his playing resume, Ewing, like Hakeem Olajuwon, was named to the NBA's 50th Anniversary All-Time Team. On February 28, 2003, the New York Knicks retired Ewing number 33 in the Madison Square Garden rafters. [105]

Ewing was hired by the Washington Wizards as an assistant coach for the 2002-03 season. From 2003-06, Ewing served as an assistant coach for the Houston Rockets and following his three-year term with Houston, he was hired by the Orlando Magic as an assistant coach. Since 2017, Ewing has been the head coach of his alma mater, Georgetown University for the men's basketball team. In addition to his playing and coaching resume, Ewing, like Hakeem Olajuwon, was named to the NBA's 50th Anniversary All-Time Team. [105]

Patrick Ewing, in addition to his historic NBA playing career, was a member of three United States Olympic gold medal teams. He first won gold with the 1984 United States Men's Olympic team at the 1984 Olympic Games in Los Angeles. In 1992, Patrick Ewing was a part of the historic 1992 United States Men's Olympic Team, which will be discussed later in this book. In the same year, Patrick Ewing won gold in the Americas Championship in Portland, Oregon.

Chapter 12

Remembering Manute Bol

Manute Bol was born on October 16, 1962 in Gogrial, South Sudan. His father was 6-8 and his mother was 6-10. The tallest member of his family was his great grandfather, who stood at 7-10. Bol was born into the Dinka tribe and lived in Sudan for most of his childhood and his teenage years. [109]

Bol started his basketball career at the age of 15. At the time of his basketball career beginning, Bol held a job in the Sudanese military. In addition, Bol played for the Sudan national team. In one of their games, Bol began to gain some attention, mostly due to his 7-7 height. The coach of Fairleigh Dickinson University, Don Feeley, spotted Bol in Sudan in 1982 and advised him to consider moving to the United States and pursuing a career in professional basketball. [109]

Bol took Feeley's advice and headed to the United States. There was a lot of mystery behind Bol. He did not have a birth certificate, no any formal documents, leading to many coaches pulling out of trying to pursue the seven-footer from Sudan. On top of having no official documents, Bol did not speak English well and needed to work on the language.[109]

Bol landed in Cleveland, Ohio in 1983 and met with Kevin Mackey, the head coach of Cleveland State. With no documents proving his age, the college believed Bol was much older than a college age athlete. He never played a game at Cleveland State. This led to his only option to pursue a professional basketball career was to declare for the 1983 NBA Draft. [112]

With all the uncertainty behind Manute Bol, it was clear there was a big chance he would go undrafted. Instead, there was one team willing to take a chance on him. The Los Angeles Clippers selected Bol with the 97th overall pick.[110] Bol was drafted into the NBA but decided he had to prove his worth and learn the English language better, so he continued to look for a college or university willing to take him on.

The NCAA questioned his eligibility for Division 1 basketball, which led Bol to try a Division II school. He enrolled at the University of Bridgeport in Connecticut. The university had a well-known English program for foreign students. Bol quickly picked up the fundamentals of the English language and played for the university's team. He played only his freshman season at the university and decided to declare for the 1985 NBA Draft. [112]

Before the 1985 NBA Draft, Bol decided to go pro and sign with the Rhode Island Gulls of the United States Basketball League in May of 1985.[110]

The move to play for the Gulls was to prove his worth against more competitive competition to assure NBA teams that he is a ready NBA prospect.

Prior to the 1985 NBA Draft, many draft experts believed Bol was not ready for the NBA and needed at least a couple more years of collegiate competition. That did not intimidate Bol and he remained in the 1985 NBA Draft and was selected by the Washington Bullets with the 31st overall pick. [110]

Bol went on to play a total of ten NBA season, splitting time with four teams: The Bullets, the Philadelphia 76ers, the Golden State Warriors, and the Miami Heat. In those 10 seasons, Bol played a total of 624 games, starting 133, and has career averages of 18.7 minutes, 2.6 points, 4.2 rebounds, and 3.3 blocks per game.[110] He earned 1985-86 All-NBA Defensive honors and was the NBA blocks champion twice.

After being waived by the Golden State Warriors in February of 1995, ending his NBA career, Bol signed a deal with the Florida Beach Dogs of the Continental Basketball Association. Bol ended his NBA career, ranking 14th all time, in recorded blocks in NBA history. He played one year before returning to the United States Basketball League, signing with the Portland Mountain Cats for one year. Bol played two years as well overseas, splitting time in Italy and Qatar. [112]

The legacy of Manute Bol's basketball career is not defined by the play on the NBA hardwood. His legacy as a player will forever be highlighted by his story and the path he took to get to play in the NBA. From a very tall kid, growing up in Sudan, to becoming an NBA player and becoming the first player from Sudan to play in the NBA, he will forever be known as a trail blazer for the country of Sudan and NBA globalization.

Following his professional basketball career, Bol was an avid social activist, giving back to his native country of Sudan. He visited Sudanese refugee camps, established a foundation for their betterment and donated huge amounts to construct schools and promote education in Southern Sudan.[111]

Manute Bol died on June 19, 2010 due to kidney failure and complications from a rare skin disorder. He was 47 years old at the time of his death and left behind his wife and his ten children. One of his children, Bol Bol, was drafted into the NBA in the 2019 NBA Draft and will play for the Denver Nuggets.

Chapter 13

The Story of Drazen Petrovic

Drazen Petrovic was born on October 22, 1964, in Sibenik, SR Croatia, SFR Yugoslavia. Sibenik is a small port town along the Adriatic Sea. [116] His father, Jovan Petrovic, was a police officer and his mother, Biserka Petrovic, was a librarian. Drazen Petrovic had one older brother, Aleksandar Petrovic, who played basketball in Europe from 1977 until 1991 before coming a coach.[116] He has coached multiple teams all over Europe and at the time of this writing, is the head coach of the Brazil National Basketball Team. One of his cousins, Dejan Bodiroga, was drafted by the Sacramento Kings with the 51st overall pick in the 1995 NBA Draft, but only played professional basketball overseas. He is a decorated European basketball professional, who won the FIBA World Championship MVP in 1998. [116]

Aleksandar Petrovic was Drazen's inspiration to pursue his basketball dreams as a child and follow in his footsteps. By the time Drazen Petrovic was 15 years old, he was getting his feet in the door with the Yugoslavian national team and began touring with the team. Soon after, still at 15 years old, Drazen Petrovic was a member of Sibenka's first team and his older brother, Aleksandar Petrovic was on the KK Cibona team, winning the Yugoslav championship and the national cup. [117]

Drazen Petrovic played with Sibenka from 1979 till 1983, reaching the FIBA Radivoj Korac Cup in back-to-back year, 1981-82, 1982-83, but lost in both appearances. [117] While at Sibeka, Petrovic's name started to gain popularity. In 1982, Petrovic, as a member of the under 18 Yugoslavia national team, won silver in the European U-18 Championship held in Bulgaria. In 1983, Petrovic won silver with the SFR Yugoslavia national team at Summer Universiade, which was held in Edmonton, Alberta, Canada. [115]

When he was 18 years old, Petrovic helped Sibenka win the Yugoslavian club championship but in the following days of the championship win, the championship was stripped from the club. The reason for the championship stripping was due to irregularities regarding refereeing and Sibenka did not want to rematch Bosna.[117]

Following the season with Sibenka, Petrovic was required to do a year of mandatory military service, which took him out of all basketball activities until 1984. That year was a big year for the young Drazen Petrovic. He joined Cibona and won multiple championships and titles in his first season. The team won the Yugoslav League, Yugoslav National Cup, which was Cibona's first European Cup championship. That same year, Petrovic led

Yugoslavia to win bronze at the 1984 Olympic Games in Los Angeles, California. The following year, 1985, Petrovic led Cibona to win the Yugoslav national cup, beating Bosna. [117]

In 1986, Petrovic got his first glance at the NBA when he was drafted in the third round by the Portland Trail Blazers but decided to decline joining the team and taking his talents elsewhere and continued playing for Cibona.[117] That season, he led the team to win another European title: 2nd tier European Cup Winners' Cup. Petrovic also led Yugoslavia to bronze in the FIBA World Cup in 1986 held in Spain. One year later, he led Yugoslavia to gold in the 1987 Summer Universiade, which was held in Zagreb, Yugoslavia and bronze in the FIBA EuroBasket held in Greece. [117]

In 1988, Petrovic decided to leave Cibona and bring on new challenges, joining Real Madrid of the ACB League for an estimated deal of four million in United States currency. Following the move, Cibona feared many of their young players would also depart which did occur. He led Real Madrid to the Spanish King's Cup and a 2nd tier European Cup Winners' Cup. Petrovic decided to only play one season with Real Madrid and that it was his time to take his talents to the NBA. Despite waiting until the end of the season to leave Real Madrid, the Portland Trail Blazers offered to buy him out of his contract to join the team that season.[117] Instead, he waited and joined Portland for the 1989-90 season. Before joining Portland, Petrovic led Yugoslavia to silver at the 1988 Olympic Games in Seoul, South Korea.

Drazen Petrovic left one of the most decorated resumes for an international basketball player in the 10 years he played overseas in Europe.

- Two-time EuroLeague champion (1985, 1986)
- EuroLeague Finals Top Scorer (1985)
- Best Athlete of Yugoslavia (1985)
- Croatian Sportsman of the Year (1985, 1986)
- Four-time Euroscar (1986, 1989, 1992, 1993)
- Two-time Mr. Europa Award (1986, 1993)
- FIBA European Selection (1987)
- Two-time FIBA Saporta Cup champion (1987, 1989)
- Two-time FIBA Saporta Cup Finals Top Scorer (1987, 1989)
- Two-time Saporta Cup Finals Top Scorer (1987, 1989)
- FIBA Korac Cup Finals Top Scorer (1988)
- FIBA EuroBasket MVP (1989)
- Spanish League Top Scorer (1989)
- Spanish Cup Final Top Scorer (1989) [117]

In his first season with the Trail Blazers, Petrovic joined a team with heavy depth at the guard position. His main role was an elite shooter and did not get the minutes he wished. He averaged 12.6 minutes per game in his rookie year to go along with 7.6 points, and 1.5 assists in 77 games off the bench. [118] Despite the lack of minutes, Drazen Petrovic made and played the best of each minute on the court. He shot .459 from three and .485 from the field.[118]

In his second season with Portland, the guard position was still full of depth and the Trail Blazers acquired Danny Ainge in a trade adding another guard to their roster. Petrovic started to gain more frustration regarding his minutes and during the tail end of the 1990-91 season, he was on his way to the New Jersey Nets in a three-team trade, which included the Denver Nuggets. [117]

Petrovic officially became a New Jersey Net on January 23, 1991. The Nets were looking for new identity in the league and their eyes on reaching the playoffs for the first time since 1966. New Jersey, prior to the season, drafted Derrick Coleman, the Syracuse big man, with the first overall pick in the 1990 NBA Draft.

Straight into a new start with the Nets, Petrovic received a much bigger role. He capped off the rest of the season averaging 20.5 minutes per game, double what he saw in Portland, and averaged 12.6 points. New Jersey ended the 1990-91 season with a 26-56 record.[118] In the offseason, the Nets drafted Kenny Anderson, a highly scouted point guard out of Georgia Tech, with the 2nd overall pick in the 1991 NBA Draft. This was the third star the Nets acquired in the past year. The following season, Petrovic became a full-time starter and received the nickname Petro due to his drive to play and start all 82 games.[118] The 1991-92 season was a breakout year for Petrovic. He shot an impressive .444 from three and a .508 from the field, establishing himself as one of the best young guards in the league. Petrovic averaged 36.9 minutes, 20.6 points, 3.1 rebounds, and 3.1 assists boosting the Nets to their first playoff appearance in five seasons. [118] New Jersey finished third in the Eastern Conference Atlantic Division and was the sixth seed in the Eastern Conference playoffs. Despite a successful season, Petrovic and the Nets were bounced in the first round by the Cleveland Cavaliers. There was no question Petrovic was the leader of the Nets. He led the team in scoring, games started and played, and led the team in shooting percentage from the field and behind the arc. [118]

The following summer, Petrovic was named the captain of the Croatian national basketball team at the 1992 Olympic Games in Barcelona, Spain. This was the first time in the country's history that they were an independent nation for an Olympic basketball sporting competition.[117] He led Croatia to the semifinals of the tournament and lost to the best team in the competition in the group stages: the "Dream Team," the 1992 United States Men's national team. Croatia won silver in the 1992 Olympic Games. [120]

Michael Jordan, who was a member of the 1992 "Dream Team" said playing against Petrovic was a thriller and he was never nervous.

> *"It was a thrill to play against Drazen,"* Michael Jordan said. *"Every time we competed, he competed with an aggressive attitude. He wasn't nervous. He came at me as hard as I came at him. So, we've had some great battles in the past and unfortunately, they were short battles."* [120]

In his final season with New Jersey and in the NBA, Petrovic continued to elevate his game to new heights. He led New Jersey to another playoff appearance with a 43-39 record, playing in 70 games and starting 67 of them. He capped the regular season averaging career-highs in minutes (38.0), points (22.3), and assists (3.5). On top of his career-highs, Petrovic shot career-highs in both from three (.449) and from the field (.518). He was named to the All-NBA Third Team but was snubbed from the 1993 NBA All-Star Game due to heavy guard depth in the Eastern Conference. [118]

Like the previous season, New Jersey finished third in the Eastern Conference Atlantic Division and was a sixth seed entering the Eastern Conference playoffs. On top of repetition, the Nets, once again, faced the Cleveland Cavaliers and was bounced in the first round.

Petrovic's legacy as a Net is historic. He was playing at his most elite level and will forever be remembered as an all-time Net great.

> *"Drazen was a large part in completing that Nets team,"* Brian Lewis of the *New York Post* said. *"You look and you say 'alright, this team has a nice young tandem in Derrick and Kenny but when you looked for the shooting, he went a long way to becoming a perfect complement for those guys. This was a guy that was kept on the bench in Portland, he was not going to get those opportunities with Clyde [Drexler] there, but to come over to New Jersey and average 20 and almost 45 percent shooting from deep, he was a perfect foil for those guys. He made that team dangerous team and one that I am convinced would have been a contender long-term if we had the chance to see Drazen's career unfold the way it should have."*

Following the season, Petrovic's contract expired and he was ready to sign a new deal. Despite a successful run with the Nets, the possibility of him not returning to New Jersey or the NBA was a high possibility. Petrovic was rumored to receiving offers from a good number of NBA teams but he was not pleased with the league's prominence.[117] In addition to several NBA contracts, Petrovic received multiple contracts from international teams, mostly across

Europe: most notably in Greece. It was also rumored that Petrovic verbally agreed to a large deal with Panathinaikos. Despite receiving multiple new contracts, he did not put pen to paper and tragedy struck. [117]

In the same summer of 1993, Petrovic traveled to Berlin to play with Croatia for a qualification tournament for the 1993 EuroBasket. Following the tournament, Petrovic decided to drive back to Croatia with his new girlfriend and her friend, Hilal Edebal, rather than fly with the team back to Zagreb. At the time, he was registered to board the plane and fly back with the team. When the flight attendant announced that the plane was missing one passenger, Aleksandar Petrovic, Drazen's older brother and the assistant coach of the team, informed the attendants that the one missing passenger was Drazen Petrovic and he made other arrangements. That night, it was thunder storming and raining hard. [119]

On the road, Drazen Petrovic's girlfriend, Klara Szalantzy, was driving a small red Volkswagen Golf car and the three were driving for hours on the Autobahn 9. While she was driving, Petrovic was sleeping in the passenger's seat next to the driver. Shortly after 5:20 p.m. central European time on June 7, 1993, a truck from the Netherlands swerved on the wet highway road, avoiding another car that cut in front of him and was heading off the road. The truck barreled its way through the median barrier that separated the northbound and southbound and was now in the middle of three southbound lanes. The truck was stopped, spread across all three lanes and the driver was waiving down oncoming cars to slow down. On the autobahn, there are very few speed limits located in certain sections of the highway. [119] According to Hilal Edebal, Klara Szalantzy was driving way too fast.

> *"Going way too fast,"* Edebal said. *"In Germany there are some speed limits, but in short places. But on the autobahn you can go as fast as a car goes."* [119]

According to the accident report, Klara Szalantzy was driving the small red Volkswagen Golf at 180 kilometers per hour, which translates to 112 miles per hour on a very wet autobahn. [119]

When Klara Szalantzy saw the truck in front of her, she lost control of the Volkswagen Golf and the car slammed into the guardrail and slid into the truck with high impact. She had enough time to reach and turned away with seconds to spare, saving her life. Her friend, Hilal Edebal, who was in the backseat, was thrown to the front seat suffering serious injuries to her brain and breaking her arm and right hip. Despite suffering the serious injuries, she survived. For Klara Szalantzy, she spent the week in the hospital and was released. She did not reveal any of the injuries she suffered. [119]

The Volkswagen Golf was left pushed into the right side of the truck and both front doors were forcefully pushed open. When rescue workers arrived on the scene of the crash, they immediately noticed two women showing signs of life and the ambulances quickly rushed them to the nearest hospital which was the Hospital of Eichstatt. The remaining person, Drazen Petrovic was still at the crash scene being attended by rescue workers and fire rescue workers. At the time of the crash, he was not wearing a seatbelt and was thrown in the direction of the truck causing him to receive deadly head trauma. According to the accident report, he died on impact. The rescue workers noticed that he was wearing a gold watch, which stopped at the exact time of the accident: 5:20. The rescue workers desperately attempted to revive Petrovic, but their efforts were not successful due to the severity of the head trauma he suffered from the crash. Drazen Petrovic was only 28 years old when he died. [119]

Hours following the fatal crash, the Croatian national team received the news that their captain, Drazen Petrovic, was killed in a car accident. Veljko Mrsic, who was one of the newest members of the team, still cries today about the fatal crash.

> *"Even now, talking about this, I start to cry,"* Mrisc said about the morning after, being around his devastated brothers. *"When I remember that we were in his bar, I just really get upset."* [119]

The following morning, Tuesday June 8, the New Jersey Nets held a press conference at the Meadowlands Arena. The press conference room was 'pin drop' quiet. Willis Reed, the Nets general manager at the time, spoke first, reading a pre-written statement. According to viewers and media at the press conference, he did not take his eyes off the paper more than two times. At the end of reading the pre-written statement, Willis Reed said "To me, it's like losing a son" to the reporters present. The Nets general manager answered several questions from the media following the statement, but he could not continue due to his emotions. [119]

Following Willis Reed, Chuck Daly, the Nets head coach, faced the media. Chuck Daly is known for his tough attitude and being one of the best coaches in NBA history, but he was a broken man that morning. John Brennan of *The Bergen Record* recalled how Chuck Daly looked and acted that morning.

> *"Chuck was as unflappable as anyone I ever dealt with, with basketball, with games, injuries,"* Brennan remembered. *"But this was devastating. He sort of had the pale look of somebody who had*

been hit so hard in the stomach, and the wind knocked out of him."
[119]

At the press conference, the Nets head coach spoke about Petrovic's aggressive and play hard attitude when they played the 1992 "Dream Team" at the 1992 Olympic Games in Barcelona. Chuck Daly addressed the conflicts the two had but how he did everything for the right reasons.

"You can't get mad at a player like that, no way," Daly said. *"Because he did everything for the right reasons."* [119]

Chuck Daly concluded his statements reminding the media even for a young man like Drazen Petrovic, who was coming off a career year and had a bright future ahead of him, nothing was promised.

"This reminds you of how precious life is," Daly told the reporters. *"And how much we take for granted."* [119]

Drazen Petrovic's death stunned not just the teams he was a part of but various leagues across the world. Aleksandar Petrovic, his older brother, described the impact his death had on the country of Croatia.

"It's hard for you to imagine here in America, because you have so many great players, but we have a country of four million; without him, basketball takes three steps back." [119]

Clyde Drexler, who was a member of the 1992 "Dream Team" that played with Drazen Petrovic during his time with the Portland Trail Blazers, talked about their relationship and the respect he had him.

"Drazen and I were very good friends," Drexler said. *"I was one of those people who welcomes him to Portland when he came from Europe. We talked about his family a lot in his restaurant, and he enjoyed his friends and he enjoyed the game of basketball. I really respect him because he worked very, very, hard. Each and every day in practice he would be the first guy to come and the last guy to leave the gym. So, anybody with that kind of dedication... you have a lot of respect for him."* [120]

Following his death, the New Jersey Nets retired his number 3 jersey and in 2002 his number 10 was retired by Cibona, the second professional club he played for overseas.[117] Drazen Petrovic was voted as the best European

Basketball player in history by players at the 2013 FIBA EuroBasket, and he was enshrined in the Naismith Memorial Basketball Hall of Fame. Petrovic also received the Olympic Order in 1993, which is highest award of the Olympic Movement regarding a sport. In 2008, Petrovic was honored as one of the 50 Greatest EuroLeague Contributors. [117]

To this day, Petrovic was a huge pioneer in the NBA globalizing as a league. Dzanan Musa, the Brooklyn Nets shooting guard/small forward has a special connection to Petrovic. Drazen Petrovic's mother, Biserka, offered Musa advice prior to joining the NBA and as a kid, Musa looked up to Petrovic.

"Probably people in the USA know a lot of nice stories about Drazen," Dzennis Musa, Dzanan Musa brother said. *"When Dzanan was drafted, he had special fillings because Drazen played there [Nets]. He was the main person for basketball globalization outside the USA. He was the first that came from ex Jugoslavia to the NBA. Still, today people talk about his work ethic. In conversations with Biserka, Petrovic's mother, she gave advice to Dzanan. Be humble and ready for your chance. Every beginning is tough and after one year everything will be different. You know Drazen's story at the beginning of his journey in the USA. Still today, Dzanan has a lot of friends who played with Drazen in the past. They were Dzanan's coaches in the past and today he has a lot of great advices from them. Drazen left something behind him and that's the passion for the basketball. When you see the Nets as an organization you can see smart decisions from people on the inside. Special culture and family feeling. Everyone wants to be there. You couldn't get any better."*

"One of the best ways I can describe him is he is the guy that changed the landscape for European players," Brian Lewis of the New York Post said. *"It was not like today, where everybody, every draft pick you see, is filled with guys whose name ends in ic or nic. That was not the landscape at that point. I am not going to say he single handedly changed it but he came pretty close. He showed that European players can not only play in the NBA but thrive and be a go to player and that knocked down a few barriers or a glass ceiling. This is obviously long before a Porzingis or a Parker and it is before Dirk. He blazed the trail for those guys. He was also the first European player to be named All-NBA."*

David Stern, the NBA's Commissioner at the time of Drazen Petrovic's sudden death, spoke highly of him and how he paved the way for other international players.

> *"Drazen Petrovic was an extraordinary young man, and a true pioneer in the global sports of basketball,"* Stern said. *"I know that a lasting part of his athletic legacy will be that he paved the way for other international players to compete successfully in the NBA. His contributions to the sport of basketball were enormous. We are all proud of the fact we knew him."* [120]

Chapter 14

Mt. Mutombo

Dikembe Mutombo, whose full name is Dikembe Mutombo Mpolondo Mukamba Jean-Jacques Wamutombo, was born on June 25, 1966 in Kinshasa, Democratic Republic of Congo, formerly known as Zaire.[122] The population of Kinshasa, which is the capital city, is around 2.5 million and has a high poverty and crime rate. His father, Samuel Mutombo, was the director of the city's high schools while his mother, Biamba Marie Mutombo, taught her kids the value of helping others and stressed to them the importance of opportunities. Dikembe Mutombo was one of 12 children. [122]

The family grew up in a six-bedroom home in the comfortable section of Kinshasa and were members of the Luba tribe. The family belonged to DR of Congo's upper class and Samuel Mutombo was educated at the Sorbonne in France. Dikembe Mutombo and his siblings were trained by their parents to value education, faith, and respect and their parents. [122]

Growing up, Mutombo aspired of becoming a successful doctor and to become fluent in nine languages: five Central African dialects, English, French, Portuguese, and Spanish. Despite having dreams of becoming a successful doctor and mastering several languages, Mutombo started playing sports in the early years of his childhood. He played soccer, practiced martial arts, and basketball. [122] When Mutombo was in his early teen years, he started to have a big growth spurt and by the time he was 17 years old, he was just short of being seven feet tall. Despite being a very tall teenager, Mutombo had little aspiration to pursue the sport of basketball. He was excelling at the goalie position in soccer and was very coordinated in martial arts.[122] Despite excelling in both soccer and martial arts, his father, Samuel Mutombo, pushed his son to give basketball a chance.

During Mutombo's first basketball practice, he fell and cracked open his chin leaving him with a noticeable scar. After the incident, Mutombo was ready to give up on basketball but after a heated argument with both of his parents, he gave basketball another chance.[122] Mutombo then joined the Zaire national team with one of his brother Ilo Mutombo. As a player on the Zaire national team, Mutombo traveled and started to learn the game of basketball from playing, analyzing his teammates and opponents, and from his brother Ilo Mutombo. After two years Mutombo started to produce on the court at a very high-level gaining notability from not just his country but the United States. A U.S Embassy employee started to read about him and saw serious potential in the young Mutombo. A former coach of Mutombo, Herman Henning, decided to introduce him to John Thompson, the head coach of Georgetown University. John Thompson was no stranger to scouting and experimenting with young international talent. He brought in Patrick Ewing just a couple years prior to finding Mutombo and later developed the Jamaican teenager into the first overall pick in the 1985 NBA Draft. After talking with John Thompson of Georgetown University, Mutombo was offered a USAID academic scholarship at the university and was on his way to the United States in 1987 at 21 years of age. [122]

When he arrived at Georgetown University, Mutombo was not fond of pursuing basketball and primarily focused on his childhood dream of becoming a successful doctor and returning to Congo. Mutombo, who was seven foot two inches tall when he arrived, had frequent meetings with John Thompson in regard to joining the basketball team but struggled to speak the English language. Due to his language barrier, Mutombo studied in the English as a Second Language Program, ESL. After talking with John Thompson, Mutombo spent his freshman season dominating the intramural basketball league at Georgetown University and was highlighted for his shot blocking ability. Following a dominant standout season in the intramural basketball league, Mutombo joined the Georgetown University men's basketball team. [122]

In his first season with the team, Mutombo split time from sitting on the bench to playing on the hardwood. He played as the second guy off the bench to Alonzo Mourning. Mutombo played in a total of 33 games and averaged 11.3 minutes, 3.9 points, 3.3 rebounds, and 2.3 blocks per game.[126] Georgetown finished the 1998-89 season with a Big East Conference record of 13-3 and an overall record of 29-5. The Hoyas won the 1989 Big East Men's Basketball Tournament and were the number one seed in the East Region of the 1989 NCAA Tournament. Georgetown lost to Duke University in the East Region final. [126]

Mutombo's junior season was a good year for him and started to develop and play better against Division 1 talent. The duo of Alonzo Mourning and Mutombo was the highlight of the Georgetown team and the duo was nicknamed the 'Twin Tower' lineup. The nickname was established due to the shot blocking and defense between the two centers and their dominance in the paint.

In his second season with the Hoyas, Mutombo played in 31 games, starting in 24 of them, and averaged 25.7 minutes, 10.7 points, 10.5 rebounds, and 4.1 blocks per game.[126] The Hoyas once again showed dominance in the Big East Tournament but were not able to win it. Georgetown lost to the University of Connecticut in the semifinals. In the 1990 NCAA Tournament, the Hoyas were the number three seed in the Midwest Region. The Hoyas did not go far in the 1990 NCAA Tournament, losing to Xavier, who were a number six seed, in the second round.

In his final season at Georgetown, Mutombo had a breakout year and established himself as a valuable NBA prospect. The 'Twin Tower' duo dominated the regular season and were easily the best center duo in college basketball. Mutombo played in 32 games for the Hoyas and averaged career-highs across the stat sheet. He averaged 34.1 minutes, 15.2 points, 12.2 rebounds, and 4.7 blocks per game.[126] Despite Mutombo's breakout year, the Hoyas did not have a good season compared to their previous seasons. Georgetown finished with a Big East Conference record of 8-8 and an overall record of 19-13. In the 1991 Big East Tournament, the Hoyas cruised to the final but were defeated by Seton Hall. Georgetown entered the 1991 NCAA Tournament as an eighth seed in the West Region and once again were bounced in the second round, losing to the University of Nevada-Las Vegas, commonly known as UNLV. [126]

Despite not being able to capture an NCAA championship, Mutombo was named the Big East Defensive Player of the Year and accomplished his goals he set when coming to Georgetown: graduate with a degree and master the seven languages. In 1991, he graduated with a bachelor's degree in linguistics and diplomacy and during the summer at Georgetown, he was an intern for the Congress of the United States and the World Bank. Despite accomplishing the goals, he set for himself and gaining professional experience as a summer intern, Mutombo made the decision to declare for the 1991 NBA Draft. [122]

The Georgetown graduate was mocked to go in the top five on numerous draft boards and had high expectations to enter the NBA and be one of the best centers on the defensive side. The Denver Nuggets was the one NBA team that had their decision made up on who they wanted to draft. The Nuggets were coming off a disappointing season and was the work team in the league when it came to opponent points per game and overall defensive rating. Denver held the fourth overall pick in the 1991 NBA Draft and there was no better player available to draft at their selection than Mutombo, who was, if not, the best defensive center in college basketball and the best defensive center in the 1991 NBA Draft class.

Mutombo was drafted with the fourth overall pick in the 1991 NBA Draft by the Denver Nuggets. He was 25 years old when he was selected by Denver and was the oldest player in the 1991 NBA Draft class. Following the selection, many analysts and draft experts across the country stated that he would only last a couple years in the league and that his dominance in college would not translate to the league.

Despite the early criticism, he made an immediate impact not just for the Nuggets but in the league. In his rookie season, Mutombo was the only rookie to play in the 1991 NBA All-Star Game and came in second, only behind Charlotte Hornets' Larry Johnson, in 1992 NBA Rookie of the Year voting. The Nuggets center was included on the 1992 NBA All-Rookie First Team.[123]

Due to Mutombo showing early signs of a bright future, Adidas quickly jumped on him for an advertisement revolved around his defensive image. The advertisement stated:

"Man does not fly… in the house of Mutombo." [121]

Mutombo played a total and started in the 71 games he played for the Nuggets in his rookie season, 1991-92, and averaged 38.3 minutes, 16.6 points, 12.3 rebounds, and 3.0 blocks per game. His 12.3 rebounds per game placed the Nuggets center in the top three in rebounding average that season. [123]

Despite the addition of Mutombo, Denver did not make a big jump in the win column compared to the previous season. In the 1990-91 season, the Nuggets went 20-62 and missed the playoffs. In Mutombo's rookie season, the Nuggets improved by winning four more games, 24-58, and did not make the playoffs. [123]

Mutombo spent a total of five seasons with Denver. The Nuggets center played and started in all 82 games in both the 1993-94 and the 1994-95 season and led the Nuggets to back to back playoff appearances in his final two seasons with the team. He played a total of 391 games as a Nugget and averaged 36.9 minutes, 12.9 points, 12.3 rebounds, and 3.8 blocks per game. [123]

In the summer of 1996, Mutombo became a free agent and was heavily considering signing a lengthy deal to stay in Denver. Despite Mutombo wanting to remain in Denver, Bernie Bickerstaff, the general manager of the Denver Nuggets at the time, was not fond of resigning the Nuggets center to a long-term deal. The Nuggets did not have the cap space to resign their rising center to a long-term deal and due to the cap space, Bernie Bickerstaff made the decision to let Mutombo walk.

For Bernie Bickerstaff, the Denver Nuggets general manager, it was clear he made a mistake and arguably his biggest mistake while with Denver by not resigning Mutombo and letting him walk in return for nothing. He did not return to the Nuggets following the 1996-97 season, which was the following season he let his rising center walk.

Shortly after Bernie Bickerstaff decided to let Mutombo walk, the free agent center signed a five-year deal with the Atlanta Hawks worth $55 million. [123] Mutombo was joining a team that had a rising sharpshooter in Steve Smith and a young core looking for the final piece to the puzzle. It was clear, after the news broke that Mutombo was on his way to Atlanta, the Hawks were considered a heavy threat in the Eastern Conference.

Steve Smith and Mutombo were one of the best duo's in the Eastern Conference and in their first season together led Atlanta to the Eastern

Conference playoffs with a 56-26 record and a second-place finish in the Eastern Conference Central Division.[131] Mutombo had a great year winning his second 1997 NBA Defensive Player of the Year, NBA All-Defensive First Team, and was named to the 1997 NBA All-Star game alongside of his Hawk teammate Christian Laettner.[123] The Hawks center finished second in the league in both rebounds and blocked shots. His teammate, Mookie Blaylock, was one of the best defensive guards in the NBA and led the league in steals that same season and was named to the 1997 NBA All-Defensive Second Team. In the playoffs of the 1996-97 season, Mutombo and the Hawks were bounced by the defending NBA champion Chicago Bulls. In his first season as a Hawk, Mutombo played and started 80 games and averaged 37.2 minutes, 13.4 points, 11.6 rebounds, and 3.3 blocks per game. [123]

Mutombo went on to spend a total of five seasons with Atlanta. He was a huge contributor on both ends of the floor and Atlanta made the NBA playoffs in four of the five seasons he was a Hawk. He played and started a total of 343 games for Atlanta and averaged 36.2 minutes, 11.9 points, 12.6 rebounds, and 3.2 blocks per game.[123] As a Hawk, Mutombo was named to the NBA All-Defensive First Team twice, 1997 and 1998, and was named the league Defensive Player of the Year the same two seasons. The Hawks big man was also a two-time NBA All-Star in his tenure with Atlanta. [123]

During the 2000-01 season, Atlanta was expected to make some splashes at the trade deadline. Many of their players were speculated to be possibly included in package deals. At the 2001 NBA trade deadline, the Hawks traded Mutombo as part of a six-player trade. The trade sent Mutombo and Roshown McLeod to the Philadelphia 76ers for Nazr Mohammed, Pepe Sanchez, Theo Ratliff, and Toni Kukoc.[123] The reason why the 76ers pursued a trade for Mutombo was due to Theo Ratliff, their big man, was out for the rest of the season due to injury. The 76ers were the top team in the Eastern Conference at the time of the 2001 NBA trade deadline and were in search of a good center to increase their odds of winning the 2001 NBA Championship.

The previous week, Mutombo played in the 2001 NBA All-Star Game and got to chance to play with his future teammate Allen Iverson and under his future head coach Larry Brown, who was his All-Star head coach that game. Ironically, the future 76ers duo of Allen Iverson and Mutombo led a late game comeback and won the 2001 NBA All-Star Game for the East, 111-110. [131]

As expected, Philadelphia made the 2001 NBA playoffs and the trade for Mutombo paid off in big ways. The 76ers were one game away from making the 2001 NBA Finals to face Kobe Bryant, Shaquille O'Neal, and the Los Angeles Lakers. In Game 7 of the Eastern Conference Finals against the Milwaukee Bucks, Mutombo had a dominant all-around game recording 23 points, 19 rebounds, and seven blocks to lead Philadelphia to the 2001 NBA Finals. [128]

In the 2001 NBA Finals, the Lakers were too much for the 76ers to handle. Philadelphia took an early lead, winning Game 1, but Los Angeles, behind the domination of Shaquille O'Neal and Kobe Bryant, won the next four games and winning the 2001 NBA Championship. Shaquille O'Neal was matched up against Mutombo and outplayed the 76ers big man. Mutombo averaged 16.8 points, 12.2 rebounds, and 2.2 blocks in the five games of the 2001 NBA Finals. [123]

Following the 2001 NBA Finals loss, Mutombo became a free agent. He was one of the best big men on the market that summer and there was no question he would be expecting another long-term deal. Shortly into free agency, Mutombo decided to remain in Philadelphia and ink a new four-year, $68 million deal. [123]

After signing a new deal, Dikembe Mutombo would only play one more year as a 76er. He played and started in 80 games for Philadelphia and averaged 36.3 minutes, 11.5 points, 10.8 rebounds, and 2.4 blocks per game. [123] The Sixers finished the regular season, placing fourth in the Eastern Conference Atlantic Division, with a record of 43-39, and were the sixth seed in the Eastern Conference playoffs. Shockingly, the 76ers were bounced in the first round of the 2002 NBA Eastern Conference playoffs by the Boston Celtics in just five games.

Following an early playoff exit, the 76ers were expected to make some moves. Mutombo was the main player on the roster that had the best chance of being dealt to the contract he signed the year prior. In the summer of 2002, the 76ers traded Mutombo to the New Jersey Nets in a three-player deal. The deal sent Mutombo to the Nets and in return, the 76ers received Keith Van Horn and Todd MacCulloch. [123]

New Jersey was coming off the 2002 NBA Finals, which they were swept by the same team that defeated the 76ers in the 2001 NBA Finals, the Los Angeles Lakers. The Nets had a great backcourt group and overall depth and needed a solid defensive big man. Mutombo was the player they had their eyes on and traded for him.

The 2002-03 season was not a good season for Mutombo health-wise. The Nets center struggled with wrist injuries and only played in 24 regular season games for New Jersey. He averaged 21.4 minutes, 5.6 points, 6.4 rebounds, and 1.5 blocks per game in the regular season. [129] Despite Mutombo only seeing action in 24 regular season games, New Jersey finished on top of the Eastern Conference Atlantic Division and second in the Eastern Conference with a 49-33 regular season record under head coach Byron Scott. [129] New Jersey was looking to return to the NBA Finals and were the two seed in the 2003 NBA playoffs. New Jersey blew past the Milwaukee Bucks, swept the

Boston Celtics, and then swept the number one seed Detroit Pistons behind the excellent play of Jason Kidd and company. In the 2003 NBA Finals, the Nets faced Tim Duncan and the San Antonio Spurs. The Nets went on to lose to the Spurs in six games and once again finish the season as NBA Finals' runner ups.

After one season in New Jersey, Rod Thorne, who was the Nets general manager at the time, and Mutombo agreed to a buyout. The Nets brought out the final two years of Mutombo's contract, making him a free agent. [131]

Now 37 years old and missing most of the previous season with a wrist injury, Mutombo signed a two-year deal with the Nets crosstown rival, the New York Knicks. Mutombo would spend only one season with the Knicks, playing in 65 games, starting 56 of them, and averaged 23.0 minutes, 5.6 points, 6.7 rebounds, and 1.9 blocks per game. [123] New York finished with a 39-43 regular season record, ranking third in the Eastern Conference Atlantic Division, and were the seventh seed for the 2004 NBA playoffs. Despite slipping into the playoffs, Mutombo and the Knicks were swept by the Nets in the first round ending their season. [130]

The following offseason, Isiah Thomas, who was the Knicks general manager at the time, traded Mutombo to the Houston Rockets as part of a four-player trade. In return for Mutombo, New York received Adam Griffin, Eric Piatkowski, and Mike Wilks. [131]

Mutombo's main role with the Rockets, at 38 years old, was to be the primary backup for Yao Ming. The Dikembe Mutombo - Yao Ming center duo was one of the most dangerous frontcourt duos in the NBA. In his first season with Houston, Mutombo played in 80 games, starting in only 2 of them, and averaged 15.2 minutes, 4.0 points, 5.3 rebounds, and 1.3 blocks per game. [123] The Rockets finished the season with a 51-31 record under head coach Jeff Van Gundy, finishing third in the Western Conference Southwest Division, and entered the 2005 NBA playoffs as the fifth seed. Despite a successful regular season, led by Tracy McGrady and Yao Ming, the Rockets were bounced in the first round by their in-state rival, Dirk Nowitzki the Dallas Mavericks in seven games. [132]

Mutombo went on to finish out his 18-year NBA career in Houston as a member of the Rockets. He played a total of five seasons with Houston and played in a total of 267 games and averaged 15.6 minutes, 3.2 points, 5.4 rebounds, and 1.1 blocks per game. [123]

On April 23, 2009, Dikembe Mutombo, at age 42, officially retired from the game of basketball, ending a Hall of Fame career. The once teenager from Congo who had his aspirations set on coming to the United States to study at Georgetown to become a doctor ended up putting together one of the most decorative international players resumes in the NBA's history.

- NBA All-Rookie First Team (1992)
- Eight-time NBA All-Star (1992, 1995, 1996, 1997, 1998, 2000, 2001, 2002)
- Three-time NBA Blocks Leader (1994, 1995, 1996)
- Four-time NBA Defensive Player of the Year (1995, 1997, 1998, 2001)
- Three-time NBA All-Defensive Second Team (1995, 1999, 2002)
- Three-time NBA All-Defensive First Team (1997, 1998, 2001)
- Two-time All-NBA Third Team (1998, 2002)
- Two-time NBA Rebounding Leader (2000, 2001)
- All-NBA Second Team (2001) [123]

In 2015, the Atlanta Hawks retired Mutombo's number 55 jersey and in less than a year later, in 2016, the Denver Nuggets retired his number 55 jersey.[131]

In the latter half of his NBA Hall of Fame career, Mutombo began to become heavily involved in humanitarian work. His work began in 1997 when he founded the Dikembe Mutombo Foundation to improve living conditions and aid his native country of the Democratic Republic of Congo. [133]

His work was highlighted throughout the NBA and across the world and Mutombo was shortly awarded the league's J. Walter Kennedy Citizenship Award, which is awarded to the player who provides outstanding service and work to communities, in 2001 and later in 2009.

In addition to his community service work, Dikembe Mutombo was elected for the President's Service Awards: a highly prestigious honor and the highest honor for volunteer service and in 1997, his foundation, the Mutombo Foundation, announced the plans to open a 300-bed hospital in Kinshasa, Democratic Republic of Congo. The hospital cost $29 million and construction began in 2004 and the project was complete in 2006. In memory of his mother, Biamba Marie Mutombo, who stressed to Mutombo as a child to value and treat other with respect, he named the new hospital the Biamba Marie Mutombo Hospital. His mother passed away due to a stroke back in 1997, the same year the plans for the hospital was announced. In 2007, the Biamba Marie Mutombo Hospital open and was officially the first hospital in nearly 40 years to open in Kinshasa, Democratic Republic of Congo. [133]

"For everything she did for her children and for her family, the value of love and giving back and sharing," Mutombo said. "Not just with you, not just with your family, but with the people you encounter in

life, with your community, and that was the kind of love my mom gave." [133]

"You're talking about impact. That's the impact that we are making," Mutombo said. *"We are touching lives. We are changing the living conditions of the people."* [133]

In 2007, Dikembe Mutombo was invited to United States President George W. Bush's State of the Union Address. At the State of the Union Address, Dikembe Mutombo was honored
for his humanitarian work and efforts to his native country. [133]

In 2009, Mutombo was named the NBA's Global Ambassador. The role had him travel the world to celebrate the game and the NBA and take part and arrange numerous charitable events. [131]

Dikembe Mutombo was awarded the Sager Strong Award on June 25, 2018, which is awarded to an individual revolved around the game of basketball that has shown courage, compassion, and faith off the court.[131] He was the second individual to win the award.

At the time of this writing, Dikembe Mutombo is serving on the Board of Trustees of the National Constitution Center in Philadelphia, Pennsylvania. The center is a museum dedicated to the United States Constitution. [131]

Dikembe Mutombo will always be remembered as one of the pioneers to the globalization of the NBA. His impact on the court has inspired many players, specifically kids from the country of Africa who have dreams of playing in the NBA that with hard work and dedication, it is possible. Off the court, Dikembe Mutombo raised the bar for former athletes to give back to the community, whether it's to their native country or to communities within the United States.

The Globalization of the NBA

Chapter 15

Detlef Schrempf

Detlef Schrempf was born on January 21, 1963, in Leverkusen, West Germany. [137] Growing up, soccer was the main sport across the continent of Europe. In West Germany, especially in Leverkusen, when Detlef Schrempf was a young kid, the sport of soccer was the main sport everyone played and dreamed of making a profession out of when they grow up.

"When I was a kid growing up in Germany, basketball was not much of a sport," Schrempf said. *"Soccer was 1, 2, and 3."* [140]

At the age of 13, Detlef Schrempf started to grow an interest to play the sport of basketball. Basketball was not a big sport popularity-wise in West Germany but one movie he watched changed his perspective on basketball.

"I was 13 and in school they put on this movie in it showed a game of basketball," Schrempf said. *"It was this game where they threw a ball into a ring; it was weird. The only thing we had was club basketball, and it wasn't much. Everything was soccer."* [140]

After viewing the movie, Detlef Schrempf picked up a basketball and the road to glory was underway. He was quite tall in his teenage years, seven feet tall, and started to pick up the sport of basketball quickly.

He began playing basketball for the Bayer Leverkusen youth teams. While on the Bayer Leverkusen youth teams, Schrempf excelled, dominating on the court. He was able to shoot, drive, and play great inside and on the other end play lockdown defense and post a good number of blocks each outing. [137]

Despite picking up basketball quickly, as said before, the sport was not common to play for kids his age in West Germany. This made Detlef Schrempf feel like an outcast compared to other kids and often time be negatively talked about and viewed.

"When I was a kid growing up in Germany, I was a complete outcast," Detlef Schrempf said. *"I was 7-foot 2, 180 pounds. I was a freak. No girls. Nothing. Many negative comments, and just this general attitude when you walk into a place. I came to America, and it was, 'ohhhhhh - look at that guy.' I had a new life here. I was totally accepted."* [140]

Detlef Schrempf came to the United States at the end of his high school years. He and his family moved to Washington and Detlef Schrempf attended Centralia High School. Centralia High School is a public high school that has produced a handful of professional athletes, but Schrempf is the only student to come out and play professional basketball in the NBA.

He played only his senior season at Centralia High School, leading the team to a state championship over one of their rivals, Timberline High School. [137]

While a senior, Detlef Schrempf began to receive notable attention from several Division 1 and Division 2 college and universities to play college basketball. One university stood out for Schrempf: The University of Washington. In the closing half of his senior season, Schrempf committed to the University of Washington to play college basketball.

As a freshman, during the 1981-82 season, Schrempf was one of the Huskies main options off the bench. Ironically, the Washington Huskies' only player who ever make it to the NBA was Detlef Schrempf, but he ranked seventh on the team in scoring with 3.3 points per game, total minutes played with 314, and games played with 28.[134] Washington finished the regular season with an overall record of 19-10 and a Pac-10 conference record of 11-7. [134] The team only played in the National Invitation Tournament but lost to Texas A&M in the second round. [137]

In his sophomore season, Schrempf received a bigger role with the Huskies. He doubled his freshman records across the boards and played in a total of 31 games and averaged 30.9 minutes, 10.6 points, 6.8 rebounds, and 1.4 assists per game as a forward.[137] The Huskies went 17-11 overall during the regular season and went 7-11 in Pac-10 competition. Due to Washington's records in Schrempf's sophomore season, the team did not advance nor participate in any postseason tournaments.

Schrempf's junior season was a breakout year for him. He received a full-time starting position at forward for Washington and produced career-high college numbers. He played in a total of 31 games, started in all 31, and averaged 38.3 minutes, 16.8 points, 7.4 rebounds, and 3.0 assists per game. [135] Washington finished with an overall record of 24-7 and a Pac-10 Conference record of 15-3. Under Schrempf's dominant junior year play, the Huskies made the 1984 NCAA Tournament for the first time since 1976. The Pac-10 did not have its own conference tournament until 1987 so the Washington Huskies and the Oregon State Beavers were named co-champions of the Pac-10 conference that season, sharing a conference record of 15-3. [135]

During his junior season, Schrempf was asked who his favorite NBA player was and why. Being a near seven-footer, Schrempf said Los Angeles

Lakers point guard, Magic Johnson, who is a global icon when it comes to the NBA.

> *"I like the way Magic plays,"* Schrempf said. *"I like the way he runs the game and his attitude toward the game, especially."* [139]

Washington's head coach, Marv Harshman, said Schrempf was the heart and soul of his team that season. He also admitted, Chris Welp, who was also from West Germany and went on to play in the NBA, was not quite as valuable as the other West German, Schrempf.

> *"Detlef is the heart of our team,"* Marv Harshman said. *"We can survive more without Welp than without Schrempf. But we play better when Chris is in there and in another year, he'll be extremely central."* [139]

In the 1984 NCAA Tournament, Washington were listed as a six seed in the West Regional bracket. The Huskies were expected to make a short run in the 1984 NCAA Tournament and if they faced three-seed Duke University in the early rounds, the Huskies were expected to be bounced. In the tournament, Schrempf and Washington cruised past the eleven seeded University of Nevada in the first round and shockingly slipped past Duke University in the second round in a two-point victory in front of the Pullman, Washington crowd of roughly eleven-thousand fans. In the Sweet Sixteen of the 1984 NCAA Tournament, Schrempf and the Huskies fell to the University of Dayton, 58-64, ending their season. [135]

In his final season with the Washington Huskies, Schrempf had his expectations set on making the NBA soon. He started and played in a total of 32 games in his senior season and averaged 36.9 minutes, 15.8 points, 8.0 rebounds, and 4.2 assists per game.[136] For the Huskies, they once again qualified for the NCAA Tournament and were listed as a fifth seed in the West Regional bracket of the 1985 NCAA Tournament. Schrempf and the Huskies finished the regular season, once again being named Pac-10 Conference co-champions with USC, both sharing a conference record of 13-5. The Huskies finished with an overall record of 22-10, which topped the Pac-10 Conference. [136]

Despite making the 1985 NCAA Tournament, Schrempf and Washington did not make it past the first round of the tournament, falling to the University of Kentucky, 55-66, ending Schrempf's college career. He left the University of Washington as a two time First-team All-Pac-10 (1984, 1985), and Third-team All-American - National Association of Basketball Coaches (NABC) in 1985. [136]

In April of 2013, Schrempf's college coach Marv Harshman died at the age of 95 and Schrempf spoke at his memorial service. During a *SI.com* feature story, Schrempf told how he talked to his coach all the time and he credits his coach for creating a basis of fundamentals for him.

> *"I talked to Marv all the time. ... He was a great man, just a true gentleman who was loved by everyone,"* Schrempf said. *He also credits the man who coached him to two first team All-Pac-10 selections for "creating a basis of fundamentals" in his game with his old school style.* [141]

Schrempf, following his senior season, declare for the 1985 NBA Draft. The former Huskie put together quite the college career at Washington and mocked to be drafted in the early selections of the 1985 NBA Draft. The Dallas Mavericks ended up drafting Schrempf with the eighth overall pick in the 1985 NBA Draft. At the time of the selection, many were stunned at the Mavericks passed on Karl Malone, a talented big man out of Louisiana Tech. Norm Sonju, the Dallas Mavericks general manager, was not attracted to the play style of Karl Malone and in a 1984 *Miami Herald* article, the general manager said the Mavericks wanted a real man.

> *"I just don't think Malone is a rebounder,"* Norm Sonju said. *"I have a problem with big men who like to shoot outside. I like a man to be where a man belongs."* [144]

The Mavericks general manager went on to bash Karl Malone, calling him a half a man, when compared to Charles Oakley, who was another dominant big man out of Virginia Union and was selected by the Chicago Bulls with the ninth overall pick in the same draft.

> *"Oakley is a man,"* Sonju said. *"Malone is more like half a man. He appears to be tougher than he is. He gets knocked down a lot. He is not a Maurice Lucas type."* [144]

For Detlef Schrempf, this put some pressure on him to perform at a high level as a rookie. He was listed as a small forward, who can play power forward. He spent a total of four seasons with the Dallas Mavericks. Schrempf played a total of 264 games with the Mavericks and averaged 19.4 minutes, 8.3 points, 3.6 rebounds, and 1.9 assists per game. [143] The Mavericks did not make one playoff appearance during that four-year span.

In February of the 1988-89 season, Dallas dealt Schrempf to the Indiana Pacers for Herb Williams, a veteran center. [143] Schrempf immediately made a clear impact on his new team, especially his outside shooting. He came off the bench but near the end of the regular season, Schrempf began to see some starting minutes with the Pacers. Indiana finished the season with a record of 28-54 and finishing in the bottom half of the Eastern Conference as the 10th seed. [143]

Schrempf went on to play a total of five seasons as a member of the Indiana Pacers, playing in a total of 354 games. In those 354 games, Schrempf averaged 33.7 minutes, 17.0 points, 8.6 rebounds, and 4.1 assists per game. [143] As a member of the Pacers, Schrempf was mostly known as the sharpshooter from behind the arc. Schrempf, as a Pacer, won back to back NBA Sixth Man of the Year awards, 1991 and 1992. In addition to winning his second NBA Sixth Man of the Year award, Schrempf was named German Player of the Year in 1992. [143]

Following the 1992-93 season, Schrempf was once again traded. Indiana dealt him to the Seattle SuperSonics in exchange for Derrick McKey and Gerald Paddio. [143]

In his first season as a SuperSonic, Schrempf was named to his first NBA All-Star team. He would go on to be named to three NBA All-Star Games during his six-year run with Seattle.

In those six seasons as a member of the SuperSonics, Schrempf played a total of 415 games and averaged 35.0 minutes, 16.6 points, 6.3 rebounds, and 4.0 assists per game. His final season with Seattle, Schrempf played only 50 games that season. [143]

Following his sixth and final season with the SuperSonics, in the summer of 1999, Seattle decided to waive Schrempf and make him a free agent. After the SuperSonics released Schrempf, he was not on the free agent market long. In fact, on the same day he was waived, Detlef Schrempf, now at age 36, signed a new deal to join the Portland Trail Blazers. [143]

Schrempf went on to finish his NBA playing career with the Trail Blazers. He was a member of Portland for two seasons, he played in a total of 103 games and averaged 20.0 minutes, 6.6 points, 4.0 rebounds, and 2.3 assists per game. [143] Due to his age and retirement overlooking his career while in Portland, Schrempf came off the bench in those two seasons and only started in three games as a Trail Blazer.

Following his second and last season in Portland, the 2000-01 season, Detlef Schrempf officially retired from the NBA. To this date, Detlef Schrempf is considered one of the most talented shooters to come off the bench and one of the top players to come from the country of Germany. He left the NBA with good honors and accomplishments.

- Two-time NBA Sixth Man of the Year (1991, 1992)
- Three-time NBA All-Star (1993, 1995, 1997)

- All-NBA Third Team (1995) [143]

While playing in the NBA, Schrempf played for the West Germany men's national basketball team at the 1983 and 1985 EuroBasket Tournament. He was also a member of the 1984 West Germany Olympic team, which took place in the United States, and played for the German Olympic men's basketball team in 1992, which took place in Barcelona, Spain. [137]

In addition to his playing career, Schrempf opened the Detlef Schrempf Foundation in 1996, a non-profit charitable organization. The foundation was focused around assisting children and families in the Northwest of the United States of America. [137]

In 2005, Schrempf returned to the NBA. He was hired as an assistant coach by the Seattle SuperSonics. Schrempf held the position till 2007.

Now retired, Detlef Schrempf has been featured in many comedy television series and participated in other television series episodes to benefit his foundation.

> *"It kind of came out of nowhere,"* Schrempf said. *"I was like, 'I'm not really into that, I'm not an actor, but if we can do it and get some exposure for our foundation, I'll do it."* [141]

Detlef Schrempf paved the way for many athletes in Germany, who had dreams of playing in the NBA. One player who heavily looked up to Schrempf growing up was Dirk Nowitzki.

When Dirk Nowitzki was drafted by the Milwaukee Bucks with the ninth overall pick in the 1988 NBA Draft, then traded to the Dallas Mavericks, he immediately began his rise to NBA stardom. Schrempf, who Dirk Nowitzki looked up to growing up, had high praise for the young Maverick.

> *"Every player, not just in Dallas or Texas, or Germany, but all over the world should look at Dirk; he has an amazing work ethic,"* Schrempf said. *"He is a super example for any player from anywhere in the world who proved that anything is possible. It opened the door for elite players that maybe a tall kid who is from a soccer country can excel in basketball."* [140]

Chapter 16

Blocked by The Iron Curtain

Arvydas Romas Sabonis was born on December 19, 1964, in Kaunas, Lithuania. Kaunas and the country of Lithuania were a part of the Soviet Union at the time Sabonis was born.[146] As a young kid, Sabonis was taller than most in his age group and the game of basketball was an opportunity he could not pass up on.

He began his basketball career at the age of 13 and two years later, at the age of 15, he joined to Soviet national junior team. As part of the Soviet national junior team, Sabonis increased his basketball skills.[146] One attribute of his game that stood out was his passing. For young big men his size, passing skills were low but Sabonis excelled by passing out to perimeter shooters and cutters.

He led the team to gold at the 1981 European Championship for Cadets in Greece.[148] Shortly after playing with the Soviet national junior team, Sabonis joined his first professional club. He signed with Zalgiris, which was a professional club located in his hometown of Kaunas, Lithuania.[149] During his time with Zalgiris, Sabonis joined the Soviet national team and became a European sensation. He joined the Soviet national team at the age of 19 in 1983. That same year, Sabonis helped lead the Soviets to a bronze medal at the 1983 FIBA EuroBasket in France. With the Soviet Union national team, Sabonis led the team to two gold medals at the 1982 FIBA World Cup in Columbia and the 1985 FIBA EuroBasket in West Germany. On top of winning two gold medals, Sabonis and the Soviets won silver at the 1986 FIBA World Cup in Spain and another bronze at the 1989 FIBA EuroBasket in Yugoslavia. [148]

With Zalgiris, Sabonis easily stood out and began to make a name for himself all around Europe. He was much different than any big man in Europe. Not only was he seven feet tall but he played the game of basketball like a guard. He spent a total of eight years with his hometown club of Zalgiris, from 1981-89, and left as an all-time great. Sabonis won three Euroscar Player of the Year awards (1984, 1985, and 1988), one Mr. Europa Player of the Year award (1985), three Lithuanian Sportsman of the Year (1984-1986), EuroBasket Most Valuable Player (1985), FIBA Club World Cup championship (1986), and three USSR League titles (1985-87). [149]

Sabonis' play and basketball skillset put him in the conversation for the best European player on the planet. With Sabonis' skillset rising, there was only one obstacle standing in his path to pursue a glorious basketball career:

119

The Iron Curtain. Due to Cold War politics associated with the Soviet Union, Sabonis was not allowed to leave Europe and play in the NBA.

Detlef Schrempf, who finished his rookie season with the Dallas Mavericks at the time of Sabonis' NBA buzz, played against him when he was 16 years old in West Germany. Schrempf believed that Sabonis was worthy of being named the best player in the world around the time of his hype.

> *"I played against Sabonis since I was 16,"* Schrempf said. *"I told everyone all the time if Sabonis was in the NBA, he would be the best player possibly ever and guys would say 'oh come on' and he would be the best center in the NBA by far."* [145]

Despite Sabonis not being allowed to take his talents to the biggest stage in North America, there was one NBA team that was willing to take the chance on him and use a first-round pick on him. That team was the Portland Trail Blazers.

> *"We had some scouts that were very into drafting the Europeans like Sabonis and I'd see film on Sabonis forever."* Portland Trail Blazers head coach Rick Adelman said. *"He was an unbelievable player."* [145]

When the 1986 NBA Draft came around, Sabonis remained a mystery player. Due to the uncertainty if he would ever step foot on an NBA court due to Cold War politics, his draft stock was unknown. It was clear as day that Sabonis had the talent to be selected with the first overall pick at the time of his European buzz but unfortunately the Iron Curtain restricted him and left teams unsure if he'll ever be available.

With the Portland Trailblazers on the clock, selecting the 24th overall pick in the 1986 NBA Draft, they were ready to take the risk. David Stern stood at the podium and announced, with a bright smirk on his face, that Arvydas Sabonis was selected. Unlike most international players watching the NBA Draft on their television or walking to the podium to shake David Stern's hand, Sabonis found out he was drafted in a unique way. The following day, Sabonis opened a magazine and one of the articles he read was that he was drafted. Despite the exciting news, Sabonis knew that the Iron Curtain was blocking him and there were minimal signs of an NBA career at the time. [146]

This was not the first time Sabonis was drafted into the NBA. One year prior, in 1995, Sabonis was selected in the fourth round by the Atlanta Hawks with their 77th pick. Despite being selected with the 77th pick, Sabonis was not of age to be selected. At the time of the 1995 NBA Draft, a player needed to be at least 21 years of age to be selected. [146]

Following his historic eight year run with one of the oldest clubs in Lithuania, Sabonis signed with Forum Valladolid of the Spanish Liga ACB league. With Sabonis moving to Spain, he faced bigger competition not only at his position but played against some of the best talent in Europe. His tenure with Forum Valladolid lasted four years, from 1989-92, and the club did not win any cups or tournaments. Forum Valladolid is no longer a basketball club and played their last season in 2015. [146] For Sabonis, it was a new opportunity in his basketball career and a way to leave the Soviet Union territory.

In 1992, Sabonis was once again on the move to a new basketball club in Europe but he did not have to go far. He joined the historic Real Madrid, which was a top team in the same league: Liga ACB. For Sabonis, this was a new opportunity to prove his dominance and be a part of a historic European club.

He spent a total of three years with the club, from 1992-95, and in those three years led Real Madrid to two Liga ACB titles capping his final season winning the 1995 FIBA European League title. In his final season with Real Madrid, the 1994-95 season, Sabonis averaged 22.8 points, 13.2 rebounds, 2.6 blocks, and 2.4 assists per game. [148]

George Karl, who coached Real Madrid for two separate seasons, the 1989-90 season and the 1991-92 season, wished he was the head coach of the team when Sabonis was wearing a Real Madrid uniform. When he was asked if he was able to come back to Real Madrid and win a championship, who would he choose to lead the team, his answer was quick and simple.

> *"When I came back, I was asked if I could do it all over and try again to bring a championship to Madrid, who would I try to get on my team?"* Karl said. *"Sabonis was my answer. The best player in Europe was Sabonis. The most difficult player to play against was Sabonis. I had actually told all the NBA scouts who had come over to Europe to see Toni Kukoc and Sabonis at that time the same thing. I told them Kukoc is good. He's an NBA player, but the best guy if you want to win is Sabonis."* [147]

Following his short stint in Real Madrid, Sabonis was 30 years old. With the Iron Curtain long gone and no longer blocking his path to compete in the NBA, he believed there was only one destination and league to play for and that was the NBA.

> *"This is it for me,"* Sabonis said in Madrid in May of 1995. *"There's nothing left for me to prove in Europe or the basketball world. Only the NBA remains."* [147]

"I decided I'm 30 years old, and Portland called me and said if you want, let's go, and I finished the contract with Real Madrid, and if I didn't come now, I didn't come ever; I don't get to feel what is NBA," Sabonis said. *"It was the last bullet, you know."* [147]

It was time for Sabonis to take his talents and play in the NBA. While with Real Madrid, Sabonis' buzz did fade a bit and his name flew under the radar. Despite the buzz slowly dropping due to his age and the possibility of him never wearing an NBA uniform, Sabonis proved his dominance at the 1988 Olympics and the 1992 Olympics in Barcelona, Spain.

The 1988 Olympics are known for being the first time USA Basketball did not qualify for a gold medal game. The reason was Sabonis and the Soviet Union. In a semifinal matchup against the United States, Sabonis dominated David Robinson in the post with a creative style of play.

"They took it right to the United States," Bill Walton said. *"They played with more imagination, more creativity. They were more assertive on offense, there was better ball movement, there was more skill."* [145]

Then in 1992, a group of basketball talent and Sabonis from Lithuania formed the Lithuanian men's national team. The formation of the team began with Saraunas Marciulionis, who at the time finished his fifth season in the NBA with the Golden State Warriors. Alongside Marciulionis, Donnie Nelson, who was an assistant coach on Golden State helped with the recruitment. Lithuania breezed through the early competition, but familiar faces arouse in the bronze medal game. The new Lithuanian men's national team faced a group of fallen Soviet Union players in the bronze medal game and Sabonis proved his dominance in a high-pressure game against some of his former teammates. In the bronze medal game, Sabonis scored 26 points and snagged 16 rebounds, leading Lithuania to the win bronze.[145] His performance was one of the best individual performances from the historic 1992 Olympics in Barcelona, Spain.

"He would have died on the court, literally," Nelson said. *"I've never seen a player play under that type of pressure."* [145]

Coming into the NBA, the Trailblazers had some worries about whether Sabonis' legs would hold up. Following the end of his Real Madrid career and the 1994-95 season, Bob Whitsitt, the Trail Blazers general manager wanted his medical staff to look at Sabonis' legs before signing him. Sabonis underwent a series of x-rays and reviewed his previous x-rays on his legs. This was not the first time Portland checked up on Sabonis' health. Before the 1988 Olympics in Seoul, Korea, Sabonis traveled to Portland to get a medical procedure on his Achilles. [147]

Dr. Robert Cook, who was the Trail Blazers team physician told Bob Whitsitt that based on his x-rays, Sabonis was not in the best of shape.

> *"He said that Arvydas could qualify for a handicapped parking spot based on the X-ray alone,"* Whitsitt said. [147]

Due to the early concerns, Portland held Sabonis on a feasible minutes restriction, especially in the first half of his rookie season.

The other concern Portland had with their 30-year-old rookie was whether he would be able to thrive and put up the same numbers he did in Europe against NBA talent. That concern quickly faded.

In his rookie season, Sabonis proved he was worth the wait and worth the risk. He played in 73 games for the Trail Blazers, starting 23, and averaged 23.8 minutes, 14.5 points, 8.1 rebounds, 1.8 assists, and 1.1 blocks per game. [150] The Portland Trail Blazers finished the season with a 44-38 record, qualifying for the NBA playoffs for their 14th straight season.

His impressive rookie season play, at age 30, earned Sabonis 1995-96 NBA All-Rookie honors. On top of earning 1995-95 NBA All-Rookie honors, Sabonis was runner up for both 1995-96 NBA Rookie of the Year and 1995-96 NBA Sixth Man of the Year award.[150] Damon Stoudemire of the Toronto Raptors won the Rookie of the Year award while fellow European import Toni Kukoc of the Chicago Bulls won the NBA Sixth Man of the Year award.

In the playoffs, Sabonis and the Trail Blazers were eliminated in the first round of the Western Conference playoffs by the Utah Jazz.

Sabonis went on to play a total of eight seasons in the NBA. All eight seasons were with the Portland Trail Blazers and they made the playoffs all eight seasons as well. In fact, all eight seasons ended with the same result: a first-round exit. [150]

Following the 2000-01 season, Sabonis refused to sign an extension with the Trail Blazers and retired from the NBA. The reason was not frustrations with the team but his physical and mental health from all 392 games he played over the eight-year span.

Instead of resigning with Portland, Sabonis shocked the world and returned to where his basketball career began. He signed a one-year deal with Zalgiris and was set to join the team in the second half of the season.[146] Instead, the "big man curse" once again caught Sabonis and he could not play. He was resting and recovering from the injuries he suffered in Portland.

Despite not playing with Zalgiris, Sabonis decided to give it one last run and he rejoined Portland for the 2002-03 season at the age of 38. The full year off benefited Sabonis and he played the most games in a single season of his NBA career in his final year. Sabonis came off the bench for Portland, playing in 78 games, and averaged 15.5 minutes, 6.1 points, 4.3 rebounds, and 1.8 assists per game. [150]

The career of Arvydas Sabonis is filled with ups and downs but the question remains what his legacy would look like if he was able to play in the NBA at 21 years of age. He entered the league at 30 and played his first NBA game at the age of 31. With Sabonis being 31 and having faced "the big man curse" of leg injuries, especially devastating Achilles injuries, early on in his career, what kind of player would Sabonis be if he was able to play in the NBA at 21?

Despite never knowing the answer to that question, Sabonis transformed the NBA. Throughout the history of the NBA, the big man position has been the key to success. In the early years of the NBA, Bill Russell, Kareem Abdul-Jabbar, and Wilt Chamberlain were the cornerstone piece to success. A dominant center who towered over everyone on the court and rose up for easy dunks and defended the paint from the 1950s to the late 1970s. Then the big man position began to receive some slack in the 1980s and 1990s with the guard position and forwards being labeled as necessities and cornerstone pieces. Despite the guard and forward positions taking the crown for success, the big man position was still a strong necessity. Hakeem Olajuwon and Patrick Ewing dominated the paint but shooting started to become a weak trend at the position but a slow evolving trend. Then there was Arvydas Sabonis. He is one of the best centers to play in the NBA and in the history of the game of basketball. Sabonis was different than many NBA centers. He was all-around. From over the head cut passes, his shooting ability from all areas of the floor, to his dominant post ups, and his lockdown defense on the other end, Sabonis paved the way for today's NBA centers like Nikola Jokic and other shooting big men from overseas like Kristaps Porzingis and most famously Dirk Nowitzki.

> *"Arvydas was Dirk Nowitzki but seven foot-four,"* Donnie Nelson said. *"Shot threes and passed the ball like Larry (Bird) and Magic (Johnson)."* [145]

> *"He was unbelievable because he was a big guy who can move, who can shoot, and who can pass,"* Dirk Nowitzki said. [145]

> *"Arvydas can read the game,"* Sarunas Marciulionis stated. *"He can play like a point guard. In those days, he can just rebound, one pass, and he finishes on the other side. It is pretty impressive."* [145]

124

Arvydas Sabonis will forever be known as that NBA player everyone wished they saw at the height of his career in the NBA. Despite the Iron Curtain blocking his path during the height of his career, Sabonis is the best European big man to play in the NBA and will forever be known as one of the key cornerstone players in NBA globalization.

The Globalization of the NBA

Chapter 17

From Sending Letters to Becoming an NBA All-Star

Rik Smits was born on August 23, 1966 in Eindhoven, Netherlands. [160] The country of Netherlands was and still is soccer dominated when it comes to sports. Rik Smits played both soccer and basketball growing up in Nederland's but at age 14 he decided to concentrate on one sport: basketball.

Rik Smits began his basketball career playing for PSV Almonte Eindhoven in Eindhoven, Netherlands. [161] The team was one of the few basketball clubs in the area. He dominated the local competition and began to rise to basketball stardom in his local area. At the age of 18, Rik Smits decided to move to the United States to attend college.[160] He decided to attend Marist College in Poughkeepsie, New York and play basketball with the Marist Red Foxes.

Marist College was not known for its college athletics at the time of Rik Smits' arrival. In 1979, Dennis Murray, the Marist College president from 1979-2016, as one of his first decisions as president decided to make Marist College jump to Division 1.

> *"One of the very first decisions I had to make when I became President in 1979 was: 'Are we going to make that big jump and become Division I?' It was a big jump in terms of cost, a big jump in terms of commitment to athletics and commitment to recruit Division I athletes to the college. I ultimately became convinced that it was the right thing to do for Marist."* [158]

For Rik Smits', it was all about the opportunity to come to the United States and see what there is to offer. Besides from basketball opportunities, Rik Smit focused around the educational opportunities in the United States.

> *"I was playing for a youth club team in the Netherlands. I was kind of out of options over there [the Netherlands] as far as schooling. I didn't know what I wanted to do. So I said, 'Hey, let me try the United States."* [158]

> *"So, I had sent some letters out to what's called the ABA USA at the time, the Amateur Basketball Association. And I said, 'Hey, I'm 7'4,*

or 7'3" at the time, young kid, interested in maybe playing some ball over in the United States. How do I go about doing that?' So, I got a letter back and they had some responses from interested schools, I think it was a NEIE school or Division III school, something like that. [158]

When Rik Smits met the coach at Marist College, Mike Perry, who came to his hometown, Perry offered Rik Smits a scholarship. He offered Rik Smits a scholarship without seeing him even touch a basketball.

"He never even saw me play, no footage or anything. But he just saw my height and offered me a scholarship. And that was it." [158]

Since Marist College was just getting its foot in the door with Division 1 competition and recruitment, the college decided it was best to recruit international players.

"The coach at the time recruited Rik [Smits]," Murray said. *"He actually recruited a number of international athletes. I think part of his strategy was that it would be difficult for a new school to recruit talented American athletes because more established programs would get them."* [158]

Rik Smits played his freshman season with the Red Foxes in 1984-85 season. He was the only player on the Marist College basketball team who was over seven feet tall. The Red Foxes went 17-12 that season and Rik Smits played in 29 games, starting in 21, averaging 26.8 minutes, 11.2 points, 5.6 rebounds, and 2.6 blocks per game. [156]

He went on to spend all four years at Marist College, playing in a total of 107 games. In those 107 games, he averaged 29.4 minutes, 18.2 points, 7.6 rebounds, and 3.2 blocks per game. Rik Smits was named the NEC Player of the Year award in both his junior and senior season, 1987, 1988. [156]

Following his senior season, Smits established himself as one of the best college centers that declared for the 1988 NBA Draft. The Los Angeles Clippers held the first pick, but it was made very clear that the Clippers were very fond of Danny Manning out of the University of Kansas. The Indiana Pacers held the second overall pick in the 1988 NBA Draft. Prior to the draft, the Pacers were looking into trading the pick as Bob Ryan of the *Boston Globe* noted in a *Chicago Tribune* story. Bob Ryan referred to the 1988 NBA Draft: Danny [Manning] and the Juniors.

Is being in the lottery any better than being No. 15? Nobody's really sure. It looks as if 7-foot-4-inch Rik Smits of Marist will be the No. 2. That's if the Pacers don't trade the pick in some deal involving Wayne Tisdale or Herb Williams. You hear the talk about trading up, trading down, trading out. [159]

Despite the trade rumors hovering over the 1988 NBA Draft, when draft day came around, Danny Manning, with no surprise was selected with the first overall pick by the Los Angeles Clippers. With the second overall pick in the 1988 NBA Draft, the Indiana Pacers selected Rik Smits.

Dennis Murray was proud of Rik Smits, who was once a teenager mailing letters to colleges and universities to play basketball to a Marist Red Fox superstar, and now the second overall pick in the 1988 NBA Draft and put Marist College on the map. Rik Smits' number 45 was retired by Marist College.

"At pro basketball games, when they introduce the players, they always mention the college the players went to. Every time he played in a major city around the world, Marist was being mentioned. People were learning about Marist. He was one of the things that put Marist on the map." [158]

Donnie Walsh, who was the Indiana Pacer President of Basketball Operations, thought Rik Smits was the perfect selection at number two.

"He was such a good shooter. And that height?" Walsh said. *"I just thought, 'He's going to be a really good NBA player.'"* [157]

In his rookie season with the Pacers, Smits quickly jumped into the starting lineup. Steve Stipanovich, who battled knee injuries since the Pacers drafted the center with the second overall pick in the 1982 NBA Draft, faced another injury set back. Following his knee injury in Rik Smits rookie season, Steve Stipanovich was forced to retire after discovering a dead spot on the bone of his left knee.

Smits immediately filled the starting center position for the Pacers. He was the starting center for Indiana for 12 seasons. In his first two seasons with the Pacers, Smits played in all 164 games for the Pacers. [153]

In the 1999-2000 season, the Indiana Pacers were the favorites to come out of the Eastern Conference and make an NBA Finals run. Led by Reggie Miller, the Pacers had a solid group of players and depth at each position. Indiana finished the regular season with an Eastern Conference best 56-26 record. [153] The Pacers entered the 2000 NBA Eastern Conference playoffs as the number one seed. In the first round, Indiana advanced, defeating the Milwaukee Bucks, winning the series 3-2. In the Eastern Conference semifinals, the Pacers cruised past the Philadelphia 76ers, winning the series 4-2. In the infamous 2000 Eastern Conference Finals, Indiana advanced to the 2000 NBA Finals, defeating Patrick Ewing and the New York Knicks, winning the series 4-2. In the 2000 NBA Finals, the Pacers faced Kobe Bryant, Shaquille O'Neal and the Los Angeles Lakers. Rik Smits faced a big test with the championship on the line: guarding Shaquille O'Neal, one of the best young centers in the league.

The Lakers quickly gained a 2-0 series lead under the Staples Center lights. The next three games were played at Conseco Fieldhouse in Indianapolis, Indiana. The Pacers won Game 3 and 5 but the Lakers escaped Game 4, winning by just two points, 120-118.[153] The Pacers flew back to Los Angeles one game away from being eliminated and losing the 2000 NBA Finals. In Game 6, the Los Angeles Laker went on to win the 2000 NBA Finals, their first championship in twelve years. The 2000 NBA Finals ended up being the closest Rik Smit would get to winning an NBA Championship in his 12-year NBA career.

Following his 12th NBA season, Rik Smits decided to retire from the NBA. During his twelve-year run, Smits underwent multiple procedures on his feet, back, and ankles. Like many NBA centers, injuries shortened Rik Smits career and forced retirement. Rik Smits twelve year run with the Indiana Pacers included a 1998 NBA All-Star selection and being named to the 1989 NBA All-Rookie First Team.

> *"I could see it coming,"* Smits said. *"My injuries were getting worse. I had my mind made up [during the playoffs] that it was time to retire."* [163]

Rik Smits will be remembered as a pioneer of NBA Globalization and the player who proved it is possible to come from a soccer dominated country and play for the biggest basketball league in the world. His son, Derrik Smits, who is eligible to be drafted in the 2019 NBA Draft after splitting time with Valparaiso University and Butler University, has expectations and the potential to be like his father. For Rik Smits, he wants his son to follow his own path and fulfil a dream.

> *"I had a great career and a great time,"* Rik Smits said. *"If he can make his living in basketball, whether that's in Europe or over here, I would love that for him. He says that's what he wants to do."* [163]

Chapter 18

Vlade Divac

Vlade Divac was born on February 3, 1968 in Prijepolje, SR Serbia, SFR Yugoslavia. [167] Growing up, Vlade Divac aspired of playing basketball and become a professional and make a living off the sport.

In his early teenage years, Vlade Divac began his youth basketball career, joining KK Elan, a local basketball club in Prijepolje. Divac recalled the moment he made the decision to leave home at the age of only 14 during the Kings' home finale against the New Orleans Pelicans in 2019.

> *"I remember when I made the big decision for myself and my family, basically,"* Divac said before the Kings' home finale against New Orleans at Golden 1 Center. *"I was just 14 years old, and I had to leave my parents to pursue basketball. It was just my mom, dad, and brother were sitting together. I was just listening - what were they going to say?- because they had the key, and they let me go to dream my dreams, and here I am on top of the world after 30 years."* [165]

He quickly developed basketball skills and thrived against local competition. His quick rise as a teenager and the talent on the court led to Divac first professional basketball opportunity. He signed with KK Sloga, a professional basketball club, which today is basking in Kraljevo, Serbia. [167] Divac made the most of the opportunity and made himself a name as one of the best young big men. He began to rise in popularity in the three years he played for KK Sloga, 1983-1986.

At the age of 18, Divac was the top player available to sign and was heavily recruited by multiple clubs. He signed with KK Partizan in 1986, a decorated club in search of finalizing a dream team in their league. In his first year with KK Partizan, the team was very successful, winning and defeating top clubs all across Europe. Divac and KK Partizan placed third in the EuroLeague and were nicknamed "Dream Team." [167] Divac was a member of KK Partizan for three years before declaring for the 1989 NBA Draft. With KK Partizan, Divac won multiple titles and championships with the club including a Yugoslavian League title. He was also awarded the 1989 Mister Europa Player of the Year. [167]

While playing for KK Partizan, Divac was a member of the Yugoslavia men's national basketball team. Divac won his first Olympic medal in 1985 at the European Championship for Cadets, also known as the U16

European Championship. A 16-year-old Vlade Divac and Yugoslavia won gold at the 1985 European Championship for Cadets, which was held in Bulgaria. Divac won a total of six gold medals, one silver medal, and two bronze medals in the span of six years with Yugoslavia. Divac and Yugoslavia also won gold at the 1995 FIBA EuroBasket in Greece and at the 2002 FIBA World Cup in the United States. At the 1996 Summer Olympic Games in Atlanta, Georgia, Divac and Yugoslavia won silver and at the 1999 FIBA EuroBasket, held in France, won bronze. [167]

At age 21, Divac declared for the 1989 NBA Draft. In his six years of professional basketball overseas, he built a reputation as one of the most valuable big men in the 1989 draft class. Divac possessed a unique skill set compared to active NBA centers in the league at the time of the 1989 NBA Draft. He can shoot consistently from the field, can make elite passes, and can create space needed to score. On the defensive end, Divac was a fearless rim protector who can swat shots into the second or third row of an arena.

Despite being viewed as one of the best centers available in the 1989 NBA Draft, many feared his game would not translate to the NBA clearly and he would need time to adjust and develop to the playstyle of the league. When the 1989 NBA Draft came around, Divac was drafted with the 26th overall pick by the Los Angeles Lakers, who were coming off a 1989 NBA Finals appearance.[170] In the Finals, the Lakers were swept by the "Bad Boy" Pistons. Following the sweep, it was clear that Lakers center Kareem Abdul-Jabbar was ready to retire from the N.BA after completing his 20th season at age 41 and Los Angeles needed a replacement. Divac was their new center but came off the bench for most of his rookie season.

Mychal Thompson, who was born in Nassau, Bahamas but grew up in the United States, was the Lakers starting center and started and played in a total of 70 games. Divac played in all 82 games, starting only five games, and averaged 19.6 minutes, 8.5 points, 6.2 rebounds, and 1.4 blocks per game. [170] His play meshed well with the Lakers and there were no early signs of disappointment. His consistent play off the bench was awarded by the NBA. Divac was named to the 1990 NBA All-Rookie First Team, which included the likes of David Robinson, Pooh Richardson, Sherman Douglas, and Tim Hardaway. [167]

Vlade Divac spent eight seasons wearing the purple and gold before being dealt in the infamous Kobe Bryant trade with the Charlotte Hornets. In those eight seasons, Divac became the Lakers full time starting center in his second season till his last season with the Los Angeles, the 1995-96 season. He played in a total of 535 games and averaged 29.0 minutes, 12.2 points, 8.5 rebounds, 2.6 assists, and 1.6 blocks per game. [170]

On July 1, 1996, the Lakers traded Divac to the Charlotte Hornets in exchange for the draft rights to Kobe Bryant, a highly talented high schooler from Lower Merion High School in Ardmore, Pennsylvania. [170]

Vlade Divac went on to play two seasons with the Hornets as their starting center. He played in a total of 145 games and averaged a career-high 32.0 minutes, 11.7 points, 8.6 rebounds, 3.3 assists, and 1.9 blocks per game. [170]

The 1998-99 NBA season was the third lockout season the league faced. On March 23, 1998, the NBA team owners voted to reopen the 1995 collective bargaining agreement. The owners wanted substantial cost control measures that would reshape the league from guaranteed contracts to a strict salary cap. The 1995 collective bargaining agreement allowed second year players to be eligible to sign huge contract extensions like Kevin Garnett, who signed a six-year, $126 million extension during the 1997-98 NBA season. The deal restricted the Minnesota Timberwolves from signing or resigning any of their players. In other words, Kevin Garnett's new extensions was the catalyst to the lockout.

> *"There is nobody in the NBA who thought it would be business as usual coming out of that season,"* says Bob Whitsitt, then the Portland Trail Blazers' president and general manager. *"If someone didn't expect a lockout for at least the summer, they didn't really know what they were doing."* [175]

The 1998-99 NBA lockout spread across 204 days, from July 1, 1998 until January 20, 1999. As Thomas Golianopoulos of *The Ringer* noted, the 204-day lockout not only costed the players in the league but the NBA as well.

> *The work stoppage was a disaster. With volatile personalities at the forefront and backbiting among players, owners, and agents, the 1998-99 NBA lockout spanned 204 days and resulted in the loss of about $500 million in total player salaries and more than $1 billion overall. Fan interest crumbled. Reputations were damaged. The NBA would never be the same. This is the story behind one of the most bitter and bizarre labor disputes in sports history.* [175]

The lockout caused an estimated $500 million in total player salary loses. [175] It was clear, prior to the lockout occurring, that the league was going to go into a lockout so many players planned and looked into other basketball opportunities.

Divac was one of the few players who played with other basketball clubs overseas while the NBA was facing a lockout. He signed a deal with the

Sacramento Kings in 1998 but decided, due to the NBA lockout, he was heading back overseas to play for a club. Divac played only two games for KK Crvena Zvezda.[170] Following the news, he was joining KK Crvena Zvezda, Divac immediately faced backlash. KK Crvena Zvezda is KK Partizan's rival, the team he played for from 1986-1989. In those two games he played for KK Crvena Zvezda, Divac earned around $500,000. [167]

On February 5, 1999, the 1998-99 NBA season officially began, following a new six-year collective bargaining agreement. Due to the lengthy lockout, the regular season ran till May 5, 1999 before the NBA playoffs began on May 8 1999. The regular season consisted of 50 games for all 29 teams. [175]

Vlade Divac, who was in his first season as a member of the Sacramento Kings, started and played all 50 games that season. In those 50 games, Divac averaged 35.2 minutes, 14.3 points, 10.0 rebounds, 4.3 assists, and 1.0 blocks per game.[170] The Kings finished the 50-game season with a 27-23 record and the sixth seed in the Western Conference playoffs. In the first round of the 1990 NBA playoffs, Divac and the Kings lost to the Utah Jazz, 3-2, ending their season. The Kings center averaged 16 points in that series and was the reason the Kings forced a decisive Game 5. Divac connected on a handful of clutch free throws in the closing minutes of Game 4 to avoid elimination.

Divac went on to play a total of six seasons with Sacramento, playing a total of 454 games. [170] With the help of Divac, the Kings were consistent contenders for an NBA championship for a majority of the six seasons. The Kings center was known for his leadership on and off the court for Sacramento. In addition, Divac teamed up with Peja Stojakovic, who will be mentioned later in this book, and Hedo Turkoglu, two international players who paved the way for their countries in the NBA.

Following his sixth season with Sacramento, Divac hit the free agent market in the summer of 2004. It was uncertain the Kings were going to resign the 36-year-old center but there was one team that wanted Divac back on their roster: the Los Angeles Lakers.

The Lakers, due to available cap space, had to release or trade a number of their well-known stars. Most notably, Shaquille O'Neal was traded to the Miami Heat, leaving Los Angeles to fill the hole at center. Divac signed a deal to join the Lakers that summer. [170]

The 2004-05 season ended up being Vlade Divac's last season in the NBA. The Lakers center suffered back injuries and only played 15 games that season. In those 15 games, Vlade Divac averaged 8.7 minutes, 2.3 points, 2.1 rebounds, and 1.3 assists per game.[170]

The following offseason, on July 14, 2007, Vlade Divac officially announced his retirement from the NBA. Vlade Divac played sixteen seasons in the NBA and was a professional basketball player for twenty-two years. At the time of his retirement, he was only one of three centers in NBA history to get 13,000 points, 9,000 rebounds, 3,000 assists, and 1,5000 blocked shots. [170]

> *"I'm happy today,"* Divac said. *"When I look back, it was a wonderful career. It was a great ride for me."* [164]

Following his retirement from the NBA, Divac accepted a position as liaison and scout for the Lakers in Europe. The Lakers, who bought out Divac's expiring contract in the 2005 offseason was now a European scout for the team. His duties were to report directly to Mitch Kupchak, who was the general manager of the Lakers and evaluate European talent.

> *"He brings a lot to the organization that benefits him and us,"* Kupchak said. *"It's not a far-fetched concept that Vlade could be a front office person or even a coach someday."* [173]

In 2006, Divac was announced as the head of operations for Real Madrid basketball club. In 2009, he was named the president of the Serbian Olympic Committee, following his rival, former president Ivan Curkovic, stepping out of the race for re-election. [174]

> *"Sports has built me as a man and taught me not just to compete, but to lead the team as well,"* Divac said. *"I'm ready to be animated and to motivate every single member of our society to contribute to the promotion of sport. Our sport will have to have a more significant place in Serbia, not to just amble along anymore. Part of our focus will be the stimulation of sport of youth, and to narrow the risk of flight of our young talents who have been leaving our country, and our sport, too early."* [174]

Vlade Divac held the position until 2017, following the end of his second-term. He was succeeded by Bozidar Maljkovic, a former Serbian basketball coach.

On March 3, 2015, Divac was hired by the Sacramento Kings as the team's vice president of basketball and franchise operations. His duties were to advise the front office, the Kings coaching staff, and areas of branding. Then, on August 31, 2015, he was named general manager.[166] At the time of this writing, Vlade Divac still hold the position as Kings general manager.

In addition to his basketball career, from player to front office executive, Divac has been a huge contributor when it comes to humanitarian work. Divac created the Group Seven Children's Foundation, which is a non-profit organization focused on raising money to children in Serbia. Group

Seven refers to the seven former players that helped make the foundation:
Dejan Bodiroga, Predrag Danilovic, Sasha Djordjevic, Vlade Divac, Zarko
Paspalj, Zeljko Rebraca, and Zoran Savic. Today, the foundation is called
Divac's Children Foundation and the foundation has close ties with the
International Orthodox Christian Charities, the IOCC. In 2007, Vlade Divac
founded the "You Can Too" humanitarian organization that assists refugees in
Serbia. [167]

Chapter 19

The 1992 'Dream Team' The Catalyst for NBA Globalization

In all sports, from amateur to professional, the term *dream* is always referenced. Becoming a professional athlete is a dream for many kids growing up. From making it to the professional leagues, winning the league's championship, and cementing their name as one of the greatest to ever play a sport has crossed the minds of every athlete in any sport.

When it comes to professional basketball, the term *dream* concentrates primarily on one team that changed the game of basketball worldwide: The 1992 United States men's Olympic basketball team, famously known as the "The Dream Team."

On April 7, 1989, FIBA, the International Basketball Federation, voted to drop restrictions on professional basketball players competing in international events.[176] This was a monumental decision by FIBA that was the first stepping stone in changing the game of basketball forever. Basketball at the Olympics portrayed the best young talent, that were not professionals at the time, to represent their country on the hardwood and play to win gold medals. For the United States, the previous Olympic basketball teams were made up of the best young college athletes. With FIBA ending restrictions on professional athletes representing their countries, the United States now had the ability to form possibly one of the greatest Olympic men's basketball teams in history.

The NBA, at the time, was rising in popularity. In the late 1970s, Magic Johnson and the Los Angeles Lakers rivaled with Larry Bird and the Boston Celtics. The rivalry included everything a basketball fan wanted to see: multiple NBA Finals matchups between the two teams, bad blood and fights on and off the court, relationship between the two poster-boys of the league, Magic Johnson and Larry Bird which carried over in the 1980s. In the 1980s, the league faced new competition.

The 1984 NBA Draft brought in fresh talent to the league and is known today as one of the best draft classes in the league's history. From Hakeem Olajuwon, Michael Jordan, Charles Barkley, and John Stockton to Otis Thorpe, Vern Fleming, and Sam Perkins, the 1984 NBA Draft brought in new talent at all positions to the league. Besides, from the 1984 NBA Draft some of the greatest players in the league's history arrived into the NBA during the 1980s such as Clyde Drexler, Karl Malone, Ralph Sampson, Isiah Thomas, Scottie Pippen, David Robinson, and the list goes on and on. [177]

The Globalization of the NBA

Following the overturn of professional basketball athletes now having the eligibility to play in the Olympics, not everyone was in favor of it. As discussed before, the Olympics has always carried the tradition of having the best non-professional basketball talent play and represent their country. The United States always sent the best college athletes to represent and bring home the gold. Those teams often dominated the Olympics but slowly the rest of the world began to catch on. There were loopholes on what determined a player to be an amateur to a professional. Many European countries had teams made up of paid professional athletes, but they were considered amateurs. Meanwhile, any player that was in the NBA was strictly considered a professional. The Soviet Union's national team was made up of paid players titled as amateurs. The Soviets, as discussed in the beginning of the book, took down the United States twice in 12 years, proving to the world that the United States does not rule the game of basketball worldwide.

> *"If you played in Europe for money, you were considered an amateur but if you played in the NBA for money, you were a professional and so our players weren't eligible,"* David Stern said in the *NBA TV The Dream Team* documentary. [176]

United States basketball professionals, born in the United States, now had the opportunity to play and represent their nation, ironically the league was not too fond of the idea in the beginning.

> *"We wanted to be good partners with FIBA to grow the sport of basketball but we [NBA] were not too anxious,"* David Stern said. *"We didn't know what it would mean, we didn't know if our players wanted to do it, we didn't know what the logistics were, but the vote passed, and NBA players were eligible for the Olympics."* [176]

The poster boy for the NBA at the time was Michael Jordan. This left the perspective of whether Michael Jordan, the face of the league at the time, would consider playing in the 1992 Summer Olympics in Barcelona, Spain. The summer for NBA players were a relaxing period of staying in shape and taking a breather from the long 82 game season. Do players want to sacrifice that couple months of break to go back and play more professional basketball?

> *"I was hoping they would not ask me to participate,"* Michael Jordan said in the *NBA TV* documentary. *"I was trying to figure out a way graciously that I can decline. I did the Olympic thing before and when Rod Thorne called me and asked me, I wasn't too about it."* [176]

This left Rod Thorne to find other great NBA players to join. Magic Johnson was the first player to publicly announce he was for it.[176] Following Magic Johnson announcing he will play for the United States Olympic men's basketball team at the 1992 Summer Olympics in Barcelona, Spain, the rest of the puzzle fell into place. As Larry Bird noted in the NBA TV documentary, if it was not for Magic Johnson stepping up first, the "Dream Team" may have not happened.

> *"I think if Magic [Johnson] was not on that team, it would have not been as spectacular as it was."* (Larry Bird) [176]

Magic Johnson was at the tail end of his career and so were many of the NBA stars that dominated the 1970s. So, for those players, it was a brand-new way to end their historic professional careers. This led the other NBA poster boy of the 1970s to join: Larry Bird. After Magic Johnson and Larry Bird joined the team, it was a snowball effect of young talent announcing their commitment to the team.

On September 21, 1991, USA Basketball announced the roster for the 1992 Olympic team. [176] The roster consisted of 12 players, 11 NBA players and one college player: Charles, Barkley, Chris Mullin, Duke University's Christian Laettner, Clyde Drexler, David Robinson, John Stockton, Karl Malone, Larry Bird, Magic Johnson, Michael Jordan, Patrick Ewing, and Scottie Pippen. [178] The coaching staff for the "Dream team" included head coach Chuck Daly, who was the head coach of the 'Bad Boy' Detroit Pistons. After Chuck Daly was announced as the head coach, there was speculation on how Michael Jordan would cooperate or want part on the team. His Chicago Bulls did not like the Chuck Daly's 'Bad Boy' Detroit Pistons but for Michael Jordan, he did not have a big problem with the decision.

There was one player that many of teammates were unsure of being a part of the team: Magic Johnson. He was coming off a forced retirement due to being diagnosed with the HIV virus. At the time, no one knew a whole lot about the HIV virus and how it could be spread. Magic Johnson was coming off a stellar performance in the 1992 NBA All-Star Game and a comeback season. In the end, Magic Johnson was left on the roster and he played.

With the 12-player roster official, there was one name left off the list that stunned the media and fans not just across the country but around the world: Isiah Thomas. He was Chuck Daly's star in Detroit and Isiah Thomas and Michael Jordan did not like each other at the time. Isiah Thomas was hurt by the decision. He deserved to be a part of the team and was the leader of one of the most famous NBA teams in the 1980s. With that said, it was clear there were two players who most certainly did not want him on the team: Scottie

Pippen and Michael Jordan. The Chicago Bulls and the Detroit Pistons were coming off a heated 1991 Eastern Conference Finals matchup, where the Bulls advanced and following their series win, Isiah Thomas the Pistons left the court early and headed straight for the locker room rather than shaking hands with the Bulls players and coaching staff.

On June 22, 1982, training camp officially began for the 1992 "Dream Team," and the snubbing of Isiah Thomas slowly diminished while their next challenge surfaced. [176] Their next challenge was how do all these NBA stars mesh and work together as a team. The 12-man roster was filled with the NBA's top talent and different egos. This left Chuck Daly and his coaching staff to determine what each of their players' roles were. With the world watching, each of the 12 players wanted to prove why he was a part of this team and show his dominance. This showed through clearly in the team's first practice. All the players were competitive as expected and wanted to prove something. A couple of days later, Chuck Daly set up a scrimmage for his talented roster to face a group made up of the best college talent at the time. The college team included the likes of Alan Houston, Bobby Hurley, Chris Webber, Eric Montross, Grant Hill, Jamal Mashburn, Penny Hardaway, and Rodney Rogers. [176] Surprisingly, the "Dream Team" played a different style of basketball. Each player overpassed the ball and did not want to be listed as a ball hog. This led to the college team's run over the "Dream Team" behind the dominance of Chris Webber and college talent basketball team. The "Dream Team" lost to the college players and the team did not want the media to have knowledge of it. The scoreboard was erased but the media quickly became aware that something wasn't right. The players on the "Dream Team" did not act right and conducted a series of awkward interviews with the media.[176] Despite losing to the college players, this was an important new perspective for the "Dream Team." The loss crushed the players egos and showed them that they can lose.

Chuck Daly conducted another scrimmage against the same college group and the outcome as very different. The "Dream Team" dominated throughout the game and at one point, the scoreboard was not running anymore. [176] After bouncing back, the "Dream Team" now had to battle qualifiers.

On June 28, 1992, the "Dream Team" began the qualifiers at the Rose Garden in Portland, Oregon. [176] The team needed to medal in the Tournament of the Americas to qualify for the 1992 Summer Olympics. For almost everyone, it seemed like it was such as easy task that it was nearly impossible for the team not to medal. Prior to every game in the tournament, the opposing teams were left in shock that not only were they facing the "Dream Team" but that they were sharing the court with them. In other words, the opposing teams were starstruck rather than afraid. In their first matchup, the Cuban men's national basketball team took pictures with the "Dream Team."

As expected, the "Dream Team" won all their games in the Tournament of the Americas, crushing all their opponents from 40 to 70 points. [178] The "Dream Team" won the gold medal and there was one common theme before, during, and after each game: pictures, handshakes, and gratitude. Following achieving gold, Larry Bird had a message for the fans and the media at center court:

> *"I just wanted to say, this is just a small step to what our goal really is; to get to Barcelona, win the gold medal, and bring it back to where it is supposed to be."* [176]

Olympics just one week away. In that week prior to the start of the competition, the team practiced in Monte Carlo, Monaco. Often, the team was swarmed by fans and media and were not just viewed as the most famous basketball team in the world but top tier celebrities. Chuck Daly compared the popularity of his team like Elvis Presley and the Beatles traveling together.

> *"It was, said Chuck Daly, coach of the 1992 team, "like Elvis and the Beatles put together. Traveling with the Dream Team was like traveling with 12 rock stars. That's all I can compare it to."* [176]

While in Monte Carlo, the players were not shy and did not try to avoid taking in the beautiful scenery. From spending time on the beaches and playing rounds of golf to enjoying the festivities, the "Dream Team" did it all. Even the head coach, Chuck Daly, viewed as an all business person, took part in the festivities. [176]

In an exhibition game against the French national team, the "Dream Team" looked like they had been practicing all the time. All the players meshed perfectly and played the game of basketball beautifully. The "Dream Team" cruised past the French national team. Despite winning easily, Chuck Daly was not pleased with how his team played. This led to a practice the following morning. In that practice, Chuck Daly made the players play a full four quarter game of basketball made up of teams of five players.[176] The practice was competitive from one on one matchups with Charles Barkley and Karl Malone, the two power forwards on the team, to Clyde Drexler and Michael Jordan. After the game concluded, the players on the losing team wanted to continue. Even though they wanted to continue, the practice concluded. Following the practice, the "Dream Team" went on the plane and flew to Barcelona for the 1992 Olympics. [176]

On July 4, 1992, the "Dream Team" arrived in Barcelona, Spain. They were swarmed by thousands of fans on the Barcelona streets and to many of the players, this was a wakeup call to how their team was viewed popularity-wise. In other words, this put pressure on the team to win the gold. There would be no excuses for losing any game in the tournament.

On July 26, 1992, the "Dream Team" faced Angola in their first game of the 1992 Summer Olympics. The 1992 Summer Olympics were the first time Angola played in basketball Olympics.[176] Heading into the game, the media viewed this matchup as possibly the biggest mismatch in Olympic basketball competition. The "Dream Team" destroyed Angola from the opening whistle and consistently went on 40 point scoring runs, leaving Angola scoreless for large amounts of time. At the end of the first half, the game was technically over. The "Dream Team" led 64-16 with another half to play.[176] During the second half, Angola started to get personal with Charles Barkley down low in the paint. Players on the Angola national team began to get physical with Charles Barkley, leaving the 'Round Mound of Rebounds' to do what he is known for, get physical and start talking trash. Charles Barkley threw an elbow, following a layup, and picked up a technical foul. Despite the rough patch in the game, Charles Barkley and the "Dream Team" won over Angola, 116-48.[176] The result was not the biggest takeaway from the game. Charles Barkley's behavior during the game shadowed over the win and was the main headline. His behavior gave the Americans a bad representation and he was referred to as 'The King of Controversy.'

> *"I thought they were playing dirty,"* Charles Barkley said. *"I told the boy, I don't know if he understood me, but 'Hey man, ease up on the elbow.' I let it go twice and then the next time I just cracked him."* [176]

On July 27, 1992, in their next game, the "Dream Team" faced Toni Kukoc and Croatia. Toni Kukoc was drafted by the Chicago Bulls in 1989.[181] There was some bad blood between Toni Kukoc with Scottie Pippen and Michael Jordan. Both Bulls were not fond of Toni Kukoc due to the Chicago Bulls organization heavily liking the Croatian. During the game, Scottie Pippen and Michael Jordan bullied and destroyed Toni Kukoc on both ends of the floor. The "Dream Team" ran over Toni Kukoc and Croatia, winning 103-70. [176]

Following two blowout performances by the "Dream Team," not everything was positive. The media began to publish stories on how this team was too good for Olympic competition and how unfair the team was. Despite the negative headlines, the team was still heavily liked by fans and received the same likeable treatment by the media.

In their third game against Brazil, the "Dream Team" once again won in blowout fashion, winning 127-83. After Brazil, came Spain. For the "Dream Team," it was yet again another blowout win, defeating Spain 122-81. The next two games were no different. The "Dream Team" defeated Puerto Rico, 115-

77, then crushed Lithuania, 127-76, to advance to the 1992 Summer Olympics Gold medal game. [176]

On August 8, 1992, the "Dream Team" faced Croatia in the gold medal game. In their previous game, just two weeks prior, the "Dream Team" crushed Croatia, winning 130-70. It was clear there was no question that the "Dream Team" would win gold but this was the last time in Barcelona that the United States could show their dominance and put on a worldwide show. The "Dream Team" defeated Croatia, 117-85, winning gold and cementing their name as the "Dream Team." [176] With the loss, Croatia won silver, followed by Lithuania winning bronze.

Players on the "Dream Team" were filled with emotion when they were awarded the gold medals at the podium despite being the favorites all along.

> *"You saw a lot of tears from players,"* Michael Jordan said. *"It was a very proud moment for me because anytime you represent your country, that is a prideful thing."* [176]

> *"All of those emotions just overcame me,"* Magic Johnson said. *"I got to be one of the guys one more time for my country. I said 'Man, I will never forget this moment.' You know if this is the end, this is how I would want to go out."* [176]

Although the 1992 Summer Olympics in Barcelona, Spain were officially over and the "Dream Team" was bringing home the gold to the United States of America, the impact was just beginning. Larry Bird and Magic Johnson retired from the NBA but the rest of the members of the "Dream Team" played in the NBA and cemented their own legacies. There was one common achievement every member of the "Dream Team" did achieve besides winning gold at the 1992 Summer Olympics: making the Naismith Memorial Basketball Hall of Fame.

Following the end of the 1992 Summer Olympics, Chuck Daly noted that all the competition knew they were facing the best team in the world. He also reflected on how the "Dream Team" will always be a landmark event for those teams and how in the future, he expects those teams to compete with the United States.

> *"They knew they were playing the best in the world,"* Daly said. *"They'll go home and for the rest of their lives be able to tell their kids, 'I played against Michael Jordan and Magic Johnson and Larry Bird'' And the more they play against our best players, the more confident they're going to get."* [176]

"Finally, there will come a day - I'm not saying it will happen anytime soon, mind you, but it's inevitable that it will happen -- that they will be able to compete with us on even terms. And they'll look back on the Dream Team as a landmark event in that process." [176]

Since the 1992 "Dream Team" and their historic run in the 1992 Summer Olympics in Barcelona, Spain, the globalization of not just the NBA but the sport of basketball grew tremendously. Prior to the 1992 Summer Olympics, the NBA was exploring ways to get international notability to the league.

On March 10, 1992, the NBA opened their first international office in Hong Kong, China and in June of the same year, opened their second international office in Melbourne, Australia.[1] In addition to the front office openings abroad, the NBA, as discussed before, set up a series of exhibition games for some of their teams in other countries. Despite venturing overseas and making small splashes, the 1992 "Dream Team" was the stamp on NBA globalization.

The sport of basketball grew worldwide and in the following years, international competition for the United States was not a breeze like it was in 1992. The future United States men's national teams did not contain the star power the "Dream Team" possessed on the court. Not just international Olympic teams began to rise in skill but so did a majority of the leagues overseas. Basketball became more accepted and was popularized in many countries in the 1990s.

There is a famous reference: The game of basketball was invented in Springfield, Massachusetts in 1891 but the modern NBA game of basketball was created in 1992 in Barcelona, Spain.

The style of basketball play was changed following the 1992 Summer Olympics. The play in the NBA before was quite simple: pound the ball to the inside and score on the offensive end. In the 1992 Summer Olympics, the "Dream Team" spread the floor and instead of having their big men camp inside and pound the ball to the basket, the big men spread the floor as well along the perimeter and shot. The style of having shooting-big men along the perimeter was a common play style and strategy for European teams. The NBA today is a shooter's league. From point guards to centers, the game has revolutionized into small ball offensive play and shooting from the perimeter.

"Now we've gone more that way, because there aren't that many good big post players to start out with," Rod Thorn, the NBA president of operations at the time. *"We didn't have what is called a stretch 4 until we started getting all these kids from Europe. The*

Nowitzki's of the world in particular, guys who could shoot the ball on the court and were big, and now everybody looks like a stretch 4."
[179]

The biggest influence the 1992 "Dream Team" had on the NBA rather than influencing the new style of offensive play was global marketing. After the dominance the "Dream Team" put on in Barcelona, Spain, the league gained new fans across the world. The NBA, as mentioned before, was the first United States professional league to play regular season games outside of the country, but the "Dream Team" brought new talent from all over the world to the league.

Kobe Bryant, who was a member of the 2008 and 2012 United States men's Olympic team, credits the "Dream Team" as the foundation for the game of basketball growing internationally.

"The global impact that they've had on the game," Kobe Bryant said. *"They really made the game or started the process of making the game as global as it is today."* [179]

Chapter 20

The Croatian Sensation: Toni Kukoc

Toni Kukoc was born on September 18, 1968 in Split, SFR Yugoslavia. Split is a small city located along the coast of the Adriatic Sea. His father worked at a shipyard along the Adriatic Sea while his mother worked in an office as a part-time employee.[181] His father was a former athlete and played soccer for a local club and passed along his passion of sports to Toni Kukoc.

Toni Kukoc played many sports in Split. He played the nation's top sports soccer and table tennis, a rising sport in Europe at the time. Toni Kukoc thrived at both soccer and table tennis, winning multiple individual honors and team awards.[180]

While thriving in soccer and table tennis, Kukoc decided to play basketball, a sport that was not very popular in the nation and was not picked up my many youths. Due to his height and skillset at a young age, Toni Kukoc quickly picked up the fundamentals of the sport.

> *"I played [ping-pong] from years eight through twelve and I was a Croatian champ,"* Toni Kukoc said. *"My dad was a soccer goalie and I played from twelve to sixteen. Then, when i was sixteen, I grew seven or eight inches during the summer and decided that basketball was the sport to pursue."* [180]

At the age of 17, Toni Kukoc began playing basketball as a member of KK Jugoplastika, a local club near Split. With KK Jugoplastika, Kukoc dominated and was a big contributor on both ends of the floor. In his six seasons with the European club, Kukoc led the team to back to back Triple Crown championships in 1990 and 1991. [184]

In 1990, Toni Kukoc was drafted by the Chicago Bulls with the 29th pick in the 1990 NBA Draft. [182] Following the selection, Toni Kukoc decided not to jump straight into the NBA and instead continue to dominate Europe. He won multiple individual honors and awards while a part of KK Jugoplastika.

- Three-time EuroLeague champion (1989, 1990, 1991)
- Four-time Yugoslavia National champion (1988, 1989, 1990, 1991)
- Two-time Yugoslav Cup champion (1990, 1991)
- Two-time Triple Crown winner (1990, 1991) [184]

Following six seasons with KK Jugoplastika, Kukoc signed with Benetton Treviso, a club in the Italian League. Kukoc immediately made an impact on the team and led the team to win the Italian League in 1992 and the Italian Cup in 1993. The 1992-93 season was the last season Kukoc would play professional basketball overseas. [184]

While playing professional basketball overseas as a member of KK Jugoplastika and Benetton Treviso, Kukoc was a member of the Yugoslavia men's national basketball team. Kukoc was a major piece to Yugoslavia's success in international and Olympic competition, winning multiple gold, silver, and bronze medals. Kukoc continued to play national team basketball for Croatia up until the 1995 EuroBasket Tournament held in Greece, where Croatia won bronze. As a member of Yugoslavia, Kukoc is one of the most decorated players to play for the team.

- 1985 FIBA Europe U-16 Championship (Gold)
- 1986 FIBA Europe U-18 Championship (Gold)
- 1987 FIBA U-19 World Cup (Gold)
- 1987 EuroBasket (Bronze)
- 1988 Summer Olympics (Silver)
- 1989 EuroBasket (Gold)
- 1990 FIBA World Championship (Gold)
- 1991 EuroBasket (Gold) [184]

As mentioned before, Kukoc was a member of the Croatian national team at the 1992 Summer Olympics in Barcelona, Spain. Kukoc and Croatia made it to the gold medal game in the tournament but suffered their second loss to the "Dream Team." Kukoc believed his Croatian national team, which included Vlade Divac and Drazen Petrovic, was the second-best team in the world.

"I would certainly say that the ex-Yugoslavian team with Vlade, Drazen, Dino and myself, that was probably the best team, I would say besides the 1992 Dream Team, in the whole world." [180]

As a member of the Croatian men's national team, Kukoc did not win any gold medals but did win a handful of silver and bronze medals.

- 1992 Summer Olympics (Silver)
- 1994 FIBA World Championship (Bronze)

- 1995 EuroBasket (Bronze) [184]

Toni Kukoc is one of the most decorated European professional basketball players to split time overseas and in the NBA. On top of his team accomplishments from championships to cups, he has quite the list of individual achievements.

- MVP Award: 1986 FIBA Europe U-18 Championship
- MVP Award: 1987 FIBA U-19 World Cup
- Three-time Croatian Sportsman of the Year (1989, 1990, 1991)
- FIBA World Cup All-Tournament Team (1990)
- Five-time Euroscar European Player of the Year (1990, 1991, 1994, 1996, 1998)
- Four-time Mister Europa European Player of the Year (1990, 1991, 1992, 1996)
- Three-time EuroLeague Final Four MVP (1990, 1991, 1993)
- EuroLeague Finals Top Scorer (1990)
- Two-time EuroLeague All-Final Four Team (1991, 1993)
- MVP Award: FIBA EuroBasket (1991)
- Two-time FIBA EuroBasket All-Tournament Team (1991, 1995) [181]

Following his final season with Benetton Treviso in 1993, Kukoc decided it was time to take his talents to the United States and play in the NBA. Jerry Krause, the Chicago Bulls general manager at the time, was obsessed with Kukoc and really wanted him to join the team following being selected by the franchise in 1990. [181]

At the time of his arrival to the Bulls, Chicago was already a top team in the NBA, and he was joining a roster that included future NBA Hall of Famers Michael Jordan and Scottie Pippen and the team was coached by Phil Jackson, who is considered arguably the greatest coach in NBA history. Chicago was also coming off three straight NBA championships. In 1993, Kukoc joined the Chicago Bulls.

Kukoc played a total of seven seasons with the Bulls, winning three NBA championships, which was another three-peat for the franchise, 1996-98. He played a total of 436 games as a member of the Bulls and averaged 29.5 minutes, 14.1 points, 4.8 rebounds, and 4.2 assists per game. [182] In addition to winning three championships, Kukoc won two individual league honors: NBA All-Rookie Second Team (1994) and the NBA Sixth Man of the Year (1996). At the time of this writing, Kukoc is the last player to win the NBA Sixth Man of the Year award and win an NBA Championship in the same season. [182]

In 1999, the Bulls began to shop and begin rebuilding their dynasty roster. Scottie Pippen was traded to the Houston Rockets beginning the dismantling of the dynasty and during the 1999-2000 season, Kukoc was traded. He was traded as part of a three-team trade which included the Golden State Warriors and the Philadelphia 76ers. Kukoc was on his way to Philadelphia, Bruce Bowen, John Starks, and a 2000 first-round pick was sent to the Bulls. [182]

Kukoc played two seasons in Philadelphia as a member of the 76ers. He played a total of 80 games and came off the bench most of his time as a 76er and averaged 23.7 minutes, 9.8 points, 3.8 rebounds, and 2.9 assists per game. [182]

Once again, Kukoc was traded to the Atlanta Hawks. The deal sent Kukoc, Nazr Mohammed, Pepe Sanchez, and Theo Ratliff to Atlanta in exchange for Dikembe Mutombo and Roshown McLeod. [182] He played two seasons with the Hawks, coming off the bench, playing in 76 games. In those 76 games, Kukoc averaged 27.8 minutes, 12.1 points, 4.2 assists, and 4.1 rebounds. [182]

After another short run, Atlanta dealt Kukoc and Leon Smith to the Milwaukee Bucks in exchange for Glenn Robinson. Kukoc played the final four seasons of his NBA career with the Bucks, playing in a total of 254 games coming off the bench. In those 254 games as a member of the Bucks, he averaged 21.0 minutes, 7.7 points, 3.3 rebounds, and 2.9 assists per game. [182]

Following the 2005-06 season, Kukoc, who was 37 years old, made it clear the only teams he would sign a new deal and continue playing with were the Milwaukee Bucks and the Chicago Bulls. Despite making it clear he only would continue playing as a member of one of the two teams, he received a handful of new deals from other NBA teams. Neither the Bucks or the Bulls offered Kukoc a new deal and on September 12, 2006, he retired from the NBA. [181]

In August of 2015, Toni Kukoc was hired by the Chicago Bulls as a special advisor to Michael Reinsdorf, the COO of the Bulls.

> *"Toni will work across the organization and his duties will be wide-ranging,"* Reinsdorf said. *"He will bring valuable perspective that comes with experience to many areas, whether it is relating to the international players on our team or sharing what it means to be a Chicago Bull when talking to partners and fans. Toni will be a strong representative of both the team's legacy and its future."* [183]

Chapter 21

The NBA Expands into Canada: The Toronto Raptors

The game of basketball has always held a place for the city of Toronto, Ontario, Canada. As mentioned in the beginning of this book, the Toronto Huskies were one of the very first basketball teams in the Basketball Association of America. The team only lasted one year, from 1946-47, but in that one year, the game of basketball was just beginning to evolve.

Around the early 1990s, the NBA were exploring adding expansion teams to their league. On April 23, 1993, the NBA announced that the league had received a formal application from Professional Basketball Franchise (PBF) (Canada). John Bitove Jr., who was the president of Bitove Investments Inc and his father, John Bitove Sr. were known for managing a Canadian food service business and were wealthy businessmen. John Bitove Sr. had always been in talks with the NBA regarding an expansion franchise in Canada in past expansion talks but in 1993, the talks were more serious than ever before. [187]

The Professional Basketball Franchise (PBF) put together a good size group to proceed with the expansion talks.

The group included Allan Slaught of Standard Broadcasting Limited; Borden Osmak, a vice president of The Bank of Nova Scotia; Phil Granovsky of Atlantic Packaging Limited; and David Peterson, former premier of the Province of Ontario, who served as chairman. Originally, Bitove and Slaight were each to own 44 percent of the franchise, with the bank holding a 10-percent stake and Granovsky and Peterson 1 percent each. The ownership group later cut in former Detroit Pistons star Isiah Thomas, who received a 5-percent share from both Bitove and Slaight. Thomas later became a club vice president and the architect of the Raptors' roster. [187]

The Professional Basketball Franchise was not alone in getting an NBA expansion team in Toronto. There were two other groups wanting to bring an NBA expansion team to the city of Toronto.

The Palestra Group, which was led by Larry Tanenbaum, a Canadian businessman, and both the Canadian Imperial Bank of Commerce and Labatt Breweries. Both Canadian Imperial Bank of Commerce and Labatt Breweries were the founders of the Toronto Blue Jays, a Major League Baseball franchise.

The other group wanting to bring an NBA expansion franchise to Toronto was a smaller group. The group was made up by Bill Ballard, Michael Cohl, and Earvin "Magic" Johnson. This small group was backed up by Metro Toronto. [187]

In July of 1993, Jerry Colangelo, the Phoenix Suns owner and the head of the NBA expansion committee all came to Toronto to meet with the groups. During each meeting Jerry Colangelo and the NBA expansion committee talked with the bidding groups about their plans for the new expansion team from designs to proposed arena sites. The PBF stood out to Jerry Colangelo and the NBA expansion committee due to their well thought out plans.

Their proposed arena site included a subway line giving fans a safer and easier way of getting to the arena when there are heavy weather conditions. The PBF group's proposed arena site location was located near the center of Toronto to appeal to major businesses to buy corporate boxes. [187] The strategy behind major businesses buying corporate boxes was a common successful trend for sports franchises in the 1980s and 1990s. Despite the new location sight, the new team was set to play their first two seasons in the SkyDome while the building of their new arena was going on.

A couple months later, on September 30, 1993, Jerry Colangelo and the NBA expansion committee awarded PBF an expansion franchise in the city of Toronto, beginning at the time of the 1995-96 season.[187] The new team was set to become the NBA's 28th team in the league.

> *"We're going to make the NBA proud. We respect the trust that they've charged us with,"* said John Bitove Jr., president of the yet-to-be-named professional basketball franchise in Toronto. [187]

Later, on November 4, 1993, the NBA Board of Governors announced that the new Toronto expansion team set a record expansion fee, which was $125 million. [188]

In addition to a new NBA franchise in the city of Toronto and the first in the country of Canada, it provided thousands of new jobs.

> *The province finally acknowledged the boost an NBA team would provide to the local economy through taxes- $81 million the first year alone, according to the Metro Toronto Convention and Visitor Association - and the creation of 4,000 jobs necessitated by construction and related activities.* [187]

Next came the creative steps to the process: coming up with the new team's name. The PBF organized a nationwide "Name Game" contest to name the team and come up with the team's colors and logo. The "Name Game" quickly became popular, generating close to 2,500 entries.

The final top-10 list was dominated by animal names: Beavers, Bobcats, Dragons, Grizzlies, Hogs (Toronto's nickname is Hogtown), Raptors, Scorpions, T-Rex, Tarantulas, and Terriers. [187]

After a successful "Name Game" contest, on May 15, 1993 the new Toronto NBA team found its colors, team name, and an established logo.

No doubt fueled by the enormous success of the movie Jurassic Park and the popularity of dinosaurs with youngsters who would grow up to be fans in the target market, the team's new moniker, the Toronto Raptors, was unveiled on Canadian national television. The franchise's logo (the work of NBA Properties) featured an aggressive, sharp-toothed little dinosaur dribbling a basketball. The team colors were to be bright red, purple, black, and "Naismith silver" (in honour of Canadian James Naismith, who invented the game of basketball in 1891). [187]

More than $20 million in Raptors gear was snapped up in the first month. By the end of 1994, the logo was hot in the marketplace, and the Raptors, still a long way from their first game, were seventh in the league in merchandise sales. [187]

One year later, after finalizing the outsides of the Toronto Raptors, the organization began to arrange their front office. On May 24, 1994, Isiah Thomas was named the franchise's first team's vice president of basketball operations. Later that year, in September, Bob Zuffelato was brought in to direct talent searches along with video experts. Bob Zuffelato, at the time of his hiring, had more than three decades of coaching, player development, and scouting experience under his belt. He served as a college head coach from 1971 till 1983 splitting time with Marshall and Boston College. After more than a decade in college, Bob Zuffelato served as an assistant coach, splitting time with the Dallas Mavericks, the Minnesota Timberwolves, and the Golden State Warriors. [187] At the time of this writing, Bob Zuffelato serves as a scout for the Toronto Raptors and has been with the franchise since his hiring in 1994. Following the hiring of Bob Zuffelato, Glen Grunwald, the former Denver Nuggets vice president, was hired as Isiah Thomas' assistant.

In the closing months of 1994, PBF ran into a roadblock with the team's new arena location. The site for the new arena was too small for John Bitove and PBF demands.

Bitove wanted a construction site large enough to house an additional 22,500-seat hockey rink, which would assure more event nights and give the structure more financial viability. This was accomplished by acquiring from Canada Post the historic Postal Delivery Building at the south end of downtown, eat of the SkyDome and still served by the subway system. [187]

Uncertainty about the arena obviously didn't deter ticket sales. At the end of 1994, the Raptors reported 50-percent deposits on 15,287 seats for the inaugural season. In February 1995, it was announced that the building would be named the Air Canada Centre. Revised plans called not only for an arena to be completed by fall 1997 but also for 200,000 square feet of adjacent office space. [187]

On May 16, 1995, the Toronto Raptors officially became an NBA franchise. [188] Shortly after the official announcement, Isiah Thomas and the Raptors organization put together its first free agent camp at Seneca College in Toronto. Brendan Malone, who served as an assistant with the Detroit Pistons and had a close relationship with Isiah Thomas as a player and as a front office executive, helped Isiah Thomas scout out free agents at the free agent camp.[187] Less than a week after the free agent camp concluded, Isiah Thomas and the Raptors hired Brendan Malone as the team's first-ever head coach.

On June 24, 1995, the NBA held an expansion draft. The Raptors and the Vancouver Grizzlies, another NBA expansion franchise, which will be talked about in this book, had a coin flip to determine which new team is awarded the first pick and the order of lottery picks in the college draft. The Grizzlies won the coin flip and decided to pick sixth in the college draft. This led to the Raptors to pick seventh in the college draft and first in the expansion draft.

With the first pick in the 1995 NBA Expansion Draft, the Raptors selected B.J Armstrong, the veteran Chicago Bulls guard. B.J Armstrong made it clear before being selected that if he was chosen, he would demand a trade to a title contending NBA team. Following the first pick, Vancouver picked second, and the two teams took turns drafting players.

Thomas filled out the Toronto roster with a combination of veterans and youngsters. He acquired proven players in the Portland Trail Blazers' Jerome Kersey, the San Antonio Spurs' Willie Anderson, the Milwaukee Bucks' Ed Pinckney, and the Miami Heat's John Salley. He also picked promising young players such as Dontonio Wingfield from the Seattle SuperSonics, B.J Tyler from the Philadelphia 76ers,

Keith Jennings from the Golden State Warriors, Oliver Miller from the Detroit Pistons, and Tony Massenburg from the Los Angeles Clippers. Others selected included Andres Guibert from the Minnesota Timberwolves, Doug Smith from the Dallas Mavericks, Zan Tabak from the Houston Rockets, and Acie Earl from the Boston Celtics. [187]

After a successful 1995 NBA Expansion Draft, Isiah Thomas the Raptors looked to complete their inaugural roster with their two picks in the 1995 NBA Draft. The 1995 NBA Draft was held in the SkyDome in Toronto, which brought out many fans wearing the new franchises uniforms.

The Raptors had the seventh and the thirty-fifth overall picks in the Draft, looking to draft young backcourt players. With the seventh pick, the Raptors selected Damon Stoudamire from Arizona, a bright point guard who was viewed as an NBA ready guard.

"They'll know who Damon Stoudamire is by the time I'm through playing," the young recruit Damon Stoudamire said confidently. [187]

With the thirty-fifth pick, the Raptors selected Jimmy King, a shooting guard out of the University of Michigan who was a member of the infamous 'Fab Five,' completing their roster for the inaugural season.[187]

The Toronto Raptors opened their inaugural season, the 1995-96 season, on November 3 in a matchup with the New Jersey Nets at the SkyDome in Toronto. In their first game, Toronto defeated New Jersey, 94-79. Despite the bright start, Toronto struggled throughout the regular season and finished their first season placing fourth in the Eastern Conference Atlantic Division and tenth in the Eastern Conference with a record of 21-61, missing the playoffs. [188]

The Raptors franchise had to wait a couple years until the feeling of winning kicked in. The 1999-2000 season was the first winning season for the franchise and also the first time in franchise history the Raptors made the NBA Playoffs. Their first playoff series win came the following postseason, the 2000-01 season, when Toronto defeated the New York Knicks in the first round of the 2001 NBA Playoffs. The 2018-19 season was a historic season for the Raptors franchise. After trading for San Antonio Spurs superstar Kawhi Leonard and dealing DeMar Derozan, who was the face of the franchise since he was drafted in 2009 in exchange. The trade, at first, left many Raptors players in anger and disappointment but Kawhi Leonard led his new team to the NBA Finals, the first time in the franchise's history.

The Toronto Raptors, behind the excellent play of Kawhi Leonard, won the 2019 NBA Championship, earning the Raptors their first NBA title in franchise history. The global impact of the championship win for the Raptors

155

spreads much farther than the franchise. Their team was made up of several international players and their championship win marked the first time in NBA history a franchise outside the United States won the title.

Pascal Siakam, who won the 2019 NBA Most Improved Player award, became the first Cameroonian player to win an NBA championship. Marc Gasol, who will be highlighted in this book, joined his brother Pau Gasol, becoming the first international-born siblings to each win an NBA championship. Jeremy Lin became the first Asian-American in NBA history to win an NBA championship. In addition to their players breaking monumental acheivements with the championship win, the Raptors general manager, Masai Ujiri, became the first African general manager to win an NBA title.

The 2019 NBA Championship win by the Toronto Raptors will always be labeled as a staple to the game of basketball growing on international levels and will always be known as a major step in the NBA globalizing.

Chapter 22

The Rise and Fall of the Vancouver Grizzlies

The country of Canada, as mentioned before, did not have a professional basketball team since the Toronto Huskies who only played one season in 1946-47 disbanded.

In 1980, Nelson Skalbania, a local entrepreneur and who was the president and majority owner of McKenzie Snowball & Skalbania, pursued the idea of having an NBA team in Vancouver but his idea quickly came up unsuccessful. After a failed attempt by Nelson Skalbania, 13 years later, Arthur Griffiths, who was the owner of the Vancouver Canucks of the National Hockey League, best known as the NHL, and the owner of Northwest Sports Enterprises, publicly announced he was pursuing to bring an NBA team to Vancouver. His announcement came in February of 1993 and, as mentioned in the previous chapter, the Toronto Raptors were founded in September of 1993. Vancouver, at the time of the announcement by Arthur Griffiths, was one of the top five most densely populated cities in the continent of North America.[189]

In addition to Arthur Griffith's pursuit of bringing an NBA team to Vancouver, he was in the works of developing a new privately-owned arena, which could hold up to 20,000 fans, for the Vancouver Canucks. The site, known as the General Motors Place, was in the downtown section of Vancouver and was ready to open for the 1995-96 season.[189]

On February 14, 1994, Jerry Colangelo and the NBA Expansions announced the preliminary approval for Vancouver to have their own NBA team and become the 29th franchise in the league. The full approval for the new Vancouver NBA team came a couple months later April 27, 1994.[189] Like the Toronto Raptors, the Vancouver franchise had to pay a $125 million fee, which was $92.5 million more than the Charlotte Hornets and the Miami Heat paid during their expansions in 1988 and 1989.

> *It was kind of a personal thing to have Vancouver come in at the same time as Toronto. Many people considered them an [underdog] originally, but they were able to rally their troops and come in at the same time. And I think timing is important, to have both east and west coast representation.* - Jerry Colangelo, (Chairman of the NBA Board of Governors, 1995) [189]

The Globalization of the NBA

Despite Vancouver becoming the 29th NBA franchise, NBA Commissioner David Stern wanted to keep the NBA a non-betting and wagering league. The provinces of British Columbia and Ontario allowed wagering on sports and David Stern required both British Columbia and Ontario to abolish any wagering on his league's games prior to the 1995-96 season.

> *To preserve the integrity of the NBA game, Commissioner David J. Stern required the provinces of British Columbia and Ontario to abolish any wagering on his league's games prior to the 1995-96 season. In British Columbia that meant removing NBA contests from the provincial government-controlled Sports Action betting games, in which players who correctly predicted the point spreads of at least three NBA games won cash prizes. In 1993, BC bettors shelled out some $1.56 million Canadian on NBA games, with a large portion of the money dedicated to health care services in the province.* [189]

> *In the end, BC Premier Michael Harcourt, himself a BC high school basketball player of some renown in the 1950s worked together with Griffiths and the NBA to achieve a final resolution. On February 9, 1994, just prior to their trip to Minneapolis, Griffiths' group agreed to contribute $500,000 per year for five years (beginning in 1995). Half of the proceeds were donated to a hospice for needy children and the other half to the BC health care system, in exchange for having all NBA games removed from Sports Action.* [189]

Following the resolution of the wagering, it was time for Vancouver to build their team's foundation. On July 22, 1994, Stu Jackson was hired as the team's first team's general manager.[189] In addition, Stu Jackson served as the vice president of basketball operations for the league's 29th franchise. Before taking the position with Vancouver, Stu Jackson held coaching positions with Providence College, Washington State University, and the University of Wisconsin. On top of his college basketball coaching resume, Stu Jackson served as the New York Knicks head coach from 1989-91, achieving an overall record of 52-45.[189] At the time of his hiring with the New York Knicks, Stu Jackson was the second-youngest coach in the league's history at 33 years old and led the team to a playoff run in 1990. At first, when Arthur Griffiths contacted Stu Jackson for the position, Stu Jackson was not interested but once they met in St. Louis, he was very intrigued.

> *I was at U of W [University of Wisconsin]. We had just finished our second year there, and had gone to the NCAA tournament, and*

*finished in the second round. At the time, over I guess that summer,
we had a very good team coming back for the following year, but I
got a call from Russ Granik at the NBA league office. They asked me
if I'd be interested in starting a franchise in Canada. I recall I said,
'Not really.'* [189]

*I met with Arthur in St. Louis, if I recall, because I was actually
coaching a summer collegiate team with USA basketball and flew in.
We had the opportunity to meet for a couple hours, and I have to say
that after meeting with Arthur, I was very intrigued.* [189]

Stu Jackson then quickly started to build the scouting department for
the new Vancouver NBA team. Larry Riley, who had quite the basketball
experience when it came to scouting and coaching on the college level, was
hired as the director of player personnel.

*In that role, he oversaw the team's scouting of professional, college
and international players and advised the team on all player-related
transactions.* [189]

Larry Riley was the head coach of Chadron State from 1976-78 and
Eastern New Mexico from 1978-88. Following his head coaching tenures at
Chadron State and Eastern New Mexico, Larry Riley served as an assistant
coach for Southeast Missouri State from 1969-70, Wisconsin-Milwaukee from
1970-73, Brevard Community College from 1973-74, and at Mercer College
from 1974-76. Larry Riley was brought into the NBA in 1988 as a scout and
video coordinator for the Milwaukee Bucks. He spent a total of six years, 1988-
94, with the Bucks organization.

*While with the Bucks he was responsible for advance scouting of
NBA opponents, CBA, USBL and college scouting. Riley originally
broke into the NBA when he was originally by the Bucks in 1988 as a
scout and video coordinator.* [189]

After building a foundation for the new Vancouver NBA team, it was
the time of the franchise to announce the teams full name. Unlike the Toronto
Raptors, letting the fans vote on a name, the franchise came up with their own
name. At first, the franchise was settled on being named the Vancouver
Mounties, but the name quickly went from a settled idea to an objection. [189] The
Royal Canadian Mounted Police, the federal and national police force of the
country of Canada, were not fond of the name and forced the franchise to come

up with new ideas. On August 11, 1994, the Vancouver Basketball Partnership officially became the Vancouver Grizzlies.

> *During ceremonies held amid totem poles at the University of British Columbia's Museum of Anthropology, Jackson and Griffiths announced the name and revealed the team logo of the fierce animal indigenous to Canada's westernmost province. Primary team colors were turquoise, bronze, and red.* [189]

Following excitement for the Vancouver Grizzlies, Arthur Griffths made a surprising announcement which stunned not just Vancouver and their new fanbase but the NBA. Arthur Griffiths announced that he will be surrendering majority control of the Vancouver Grizzlies, the Vancouver Canucks, and General Motors Place to John McCaw Jr.

> *On March 7, 1995, Griffith announced that he had surrendered majority control of the Grizzlies, the Canucks, and General Motors Place to Seattle's John McCaw Jr, a minority shareholder whose family had made its fortune through McCaw Cellular, a wireless-communication giant that had recently completed a multibillion-dollar merger with AT&T.* [189]

> *The move gave McCaw 60-percent ownership in a collective now known as the Northwest Entertainment Group, of which Griffiths remains CEO and chairman.* [189]

The move did stun most of the NBA and the Vancouver franchise, but it did not leave the franchise is a shaky position. The Vancouver Grizzlies were set to draft their franchise's first players in June of 1995 and were still in need of hiring their coaching positions. The Grizzlies waited until only five days before the 1995 NBA Expansion Draft to sign their first head coach. On June 19, 1995, Stu Jackson hired Brian Winters as the franchise's first head coach. [189] Brian Winters was drafted with the 12th overall pick in the 1974 NBA Draft by the Los Angeles Lakers, splitting nine seasons between the Lakers and the Bucks. Following his nine years as a player, Brian Winters served as an assistant coach at Princeton University from 1984-86 before making his return to the league. He served as an assistant with the Cleveland Cavaliers from 1986-93 and an assistant for the Atlanta Hawks from 1993-95 before coming to the Vancouver Grizzlies.

When the 1995 NBA Expansion Draft came around, as mentioned before, the Toronto Raptors were awarded the first overall pick due to winning a coin flip. Players available for selection were only one select player from each of the 27 NBA teams. Each team had the chance to lock eight of their players, making them unselectable for the Toronto Raptors and the Vancouver Grizzlies. As mentioned in the chapter prior, the Toronto Raptors, due to winning the coin flip, selected B.J. Armstrong from the Chicago Bulls with the first pick in the 1995 NBA Expansion Draft. B.J. Armstrong refused to play for the Toronto Raptors and played for the Golden State Warriors during the 1995-96 season.

With the second pick in the 1995 NBA Expansion Draft, the Vancouver Grizzlies selected Greg Anthony from the New York Knicks as their second player. Kevin Pritchard signed with the Vancouver Grizzlies a couple days before the 1995 NBA Expansion Draft.

As the draft progressed, the Vancouver Grizzlies selected the following players from NBA teams. The team included a mix of young and veteran players.

> *Among the top players selected by the Grizzlies during the expansion draft were Indiana Pacers guard Byron Scott, Cleveland Cavaliers guard Gerald Wilkins, and Utah Jazz swingman Blue Edwards. Other NBA veterans included Charlotte Hornets forward Kenny Gattison, New Jersey Nets center Benoit Benjamin, and Washington Bullets forward Larry Stewart. Vancouver also selected Rodney Dent from the Orlando Magic, Antonio Harvet from the Los Angeles Lakers, Reggie Slater from the Denver Nuggets, Trevor Ruffin from the Phoenix Suns, Derrick Phelps from the Sacramento Kings, and Doug Edwards from the Atlanta Hawks. Prior to the expansion draft, Vancouver had signed free-agent point guard Kevin Pritchard [formerly of the Miami Heat] as its first-ever player.* [189]

Following a good expansion draft by the Vancouver Grizzlies, it was time for the franchise to complete their roster for their inaugural season. On June 28, 1995, the 1995 NBA Draft was held at the SkyDome in Toronto. [193] The Vancouver Grizzlies held the 6th and 36th picks in the 1995 NBA Draft and had their eyes on selecting a big man with their 6th pick. With the 6th pick, the Vancouver Grizzlies selected Bryant Reeves, a highly scouted center out of Oklahoma State. [193]

> *At the 1995 NBA Draft held in Toronto's SkyDome on June 28, the Grizzlies tabbed Oklahoma State's 7-foot, 292-point center Bryant "Big Country" Reeves as their first-ever college draft pick. Reeves was the first true center selected and the sixth player taken overall. Jackson said he was delighted to get a player of Reeves's offensive capabilities and predicted that the young recruit would grow into one*

of the NBA's top centers. Looking for ways to sell the game in an untested NBA market, the Grizzlies also felt that Reeves was an especially solid citizen with the country charm to win over new fans. [189]

With the 36th pick in the 1995 NBA Draft, the Vancouver Grizzlies selected Lawrence Moten, a shooting guard out of Syracuse University, completing the roster for their inaugural season. [193]

As expected, the Vancouver Grizzlies did not have a good first year as a franchise. The team did start off on the right foot, winning their first two games, one on the road and one at home at the General Motors Palace. He averaged 13.3 points per game and 7.4 rebounds per game making him a fan favorite and made the NBA's All-Rookie Second Team. [193] Despite becoming a fan favorite and a promising rookie big man, he did not help the Vancouver Grizzlies draw large crowds at the General Motors Palace.

In their first season, the Vancouver Grizzlies lost 23 consecutive games, which at the time of this writing, stands as the league's worst single game losing streak in history. The Vancouver Grizzlies finished their first season with an overall record of 15-67 and an average attendance of less than 18,000 at home. [193]

The 1998-97 season, the Vancouver Grizzlies second season, was not much better at all. In the 1996 NBA Draft, the Vancouver Grizzlies held the 3rd, 22nd, and the 51st overall picks. Stu Jackson and the Grizzlies selected Shareef Abdur-Rahim, a versatile power forward out of the University of California Berkeley, power forward Roy Rogers out of the University of Alabama with the 22nd pick and shooting guard Chris Robinson out of Western Kentucky University with the 51st overall pick. [189]

The franchise mirrored their inaugural season, finishing with a record of 14-68. During their second season, Brian Winters was fired following a disappointing record of 8-35 at the time of his firing: January 24, 1997. Stu Jackson filled in the vacant head coaching position and finished the season winning only six of the remaining 39 games. [189] Despite another disappointing season, leaving their new fans wondering if success will ever be achieved in Vancouver, there were some bright signs from their young talent. Forward Shareef Abdur-Rahim, a contender for the Rookie of the Year, and second-year center Bryant "Big Country" Reeves were the focal points of the Grizzlies' offense, and they responded by finishing the season as one of the league's highest-scoring frontcourt duos.

Following two early disappointing seasons, the Vancouver Grizzlies began to turn in the right direction. In the 1997 NBA Draft, the Vancouver Grizzlies held the 4th and 53rd picks. With the 4th pick, the Vancouver Grizzlies selected Antonio Daniels, a promising point guard out of Indian Hills

Junior College, followed by C.J. Bruton, a shooting guard from Bowling Green State University. The team also traded Rodrick Rhodes to the Dallas Mavericks for Sam Mack, Otis Thorpe, and a 2003 first round pick. [189]

The Vancouver Grizzlies finished their third season with an overall record of 19-63 under their new head coach Brian Hill. [189] At the trade deadline, the Vancouver Grizzlies acquired Sacramento Kings guard Bobby Hurley and Michael Smiths, giving up Chris Robinson and Otis Thorpe.

Shareef Abdur-Rahim provided a well needed boost and rose as one of the league's best young players. In his second season, Shareef Abdur-Rahim was nicknamed "the Future" and was the player fans hoped can bring success to Vancouver.

> *Nicknamed "the Future," Abdur-Rahim proved at the age of 21 that his future is now. The second-year pro improved upon his rookie season in nearly every statistical category, in nearly identical minutes. His scoring average soared to 22.3 points, sixth in the NBA, and his shooting improved to 48.3 percent. The versatile forward also averaged 7.1 rebounds and 2.6 assists per game.* [189]

In their fourth season, the 1998-99 season, the Vancouver Grizzlies won only eight of their 50 games that season. The 1998-99 season was cut to only 50 games due to the league facing a lockout. The Vancouver Grizzlies stuck some gold in the 1998 NBA Draft, selecting Mike Bibby, a talented point guard out of the University of Arizona. In addition to Mike Bibby, with the 56th pick in the 1998 NBA Draft, Vancouver selected J.R. Henderson, a small forward from the University of California, best known as UCLA. [189]

The following season, the 1999-2000 season was a brighter season for the Vancouver Grizzlies but not before some drama surfaced in the offseason. The Vancouver Grizzlies selected Steve Francis, a talented point guard, who spent only one year at the University of Maryland, with great upside with the second pick in the 1999 NBA Draft. Steve Francis was not pleased with his draft selection and said at the time of his selection, he expressed immediate frustration. Jeffrey Fried, Steve Francis' player attorney and agent, was not pleased either and knew the remaining of the summer of 1999 would not be an easy ride. [192]

The selection came as a surprise due to the franchise drafting Mike Bibby, a point guard, in last year's draft and he had a good rookie season. Steve Francis went on record saying he wanted to be selected with the first pick, which was held by the Chicago Bulls, and he would not be interested in being a part of the Vancouver Grizzlies organization. Jeffrey Fried and Nate Peake, Steve Francis' manager, believed prior to the selection, their client would fall to the Charlotte Hornets, who held the third overall pick. [192]

Despite being on record saying he would not be pleased as a member of the Vancouver Grizzlies organization, Steve Francis decided he would play but, in the end, he was on his way to the Houston Rockets. The rookie point guard had an unknown incident at the airport, leading to him being a part of the biggest trade in the league's history in August of 1999.

The trade included three teams, the Houston Rockets, the Vancouver Grizzlies, and the Orlando Magic, and eleven players. The deal sent Steve Fancis and Tony Massenburg to the Houston Rockets, Antoine Carr, Brent Price, Michael Dickerson, and draft picks to the Vancouver Grizzlies, and Lee Mayberry, Makhtar N'Diaye, Michael Smith, and Rodrick Rhodes to the Orlando Magic. [191]

Two decades later, Steve Francis does not regret his actions following his draft selection and being dealt. In March of 2018, Steve Francis wrote a story with *The Players' Tribune* documenting and focusing around his story and highlighting his time with the Vancouver Grizzlies.

> *"Now, I know people in Vancouver are still pissed off at me for forcing a trade out of there. I damn near cried when I got taken by the Grizzlies at No. 2,"* Francis wrote. *"I was not about to go up to freezing-ass Canada, so far away from my family, when they were about to move the franchise anyway. I'm sorry but ... actually, I'm really not even sorry."* [190]

Steve Francis went on to win the 2000 NBA Rookie of the Year Award as a member of the Houston Rockets and go on to play eleven years of professional basketball, splitting time with three NBA teams and capping his career with the Beijing Ducks of the Chinese Basketball Association in 2010. [191]

With Steve Francis dealt to Houston, the 1999-2000 season was a promising season for the Vancouver Grizzlies. Other than Steve Francis, the Vancouver Grizzlies held two additional picks in the 1999 NBA Draft, but both were second round picks. With the 37th pick, the Vancouver Grizzlies selected Obinna Ekezie, a Nigerian native who was a center. Obinna Ekezie played at the University of Maryland and had a chance to be selected in the first round. The Vancouver Grizzlies picked Antwain Smith with the 51st pick in the 1999 NBA Draft. Antwain Smith was a power forward from LSU. [191]

The franchise hired Lionel Hollins as their head coach following the first 22 games of the season. Brian Hill went 4-18 before being fired. The Vancouver Grizzlies finished with an overall record of 22-60, placing last in their division and 27th in the N.BA in fan attendance. In the following offseason, the summer of 2000, Lionel Hollins was fired and replaced by

Sidney Lowe, a former NBA player who held assistant coaching positions with the Minnesota Timberwolves and the Cleveland Cavaliers.

The 2000-01 season was the final season the franchise played in Vancouver before relocating to Memphis, Tennessee. In the 2000 NBA Draft, the Vancouver Grizzlies were granted the second overall pick. The Vancouver Grizzlies were fond of Kenyon Martin, a strong power forward from Cincinnati. The franchise was invested in drafting a talented big man who could play either the power forward or center position. Kenyon Martin, as expected, was selected first overall by the New Jersey Nets. With the second overall pick, the Vancouver Grizzlies selected Stromile Swift, a sophomore from LSU. Stromile Swift was a versatile power forward who could also play at the center position. The second overall pick was the only draft pick the Vancouver Grizzlies held in the 2000 NBA Draft. [191]

In their final season in Vancouver, the Grizzlies finished with an overall record of 23-59, which was the best overall record the franchise accomplished at the time.

The Vancouver Grizzlies began talks about relocation during the 1999-2000 season. The franchise was not doing well with fan attendance on top of struggling to finish with at least a .500 record. The other Canadian franchise, the Toronto Raptors, on the other hand, were becoming one of the most popular franchises, highly due to the Vinsanity effect. Vince Carter, arguably single handedly, took the franchise to league stardom, despite not being championship contenders till the early 2000s. He helped the Toronto Raptors go from near the bottom in fan attendance to becoming the league's best team when it came to fan attendance in the early 2000s.

The question remains is how could an NBA team in Vancouver, one of the most populated cities in Northern America fail and relocate? The main reason was the snowballing of events leading to financial issues with the franchise.

As mentioned before, the Vancouver Grizzlies drafted Bryant Reeves, the big man from Oklahoma State. Bryant Reeves received and signed a contract worth $64 million over six years.[191] The Vancouver Grizzlies big man never lived up to the potential the franchise hoped for, in fact, he was never an all-star.

To tie in with Bryant Reeves contract was fan attendance at the General Motors Place. During their first season, the Vancouver Grizzlies attracted an average of 17,000 fans per home game.[191] Following their first season, the attendance started to drop lower and lower. Due to the consistent drop in fan attendance at home, the franchise lost millions of dollars.

In 1999, Bill Laurie, who was the owner of the St. Louis Blues of the National Hockey League, the NHL, had serious intentions to buy the Vancouver Grizzlies and move the franchise to St. Louis, Missouri.[191] As mentioned before, the team was sold to Michael Heisley instead, but he was invested as well to relocate the franchise to a small market city in the United States. Prior to Michael Heisley purchasing the franchise, John McCaw Jr. attempted to sell the team to Dennis Washington, the owner of Seaspan ULC, formerly known as Seaspan Marine Corporation, which was based in the Pacific Northwest area. [189]

Despite new ownership all agreed to be open to relocate the franchise, David Stern, the NBA Commissioner at the time, was not open to the move. He wanted the franchise to remain in Vancouver.

Then in January of 2001, first, Bill Laurie paid John McCaw Jr. an undisclosed amount to drop the deal. Four days later, the deal became official between Michael Heisley and John McCaw Jr. The Vancouver Grizzlies were sold to Michael Heisley for $160 million dollars. Michael Heisley stated that he was invested to keep the franchise in Vancouver, and he was on the same page as David Stern. [189]

Following Michael Heisley's purchase, the relocation talks started to heat up. The Vancouver Grizzlies president of basketball operations, Dick Versace, publicly came out and said that his franchise was losing roughly $35 to $40 million each season but many league officials doubted the claim.[189] One person who doubted the claim was the Toronto Raptors CEO Richard Peddie. As mentioned before, the Toronto Raptors were becoming a successful franchise, highly due to the attraction of Vince Carter and the Vinsanity effect. Following the claims, Michael Heisley claimed that the Vancouver Grizzlies had lost over $80 million dollars. On top of Michael Heisley's claims, Dick Versace backed his new owner stating the franchise was not being supported well enough by the nearby business operations in Vancouver.

On top of the front office claims, as mentioned before, the moves and draft picks the franchise made over their six-year span was a huge hit to their financial situation. From Bryant Reeves' giant contract to drafting players that never lived up to expectations, the Vancouver Grizzlies franchise had trouble attracting fans to the General Motors Place. On the other hand, the Toronto Raptors struck gold drafting Vince Carter, which resulted in consistent sell-out crowds and a massive increase in sales.

Then, in February of 2001, Michael Heisley and the Vancouver Grizzlies front office started to adventure into the United States for potential relocation targets. David Stern and the NBA set Michael Heisley and the Vancouver Grizzlies a strict March 1, 2001 deadline to apply for relocation. The deadline was pushed back to March 26, 2001 due to the Charlotte Hornets, who were another NBA team at the time looking to relocate. [191]

Following the relocation talks heating up, multiple cities, led by wealthy businessmen contacting Michael Heisley to lure the franchise to their cities. Pitt Hyde, who was the CEO and founder of AutoZone, which is a car sales place, strongly wanted the franchise to move to Memphis, Tennessee. Pitt Hyde, in efforts to lure the franchise to Memphis, offered to purchase at least 50% of the team. [191] On top of Pitt Hyde's strong sales pitch, the city of Memphis had an arena for the team to play in until a new site was built. The arena was called the Pyramid Arena. The city of Memphis wanted to lure the Vancouver Grizzlies to their city, highly due to their most recent relocation of an American sports franchise, the Tennessee Titans of the National Football League. The Tennessee Titans moved to Nashville, Tennessee, moving out of Memphis, leaving the city without a popular professional sports team. Despite the other cities trying to lure the Vancouver Grizzlies franchise, the city of Memphis, Tennessee always held a commanding lead in the race. [191]

Another United States city that had their eyes peeled on luring the Vancouver Grizzlies was New Orleans, Louisiana. Marc Morial, the mayor of New Orleans reached out to Michael Heisley to lure the franchise to his city. The city of New Orleans was looking to attract an NBA franchise for a couple years and the city offered the franchise most cities could not offer: an established arena. The Smoothie King Center was built in 1999 and was ready to be played in if the Vancouver Grizzlies were to relocate there.[189] On top of the new arena, Metrovision had a strong foundation for most business inquiries when it came to tickets and suites. This appealed to Michael Heisley.

The other two cities, which were considered long-shots for Michael Heisley were Anaheim, California and Buffalo, New York. The city of Anaheim was a unique relocation option for the Vancouver Grizzlies. The city attempted to lure the Houston Rockets, who looked into relocation but remained in Houston in 2000 and the city, like New Orleans, had an established arena: Arrowhead Pond of Anaheim, which is known today as the Honda Center. In addition to their established arena, the state of California had a number of successful American professional franchises: three of them were NBA franchises, the Los Angeles Clippers, the Los Angeles Lakers, and the nearby Sacramento Kings, who relocated in 1985. [191]

The city of Buffalo, like Anaheim, had an established arena called the HSBC Arena, where the Buffalo Sabres of the National Hockey League played. Buffalo had an NBA team for an eight-year span, the Buffalo Braves from 1970-78, before Paul Snyder, who was the Buffalo Braves team owner, had disagreements with owners of Buffalo's other sports teams. The disagreements were due to the home venue, the Buffalo Memorial Auditorium. Paul Snyder did not like how the Buffalo Memorial Auditorium was the only arena for Buffalo's professional sports teams at the time, but the city opened the HSBC Arena shortly after.[189] The Buffalo Braves later relocated to San Diego in 1978 and were named the San Diego Clippers, who are known today as the Los Angeles Clippers.

Anthony Masiello, who was the Mayor of Buffalo expressed interest in bringing back an NBA team to Buffalo and had his eyes on luring the Vancouver Grizzlies. In the end, it was only a thought by Anthony Masiello and the thought did not reach any talks.

The four major cities that offered high bids for the relocating Vancouver Grizzlies were Anaheim, Memphis, and New Orleans. Out of those three cities, Anaheim was the only location that offered a solid foundation regarding an arena.

After a long waiting game, leaving the Vancouver Grizzlies' fans and players wondering where they will see their team land, on March 26, 2001, Michael Heisley announced that Memphis will be the franchises new home.[191] When the dust settled and Michael Heisley chose Memphis, the other city that received a lot of interest was Louisville.

Despite Michael Heisley choosing Memphis as the franchise's new home, the NBA relocation committee did not approve of the move till July 3. The NBA Board of Governors decided on July 3, 2001 in a unanimous decision to finalize the relocation of the Vancouver Grizzlies to Memphis, Tennessee.

The Vancouver Grizzlies finished off their final season in Vancouver with an overall record of 23-59, placing 13th in the Western Conference. The franchise's overall record in their six seasons in Vancouver recorded a record of 101-359 (.220). [189]

Since the relocation to Memphis, Tennessee, the Grizzlies franchise has played a total of 18 seasons in Memphis, Tennessee. Since their first season in Memphis, the 2001-02 season, the franchise holds an overall record of 691-769 (.473%). [191] The franchise is yet to covet their first NBA Championship at the time of this writing.

Chapter 23

The Forgotten Team: 'The Dream Team II'

The 1992 United States Men's Olympic Basketball Team, also known as "The Dream Team," cemented the game of basketball across several borders around the world. It was the first time in men's Olympic basketball history that NBA professionals were able to participate in Olympic competition, rather than the top college players in the country representing the United States. As mentioned before, "The Dream Team" did not only win the gold but destroyed their competition and proved their basketball dominance.

The 1994 World Championship was the first time NBA players were eligible to play and represent the United States in FIBA competition. FIBA, as mentioned before, stands for the International Basketball Federation and is an association of national organizations focused around the game of basketball.

The 1994 World Championship was the next big international tournament for the United States to show the world once again that the game of basketball is dominated by the United States. The team was immediately named "The Dream Team II." To Rod Thorn, who was the NBA's Executive Vice President of Basketball Operations and part of the team selection committee, there was not a lot of pressure for the team to live up to the expectations or perform at the same level as the original "Dream Team" in 1992 in Barcelona, Spain.

> *"From the NBA's perspective, there wasn't a concern about them being called the "Dream Team II," Rod Thorn said. "While everyone witnessed the Dream Team's dominance in Barcelona, the rest of the world in 1994, from a competitive standpoint, still had some catching up to do, and the pressure was minimal on the USA team. The coaching staff had a lot of flexibility with varying lineup combinations based on competition."* [197]

The United States Men's basketball roster featured a mix of talented NBA All-Stars and the league's rising young talents. The twelve-man roster did not feature any players from the original 1992 "Dream Team" roster. Jim Tooley, the director of the Men's National Team, organized a committee made up of general managers and former players to decide on which players deserved invitations to the team.

> *"We had a committee made up primarily of NBA general managers and some former players,"* Jim Tooley said. *"So [in the summer of 1993], we all met in La Jolla, California, and started talking about team needs. We didn't have a pool of players back then like we do now - not much continuity, which we know now is big."* [197]

169

"We knew there were some players like Isiah Thomas and Joe [Dumars] and Dominique [Wilkins] that weren't able to be a part of the 1992 Dream Team, so we wanted to invite them. Then we talked about how to fill out the rest of the roster with a mix of generations and skill sets. We had king of identified who we wanted. There weren't many heated discussions at all." [197]

The Dream Team II: Alonzo Mourning, Dan Majerle, Derrick Coleman, Dominique Wilkins, Joe Dumars, Kevin Johnson, Larry Johnson, Mark Price, Reggie Miller, Shawn Kemp, Shaquille O'Neal, and Steve Smith.

The head coach of the 1994 United States Men's World Championship team was Don Nelson, who at the time of the tournament was the head coach of the Golden State Warriors. As a player, Don Nelson won five NBA championships with the Boston Celtics and played a total of 14 seasons in the league, splitting time with three franchises: the Chicago Zephyrs, today known as the Washington Wizards, the Los Angeles Lakers, and the Boston Celtics. His number 19 jersey is retired by the Boston Celtics.

As a coach, Don Nelson won three NBA Coach of the Year awards and coached in the NBA All-Star Game twice. The NBA recognizes Don Nelson as one of the league's top ten coaches in their history.

To Don Nelson, he was surprised that USA Basketball selected him as the head coach of 'The Dream Team II,' but he took the opportunity and called it an honor.

"I really don't know why they chose me, to tell you the truth," Nelson said. *"But I do know I always wanted to coach a U.S. national team. I didn't really have any conversations with [the league or USA Basketball] in advance of them choosing me. But, heck, it was an honor."* [197]

The roster was set for the 1994 United States Men's team but once announced, there was one position that left everyone wondering who would start: the center position. Alonzo Mourning proved his worth at the center position and completed his second season in the NBA. In his first season, he was honored to the 1993 NBA All Rookie First Team. Shaquille O'Neal, on the other hand, had an advantage over Alonzo Mourning. He was a two time All-Star and won Rookie of the Year over Alonzo Mourning. Due to Shaquille O'Neal's leverage over Mourning, many believed the starting center for the 1994 United States Men's basketball team should be Shaquille O'Neal.

When it came time for the 1994 United States Men's to begin practices and preparation for the upcoming tournament, the practices were very competitive according to some players.

"Our practices were the ultimate pickup games," Reggie Miller said. *"I mean, they were officiated as structured, but it's in terms of you going against guys at the top of each position. One of the guys I always looked up to and always had problems guarding and being by*

was Joe [Dumars]. I picked his brain. You were picking everyone's
brains because you knew you had to play these guys the next seasons
- I was looking for tells." [197]

Alonzo Mourning never matched up against Shaquille O'Neal in college but a rivalry was always established between the two because of their talents at the center position. For Alonzo Mourning, he wanted to prove his worth against Shaquille O'Neal.

> *"We never really played each other in college, but we always had*
> *that rivalry of being the two best young centers of our generation,"*
> Mourning said. *"We were drafted together. He was picked first, me*
> *second. The NBA kind of highlighted every game we played. He won*
> *Rookie of the Year, I was runner-up even though I felt like we should*
> *have shared the honor with me getting my team into the playoffs. So,*
> *yeah, everyone there was trying to prove something in those*
> *practices. And with me and Shaq, when practice started, boy, we'd*
> *butt heads like some bulls. We were all alpha males. You were*
> *carving out space, saying, "This is my territory."* [197]

The 1994 FIBA World Championship was the 12th FIBA World Championship and out of those 12, the United States Men's teams have only one twice. The tournament ran from August 4, 1994 until August 14, 1994 and the games were held in three different venues: Maple Leafs Gardens and SkyDome in Toronto, Canada, and the Copps Coliseum in Hamilton, Canada. Maples Leafs Gardens held 16,540 seats, SkyDome held 28,7000 seats, and Copps Coliseum held 18,440 seats. The 1994 F.I.B.A World Championship was originally planned to be held in Belgrade, Yugoslavia but due to the United Nations formatting limitations on sporting events, the tournament was moved to Toronto, Canada in 1992. [201]

Other than the United States, there were a total of fifteen nations that participated in the tournament: Angola, Argentina, Australia, Brazil, Canada, China, Croatia, Cuba, Egypt, Germany, Greece, Puerto Rico, Russia, South Korea, and Spain. Initially, North Korea was going to take part in the tournament but withdrew and was replaced by South Korea. [201]

All fifteen nations were placed into four groups and followed the same format as traditional international tournaments. Brazil, China, the United States, and Spain were placed in Group A. Group B included Australia, Croatia, Cuba, and South Korea. Angola, Argentina, Canada, and Russia filled Group C while Egypt, Germany, Greece, and Puerto Rico filled Group D. [201]

The United States topped Group A, ending with a 3-0 record followed by China, which went 2-1. Both teams advanced to the second round. Croatia and Australia advanced to the second round in Group B, Russia and Canada came out of Group C, and Greece and Puerto Rico advanced to the second round out of Group D. [201]

The second round of the 1994 FIBA World Championship included four groups as well but two of those four groups were playing just for placement. Group I and Group II were the eight teams that advanced to the second round while the other eight teams that did not score enough to place in the top two places of their group were placed into Groups III and IV. [201]

Group I of the second round featured Australia, Puerto Rico, Russia, and the United States while Group II featured Canada, China, Croatia, and Greece. Group III included Argentina, Egypt, South Korea, and Spain while Group IV held Angola, Brazil, Cuba, and Germany. Only teams in Group I and Group II can qualify for the semifinals if they finish in the top two of their groups. The third and fourth place teams in Group I and Group II will qualify for the 5-8 placement bracket. [201] For Group III and Group IV, the top two finishers in each of those groups will qualify for 9-12 placement while the bottom two teams in Group III and Group IV will compete for 13-16 placement.

The United States and Russia advanced to the semifinals in Group I. The United States finished on top with a record of 3-0 while Russia went 2-1, losing to the United States in their final game of the second round of August 12, 1994, 111-94. In Group II, Croatia finished on top with a 3-0 record followed by Greece with a 2-1 record. Both advanced to the semifinals. [201]

In the semifinals, Russia faced Croatia while the United States faced off against Greece. Russia went on to slip past Croatia, 66-64, to advance to the 1994 FIBA World Championship while the United States steamrolled their way, beating Greece, 97-58, to join Russia in the finals. In the third-place game, Croatia defeated Greece, 78-60, to win bronze. [201]

In the 1994 F.I.B.A World Championship game, the United States and Russia faced off in the SkyDome in Toronto, Canada on August 13, 1994. As USA Basketball said it best, the 1994 'Dream Team II' saved their best game for last.

> *Saving its best game for last, the USA dominated the gold medal contest from start to finish as it trounced Russia 137-91. Playing in front of a World Championship record crowd numbering 32,616, the USA hit 16 of its first 17 shots and led 25-10 with the games less than five minutes old and never looked back. [Dominique] Wilkins led the offensive attack with 20 points, while [Shaquille] O'Neil added 18 points and 10 rebounds and Mourning and Kemp accounted for 15 and 14 points respectively. The USA's 137 points were the second most ever by a USA team in the World Championships.* [197]

Don Nelson recalled the star stuck looks on the opposing players faces before almost every game during the 1994 FIBA World Championship. He also added how there was only one close game for the United States in the tournament, but his team still won by 15 but the press treated the win as a loss.

> *"Either way, teams were star-struck before the game or after the game because we beat everybody decisively,"* Nelson remarked. *"I remember when we played Spain, that was the only close game we had. We had a big lead, and I was trying to play some of the guys that didn't get a chance to play as much. I tried to have a nine or 10-man rotation. Spain ended up coming within 14 points, and you would*

have thought we had lost the world title the way the press treated the game - that we only won by 15 points. That was the only close game we had, and I wouldn't even call that close really." [197]

As mentioned before, Shaquille O'Neal won the tournament MVP award and to his coach, Don Nelson, he was the main leader of the team. It was not just his actions on the hardwood that established him as the leader but his off the court actions.

"Shaq was our leader," Nelson said. *"He set the tone. He kept everyone committed, but loose, too. His Shaq FU stuff was out then, and he always had jokes. But it was playful in the right way because when the games started, boy, was he dominant. And I also always had the issue of minutes when dealing with a team that talented, and he even helped in that way by volunteering to come off the bench some games. He really made my job easier."* [197]

"I remember the thing that put our whole team at ease was the fact that (Shaquille) asked to come off the bench. He didn't want to start, so I could start Alonzo Mourning or one of the other bigs I had. Shaq was in his own way the leader of that team. Not starting was one of the leadership things that he did, but he was there for every practice, worked hard and really set the tone. I remember the first time we just took some laps around the gym, he led the entire team in wind sprints. That just set the tone for the whole thing." [197]

There is no debate 'The Dream Team II' dominated the 1994 FIBA World Championship and once again, delivered gold to the United States. Despite their domination, the team always and to this day, will be stuck in the shadows of the original 1992 'Dream Team.' The team did not beat their opponents by the margin the original 'Dream Team' did and did not necessarily have the established star power and legacies that the 1992 team had.

But where did the 'Dream Team II' nickname come from? The media created the nickname for the 1992 United States Men's basketball team, but this time, Jim Tooley and USA Basketball cemented the nickname for the 1994 team.

"We - USA Basketball - were the ones that decided to dub the new team "Dream Team II," Tooley said. *"Whereas the first time, it was media that gave the original team that nickname. And we kind of put the second team in an unfair position."* [197]

"I don't think they liked being compared, to be honest. So much of the original team was about ambassadorship, and the new team just couldn't live up to it. Some of the younger guys didn't quite understand etiquette. We'd be up 20, and guys were showing out after dunks. I remember Nellie [Don Nelson] telling the guys, "Come on, act like you've been there before." [197]

To the players of the 1994 'Dream Team II,' most realize and knew from the start, to exceed expectations and prove their dominance over the 1992 'Dream Team' was near impossible.

"There were a lot of eyes on us, man," Alonzo Mourning said. *"They wanted to see what we were gonna do and how we would represent our country. We were younger, yeah, and somewhat immature. But, hey, we were out there having fun. That was just the way we did it."* [197]

"Some people said some of the antics were classless, that we should have held back. But when I'm out there screaming after rebounds and dunks - those are primal noises. It's no disrespect. When I would flex after a block...that's me enjoying the game. That's a release." [197]

As highlighted by Alonzo Mourning, the 1994 'Dream Team II' was constantly knocked for their immaturity on the court. Unlike the 1992 'Dream Team,' the 1994 'Dream Team II' was a lot younger and was filled with young NBA talent and the next generation of superstars in the league. Often, after huge slams, acrobatic blocks, or continuous offensive sequences of scoring, the players would express their feelings on the court by jumping, screaming, and dancing. Due to the 1994 'Dream Team II' having heavy comparisons to the 1992 team, the immaturity was highlighted in multiple media reports throughout the tournament.

For Mark Price, he believes that the team never received the respect about how good of a basketball team the 1994 'Dream Team II' really was. His reasoning behind his claim was that a team of young talent could not follow the 1992 'Dream Team' that was full of legends.

"I think we never really got the respect for how good we were as a basketball team," Price said. *"When you follow a team full of legends, no matter what, you probably won't get your just due. That's probably my biggest beef because we were really good."* [197]

In the end, the 1994 'Dream Team II' was a team destined to fail if their mission was to live up and overcome being in the shadows of the 1992 'Dream Team.' The nickname, 'Dream Team II' should have not been established and should have been retired by the original cast in 1992.

Despite not living up to their hype or overcoming the shadows of the 1992 'Dream Team,' the team showed that the United States clearly runs the basketball game, on an international level, over all the other countries. By having a completely different roster than the 1992 'Dream Team' come out and prove their dominance, and a much younger roster, the United States showed the world that they will continue to run the sport of basketball.

Chapter 24

The 1995 NBA Draft

The 1995 NBA Draft was the first time in the league's history that a draft was held outside the borders of the United States. This was also the first NBA Draft that featured the two new expansion teams in the league: the Toronto Raptors and the Vancouver Grizzlies. As mentioned before, the country of Canada began to establish their new chapter in the NBA after Jerry Colangelo and the NBA announced that Toronto would have its first NBA team since 1947. The team was named the Toronto Raptors and their colors represented and honored Canadian Dr. James Naismith, the inventor of basketball: bright red, dark purple, and silver. The Raptors did not stand as the only NBA team in Canada for long. On other side of Canada, in Vancouver, the Vancouver Grizzlies were established as an NBA franchise.

On June 28, 1995, the SkyDome in Toronto, Ontario, Canada hosted the 1995 NBA Draft.[193] The SkyDome was the new home of the Toronto Raptors.

The 1995 draft class was filled with young talent and some players classified as being franchise changing players. The class was highlighted by Kevin Garnett, a high school power forward. The draft featured a total of 58 selections incorporated in two rounds. Out of those 58 selections, four of the selections were international players. [193]

It did take some waiting but with the 22nd pick in the 1995 NBA Draft, the Charlotte Hornets selected George Zidek, a seven-foot center born in Gottwaldov, Czechoslovakia. He was the first ever Czech player drafted into the NBA.[193] George Zidek grew up playing professional basketball alongside his father Jiri Zidek. Both of them played USK Slavia Prague in their native Czechoslovakia and led their team to the EuroLeague Finals in the late 1960s. To this date, George Zidek and Jiri Zidek are the only father and son duo to lead a team to the EuroLeague Finals. [196]

George Zidek came to the United States in 1991 and enrolled at the University of California, Los Angeles, known as UCLA, to play on the UCLA Bruins Men's basketball team. George Zidek spent all four years at UCLA and capped off his final season as a Bruin winning the 1995 National Championship. He was the starting center for the Bruins that season and in the 1995 National Championship win.

As a professional basketball player in the NBA, he did not last too long. He only played three seasons in the league before taking his basketball talents overseas. In those three seasons in the NBA, Zidek split time with the

Charlotte Hornets, the Denver Nuggets, and the Seattle SuperSonics. He went on to only average under four points per game.

Following his three-year tenure in the league, Zidek spent the final seven years of his professional basketball career with six different basketball clubs: Zalgiris, Fenerbahce, Real Madrid, Alba Berlin, Prokom Trefl Sopot, and CEZ Nymburk. The only professional basketball championship he achieved was with Zalgiris in 1999, winning the EuroLeague. [196]

Nine selections following George Zidek being selected 22nd overall by the Charlotte Hornets, with the 31st selection, the Chicago Bulls selected Dragan Tarlac, a center from Novi Sad, SR Serbia, SFR Yugoslavia.[193] Unlike Zidek, Dragan Tarlac did not play college basketball in the United States. He began his professional basketball career with Crvena Zvezda for two years, 1990-92, then played as a member of the Greek powerhouse, Olympiacos, from 1992-2000. [196]

Dragan Tarlac did not have expectations to remain in the NBA long after he was selected by the Chicago Bulls. His game and play style did not fit well, especially on the offensive end, against traditional NBA centers and, as expected, he only lasted one season. Following his rookie season with the Chicago Bulls, he took his basketball talents overseas to join Real Madrid. Tarlac spent two seasons with Real Madrid before ending his career with CSKA Moscow in 2003-04. [196]

Despite busting out of the NBA after only one season, Tarlac ended his career with a decorative basketball resume overseas. He won the EuroLeague in 1997 as a member of Olympiacos and won the Greek League Championship in five of his eight years with the club. In addition, Dragan Tarlac won multiple Greek Cups with Olympiacos, the Triple Crown in 1997, and ended his career on top winning the Russian Championship with CSKA Moscow in 2004. [196]

With the 51st pick in the 1995 NBA Draft, the Sacramento Kings selected Dejan Bodiroga, another international player born and raised in Yugoslavia. [193] Dejan Bodiroga never played with the Sacramento Kings after being selected in the 1995 NBA Draft but played a total of 18 years as a professional basketball player overseas, splitting time with eight clubs.[196]

Like Tarlac, the final two international players that were selected in the 1995 NBA Draft never played for their NBA team. Constantin Popa, a center from Romania, was drafted with the 53rd overall pick by the Los Angeles Clippers and with the next pick, Eurelijus Zukauskas, a center from Lithuania, was selected by the Seattle SuperSonics. [193]

Overall, the 1995 NBA Draft was another big step in the league globalizing the game of basketball. From two Canadian NBA teams making their first draft selections filled with Canadian fans under the SkyDome lights in Toronto to five more international players being drafted into the league from three different countries, it was a success for the league.

The Globalization of the NBA

Chapter 25

The Kid from Canada

Stephen John Nash was born on February 7, 1974 in Johannesburg, South Africa.[204] When Steve Nash was less than two years old, his family moved from Johannesburg, South Africa to Regina, Saskatchewan, the capital city of the Canadian province, Saskatchewan. Steve Nash and his family did not settle in Regina for long. They moved, once again, to Victoria, British Columbia, and settled there. [205]

His father, John Nash, was a professional soccer player in South Africa. Steve Nash, due to his father playing soccer at a high level, fell in love with the sport growing up. Steve Nash's brother, Martin Nash, played professional soccer as well and scored a total of 38 goals for the Canadian national team. [205]

Despite the interest level in soccer as a young kid, Steve Nash had an interest in playing ice hockey. Ice Hockey in Victoria, British Columbia, and in the county of Canada is a major sport which is picked up by many kids at early ages. Nash began playing ice hockey around the age of eight years old.

Nash picked up the game of basketball when he was 12 years old. As a young kid, Nash's interest started to grow towards the game of basketball and before he went to high school, he strongly believed he could make a professional career as a basketball player. At that time in his life, Nash ruled out the sport of ice hockey; it was between basketball and soccer. Nash recalled his passion for both soccer and basketball, but it was his unique perspective growing up around soccer that made him great at basketball. In the end, Nash pursued basketball.

"Obviously they're completely different sports - one's with your feet, one's with your hands - but as far as spacing, connectivity with your teammates, movement, passing, defending, there are similarities," Nash said. *"I probably wouldn't have been an NBA player if I didn't bring a unique perspective born in soccer to the game of basketball."* [204]

"In soccer, you always have to have your head on a swivel and be thinking before you get the ball. You have to see where you're going to go with it or what your options are before you get it. And that's not the way a lot of kids grow up playing basketball. So that have me an awareness and a mentality to be a step ahead of the defense and be

*predicting angles and opportunities before they arise. So, it's
something that I transferred over."* [204]

Steve Nash played the first three years of his high school career at
Mt. Douglas High School but was forced to transfer due to his grades. Nash
then transferred to St. Michael's University School, which is a private boarding
school in Victoria, British Columbia. Due to his transfer halfway into the
school year in 1990, Nash was not able to play basketball his junior year. [205] He
described the penalty as difficult, but it made him work harder.

*"I just loved basketball so much and played so much and worked so
hard - to be punished for transferring schools - it was a difficult
year,"* Nash said. *"But it was something I had to do. I wouldn't be
where I am today if I hadn't made that move. It's that simple."* [204]

While at St. Michael's University School, Nash excelled in
basketball, soccer, and rugby. He picked up rugby at the school but never had a
serious interest in the heavy contact sport.

Basketball was Nash's main sport in high school, and he excelled at a
high level, leading the school to multiple tournaments and championship
games. In his senior year, Nash was awarded the province's Player of the Year,
which is given to the best high school basketball player in the specific province
of Canada. [205]

Despite the success in high school, Nash struggled to be recruited by
big name colleges with great basketball programs. Ian Hyde-Lay, Nash's high
school coach, sent out multiple highlight tapes and lists of his notable
accomplishments and stat lines to universities in the United States but did not
hear back from any colleges or universities.

*"It was frustrating because I was watching college basketball on TV
all the time thinking that I could play with this guy and that guy, that
I could play at certain schools and no one would ever show any
interest,"* Nash said. [204]

After hearing nothing from colleges and universities, Santa Clara
University came calling. Dick Davey, who was the head coach at Santa Clara
University, watched Steve Nash in person and immediately wanted to St.
Michaels University School guard on his team.

*"After seeing him I was nervous as hell just hoping that no one else
would see him,"* Davey said. *"It didn't take a Nobel prize winner to*

*figure out this guy's pretty good. It was just a case of hoping that
none of the big names came around."* [205]

Steve Nash then declared to Santa Clara University with a basketball
scholarship. He spent three years at the university, leading the Broncos to
multiple NCAA Tournament appearances. [202] In his junior season, Nash set
school records and led the West Coast Conference, WCC, in both scoring and
assists. The only player to lead the WCC in both scoring and assists prior to
Nash was John Stockton, who played at Gonzaga nearly a decade before Nash
enrolled at Santa Clara University. [202]

After four successful seasons at Santa Clara University, Nash decided
that he would declare for the 1996 NBA Draft. [205] He graduated from Santa
Clara with multiple college and NCAA honors in those four years of play:

- Three-time WCC Champion
- Two-time WCC Player of the Year
- Two-time WCC All-WCC First Team
- Santa Clara's All Time Leading Scorer (1,689 points)
- Santa Clara's All Time Leader in Steals (147)
- Santa Clara's All Time Leader in Assists (510)
- No. 11 retired by Santa Clara [204]

Nash was projected to be selected within the early first round,
ranging from picks 10 to 20. One team that was looking for a point guard was
the Phoenix Suns. The Suns needed depth at the point guard position and Nash
seemed to be the perfect fit coming off the bench.

It did not take too long for Nash to be drafted into the NBA. From an
unrecruited high school kid, he was selected with the 15th pick in the 1996
NBA Draft by the Phoenix Suns. [203] Danny Ainge, who was the Phoenix Suns'
assistant coach at the time, called Steve Nash to let him know that he will be a
member of the Suns organization. Not all the Suns fans were pleased with the
selection, highly because not many even knew of the Santa Clara point guard.

> *"Meanwhile out west in Phoenix, the announcement by Suns assistant
> coach Danny Ainge was met with a storm of jeers and catcalls from
> fans gathered at the America West Arena who knew little of the 6-3
> pound Canadian."* [204]

Despite hearing mixed emotions from the Suns fans after the
selection, Nash was not affected by it. He was ready to prove the doubters
wrong and was ready to gain the city of Phoenix's trust behind the selection.

"I don't look like I'm going to be a tremendous basketball player on appearance," the rookie said with a smile. "I probably would've booed myself too, but I'm going to be a really good player and I'm going to help the team a lot. I have a lot of faith in myself and hopefully they'll enjoy watching me play. They want to win and I wouldn't want fans who just sat back and didn't care, so I'm excited to be in a passionate city." [204]

As a rookie, Nash did not play many minutes and came off the bench for the Phoenix Suns. He played in 65 games and only started in two of the games. In those 65 games, Steve Nash averaged 10.5 minutes, 3.3 points, 2.1 assists, and 1.0 rebounds.[203] Due to his lack of playing time, many Suns fans did not expect Nash to become what Danny Ainge dreamt of him being. Then came his second year in the NBA.

Nash received a bigger role off the bench in his second season playing in a total of 76 games and started in nine of them. In those 76 games, Nash averaged 21.9 minutes, 9.1 points, 3.4 assists, and 2.1 rebounds. [203] His second season in the NBA, the 1997-98 season, was impressive to other NBA teams and there was speculation that due to his role on the Suns, playing behind Jason Kidd, that he could be shipped to another team.

Following the 1998 NBA Draft, the speculations became a reality. The Phoenix Suns traded Nash in a package deal to the Dallas Mavericks. The deal sent Nash to the Dallas Mavericks in exchange for Bubba Wells, Martin Muursepp, and a first-round pick. [203] The first-round pick dealt to Phoenix ended up being Shawn Marion.

Nash's first season with the Dallas Mavericks was a short one due to the 1999-2000 NBA lockout. In addition to the season being cut, Nash missed 25 games with an ankle injury. The Mavericks ended their first season with Nash winning 19 of the 31 games but missing the playoffs. He played and started in all of his 40 games and averaged 31.7 minutes, 7.9 points, 5.5 assists, and 2.9 rebounds per game. [203]

Nash would spend five more seasons with the Dallas Mavericks. In those five seasons, he picked up his game and became one of the most talented point guards in the NBA and began to make a household name for himself in Dallas, becoming a fan favorite. Nash helped lead the Mavericks to two playoff appearances in back to back seasons, 2001-02 and 2002-03, but both playoff runs were short runs. He was named an All-Star in 2002 and 2003 and was named to the NBA All-NBA Third Team those seasons as well.

Following the 2003-04 season, Nash entered his first summer as a free agent. Mark Cuban, who was the owner of the Dallas Mavericks, was not too fond of offering Nash a long-term extension due to the current salary cap situation. Instead, Mark Cuban and the Dallas Mavericks wanted to build a younger roster around Dirk Nowitzki and Mark Cuban was hesitant on locking up Nash to a long expensive contract. Mark Cuban offered Nash a four-year deal worth only $9 million. [204] On the other hand, another familiar team came calling for Nash: The Phoenix Suns. The Suns were coming off a disappointing season but had bright young talent with superstar potential. Shawn Marion, the first-round draft pick acquired for Nash in the trade that sent the Suns point guard to Dallas, began to show superstar potential. In addition, the Suns had a hole at the point guard position, due to Jason Kidd leaving for New Jersey and his replacements not filling his shoes.

The Phoenix Suns offered Nash a six-year deal worth $63 million, one of the highest contract offers he received that summer. [204] Before accepting the contract and returning to Phoenix, Nash approached Mark Cuban and asked if he was willing to match the Suns contract and if the Mavericks did, he would remain in Dallas. Mark Cuban did not match the deal which led to Steve Nash signing the four-year $63 million deal to return to Phoenix.

In his first season back in a Suns uniform, Nash had the best year of his NBA career. Phoenix, under Mike D'Antoni, ran an offensive system Nash fit perfectly in. On top of the offensive system, Nash was surrounded by good offensive and defensive players that meshed with his offensive skillset. During the 2004-05 season, the Suns achieved an overall record of 62-20, which was an NBA best and lead the league in scoring per game. Steve Nash was the leader of the Suns in his first season back and averaged 34.3 minutes, 15.5 points, 11.5 assists, 3.3 rebounds, and 1.0 steals per game. He played and started in a total of 75 games. [204]

Phoenix faced the Memphis Grizzlies in the first round of the Western Conference playoffs. In the first-round matchup, Nash and the Suns swept the Grizzlies in four games to advance to play his former team: Dirk Nowitzki and the Dallas Mavericks. For Nash, he was ready to prove Mark Cuban and the Dallas Mavericks that he was worth the long extension the previous summer and make the franchise regret their decision to let him walk.

In the Western Conference semifinals, Nash and the Suns had their way. Phoenix defeated Dirk Nowitzki and the Dallas Mavericks in six games, 4-2, to advance to the Western Conference Finals. [204]

The Suns were only four games away from advancing to the 2005 NBA Finals. Those four wins needed to advance were not easy wins for Nash and the Suns. The San Antonio Spurs, led by Tim Duncan, had a great team filled with veterans and young talent hungry for another NBA championship. The Spurs, led by head coach Gregg Popovich, won the 2003 NBA championship and were considered the favorites to win the series and advance to another NBA Finals. For Nash and the Suns, this was the first time since 1993 Phoenix was in the Western Conference Finals.

As expected, the San Antonio Spurs defeated Nash and the Suns in five games, 4-1, to advance to the 2005 NBA Finals. In the end, the San Antonio Spurs went on to covet another NBA championship and win the 2005 NBA championship. [204]

Despite coming just short of an NBA Finals appearance and a chance to win his first NBA championship, the 2004-05 season was a historic run for Nash. The Phoenix Suns point guard was considered a slim favorite to win the 2005 NBA Most Valuable Player Award. The only other player to win the award over Nash was Shaquille O'Neal of the Miami Heat.

Nash narrowly edged out Shaquille O'Neal to win the 2004-05 NBA Most Valuable Player Award. The other players who received votes for the award were Dirk Nowitzki of the Dallas Mavericks, Tim Duncan of the San Antonio Spurs, and Allen Iverson of the Philadelphia 76ers. [210]

The 6-3-point guard, who returned this season to Phoenix where he spent the first two years of his career, totaled 1,066 points to narrowly edge out Shaquille O'Neal (1,032 points) of the Miami Heat in MVP voting. The 34-point difference is the fourth-closest voting margin since median began voting on this award in 1980-1981. Rounding out the top-five in voting for MVP were Dallas' Dirk Nowitzki (349 points), San Antonio's Tim Duncan (328 points), and Philadelphia's Allen Iverson (240 points). [210] A panel of 126 sportswriters and broadcasters throughout the United States and Canada voted for the prestigious award. Players were awarded 10 points for each first-place vote, seven points for each second-place vote, five for third, three for fourth and one of each fifth-place vote received. In addition to winning MVP, Steve Nash joined a very selective group of former winners in multiple categories. [210]

> *"The three-time NBA All-Star averaged 15.5 points (.502 FG%) and an NBA-best 11.5 assists in 34.3 minutes per game. The Suns enjoyed a 60-15 record when he was in the lineup this season as he helped guide the team to its first division title since 1994-95 and its fourth overall (1980-81, 1992-93, 1994-95). Nash is one of only seven players since 1970 to notch double-figures in assists in 14 or more consecutive games (John Stockton, Magic Johnson, Nate Archibald, Isiah Thomas, and Kevin Porter)."* [210]

> *"Nash is in the company of Bob Cousy (1956-57), Oscar Robertson (1963-64), Johnson (1986-87, 1988-89 and 1989-90), Michael Jordan (1990-91, 1992-93, 1995-96, 1997-98), and Allen Iverson (2000-01) as the only guards in NBA history to be named NBA MVP. He is also the fourth player in NBA history to lead the league in assists and win the MVP award in the same season (Cousy, Robertson, and then Johnson in 1986-87.*

*Nash (Canada) is in select company as he joins Hakeem Olajuwon
(1993-94, Nigeria) as the only international players to win the
award."* [210]

It did not take Steve Nash long to covet yet another NBA Most
Valuable Player Award. The 2005-06 season was a rollercoaster ride for the
Suns. Amare Stoudemire, Nash's right-hand man in the front court suffered a
serious knee injury during the regular season was sidelined for most of the year.
Due to his injury, Nash and the Suns were not expected to repeat the success
they had the previous season.

Despite the early negative projections, Nash proved the doubters
wrong and led the Suns to yet another impressive season. Phoenix finished the
2005-06 season with a 54-28 record and won their division led by Nash, the
reigning league Most Valuable Player. [203]

In the Western Conference Playoffs, Nash and the Suns faced Kobe
Bryant and the Los Angeles Lakers. The Suns quickly fell to a 3-1 deficit and
was one loss away from facing a first-round exit. Nash and the Suns had other
plans, winning the next three games, defeating Kobe Bryant and the Los
Angeles Lakers in seven games, 4-3, to advance to the Western Conference
semifinals to face the Los Angeles Clippers. As the Suns did in the first round,
Nash led his team to the Western Conference Finals, defeating the Los Angeles
Clippers in seven games, 4-3, to face the Dallas Mavericks; Steve Nash's
former team.

As expected, the Dallas Mavericks took the series over Nash and the
Suns in six games, 4-2, to advance to the 2006 NBA Finals to face the Miami
Heat.

Prior to the 2006 NBA Playoffs, Nash was awarded his second NBA
Most Valuable Player Award, joining the company of Magic Johnson as the
only guards to win back to back Most Valuable Player Awards. The other
players to receive votes for the 2005-06 NBA Most Valuable Player Award
were LeBron James of the Cleveland Cavaliers, Dirk Nowitzki of the Dallas
Mavericks, Kobe Bryant of the Los Angeles Lakers, and Chauncey Billups of
the Detroit Pistons.

*"Steve Nash of the Phoenix Suns was named the winner of the
Maurice Podoloff Trophy as the NBA's Most Valuable Player for the
2005-06 season, the NBA announced today. He joins Hall of Famer
Magic Johnson as the only point guards in the league's history to
capture multiple MVP Trophies and becomes one of nine players to
win the award in consecutive seasons. The 10-year NBA veteran
totaled 924 points, including 57 first place votes, from a panel of 125
sportswriters and broadcasters throughout the United States and*

> *Canada. Players were awarded 10 points for each first-place vote,*
> *seven points for each second-place vote, five for third, three for*
> *fourth and one for each fifth-place vote received. Rounding out the*
> *top five in voting for MVP were Cleveland's LeBron James (688*
> *points), Dallas' Dirk Nowitzki (544 points), the Los Angeles Lakers'*
> *Kobe Bryant (483 points) and Detroit's Chauncey Billups (430*
> *points). Nash averaged career-highs in points (18.8), rebounds (4.2),*
> *minutes (35.5), field goal percentage (.512) and free throw*
> *percentage (.921)."* [212]

Steve Nash went on to spend an additional six seasons with the Phoenix Suns before being traded to the Los Angeles Lakers in a sign and trade deal. As a Sun, Steve Nash played in a total of 744 games and averaged 30.6 minutes, 14.4 points, 9.4 assists, 3.1 rebounds, and 0.7 steals per game. [203] His number 13 jersey was retired by the Phoenix Suns following his retirement from the NBA in 2015.

Before signing with the Los Angeles Lakers to team up with Kobe Bryant, Steve Nash had interest in signing with the Toronto Raptors. On July 11, 2012, the Los Angeles Lakers and the Phoenix Suns agreed on a sign and trade deal which sent Steve Nash to Los Angeles, reuniting with former head coach Mike D'Antoni, in return for four draft picks. [203] The main reason for the sign and trade was Steve Nash wanting to give back to the Suns organization.

Nash went on to finish his NBA career with the Los Angeles Lakers and spent two seasons with the franchise. Due to the infamous Wilt Chamberlain wearing number 13 for the Los Angeles Lakers and the franchise retiring his number, Nash changed his jersey number from 13 to 10.

In his first season with the Los Angeles Lakers and his 17th NBA season, Nash was not in the best of shape health-wise. The Lakers point guard was suffering from back concerns, but it was not his back that sidelined him in his first season as a Laker.

In just the second game of the regular season, Nash suffered a left leg fracture, which sidelined him for the next seven weeks. Despite missing seven weeks, Nash went on to play a total of 50 games, starting all 50, and averaged 32.5 minutes, 12.7 points, 6.7 assists, 2.3 rebounds, and 0.6 steals per game. His 32 games missed was a career high and 6.7 assists per game was a career low for Nash. [203]

In his final season, Nash was facing the injury bug in multiple parts of his body. He suffered from nerve problems in his left leg from the previous season and his back was getting worse. Nash played in a total of only 15 games for the 2013-14 season and averaged 20.9 minutes, 6.8 points, 5.7 assists, 1.9 rebounds, and 0.5 steals per game before getting shut down by Mike D'Antoni in the second half of the season. [203]

Nash wanted to have one last run in the NBA and play for the Los Angeles Lakers in the 2014-15 season. Just prior to the start of the season, Nash's back gave out on him and he was ruled out for the entire season. He only played in a handful of preseason game. Nash was clearly disappointed that he could not play in his final season, but he still supported his team throughout the regular season.

> *"Being on the court this season has been my top priority and it is disappointing to not be able to do that night now,"* said Nash. *"I work very hard to stay healthy and unfortunately my recent setback makes performing at full capacity difficult. I will continue to support my team during this period of rest and will focus on my long-term health."* [213]

Mitch Kupchak, the General Manager of the Los Angeles Lakers, expressed his disappointment with the news that Steve Nash would be shut down for the 2014-15 season and thanked his efforts to fight through injuries and his efforts to return to the hardwood and wear the purple and gold.

> *"As disappointed as we are for ourselves and our fans, we're even more disappointed for Steve,"* said Lakers General Manager Mitch Kupchak. *"We know how hard he's worked the last two years to try to get his body right for the rigors of the NBA, and how badly he wants to play, but unfortunately he simply hasn't been able to get there up to this point in time. Steve has been a consummate professional, and we greatly appreciate his efforts."* [213]

On March 21, 2015, Nash retired from the NBA as a player but did not leave the game and the league he loved. In September of 2015, Nash was hired by the Golden State Warriors as a consultant, specializing in player development. He went on to be a part of two championship teams with the Warriors in back to back seasons, the 2015-16 season and the 2016-17 season.

On March 31, 2018, Nash was inducted into the Naismith Basketball Hall of Fame. His class included Charlie Scott, Grant Hill, Jason Kidd, Maurice Cheeks, and Ray Allen.

> *"I was never even supposed to be here,"* said Nash, who was born in South Africa and grew up in Canada and went on to win back-to-back NBA MVP awards. *"Play the long game. You don't have to be the chosen one. If you're patient, the plateaus will become springboards."* [214]

On top of his historic NBA career, Steve Nash won a handful of medals as part of the Canadian men's basketball national team and retired from international competition in 2007. Steve Nash was the general manager of the Canadian men's national basketball team from 2012 till 2019 and at the time of this writing is a co-owner of the Major League Soccer (MLS) franchise, the Vancouver Whitecaps since their establishment in 2011. [206]

There is no debate Steve Nash will always be remembered as one of the greatest all around NBA point guards in the league's history. Besides from his NBA legacy, Steve Nash paved the way for Canadian and international basketball athletes who have dreams and aspirations of lacing up the shoes and wearing an NBA uniform. From being born in Johannesburg, South Africa and being raised in Victoria, British Columbia, Canada, being a kid with NBA dreams, Steve Nash will always be remembered as a Canadian pioneer when it comes to NBA globalization.

Chapter 26

The Best European Import

Dirk Werner Nowitzki was born on June 19, 1978 in Wurzburg, West Germany.[219] Since birth, the sport of basketball was engraved in his life. Dirk Nowitzki came from a sports family. His mother, Helga Nowitzki played professional basketball for the West Germany national team in 1966 and participated in the 1966 EuroBasket Women Championship which was a part of F.I.B.A. His father Jorg Werner was a professional handball player and during the prime of his career, played represented the country of Germany on an international level and was a member of their top-level roster. His older sister Silke Nowitzki grew up to become a star in the sport of track and field. Following her professional athletic career, she took on a role with the NBA covering the league on international television. [219]

With athletics surrounding Dirk Nowitzki growing up, he quickly became accustomed to sports. Despite gaining an interest in sports as a young kid, it was not until he was 13 years old when he began his basketball career as a youth.[219] Nowitzki was taller than most of the other kids his age and under the mentorship of his mother, he quickly adjusted to the game of basketball. His talent on the court was quickly scouted by a variety of teams. From local basketball teams to second division German professional teams were interested in picking up the tall teenager.

At age 15, Nowitzki joined DJK Wurzburg, a German sports club known primarily for their basketball success. The club is a popular attraction for young talented basketball players in the country of Germany. Holger Geschwinder, a former professional basketball star from Germany, led DJK Wurzburg and lured Nowitzki to their team at age 15 after he watched him play a couple of times. [219]

Nowitzki joined DJK Wurzburg in 1994 and spent a total of four years with the club. At the time of his arrival, DJK Wurzburg was a second-tier level league team, a part of the Second Bundesliga. His first season with the team was a struggle for Nowitzki. He struggled academically and had trouble balancing both basketball and schooling, which led to him being benched in games and getting limited minutes. [219]

In his second season, the 1996-97 season, Nowitzki broke out and showed he had the potential to become one of the best young German basketball players. He became a consistent starter on DJK Wurzburg and was their top offensive weapon. He shot the ball well, but he excelled in the frontcourt, driving, and in transition.

By the age of 18, Nowitzki had grown to nearly seven feet tall and his basketball skill set developed to a high level. His final two seasons with DJK Wurzburg were nothing but impressive but he began to catch the eyes of NBA scouts in 1997.

Nowitzki decided to participate in the Nike Hoops Heroes Tour which was held in his native country of Germany in 1997.[220] The rising star in Germany competed with some of the NBA's best talents at the time. The game included talents such as Charles Barkley, Michael Jordan, and Scottie Pippen. To Nowitzki this was a golden chance to put his name on the map and establish him as a possible future NBA star or to make himself in the conversation for colleges and universities to recruit him. [220]

The unknown kid playing for DJK Wurzburg and was only known within the borders of Germany life changed forever after the show he put on at the Nike Hoops Heroes Tour.

Charles Barkley, a member of the infamous 1992 'Dream Team' and a decorated NBA player on track to be in the Naismith Memorial Hall of Fame, knew better than anyone about the talent overseas. To him, he was in complete shock after the show Nowitzki put on. According to Charles Barkley, Nowitzki finished with around 52 points.

> *"Dirk was kicking our ass,"* Barkley said. *"He's got like twenty-five at halftime, and me and Michael (Jordan) were like 'Scottie, you gotta pick it up a bit.' He's mad. C'mon, lock him down in the second half, lock him down in the second half."* [220]

> *"Dirk finished with like 52."* [220]

Following the game, Charles Barkley was intrigued to find out more about this young German teenager named Dirk Nowitzki. Despite wanting to find out more about Nowitzki, Charles Barkley confidently wanted him to take his talents to the United States and join his alma mater, Auburn University to play basketball. There was one thing in the way of Nowitzki expanding his talents after a life changing game. In the country of Germany, he as well as every teenager were required to serve time in the military.[219] As required, Nowitzki had to serve mandatory military service with Bundeswehr, an armed service of the country of Germany, which lasted from September 1997 until June 1998. [219]

Charles Barkley asked the young Nowitzki what his future plans were going to be. Nowitzki immediately responded telling the former NBA Most Valuable Player that he was heading to the military.

"He says, 'I have to go in the army,'" Barkley recalled. *"I said, 'Dude, you can't go in the army playing like that."* [220]

Following the humble response from Nowitzki, Charles Barkley knew he could not let him slide, especially with him having no recognition outside his native Germany borders. Charles Barkley acted and called Nike to help convince Nowitzki to commit to Auburn University. He went as far as to tell Nike to give the kid whatever he wants.

"I call Nike, I say find out about this kid, tell him I'll give him anything he wants to go to Auburn," Barkley said. *"Just tell him, anything he wants, we'll get it done."* [220]

Despite being recruited by the best college basketball player to come out of Auburn University, Nowitzki stayed back and served his military service.

Charles Barkley strongly believes to this day that if Nowitzki committed to Auburn University, he would have done well.

"He would have done good at Auburn, we would have taken care of him, we in the SEC," Barkley said. [220]

If Nowitzki did end up committing to Auburn, the school, Nike, and Charles Barkley would have been in for a rough ride. Clearly, the impact Nowitzki could have made on the hardwood facing SEC competition consistently would have been impeccable. On the other side of it, if the NCAA were to find out about the behind the scenes recruitment of Nowitzki by Charles Barkley and if Nike participated in the negotiations, major recruitment violations would have been handed out. Overall, the risk was slim to no concern for Charles Barkley. He was one of the first to discover the talent Nowitzki possessed on the court with a basketball. In the end, Nowitzki became not only a global icon but at the time of this writing, one if not the best European basketball imports in the NBA's history.

After a life changing Nike Hoops Heroes Tour in 1997 and following his military service, Nowitzki was ready to take on more NBA competition at the Nike Hoops Summit in March of 1998 in San Antonio, Texas. This was the first time Nowitzki stepped on American soil and he can to impress and put on another show. At the Nike Hoops Summit, held at Alamo Stadium, NBA scouts were hidden with the fans, coaches, and general managers in attendance ready to watch this kid from Germany named Dirk Nowitzki. The event, at the time, was the biggest attraction to watch top talent affiliated with U.S. men's basketball. [220]

As expected, Nowitzki proved he was not a fluke and scored a total of 33 points on 50 percent shooting to go along with 14 rebounds and three steals for the international team.[220] Beside from his impressive stat line, scouts were fond of his ball handling, shooting, and his quickness for a player his size.

Following the Nike Hoops Summit, Nowitzki began to hear from multiple European and international clubs as well as colleges and universities. Nowitzki was even recruited by NBA teams.

Right around the corner, following the Nike Hoops Summit was the 1998 NBA Draft. Nowitzki felt confident in himself and decided not to take the traditional route to the league, going from a college or university then declaring for the following year's NBA Draft. Instead, Nowitzki declared for the 1998 NBA Draft, making him available for selection to any of the teams, depending on where he goes. [219] His draft stock constantly changed throughout the mock drafts. His highest projection saw him going in the top five, but most mock drafts saw Nowitzki landing outside of the top ten.

The 1998 NBA Draft was held at the General Motors Palace in Vancouver, British Columbia, Canada on June 24, 1998.[221] Out of all the players in the draft class, Nowitzki was clearly the most intriguing prospect. From once being an unknown teenager playing with DJK Wurzburg to a projected lottery pick in an NBA Draft in little over than a year raised eyebrows across the world, especially with Nowitzki skipping the traditional college route to get to the NBA Draft. The question remained which team would take the chance on Nowitzki.

He did not have to wait long to hear his name called by David Stern, the NBA Commissioner. With the ninth pick in the 1998 NBA Draft, the Milwaukee Bucks selected Nowitzki.[221] Despite being selected by the Milwaukee Bucks, Nowitzki's new home was not going to be Milwaukee.

As mentioned, Nowitzki was on his way to the Dallas Mavericks as part of the Steve Nash trade.[221] Unlike most lottery picks, Nowitzki was joining a team that was familiar with winning but had only won one division title since 1987. [218] With the acquisition of Steve Nash and Nowitzki, the Dallas Mavericks were considered a dangerous Western Conference team.

Nowitzki had to wait some time until he made his NBA debut due to the 1998-99 NBA lockout. With lockout negotiations putting the 1998-99 season on hold, Nowitzki decided to return to DJK Wurzburg and play for the team. He played a total of 13 games and once the NBA lockout concluded he returned to Dallas and was ready to make his debut. [219]

As expected, Nowitzki's game did not translate over to the NBA right away. He needed time to adjust to elite competition and work on his game, especially his defense. He entered his rookie season as a power forward, matching up against opposing players his size but with more physical and bigger.

On top of Nowitzki's early struggles, the Dallas Mavericks, with the acquisition of Steve Nash, took some time to build chemistry between players. The 1998-99 shortened season was not a pretty one for the Dallas Mavericks, ending their season with only 19 wins and did not make the 1999 Western Conference playoffs.[218] For Nowitzki it was one of the worst seasons of his career. He played in 47 of the 50 games, starting in 24 of them, and averaged 20.4 minutes, 8.2 points, 3.4 rebounds, and 1.0 assists per game.[221] Following his rookie season, his name was circulating in the NBA Draft bust conversation, but Nowitzki quickly proved the doubters wrong.

The 1999-2000 season was filled with new beginnings for the Dallas Mavericks franchise. Ross Perot Jr sold the team to Mark Cuban for $285 million and their new owner had a plan for his new franchise. The most valuable part of Mark Cuban's new plan for his newest investment was to support. Unlike most owners, Mark Cuban attended all 82 games of the 1999-2000 season, sitting courtside with his players. [218]

As for Nowitzki, he had a chip on his shoulder to come out his second season with the Dallas Mavericks and live up to his hype. To say the least, Nowitzki proved the early doubters wrong. The Dallas Mavericks went from 19 wins the previous season to 40 wins in the 1999-200 season which was one of the biggest wins jumps in franchise history.[218] Despite the huge jump, the Dallas Mavericks came just shy of the 2000 Western Conference playoffs.

A big reason for their tremendous turnaround was Nowitzki. In the 1999-200 season, Nowitzki played in all 82 games, starting in 81 of them, and averaged 35.8 minutes, 17.5 minutes, 6.5 rebounds, and 2.5 assists per game.[221] His turnaround season earned Nowitzki credit to be a serious candidate for the NBA's Most Improved Player Award. Despite becoming a serious candidate for the honor, Nowitzki came just short of the award, losing to Indiana Pacers shooting guard Jalen Rose, who also had a tremendous jump. Following his second season in the NBA, Nowitzki began his Hall of Fame worthy resume only some international players can only dream of.

Dirk Nowitzki went on to play a total of 21 seasons in the NBA with only one team: the Dallas Mavericks. At the time of this writing, Nowitzki is the only player in NBA's history to play 21 seasons with one team.[221] Kobe Bryant ranks second, playing a total of 20 seasons with the Los Angeles Lakers. On top of playing 21 seasons with one team, Nowitzki is only one of five players to play 21 seasons in the league. The other four players to play 21 seasons in the NBA are Kevin Garnett, Kevin Willis, and Robert Parish. Vince Carter, at the time of this writing, is playing for the Atlanta Hawks in his 22nd season, which is an NBA record.

In his home final game, which took place on April 9, 2019, Nowitzki showed the sellout crowd filled with fans that supported him for over two decades that father time was not going to affect him. In his final game under the

American Airlines Arena lights, Nowitzki scored 30 points, which included his signature moves: the infamous one-legged step back and his high arcing three-point shot.[217] Following his final home game, Nowitzki addressed the crowd and confirmed that he will not be returning for a 22nd season, calling it a career.

> *"As you guys might expect, this is my last home game,"* Nowitzki said wiping tears from his eyes. [217]

After one of the greatest last home games in the NBA's history, it was time for Dirk Nowitzki to lace up some last time. On April 10, 2019, Nowitzki and the Dallas Mavericks traveled to San Antonio, Texas to face their in-state rival, the San Antonio Spurs. Over the span of Nowitzki's career, usually the environment in San Antonio for his team was hostile and filled with boos and negative chants. For Dirk Nowitzki's last game, it was the opposite. That night, no matter if you attended the game or watched it live on television, it was history in the making and a special sight that will come around very few times. Gregg Popovich, the San Antonio Spurs head coach, who is known for being a man of few words but one of the greatest coaches in the NBA's history, felt not only honored but blessed to be a part of Dirk Nowitzki's final game.

> *"Everybody - players, fans, coaches and staff got to witness history, watching him play his last game,"* San Antonio Spurs Head Coach Gregg Popovich said. *"He played a fine game, which was great. It's not surprising ... I feel honored and blessed to have been able to watch him all these years because he's one of those consummate professionals and he never wavered from that."* [228]

Throughout the game, every time the ball was in Dirk Nowitzki's hands, the crowd erupted, wanting him to shoot wherever he was on the floor. He finished his final NBA game recording a double-double with 20 points and 10 rebounds. Unfortunately, the Dallas Mavericks could not pull out the win and lost 105-94 against the San Antonio Spurs. [228]

In those 21 years as an NBA player, Dirk Nowitzki proved he was the best European import to play in the league. He accomplished almost everything an NBA player can dream of and built a Hall of Fame resume. Nowitzki will be enshrined into the Naismith Memorial Hall of Fame once eligible.

- 14-Time NBA All-Star (2002-2012, 2014-15, 2019)
- Three-Time NBA All-Third Team (2001, 2004, 2012)
- Four-Time NBA All-NBA First Team (2005-2007, 2009)

- Five-Time All-NBA Second Team (2002-2003, 2008, 2010-2011)
- NBA Three Point Shooting Contest Champion (2006)
- NBA Most Valuable Player (2007)
- NBA Champion (2011)
- NBA Finals MVP (2011)
- Sixth in NBA All-Time Point Leaders (31,560) [221]

On top of his NBA Hall of Fame resume and being arguably the best stretch four in NBA history, Nowitzki has a decorated international career with Germany and FIBA. He began his national basketball team career back in 1997 as a member of the German national basketball team. He immediately became the team's top offensive weapon, especially shooting. He played a total of 86 games for the German national team and averaged 31.4 minutes, 21.5 points, 7.1 rebounds, and 1.8 assists per game.[222] Nowitzki participated in a total of 14 international tournaments in his international career before announcing his retirement in 2016.

Nowitzki and Germany never won gold in the 19 years he was a part of the team but won bronze at the 2002 FIBA World Championship, which was played in the United States, and silver at the 2005 FIBA European Championship, also referred to as EuroBasket, which was held in Serbia and Montenegro. [221]

There is no question, Nowitzki will go down as one of the best stretch four players in the NBA's history. In fact, Nowitzki was the player who made the stretch four position a common trend in the NBA today.

His legacy is much more than basketball. Nowitzki became the fourth German born player to reach the NBA and earned a total of $242 million in career contract earnings.[222] On top of his career contract earnings, Nowitzki is a longtime Nike endorser, which traces back to Charles Barkley in 1997 when the NBA Hall of Famer saw Nowitzki play at the Nike Hoops Heroes Tour in Germany.

As mentioned before, Dirk Nowitzki's legacy starts with one simple basketball move on the hardwood: the one legged fadeaway jumper. That one move is trademarked and became popular in the NBA because of Nowitzki but why is that move so significant in NBA history? The answer is easy. He changed the perspective of big men in the league.

Today, the NBA has turned into a shooters league. When Nowitzki came into the NBA back in 1998, it was uncommon but a clear plus if a big man could shoot outside the paint and especially from three. Nowitzki was a big reason why big men today need to learn how to shoot and come into the NBA with an established shot.

Nowitzki, once he found his niche in the NBA with moves such as the one legged fadeaway jumper and his high arcing three-point shot, the league adjusted around him rather than having him change his game. That is because what he brought to the league became a trend. Many coaches did not appreciate the moves and skill set Dirk Nowitzki established throughout the NBA and it's 30 teams. Despite not appreciate it, they must respect it.

European players back around the time Nowitzki came into the NBA were commonly referred to as 'soft' or 'just a shooter.' Nowitzki finally buried that stereotype back in 2011 when he led the Dallas Mavericks to their first NBA championship, defeating arguably the best 'Big Three' in NBA history at the time. When LeBron James announced his free agent decision to take his talents to South Beach and join the Miami Heat, many and if not everyone, believed the Miami Heat would win the 2010-2011 NBA Championship. The Dallas Mavericks, led by Nowitzki, were filled with toughness, from playing hard to playing through small injuries, and ending their historic playoff run lifting the NBA championship. That was the narrative behind their first championship in franchise history: toughness.

Robin Lundberg, host at Sports Illustrated, CBS Sports Radio, and Sirius XM, believes Nowitzki leading the Dallas Mavericks to the 2011 NBA Championship defined how the NBA world looks at international players. In addition, Lundberg compares Nowitzki's impact on the game of basketball to hip-hop legend Outkast's impact on the culture of music during the mid-1990s.

"In a way, the 2011 NBA Finals completely legitimizes international basketball forever," Robin Lundberg said. *"Up until that point, the ignorant stereotype of players from overseas continued to plague Dirk Nowitzki. He was labeled soft despite his resume up until that point. Afterwards, his status was cemented, and he became the upside comparison for international prospects. Dirk was innovative, not only as the greatest European import ever but also as a sweet shooting big man on the perimeter. It kind of reminded me of the mid 90s when East and West hip hop were hot and then other sounds began infiltrating the scene. To me, Dirk was like Outkast. He may have been from a different region, but he was undeniably dope."*

With all being said, Nowitzki has not only proved he was the best European import player the NBA has ever seen but he is also the NBA's most important European player ever. Without Nowitzki, the play style in the NBA, being a heavy shooters league, may have not transformed this early.

From a young German teenager, moving halfway around the world to chase a dream, he succeeded. The impact Dirk Nowitzki made on the NBA is bigger than basketball. Clearly, he is the greatest player to wear a Dallas

Mavericks uniform, but he will forever be known as the greatest European pioneer in NBA globalization history.

Chapter 27

The Sharpshooter who Defined the 'Soft' Stereotype

Predrag "Peja" Stojakovic was born on June 9, 1977 in Pozega, Croatia, which today is located on the Croatia border.[231] At the time of his birth, Croatia was a part of Yugoslavia. Shortly into his childhood, Stojakovic and his family fled Porzega and moved to Belgrade, Yugoslavia due to the Yugoslav wars but his father remained in Porzega to fight for the Army of the Republic of Serbian Krajina. His border town of Porzega was considered very dangerous to live in and many residents, if they had the money, moved. [231]

Stojakovic began working at a very young age at his family's grocery store. He would work right after school and help run the grocery store.[231] While building a strong work ethic at a young age, Stojakovic always dreamed of becoming a professional athlete.

Unlike most of his friends, Stojakovic had his growth spirt early in his life. By his early teenage years, Stojakovic was over six feet tall and played handball, soccer, and volleyball.[231] He excelled at the three sports due to his height but by age 13 Stojakovic was introduced to a new sport: basketball.

Belgrade was known for the sport of basketball. [231] The sport was quite popular in the area and Stojakovic played against various forms of competition growing up. A number of local coaches began to scout Stojakovic and envisioned great potential in the young kid, mainly due to his height and quickness. On top of his skillset, Stojakovic's work ethic played a big role in his success at a young age and that was valuable for many local coaches.

Despite being taller than most kids his age, Stojakovic worked on his shooting more than his inside play. In Yugoslavia and all across Europe, shooting was always viewed as a valuable attitude in the game of basketball and Stojakovic quickly mastered an outside touch from behind the three-point arc.

At the age of 15, Stojakovic joined his first professional basketball club. He joined KK Crvena Zvezda.[231] His skillset began to grow, and his basketball IQ rose quickly, facing the best young talent in the international circuit. At the time, Stojakovic was six foot- seven and he was not done growing.

Stojakovic did not resign with Crvena zvezda and instead, was on his way to Greece with his family at the age of 16. [231] He was able to obtain citizenship in Greece, along with his family, with the aid of his new team.

Stojakovic signed a three-year deal with PAOK Thessaloniki, a rising team in the Greek League. The team, in addition to signing Stojakovic, gave him and his family a five-year personal services deal. The personal services deal helped his family with expenses and living conditions. [231]

He did not play the first season, the 1993-94 season with PAOK Thessaloniki due to a playing permit. Stojakovic needed a playing permit to play for the Greek club from the Greek government. Despite sitting out the first season, the time off did not hurt him. The following season, the 1994-95 season, Stojakovic was named a starter for the team after a few games. He quickly made a name for himself in the country of Greece and was treated as one of the league's best players. Stojakovic was a fan favorite and PAOK Thessaloniki treated him very well. With the Greek Club, Stojakovic led the team to win the 1995 Greek Cup and played in the 1996 FIBA European Cup, which is one of the highest achievements for a team across Europe. [231]

One player quickly grew interested in Stojakovic and saw a bright NBA future in the young European sharpshooter: Byron Scott. Scott was playing for the Greek powerhouse, Panathinaikos, and was in the near end of his playing career.

Like many European players with bright NBA futures ahead, Stojakovic faced troubles with his club's contract. He was in the last year of his playing deal with PAOK Thessaloniki but his personal services deal was still active. [231] With early worry that Stojakovic could be stuck in Greece, the worry was soon put to rest and Stojakovic was able to be selected in the 1996 NBA Draft. He left Europe with a strong resume which included being named the 1994 Yugoslavian Most Valuable Young Player, two cup championships, the 1998 Greek League Most Valuable Player, and the 1998 FIBA EuroLeague Top Scorer. [231]

Stojakovic always dreamed of making the NBA and playing for a team. When he was 15 years old, Detlef Schrempf was drafted in the NBA, breaking another barrier for Europeans and proving an NBA dream can become a reality. As a young child, Stojakovic would tune in to any NBA offered on Yugoslavian Television and loved watching Michael Jordan and the Chicago Bulls and he modeled his game after Chris Mullin and Charles Barkley.[231]

He was initially drafted in the 1996 NBA Draft by the Sacramento Kings with the 19th overall pick but, as discussed before, was not able to play until the 1998-99 season. [232] The Kings signed the European star prior to the 1998-99 season, which was a lockout year for the league.

At the time of his arrival, Sacramento was one of the best teams in the Western Conference and were considered a team that could make a run at the championship. In addition to Stojakovic joining the Kings, Vlade Divac signed with the Kings as a free agent. Divac and Stojakovic were good friends and were expected to play very well alongside each other.

Stojakovic came off the bench in his first two seasons with Sacramento. He quickly became the Kings sixth man off the bench and averaged 22.5 minutes per game.[232] It was clear that Stojakovic was a sharpshooter from three, but his form was unique. Instead of tucking in his left elbow, Stojakovic shot the ball crooked. Despite a crooked shot, Stojakovic made his form look smooth and his shots rarely glazed the rim.

The 2000-01 season was a breakout season for Stojakovic. He was released off the bench and became a starter for the Kings. He played in 75 games, starting all 75, and averaged 38.7 minutes, 20.4 points, 5.8 rebounds, 2.2 assists, and 1.2 steals per game. [232] On top of his strong numbers, Stojakovic was one of the most consistent shooters in the league. He shot .400 from three and .470 from the field, which is very rare for a stretch three in the NBA. [232] His breakout play earned Stojakovic heavy consideration for the 2001 NBA Most Improved Player award but finished runner up to Tracy McGrady of the Orlando Magic.

The Sacramento Kings finished the season with a 55-27 record and easily clinched the Western Conference playoffs.[232] In the playoffs, the Kings cruised to the Western Conference semifinals but faced Kobe Bryant, Shaquille O'Neal, and the Los Angeles Lakers. The Kings ended the season on a humiliating note, getting swept by the Lakers.

Following his breakout season, Stojakovic put up another year of consistent numbers, earning the fourth-year European his first All-Star appearance. Stojakovic felt being named to the All-Star team was not just a personal accomplishment. It traces back to his European roots.

> *"Being part of that game, it makes you feel like you're part of something big,"* Stojakovic says. *"Especially for me, being from Europe."* [238]

Not only was Stojakovic named to the 2001-02 Western Conference All-Star team but he was chosen to compete in the NBA Three-Point Shooting Contest. The 2002 NBA Three-Point Shooting Contest is considered one of the best in the history of the NBA. Along with Stojakovic, the contest featured Mike Miller, Paul Pierce, Quentin Richardson, Ray Allen, Steve Nash, Steve Smith, and Wesley Person. Stojakovic kept his cool in each round of the contest and won. He became the first European-born player to win an NBA All-Star Weekend competition event.[231] The following year, Stojakovic successfully defended his title in the 2002-03 NBA Three-Point Shooting Contest. The contest featured Antoine Walker, Brent Barry, David Wesley, Pat Garrity, and Wesley Person. [231]

Stojakovic would go on to play a total of eight seasons with the Sacramento Kings playing in a total of 518 games. In those 518 games, he averaged 34.2 minutes, 18.3 points, 5.0 rebounds, 2.0 assists, and 1.0 steals per game. [232] In those eight seasons, Stojakovic created a outstanding resume, highlighted by his consistent sharpshooting. He was a three time All-Star, named to 2004 All-NBA Second Team, two-time NBA Three-Point Shooting Contest champion, and led the league in NBA Three-Point field goals in 2004. [232] In addition to his multiple league honors, he finished fourth in the 2004 NBA Most Valuable Player voting.

He holds many records in multiple statistical categories for the Sacramento Kings. He ranks first in Sacramento Kings franchise history in three pointers made (1,070) and attempts (2,687). Stojakovic ranks first as well in free throw percentage (.893). He also ranks third on the Kings all-time scoring list with 9,498 points scored, fourth in field goals made (3,352), attempted (7,269), and sixth in steals (543). [232] On December 16, 2014, the Sacramento Kings retired Stojakovic's number 16 jersey. [231]

Like many NBA stars and valuable role players, Stojakovic was traded at the NBA trade deadline on January 25. 2006. The trade sent Stojakovic to the Indiana Pacers for Ron Artest. [232] The trade was one of the main trades that occurred at the deadline. Stojakovic played and started the remaining 40 games for the Pacers but following the 2005-06 season, he would enter NBA Free Agency.

In free agency, it was unlikely Stojakovic was going to sign a deal to remain with the Indiana Pacers. The Pacers had Danny Granger, who was coming off an impressive rookie season and earning 2005-06 NBA All-Rookie Second Team honors.

Shortly into free agency, Stojakovic agreed to a five-year $64 million deal with the New Orleans Hornets. [232] Unfortunately for Stojakovic, he got his first taste of the injury bug in the NBA. He only played in the first 13 games of the NBA season, missing the remaining 69 games of the 2006-07 season.[232] He aggravated a protruding disc in his back.

Stojakovic went on to play five seasons with the New Orleans Hornets, who became the Oklahoma City Thunder after relocating prior to the 2008-09 season. He played a total of 219 games averaging 13.2 minutes, 15.5 points, 4.4 rebounds, and 1.4 assists per game before being shipped to the Toronto Raptors. [232]

On November 20, 2010, the Thunder shipped Stojakovic along with Jerryd Bayless for David Anderson, Marcus Banks, and Jarrett Jack. [232] His Raptors tenure was cut to two games due to a serious knee injury and he was released in January of 2011.

Just a couple days after being released, Stojakovic was picked up by an NBA team. The Dallas Mavericks, who had six international players at the time of his arrival, signed Stojakovic to a deal. He joined Alexis Ajinca, J.J

Barea, Rodrigue Beaubois, Ian Mahinmi, Dirk Nowitzki, and Sasha Pavlovic as international players on the roster. [232]

Stojakovic was a big contributor in the Dallas Mavericks championship run, splitting time off the bench and starting. Off the bench, Stojakovic provided instant offense and was a major shooting threat on the perimeter. He ended his NBA career winning the 2011 NBA Championship, defeating the infamous Big Three of Chris Bosh, Dwayne Wade, and LeBron James of the Miami Heat, coveting the Mavericks first championship in franchise history.

He officially announced his retirement in December of 2011 due to lingering injuries to his back and neck.

> *"When you start competing against your body more than you're preparing for the actual game,"* Stojakovic said, *"it's a wakeup call."* [234]

> *"I feel so blessed to have been given the athletic gifts to play professional basketball,"* Stojakovic said. *"I have always loved the game and have great respect for it and I know the time is right to step away. I promised myself a long time ago, if it came to a point where my heart and body were not 100 percent committed, I would step away. I have reach that point and I know the time is right to retire."*
> [234]

On top of his NBA career, Stojakovic led Yugoslavia to three medals. In the 1999 FIBA EuroBasket, held in France, Stojakovic and Yugoslavia won bronze. Two years later, at the 2001 FIBA EuroBasket in Turkey, the team won gold and the following year, 2002, at the FIBA World Cup, held in Indianapolis, Stojakovic and Yugoslavia won another gold medal. Stojakovic was named the FIBA EuroBasket Most Valuable Player and earned All-Tournament honors for the 2002 FIBA World Cup. [231]

At the time of this writing, Peja Stojakovic is the assistant general manager of the Sacramento Kings. His responsibilities include keeping abreast of domestic and international talent pools available to the Kings as well as general manager and fellow countryman Vlade Divac with the team's scouting efforts. [233]

Peja Stojakovic's legacy often goes unnoticed when compared to other European forwards like Dirk Nowitzki, Toni Kukoc, Manu Ginobili and others. The story of Peja Stojakovic puts him apart from many other European imports. From coming from Yugoslavia, being forced to leave the town of Pozega due to bomb and war activity, heading to Greece and becoming one of the best young European players, and topping his career with a historic thirteen year run in the NBA, Stojakovic paved the way for European players.

He is a trail blazer who's playing style differed from other past European players. When he came into the league, like most European players, Stojakovic was referred to as soft and just another shooter. To him, being called soft was never a distraction nor did he know what the reference meant when talking about fights on the hardwood court.

> *"I haven't seen many people fight on NBA floors,"* Stojakovic said. *"I never thought about it that much. I always looked at it that you step on the floor and do the best that you can. I don't think you can label somebody like that. I don't even know what soft means. At the end of the day it's a game and either you can play, or you cannot play. My coach when I was young used to talk about our ceiling. We all have different ceilings and your goal is to reach it."* [238]

His niche in the league was clearly shooting but he established himself as one of the best shooters the NBA has ever seen.

Throughout his NBA career, Stojakovic was never gifted or handed anything. According to himself, he had to prove everything.

> *"I wasn't given promises in my career,"* he says. *"I was always proving myself, every day of every year."* [238]

Overall, the legacy of Peja Stojakovic is not over. He is the assistant general manager of the Sacramento Kings, who today are run by an Indian-born owner, Vivek Ranadive and their general manager is Stojakovic's fellow countryman Vlade Divac. The franchise that opened the doors and he left there with his number hanging in the rafters.

> *"He was one of those Europeans who kind of paved the way for me and others,"* Kristaps Porzingis said. [236]

> *"Peja will go down as one of the great shooters in the history of the NBA,"* NBA Commissioner David Stern said in 2011. *"His success was the result of a tireless work ethic and an unquenchable desire to be the best at what he did. Peja's legacy, however, goes way beyond his 3-point skills and that elusive Finals title he won last season with the Dallas Mavericks. Peja was part of the wave of international stars that helped introduce the world to the NBA game and inspired thousands of fans to begin playing the sport of basketball."* [236]

Chapter 28

The San Antonio Spurs 'Big Three' Dynasty

For an NBA team or for any organization to be referred to as a dynasty is not proven in one season. An NBA dynasty is a team that has won multiple titles in a short period of time. There are a few NBA teams that have earned the right to be called a dynasty.

The first dynasty the league witnessed was the Boston Celtics, dating back to the 1950s. Led by one of the greatest players in the NBA's history Bill Russell, the Celtics dominated over two decades of play. Their dynasty lasted from 1957 until 1969, winning 12 NBA championships, which included 10 straights, 1957-66.

Other historic NBA dynasties include Magic Johnson and the showtime Los Angeles Lakers, who dominated from 1980 until 1988, Larry Bird and the Boston Celtics from 1981-1986, Michael Jordan and the Chicago Bulls from 1991-98, and most recently the Golden State Warriors from 2015-2019.

Compared to those five iconic NBA dynasties, there is one dynasty that sticks out in NBA history. That is the San Antonio Spurs dynasty, which won five championships from 1999-2014.

The making of the dynasty dates back to March 26, 1993. Peter M. Holt, a local businessman, and a group of 22 investors purchased the franchise from Red McCombs for $75 million. [240] At the time of the purchase, the Spurs were a good team, but they were looking to win their first championship.

Now under new ownership, the Spurs made some changes heading into the 1994-95 season, bringing in Bob Hill, the former head coach of the Indiana Pacers. That season, led by David Robinson, the Spurs finished with the league's best record, 62-20, and had high hopes for a championship run.[240] Robinson was named the NBA Most Valuable Player that season, but when playoff time came around, the Spurs ran into Hakeem Olajuwon and the Houston Rockets in the Western Conference Finals. They would lose to the Rockets, who became the NBA champions that year.

In the 1995-96 season, San Antonio had a repetitive year, breezing to the Western Conference playoffs, but lost in the Western Conference semifinals to the Utah Jazz. After two successful seasons disaster struck, and the Spurs went from consistent playoff contenders to rock bottom.

The 1996-97 season was a year the San Antonio franchise does not want to look back on. The team went from 59-23 the previous year to 20-62. [240] Before the season, as mentioned earlier in this book, Dominique Wilkins returned to the NBA, signing a deal with the Spurs. San Antonio took a major blow, losing their star David Robinson for 76 games due to a back injury. [240]

Only after 18 games, the Spurs made a head coaching change, the first step in forming a future NBA dynasty. Bob Hill was replaced by Gregg Popovich, who was an assistant for the Golden State Warriors at the time but served as an assistant for the Spurs from 1988-92. The 1996-97 season was the worst year the Spurs franchise had. In fact, that was the only time the franchise missed the NBA playoffs. [240] Despite all the negatives behind a disastrous year, there was a very bright future on the horizon.

The Spurs won the 1997 NBA Draft Lottery and were awarded the first overall pick. It was very clear what player the Spurs were going to select week prior to the 1997 NBA Draft: Tim Duncan, a power forward from Wake Forest University. He stayed all four years in college, being named the Atlantic Coast Conference, ACC, Player of the Year two times, and led Wake Forest to an overall record of 97-31 record. [240]

It was clear Tim Duncan was the guy San Antonio wanted. When the 1997 NBA Draft came around, David Stern walked to the podium to announce the first pick. The San Antonio Spurs selected Tim Duncan from Wake Forest University.

In that moment, the Spurs and the NBA knew something special was on the horizon: the front court duo of David Robinson and Tim Duncan. Cleary Robinson was coming back from a devastating back injury from the previous season and there were questions if he can still play at an elite level.

The following season, the San Antonio Spurs, led by the front court duo of Robinson and Duncan and surrounded by great role players in Avery Johnson, Monty Williams, and Jaren Jackson to name a few. The Spurs, in Duncan's rookie season, finished with a 56-26 record, making the Western Conference playoffs. Duncan averaged a double-double in his rookie year with 21 points and 12 rebounds, earning him First Team All-NBA and winning the NBA Rookie of the Year award. [240]

The 1998-99 season was a historic season for the San Antonio Spurs franchise. The front court duo of Robinson and Duncan clicked even better than their first season together. As mentioned before, the 1998-99 season was an NBA lockout season, which resulted in a 50 games season. In those 50 games, the Spurs, led by Robinson and Duncan, finished with a 37-18 record, [242] clinching yet another playoff appearance but the question remained: Can the Spurs finally win it all?

The Spurs, due to their impressive regular season record, entered the playoffs as the number one seed. In the first round, the Spurs defeated the

Minnesota Timberwolves three games to one to advance to the Western Conference semifinals. In the semifinals, San Antonio swept Kobe Bryant and the Los Angeles Lakers to advance to the Western Conference Finals. In the Western Conference Finals, the Spurs faced off with the Portland Trail Blazers. The Trail Blazers had the talents on Arvydas Sabonis, Jermaine O'Neal, Rasheed Wallace, and valuable role players but to many the Spurs were destined for the 1999 NBA Finals. As expected, San Antonio blew past Portland in a sweep to advance to the 1999 NBA Finals, led by the passing of Avery Johnson and Tim Duncan's elite all-around game. [243]

In the 1999 NBA Finals, San Antonio was four game away from finally winning their first NBA Championship. They faced Patrick Ewing and the New York Knicks. It took only five games for the San Antonio to win their first NBA Championship. With the Finals win, the San Antonio Spurs finally got over the hump but there was a brighter future awaiting. After the Finals win, Tim Duncan expressed his love for San Antonio, and it was exactly what the Spurs organization and their fans wanted to hear. In addition, Duncan reassured this title win is not a one hit wonder.

> *"I love San Antonio,"* Duncan said. *"It's a great place. I would love to be there the rest of my career. We've given them a good reason to keep us there."* [244]

> *"We'll be ready to go next year,"* Duncan said. *"There will be a lot tougher teams in the West that are going to challenge us for it, but we'll be right back up there."* [244]

Before the Spurs could prove their title win was not just a one-time thing, the 1999 NBA Draft came around. In the 1999 NBA Draft, the Spurs added another piece to their historic future dynasty. With the 57th pick in the 1999 NBA Draft, the San Antonio Spurs selected Manu Ginobili, a shooting guard from Virtus Bologna in Italy.[240] At the time of the selection, rarely anyone knew who Ginobili was including Duncan himself. In March of 2019 at Manu Ginobili's jersey retirement ceremony in San Antonio, Duncan reflected on the story when he heard about Ginobili being selected.

> *"I'll tell you this one story,"* Duncan said in front of the San Antonio Spurs crowd. *"I got that call from Pop [Popovich] every year I watch the draft. I sit at home and tell everyone all day long that I am not watching the draft. I sit at home and watch the draft and we pick people we never heard of. Sitting there, Manuel Ginobili... Who did we just pick? 'Oh he is going to be great, he is this and this,' ok Pop whatever."* [245]

Little did Duncan know that Ginobili was going to be not only one of the greatest players to wear a Spurs jersey but one of the greatest international players to play in the NBA.

Then came the final piece of the Spurs historic trio of their future dynasty. In the 2001 NBA Draft, the Spurs organization, once again, took a gamble and drafted an international talent. With the 21st pick in the 2001 NBA Draft, the San Antonio Spurs selected Tony Parker, a point guard from Paris Basket Racing in France. [240]

Fast forward to the 2002-03 season. Before the 2002-03 season, David Robinson announced that it will be his last season and he will be retiring. For any NBA legend and future Hall of Famer, there is no better way to end an NBA career than winning it all. The Spurs were motivated to send David Robinson into retirement with one more ring.

That season, the 2002-03 season was Parker's second season and Ginobili's rookie year. Parker played in a total of 77 games, starting in 72 games, and averaged 29.4 minutes, 9.2 points, 4.3 assists, and 2.1 rebounds per game earning him NBA All-Rookie First Team honors. [246] Ginobili was coming into his rookie season in the NBA as a bench player ready to prove his worth in the NBA. Parker was ready to exceed expectations and prove his worth as being the starting point guard for years to come.

The Spurs finished the 2002-03 regular season with 60 wins and 23 losses, easily clinching yet another playoff appearance and a step closer to winning a championship.[247] In the playoffs, the Spurs blew past the Phoenix Suns 4-2, then Kobe Bryant and the Los Angeles Lakers 4-2, and advanced to the 2003 NBA Finals to face Jason Kidd and the New Jersey Nets.

In the 2003 NBA Finals, the San Antonio Spurs defeated the New Jersey Nets, 4-2, to covet their second NBA Championship. [247] They accomplished the perfect ending to David Robinson's NBA Hall of Fame career.

With David Robinson gone, it was not all sorrow for the Spurs. After a successful season and with Parker and Ginobili proving their worth, it was the beginning of the San Antonio Spurs dynasty, led by Tim Duncan and two talented international players in Tony Parker and Manu Ginobili. The trio was named 'The Big Three.'

The 2002-03 season was the beginning of something special for the Spurs. Duncan was awarded the 2002-03 NBA Most Valuable Player Award and won his second ring. Parker played and started all 82 games of the regular season, averaging 33.8 minutes, 15.5 points, 5.3 assists, and 2.6 rebounds.[246] Manu Ginobili played in 69 games, starting only five, averaging 20.7 minutes, 7.6 points, 2.3 rebounds, 2.0 assists, and 1.4 steals per game, earning him All-NBA Rookie Second Team honors. [251]

Following their 2002-03 NBA Championship, the value and vision of the NBA's newest trio was unknown. They certainly proved they can win, and their play styles meshed together but the word dynasty revolving around the trio was not stressed.

'The Big Three' would go on to win a total of five NBA Championships and make the San Antonio Spurs one of the most successful organizations in all American professional sports. In addition to the Spurs success, the 'Big Three' were never overcome by the infamous battle of egos. All three stars maintain their roles with the team and never had any problems with their roles.

"It's very unique," Ginobili said. *"I don't think that it's happened to many teams in history where three players have played together for so long and in a successful manner like this where no one is egotistical and trying to demand things."* [253]

"We have no ego and we didn't let money affect, you know, our dynasty." [253]

With all being said, where does the 'Big Three' and the San Antonio Spurs dynasty rank in the league's history. First, just start off the legacy of all three players.

Tim Duncan's nickname is "The Big Fundamental" for a reason. His playstyle on the hardwood was not anything fancy. He played like a traditional power forward from simple post moves to mid-range jump shots. His fundamental style of play over his nineteen-year career with the San Antonio Spurs established Duncan as arguably the greatest power forward in the NBA's history. His NBA resume across those nineteen years can prove that. He is a two-time NBA Most Valuable Player, five-time NBA Champion, three-time NBA Finals Most Valuable Player, 15-time NBA All-Star, 10-time All-NBA First Team, eight-time NBA All-Defensive First Team, and a 10-time NBA All-First Team. [254]

In addition to his personal NBA honors, Duncan ranks 14th in NBA all-time scoring with 26,496 points, sixth in rebounds with 15,091 rebounds, and fifth in blocked shots with 3,020 blocks. [254]

Duncan is only one of four players in NBA history to win three NBA Finals MVP awards. The other three players are Magic Johnson, Michael Jordan, and Shaquille O'Neal. In other words, Tim Duncan is the only power forward to achieve that mark.

His number 21 jersey is retired at both Wake Forest and for the San Antonio Spurs. In addition to his NBA career, Duncan played as a member of the United States men's Olympic team, winning three gold medals and two bronze medals over a span of 10 years.

In July of 2019, the San Antonio Spurs announced that Tim Duncan was hired as an assistant coach under his former coach Gregg Popovich, continuing his legacy as a San Antonio Spur. Duncan and Popovich are the only two who have been a part of every Spurs championship.

> *"It is only fitting, that after I served loyally for 19 years as Tim Duncan's assistant, that he returns the favor."* [250]

Then there is the point guard of the dynasty, Tony Parker. Once a professional from France, Parker is now retired from the sport of basketball after a historic 18-year career in the NBA. His legacy is not just what he did for the San Antonio Spurs, being a part of four championships and the floor general for that dynasty. He was a trail blazer in NBA globalization and is one of the greatest international players in the league's history.

Following the 2018-19 NBA season, Tony Parker announced his retirement in San Antonio, Texas, where he arrived as a teenager and started his legacy.

> *"I'm going to retire,"* Parker told The Undefeated. *"I decided that I'm not going to play basketball anymore."* [255]

> *"A lot of different stuff ultimately led me to this decision,"* Parker said. *"But, at the end of the day, I was like, if I can't be Tony Parker anymore and I can't play for a championship, I don't want to play basketball anymore."* [255]

In Parker's 18 years in the NBA with two NBA teams, he played in 1,254 games and averaged 15.5 points, 5.6 assists, and 2.7 rebounds. [246] Not only did Parker win four NBA titles but he became the first European player to win the NBA Finals Most Valuable Player award in 2007. Parker scored a total of 19,473 points, ranking 53rd all time, 7,036 assists, ranked 17th all-time, and he finished his career with a 49.1 shooting percentage, which is very impressive for a point guard. [246]

His number 9 jersey will certainly be retired by the San Antonio Spurs and he will join the other two members of the 'Big Three' in the rafters. Parker believes the 'Big Three' trio will always be remembered.

> *"We're always going to be remembered together,"* Parker said. *"But it was great to share that moment with them. It's crazy. We came from three different backgrounds and came together. And to see*

Timmy's jersey retired and then Manu ... it was very emotional to go to Manu's jersey retirement, and you go through all the moments and you think about what you're going to say. It was just nice to share the moment with them." [255]

When it comes to the impact Parker made on the globalization of the NBA, he believes he was a good ambassador for French basketball. In his thirteen years as a member of the France men's basketball team, he won two gold medals, one silver, and three bronze medals. Parker is arguably the best player to ever lace up for the France men's basketball team.

"People don't realize that I grew up with nothing," Parker said. *"We had nothing growing up, and it was rough times. But I think that's what gave me the motivation to make it in life because I wanted my family to have a better life. And I think Pop saw that very early in me when he first interviewed me. I think that's why Pop was so hard on me, because he knew that I will stay motivated and wanted to make it whatever happened. And he threw everything at me, and I was always there ready to go."* [255]

"I hope that I had a good impact with Dirk [Nowitzki] and Pau [Gasol]," Parker said. *"After we arrived, it exploded. Now you have more than 80 international players, 12 French guys in the NBA. So I always took it seriously, my role of being a good ambassador for French basketball."* [255]

Then there is Manu Ginobili, who has one of the greatest NBA stories in the history of the league. Being drafted with the 57th pick in the 1999 NBA Draft to becoming one of the best small forwards the league has seen in recent years, Ginobili has been through it all.

His legacy began after a successful rookie year in the NBA. Following the first season, Ginobili did not let ego get to him and he embraced the sixth man role. In his first two seasons, he started only 44 of the 146 games he played in. [251]

Everyone acknowledged Ginobili as San Antonio's secret weapon off the bench until the 2004 Olympic Games in Athens, Greece. He played and represented Argentina and in the semifinal's matchup against his teammate Tim Duncan and the United States, he scored 29 points leading Argentina to the 2004 Olympic Finals, where they defeated Italy to win it all. [253]

Despite leading Argentina to gold on the world biggest stage when it comes to international competition, Ginobili always embraced the sixth man role throughout his fifteen-year NBA career with the San Antonio Spurs. He came off the bench for 708 of his total 1,057 regular season games. In fact, the Spurs had a .708 winning percentage (918-378) when Ginobili came off the bench. [251]

In those fifteen years in the NBA, Ginobili is a four-time NBA Champion, two-time NBA All-Star, 2008 NBA Sixth Man of the Year, and his number 20 jersey retired by the San Antonio Spurs. In addition to his NBA accomplishments, before he came to the NBA, Ginobili played seven years overseas with four basketball clubs. [251]

His legacy is much bigger than basketball. Ginobili established himself as an NBA globalization pioneer coming from Argentina, which is not a popular country when it comes to producing NBA talent. The biggest takeaway from his basketball career was that he played with a non-selfish style of play and never had an ego.

> *"You embody how basketball is meant to be played,"* Steph Curry tweeted following the Ginobili's retirement.

The San Antonio Spurs dynasty differs from the previous and current NBA dynasties we have seen or are witnessing. At the beginning of the dynasty, the perception of international players was not as high as it is in today's NBA. The Spurs brought new light on international talent during their dynasty. They drafted Manu Ginobili with the 57th pick and developed him into one of the best international players and the best sixth man players in the NBA's history while Tony Parker was the floor general for the dynasty and the play maker behind the four championships. The 'Big Three' of Tim Duncan, Tony Parker, and Manu Ginobili will go down as one of the best trios we have ever seen in NBA history, but they will also go down as the trio that evolved the game of basketball globally.

Chapter 29

The Global Logo of Basketball

Yao Ming was born on September 12, 1980 in Shanghai, China.[256] When Ming was born, he was five kilos (11 pounds), which is almost twice the size of a normal infant. His parents, Yao Zhuyuan and Fang Fengdi were both professional basketball players and the game of basketball was quickly brought upon Ming at a young age. His father, Yao Zhiyuan was selected to the Shanghai basketball team strictly because of his height while his mother Fang Fengdi started playing the sport at 15 years of age and was selected to the Chinese national team and was the starting center during the 1970s.[256]

By the time Ming was only four years old, he was over a meter tall (a little over 3 feet) and by the age of eight he was approaching two meters. Ming towered over his fellow classmates growing up and by the age of 12 Ming was introduced to a famous basketball coach in his area. [256] Ming played in front of the coach and following the short show, the coach told his mom that basketball was not a good option for Ming due to his lack of balance and his body structure.

Despite the harsh criticism, Ming continued to follow in his parents' footsteps and play basketball. When Ming was 13 years old, he joined the Shanghai Sharks junior team and played with the team till he was 17 years old. Following his four-year stint with the junior team, Ming joined the Shanghai Sharks. In year two, Ming faced his first devastating sports injury. He broke his foot for the second time in his life. He only played 15 games that season, scoring a total of 304 points and 101 rebounds. [259]

Ming played a total of five seasons with the Shanghai Sharks. He played in a total of 136 games and averaged 23.2 points, 15.6 rebounds, and 1.8 assists. In those five seasons, Ming was the Chinese Basketball Associations leading rebounder and blocks for his final three seasons, won the Chinese Basketball Association Dunk contest twice, and was the Chinese Basketball Association Most Valuable Player in 2001. In addition, Ming won a championship with the Sharks in 2002. [259]

After five seasons in the Chinese Basketball Association, Ming was pressured to enter the 2002 NBA Draft. The pressure came from the Chinese Basketball Association itself to show the talent it could produce. The Houston Rockets won the 2002 NBA Draft Lottery and the franchise is well known for choosing big men when they had the first overall pick. From Elvin Haynes, Hakeem Olajuwon, to Moses Malone, the Rockets were very familiar with drafting a big man at No. 1. As the 2002 NBA Draft crept closer and closer, it seemed like history was going to repeat itself.

As the 2002 Draft approached, the Rockets kept that trend going by using their No. 1 overall pick in that draft to thing big again.

On June 27, 2002, the 2002 NBA Draft took place and it was almost certain throughout the NBA that Yao Ming was going to become a Houston Rocket. As expected, David Stern walked to the podium and announced that the Houston Rockets selected Yao Ming. Ming became the highest draft pick to come directly from an international league. Ming was watching the draft alongside his family back in Beijing, China so no one would be able to witness a picture of David Stern and a young 7'6" Yao Ming next to each other at the draft.

"This is now a new start in my basketball life," Yao said from Beijing through an interpreter. *"This is a new league in front of me for me to play, so it will be a new challenge for me."* [260]

"I remember the exhilaration of calling his name as the first pick ... and contemplating that he would be a bridge between Chinese fans and American fans," NBA Commissioner David Stern said. *"That all happened with a wonderful mixture of talent, dedication, humanitarian aspirations and a sense of humor. What a wonderful combination."* [260]

Michael Goldberg, a member of the Rockets legal counsel, received a letter that Ming was officially up for grabs the night before the 2002 NBA Draft. There was some concern that Ming might not be able to be drafted. After hearing the news, he relayed the message over to Carroll Dawson, the Houston Rockets general manager.

"I thought I'd scream but I just fell back in bed and looked at the ceiling," Dawson told the Associated Press. *"I just felt such a great relief. The whole franchise wanted this so badly. I just felt that it would all be worked out."* [261]

In addition to Yao Ming being selected, the Rockets were not finished drafting international talent. They selected Bostjan Nachbar, a 6-9 forward from Bennetoon Treviso of the Italian League with the 15th overall pick.[260] In fact, the Rockets were not the only team drafting international talent in the early first round. Five of the first 16 picks came from overseas as a record 17 foreign-born players were selected.

Cuttino Mobley, the Rockets point guard was thrilled with the selection of Ming and saw no worries with the addition.

> *"He'll have to fit in with us,"* Mobley said. *"He's a very skilled player and that's fun, and he can pass the ball too. We'll feel him out after he gets here. I'm sure everything will work out... He's the No. 1 pick and he has skills, he's not just your average 7-6 dude."* [261]

When Ming was introduced to his teammates, he was very shy. Steve Francis, who was one of the main leaders on the Rockets team, told Ming not to worry about being shy. Francis told Ming that we have been waiting to get a player like you.

> *"I'm so sorry, I'm a little bit shy,"* Yao said to Steve. [263]

> *"Don't worry, Francis said, and then gave him a big friendly hug, "We've been waiting for you. We need you."* [263]

In his rookie season, Ming impressed and showed he was worth the risk being drafted number one. He averaged 13.5 points, 8.2 rebounds, and 1.8 blocks per game, helping Houston finish the regular season with a 43-39 record. [263] Ming was named to the Western Conference All-Star team in his rookie season and he was named to the NBA All-Rookie First Team. He came up short in the NBA Rookie of the Year voting to Amar'e Stoudemire of the Phoenix Suns.

Ming's best memory from his rookie season was when the Rockets organized a Chinese New Year party in February.

> *"In February of my first year I was getting more comfortable on the court and I was getting to know my teammates,"* Ming said. *"For Chinese New Year, the Rockets arranged a surprise party in my honor. It was a game day, and they knew that in China everyone would be getting one or two weeks of vacation, like Christmas. I didn't know they were planning anything. Right before the game, Nelson Luis, our p.r. manager, asked me to come to this office to answer some questions. He was just trying to stall me. When I walked into the locker room after leaving his office, there was Chinese New Year's music playing and everyone was singing. It was a true surprise. Rudy walked up to me and handed me an envelope. I pulled out the one-dollar bill that was inside. Everyone laughed. Steve gave me one of his high fives. My hand was stinging again. I couldn't stop*

smiling. All these years later, it is still a very, very warm memory." [264]

Ming went on to play a total of eight seasons with the Houston Rockets and in the NBA. Like many big men, Ming was plagued by foot injuries. He missed all 82 games of the 2009-10 season. [263] Prior to the season, the Rockets filed for a disabled player exception, which would allow Houston to have enough money to sign another free agent and Ming's contract to weigh less on their salary cap.

On July 20, 2011, Yao Ming announced his retirement from the game of basketball in Shanghai, China. Ming said the reason for the early retirement was due to his foot injuries.

> *"At the end of the last year, my left foot had a third fracture,"* Ming said. *"Today, I need to make a personal decision. I will stop my basketball career and I will formally retire. Today, thinking back and thinking of the future, I have been very grateful. First of all, I need to be grateful to basketball. It has brought me happiness to many people including myself."* [257]

> *"Life is my guide. Just follow it and it will open doors. Out of each door, there will be a beautiful world outside. Since I am retired, one door is closed. But a new life is waiting for me. I have left the basketball (court), but I will not leave basketball."* [257]

Jeff Van Gundy, Ming's former coach with the Houston Rockets, had high praise when talking about Ming's playing career.

> *"People are saying he was pretty good,"* Van Gundy said. *"No, he was dominant. He could play. You can make the case he didn't do it for long enough to be considered an all-time great. But this guy is dominant when he played. In his age group, he was the best center, when healthy."* [257]

> *"People forget what kind of pressure he was on when he came over here, not totally comfortable with the language to start off with and being the first pick in the draft,"* Van Gundy said. *"People hoped he would fail. Some of the then-Rockets players wanted to trade the pick for Lamar Odom. They guy was under enormous pressure. He handled every bit of it with grace and wisdom, and he handled it flawlessly."* [257]

Ming ended his NBA playing career with a decorative resume. He was an eight-time NBA All-Star, three-time All-NBA Third Team, two-time All-NBA Second Team, and his number 11 jersey is retired by the Houston Rockets. He played in a total of 486 NBA games and averaged 32.5 minutes, 19.0 minutes, 9.2 rebounds, 1.9 blocks, and 1.6 assists per game. Due to his injuries, Ming missed a total of 180 games. [263]

In addition to his NBA playing career, Ming was the face of the Chinese men's national basketball team for four years. In those four years, Ming was three gold medals at the FIBA Asia Cup, 2001, 2003, and 2005, and one silver medal at the 2002 Asian Games in Buscan, South Korea. [256]

Despite retiring as a player, Ming did not step away from the game of basketball. David Stern needed to keep Ming revolved around the NBA and saw him as a monumental figure that can grow the sport of basketball.

"I'm utterly thrilled that we're contemplating working with Yao as we continue to grow the sport of basketball," Stern said. *"We have a full force in China. We think Yao is equally committed. I think we'll find ways to work together. We know him and we know his hopes for Chinese Basketball."* [266]

In September of 2016, Yao Ming was elected into the Naismith Memorial Basketball Hall of Fame. In his Hall of Fame class, he was inducted alongside Shaquille O'Neal and other NBA greats.

In his second to last season in the NBA, Ming brought his former team, the Shanghai Sharks, to help them with their finances. The team was doing well financially at the time and feared bankruptcy.

In 2017, Yao Ming was named the president of the Chinese Basketball Association. The CBA voted unanimously to appoint Ming was their president. Ming was set to transform the league which was led by government bureaucrats over the past two decades. Ming said he would introduce scientific training methods to Chinese clubs, improve the tactical education of players and forge exchanges with leagues in the United States, Europe, and elsewhere.

"Our next move will be to borrow from international advanced experience, to thoroughly study China's actual conditions and carve ourselves a path of innovation," Ming said. [266]

"For many years we haven't seen any admirable or acceptable reform measures introduced by the CBA," Yang Ming, a Chinese sports commentator said. *"Yao Ming is not only a brilliant player, but intelligent with his independent ideas."* [266]

The legacy of Yao Ming stretches far from his play on the hardwood. Ming is the global symbol of basketball. His arrival into the NBA was monumental and he helped bridge the NBA to basketball all over the world.

"What's striking to me is the powerful impact Yao made here in America," Clayton Dube, an expert on economic and political change in China and the associate director of the University of Southern California's U.S. – China Institute. *"That shouldn't be overlooked. He just really exemplified all that could be good in a person. That made a big difference."* [269]

"You have to understand, before him, basketball wasn't popular in China, Tracy McGrady, Ming's former teammate said. *"I had made trips before he came into the league, and there was basketball, but it wasn't a part of the Chinese culture. Now, there's over 300 million people in China playing because of Yao Ming. I saw it. I felt it. That is his legacy. He brought NBA basketball to China and I will forever be thankful that I was able to be a part of it."* [269]

Ming's presence in the NBA was not just felt in China and across the world. In fact, many experts believe the Rockets franchise, that was sold for $2.2 billion was highly due to Ming and his time playing with the franchise a decade before.

"In 2017, the Rockets were sold for a record $2.2 billion, a value that many experts said could have never been reached without Yao Ming." [269]

Ming, outside of his play on the court, played a huge role in the NBA globalizing their game across the world, especially in China. Despite his image, what will his legacy be based on his play on the court?

His playing career was cut short due to the big man curse: lower body injuries. Despite being forced to retire early due to foot injuries, Ming was the perfect center for the game of basketball. His play style was unique yet fundamental and he proved his dominance on the hardwood when healthy. Ming had a great touch at the rim and was quick on his feet compared to other 7-6 centers. If Ming stayed healthy throughout his playing career, the question would rise, on the topic of one of the greatest players to play the game.

Overall, Ming will always be remembered as the NBA globalization pioneer who bridged the game of basketball from North America and the NBA to overseas in Europe and China. He brought the NBA millions of new fans and his legacy will forever be remembered as an NBA globalization pioneer.

> *"Yao Ming was more than a bridge between the East and West,"* Diamond Leung of The Athletic said. *"He was a symbol of hope, enabling talented players around the world to believe their basketball dreams were possible. The NBA became a more accepting place because of him. And in his role as a humanitarian, he continues to leave a legacy."*

Chapter 30

The Brothers from Barcelona

Pau Gasol Saez was born on July 6, 1980 in Barcelona, Spain.[270] His younger brother, Marc Gasol Saez, was born on January 29, 1985 in Barcelona, Spain.[272] Both of their parents worked in the medical field while Pau and Marc grew up. Their father, Agusti Gasol, worked as an administrator while their mother, Marisa Gasol, worked as a doctor. [270] In addition to their work in the medical field, both of their parents played second-division basketball in Spain. The Gasol brothers spent a good amount of their childhood in Cornella, Spain before moving to Sant Boi de Llobregat, a suburb of Barcelona.[270]

Pau's sports career began when he was a young kid playing two sports: soccer and rugby. When Pau grew taller, he picked up the game of basketball but never considered pursuing the sport on the level his parents did. He wanted to become a doctor and join the medical field, following in his parents' footsteps.[270] Despite not wanting to pursue basketball, Pau was very talented compared to the other kids growing up and local coaches and teams started to take notice.

At the age of 16, Pau joined CB Cornella, a feeder club for FC Barcelona.[270] He quickly was promoted to the FC Barcelona junior team then joining the senior team. Pau spent a total of three seasons with FC Barcelona, winning multiple individual and team awards and honors. He is a two-time Spanish League champion and was named the 2001 Spanish League Finals Most Valuable Player. [270]

Following the 2000-01 season, Pau declared for the 2001 NBA Draft. He was well liked by multiple lottery teams and was expected to be selected anywhere in the top 15. When the draft came, Gasol was selected third overall by the Atlanta Hawks but Atlanta was not where he would be playing. His draft rights were a part of a trade that sent him to the Memphis Grizzlies in exchange for Shareef Abdur-Rahim. [274]

While Pau was on his way to Memphis and joining the Grizzlies, his family moved to Memphis. His younger brother Marc attended Lausanne Collegiate School, which is one of the most expensive private schools in Memphis, and following his graduation departed back to Spain to join Pau's former basketball club, FC Barcelona.[276] The high school retired Marc's number 33 jersey following his NBA Draft selection in 2008.

"I think you could say I took a step back in my development," Gasol says of his move from Barcelona to Tennessee. *"In Barcelona, I was*

with the best players in the country, so some of them were close to my
size. Here, I was taller than everyone, so I could score whenever I
wanted. The competition wasn't the same. I wasn't practicing as
much; I was gaining weight." [269]

Marc played with FC Barcelona's youth club when he was six years old while his brother Pau began to become one of Spain top prospects. Marc played three seasons with FC Barcelona before moving to Girona, another top-level team in the same league. With Girona, Marc excelled and was named the ACB's Most Valuable Player in 2008. [276]

Marc, following the 2007-08 season, declared for the 2008 NBA Draft in hopes of joining his older brother in the NBA. Unlike his brother Pau, Marc was not highly scouted by NBA teams and was projected to be a late second round pick. He was selected by the Los Angeles Lakers with the 48th overall pick in the 2008 NBA Draft [275], but like his brother, he was traded. Ironically, a couple months later, he was traded to the Memphis Grizzlies, the team where his brother Pau played and finished his seventh season. Once the trade details became public, Marc was in fact traded for his brother Pau. The Grizzlies traded Pau Gasol and a 2010 second round pick to the Lakers in exchange for a 2010 Aaron McKie, who ironically signed a deal with the Lakers the day before, Jarvaris Crittenton, Kwame Brown, and two first round pick. [273]

For the Lakers, this was their final piece to a championship puzzle. Pau was not viewed as a rental for the Lakers either. He was not only a piece to a championship but a long-term player.

> *"We're extremely pleased to be able to make this trade,"* Mitch
> Kupchak, the Lakers general manager said. *"Pau is a proven player*
> *of all-star caliber in this league who can score and rebound and he's*
> *still a young player. We feel this move strengthens our team in the*
> *short term as well as the long term."* [273]

In the seven seasons Pau spent with the Grizzlies, he averaged 18.8 points and 8.6 rebounds and was named an NBA All-Star in 2006 and won the NBA Rookie of the Year for the 2001-02 season. [274]

For Marc, this was a great opportunity for him in Memphis. Due to his brother now on his way to Los Angeles, the center position needed to be filled and he was granted a starting job. Marc played all 82 games his rookie season, starting in 75, and averaged 30.7 minutes, 11.9 points, 7.4 rebounds, and 1.7 assists per game.[275] His strong rookie year earned Marc Gasol 2009 NBA All-Rookie Second Team.

Marc Gasol went on to play eleven seasons with the Memphis Grizzlies, playing a total of 769 games for the franchise. Out of those 769 games, Gasol started 762 games and averaged 33.7 minutes, 15.2 points, 7.7 rebounds, 3.4 assists, and 1.5 blocks per game.[275] In those eleven seasons, Gasol proved he is in the conversation for the best Grizzlies player all time. He is the franchise leader in multiple statistical categories. Gasol ranks first in minutes played (25,917), field goals made (4,341), 2-Pt Field Goals made (4,040), 2-Pt field goals attempted (8,103), free throws made (2,701), field goals attempted (3,474), defensive rebounds (4,624), total rebounds (5,942), and blocks (1,135). [275] His older brother Pau ranks first in blocks per game with 1.8 blocks. [274]

Both careers of Pau and Marc are similar yet different. Pau, who will be entering his 19th season in the NBA come October, has been a part of five NBA teams. He spent the first seven years of his career with the Memphis Grizzlies, the next seven with the Los Angeles Lakers, two with the San Antonio Spurs, two with the Chicago Bulls, and one with the Milwaukee Bucks. The 2018-19 season did not serve well for Pau as he missed a total of 79 games due to a stress fracture in his foot.[274] In July of 2018, Pau signed a one-year deal with the Portland Trail Blazers, and it is expected to be his last season playing in the NBA. [274]

In his eighteen years in the NBA, Pau has accomplished everything a player can dream of except an NBA Most Valuable Player Award. He is a two-time NBA Champion, a six-time NBA All-Star, named to the All-NBA Second Team twice, and named to the All-NBA Third Team twice as well. Prior to the upcoming 2019-20 season, Pau has played in a total of 1,226 NBA games and has career averaged of 33.4 minutes, 17.0 points, 9.2 rebounds, 3.2 assists, and 1.6 blocks per game. [274]

His younger brother Marc has a decorative NBA resume as well. He won his first NBA Championship with the Toronto Raptors during the 2018-19 season. In addition to his NBA title, Marc is a three-time NBA All-Star, the 2013 NBA Defensive Player of the Year, named to the All-NBA First Team in 2015, and the 2013 All-NBA Second Team. Marc has played a total of eleven seasons in the NBA, splitting time with the Memphis Grizzlies and the Toronto Raptors, and played in a total of 769 games. His career averages are 33.4 minutes, 15.0 points, 7.7 rebounds, 3.4 assists, and 1.5 blocks per game. [275]

After Marc Gasol and the Toronto Raptors were crowned the NBA Champions for the 2018-19 season, not only did the Raptors win their history making title but there was another historic event. Marc and Pau became the first brother in NBA history to both win at least one championship. In fact, Marc won his first NBA Championship on the 10th anniversary of Pau's first NBA championship back in 2009 with the Los Angeles Lakers. [277]

Following Marc's first NBA Championship win, Pau Gasol took to Twitter to publicly congratulate his brother.

Who would have thought? Hours upon hours playing the sport we love since when we were little kids, dreaming of making it big. And now, how wonderful is it that we get to live moments like this one? Enjoy every minute of this historic accomplishment Marc Gasol!

On top of both of their decorative NBA resumes, both Gasol brothers have played for the Spain men's national team. Pau played a total of 16 years for Spain, winning four gold medals, four silver medals, and three bronze medals while Marc has played a total of 10 years, winning three gold medals, three silver medals, and two bronze medals. [274]

The legacy of the Gasol Brothers is much more than the game of basketball. Pau Gasol was a trail blazer for the country of Spain, becoming one of the first players to come over from the country and play in the NBA. Marc Gasol followed his older brother's footsteps and is coming off capturing his first NBA Championship with the Toronto Raptors.

For both brothers, their NBA legacy is not set in stone. It is likely the 2019-20 season will be Pau Gasol's last with the Portland Trail Blazers. Marc, on the other hand, is showing no signs of slowing down and is projected to play a good number of seasons before calling it a career. With their NBA legacies still growing, the Gasol brothers are trail blazers for the country of Spain, proving there is a path to the NBA. On the global scale, outside of their play on the NBA hardwood, the Gasol brothers, as mentioned before, are two of the best players to play for the Spanish men's national team. Overall, the legacies of the Gasol brothers will be forever remembered around NBA globalization.

Chapter 31

The Power of Social Media

The National Basketball Association is one of the most global leagues in the world. Compared to other American professional leagues such as the National Football League and Major League Baseball, the NBA is holding its ground on being the most popular American sports league worldwide. In fact, the sport of basketball is second to soccer in worldwide popularity, largely due to the success of the NBA.

There are many reasons why the NBA has become such a worldwide league, gaining interest from hundreds of countries around the world. It is clear the main reason for their worldwide success is their international talent playing in the league. All the international players listed in this book have either paved the way for fellow countrymen to follow in their footsteps and pursue an NBA dream or are currently representing their country and helping the league grow more worldwide. Besides from the international talent who help grow the NBA worldwide, another huge reason to the league's global success is the power of social media.

Not every fan is not privileged or given the chance in their lives to attend a live NBA game. Due to the league hosting their games inside the United States borders for a huge majority of each season, fans around the world tune into social media to catch up and follow their favorite team. Social media allows fans from all over the world to check what is happening daily in the NBA without any expense. From seeing final scores of games to watching highlights from games, fans do not miss a beat, even if they are a couple thousand miles away or halfway across the world.

> *"From a fan standpoint, [technology] is how we bring our game to our fans on a global basis,"* NBA Commissioner Adam Silver said. *"Only a small percentage of our fans, probably one percent actually experience our games in person, in arenas."* [281]

The NBA has been the most tweeted-about sports league since 2018, according to Twitter themselves, with more than 100 million NBA-related tweets per regular season.[281] Social media platforms will continue to grow each year, with new people joining every day. But why is social media so important for the NBA?

LeBron James, who has been the face of the NBA since his arrival in 2003, has a combined social media following of 94 million at the time of this writing, between the social media platforms of Instagram and Twitter. On the social media platform, FaceBook, James has over 23 million followers as well. That combines to over 100 million in social media followers from all over the world. The NBA's social media accounts, across those same three social media platforms, have a combined 105 million followers.

The NBA is a league driven by the players, rather than the teams and the league itself. Fans across the world are given the opportunity to chat about, like, and follow their favorite players, teams, and the league through social media, giving them a feeling of being a part of the league. When James posts or tweets on any of his social media platforms, hundreds of thousands of his social media followers' comment and like his postings. On top of social media allowing fans to engage with the poster boy of the NBA and other NBA stars and players, social media allows the NBA's players to showcase their lives off the hardwood court.

The NBA was an early adapter to the power of social media when the platforms began to grow in popularity in the late 1990s and early 2000s. On top of their early action, the league does not have many restrictions on what their players can post or talk about on social media. In other words, the league offers transparency to their athletes when it comes to social media.

In recent years, NBA athletes have taken to social media to express their thoughts on the United States and political issues across the world. In 2014, NBA players across the league took to social media to discuss the killing of Eric Garner. In addition to the social media postings related to the Black Lives Matter movement, many of the league's players wore 'I can't breathe' shirts, which was directed towards the Eric Garner incident, to support their stand towards the political issue. The NBA did not protest or limit the peaceful political protests by their players and supported their players stances.

Another example came in 2016 at the ESPN Awards, called the ESPY's. At the 2016 ESPY's, four of the NBA's most popular players took the stage, wearing black suits, and spoke out about racial tensions in the United States. The NBA, once again, supported these four players.

But why is this important? It is very important because the NBA does not struggle with social media postings by players often at all. The National Football League, in the recent years, has struggled with player protests not just on social media but on their sidelines. When compared to other American sports leagues, the players of the NBA have a reputation of being more vocal on political and social issues than any other group of professional athletes. The reason is their league backs their players on social media and does not apply a written rule on what players can and cannot say online or on the big stage.

Another side of social media, that is very beneficial to the NBA, is marketing. The league has done a brilliant job of marketing their teams, players, and sponsors on their social media platforms, with the help of their social media followers.

Back in 2017, the NBA agreed to allow their teams to sell jersey sponsorships, with patches of the business logos near the players' left shoulders on their jerseys. [280] The move was bound to happen, with soccer teams and other professional sports teams across Europe, adopting the business strategy early on, dating back to the 1960s. [260] With the new business move, the NBA became the first league in the big four professional sports leagues in the United States to allow sponsors for their uniforms.

After one season, the NBA's decision to allow sponsorship paid off. Here is an example of the success behind a sponsor patch.

> *IEG/ESP, a division of ad agency WPP that tracks sponsor spending and ROI on the major US sports leagues, came out to say the jersey patches accounted for $137 million of the year's total $1.12 billion, that's a small portion, but that was all just in one NBA season. When this report came out, nine teams did not have sponsors on their jerseys. Going into this season [2018-19], only two teams (Indiana Pacer & Oklahoma City Thunder) do not have sponsors on their logos.* [280]

During the 2018-19 NBA season, the Indiana Pacers partnered with Motorola as their jersey sponsor while the Oklahoma City Thunder partnered with Love's Travel Stops and Country Stores, making all 30 NBA teams have a jersey sponsor. [280]

The business behind the jersey sponsorship patch spreads much further on social media platforms. During an NBA game, it might be hard for viewers to look at what company is represented on their favorite team's jersey. With the power of social media, the business behind the patch goes a long way. Pictures posted, videos of gameplay, and other postings from the game allow viewers to see the patch and investigate it.

Jeff Katz, the General Manager of GumGum Sports, analyzed the exposure from social media platforms and discovered that social media brought in 76 percent of the media value, compared to 24% from television broadcasts.

> *"The jersey patch is just such a unique asset," Katz said. "Especially because during a game, the gameplay is so fast that it might be tough to pick up the jersey patch in a clear way, but on social media,*

typically when you're posting about players, you include a photo that has a player wearing a game jersey, and those are often showcasing the jersey patch. Then with highlight clips as well, they often have a slow-motion and close-ups of players doing spectacular things. It's a tremendous asset that is really defined by social." [280]

Nielson Sports, a company that measures the value of sponsorship, considering the quality of exposures and audience size, analyzed the 2017-18 NBA season and the impact social media made for the league's and their team's sponsors. This was their analysis.

2017-18 NBA season

1.1million- Logo appearances tracked on social media

$490 million- Media value generated via social media for sponsors

20% to 50%- Range of social media's share of total media value

1.5 billion- Fan interactions across Facebook, Twitter, Instagram, and YouTube [280]

As mentioned before, not only does the NBA, their teams, and their players gain more social media followers each day on multiple platforms, but new people join social media every day and those numbers from the 2017-18 season have grown tremendously.

Overall, the power of social media helps the NBA relate and grow their league across the world every single day. From giving their fans access to see what their favorite players are doing off the court, see their interests, and their lifestyles to opening new business partnerships and opportunities for the league, social media is a huge benefactor for the NBA to grow more worldwide every day.

Chapter 32

Faces of NBA Globalization Today

Throughout this book, from the trail blazing players who paved the way for their countries, to players who helped boost the globalization of the NBA, to historic events, the trend of international players coming to play in the NBA has been a historic process. In the history of the NBA, international players faced many types of adversity. From the stereotype of being called 'soft,' or too often being over-hyped, to being listed as a bust early on in their playing careers, the road for international players is not an easy travel.

Prior to the start of the 2018-19 NBA season, there were a total of 108 international players from a record-tying 42 different countries and territories in the league. [284] The number of international players in the NBA equivalents to around 25 percent of the league's total number of players.[284] Out of those 108 international players, Canada led the way with 11 players, followed by Australia with nine, France with nine, Spain with seven, and the countries of Croatia, Serbia, and Turkey each having five players.[284] From a continent standpoint, Europe had 65 players representing in the NBA on opening-night rosters, which is a record. [284]

On top of the 108 international players in the NBA, there are five foreign-born NBA team owners in the NBA. In May of 2010, Russian billionaire Mikhail Prokhorov purchased the New Jersey Nets franchise, becoming the first foreign-born NBA owner.[282] In August of 2018, Prokhorov sold the Nets franchise to Joseph Tsai, the Executive Vice Chairman of Alibaba Group for an NBA-record $2.35 billion. Tsai became the first Chinese owner of an NBA franchise.[282] The other four foreign-born NBA owners are …

- Micky Arison of the Miami Heat (Israel)
- Erik Thohir of the Philadelphia 76ers (Indonesia)
- Vivek Ranadive of the Sacramento Kings (India)
- Larry Tanenbaum of the Toronto Raptors (Canada) [282]

In recent years, there was one event that showcased how the league and their teams were starting to fully invest in global talent. That event was the 2016 NBA Draft.

The 2016 NBA Draft will forever be highlighted as an international dream. The 2016 draft class was full of depth and headlined some of the brightest prospects. Fifteen international players were among the first 30 picks, which set an NBA record for most foreign-born players selected in the first round of an NBA Draft.[285] The previous record was 12 international players in the first 30 picks at the 2013 NBA Draft.[285] Overall, there were not only fifteen international players taken in the 2016 NBA Draft. There was a total of 27 international players selected in the 2016 NBA Draft. The draft consisted of 60 picks so 45 percent of the players selected were international players. [285]

Fast-forward to the most recent NBA Draft, the 2019 NBA Draft. The country of Canada made history, setting the record for most draftees from a non-U.S. country in one NBA Draft with six players. [286] In fact, just one week prior to the 2019 NBA Draft, the Toronto Raptors won the country of Canada their first NBA championship. The previous record for most non-U.S. draftees in one NBA Draft was held by the country of France with five players back in 2016. [285]

RJ Barrett of Duke University was drafted third overall by the New York Knicks, kicking off Canada's historic night. With Barrett being selected, he joined fellow Canadians Anthony Bennett (2013), Kelly Olynyk (2013), Andrew Wiggins (2014), Nik Stauskas (2014), Trey Lyles (2015), Jamal Murray (2016), and Shai Gilgeous-Alexander (2018) as NBA Lottery picks.[286] This also marked the sixth time in the last seven years a Canadian was drafted in the first round of an NBA Draft.[286]

The Canadian players that were available to be drafted were Virginia Tech's Nickeil Alexander-Walker, Michigan's Ignas Brazdeikis, Syracuse's Oshae Brissett, Gonzaga's Brandon Clarke, Arizona State's Luguentz Dort, Florida State's Mfiondu Kabengele, Iowa State's Marial Shayok, and Vanderbilt's Simi Shittu.[286] Ironically enough, Brazdeikis was drafted by the New York Knicks, uniting the two Canadians, Barrett and him, on the same NBA team.

> *"It feels great,"* Barrett said following his selection by the New York Knicks. *"Canadian basketball is really on the rise. You see we have - - like you said, probably six, maybe more, in this draft this year. We have probably four of us going in the first round. So, it's just amazing. Canada basketball is on the rise. We're going to have to cut some NBA players from the team this summer. But it's great."* [286]

> *"It's amazing to be Canadian,"* Barrett said. *"We take a lot of pride. That's why I've got my Canadian flags on this side of my [draft] jacket. To put it on for our country, that means a lot."* [286]

Ironically, Barrett did not play for the Canadian men's national team in the 2019 FIBA World Cup.

Barrett's father, Rowan Barrett is the general manager of Canada Basketball and during his playing career, captained the Canadian men's national team at the 2000 Olympic games. To see the country of Canada, succeed in the 2019 NBA Draft, Rowan Barrett called it a momentous day for the country of Canada and the players drafted.

> *"Today is a momentous day for all our Canadian players drafted into the NBA,"* Barrett said. *"With a record number of Canadians selected in the 2019 NBA Draft, this exemplifies our players reaching for the highest levels in the sport. This growth has not happened overnight and is result of many years of planning, programming, and winning. In addition, recognition needs to be shown to all the coaches within the provincial/territorial sport organizations, clubs, and national team programs for providing these athletes with an opportunity to develop their talent and skills for this moment. As we look at these athletes and those coming behind them, it is exciting to know that our Olympic teams will be well positioned to compete over the next three cycles."* [286]

Canada was the country, outside of the United States borders, that highlighted the 2019 NBA Draft but there was another country that made history as well. Rui Hachimura of Gonzaga became the first Japanese-born player to be drafted into the NBA.[286] Prior to Hachimura, there have only been two Japanese-born players to have appeared in a regular-season NBA game: Yuta Watanabe and Yuta Tabuse.

Yuta Watanabe played in a total of 15 NBA games last season with the Memphis Grizzlies but spent most of the season with the Grizzlies G League affiliate the Memphis Hustle. Tabuse, on the other hand, played in only four regular season games for the Phoenix Suns in 2004. Both players went undrafted and signed undrafted free agent deals.

Hacimura was selected with the ninth overall pick in the 2019 NBA Draft by the Washington Wizards, after a successful three year run with Gonzaga.

> *"It's crazy. It's unreal. It means a lot to me, my family and my country ... I'm just thankful,"* Hachimura said. [286]

The 2019 NBA Draft brought in new international talent into the NBA. As mentioned before, there were a total of 108 international players from 42 different countries prior to the 2019 NBA Draft. Clearly, all 108 international players plus the new additions following the NBA Draft represent their countries on the hardwood and play different roles in boosting the NBA more globally but there are only a handful of active players that are the faces of NBA globalization today. The players that best fit as the active faces of NBA globalization are the best player from each country outside the United States. For this list, Giannis Antetokounmpo and the country of Greece will be explained in the following chapter. The country of Spain was left off and can be found in *The Brothers from Barcelona* chapter.

Ben Simmons - Australia

As just mentioned, Ben Simmons was drafted first overall in the 2016 NBA Draft by the Philadelphia 76ers. Simmons was born in Melbourne, Australia on July 20, 1996. His father, Dave Simmons, is American but played professional basketball overseas in Australia in the National Basketball League at the time of his son Ben Simmons birth. [287] He played a total of 13 seasons in the NBL.

Ben Simmons thrived playing the sport of basketball since he was seven years old. He played with Australia's under-12 team at the age of seven and as he grew up, he continued to grow and become more elite on the hardwood.

In high school, Simmons played with multiple Australian basketball clubs and participated in practices with the Australian men's national team, the Boomers. He helped Australia win silver at the 2012 FIBA World U17 Championship, held in Lithuania and gold at the 2013 FIBA Oceania Championship, held in Australia and in New Zealand.[287] In addition, Simmons was commonly invited to basketball camps in the United States. The camps featured some of the best high school talent in the world.

Instead of playing in Australia's National Basketball League like his father, Simmons decided to declare to Louisiana State University to play college basketball. He spent only one year at LSU before being drafted first overall by the Philadelphia 76ers in 2016. [287]

Simmons missed the 2016-17 season due to a lingering foot injury he suffered in training camp. In the 2017-18 season, Simmons won the NBA Rookie of the Year Award, playing in all 81 games and averaged 33.7 minutes, 15.8 points, 8.1 rebounds, and 8.2 assists per game. [287]

At the time of this writing, Simmons is entering his third season in the NBA and in July of 2019, the 76ers inked him to a new extension worth $170 million over five years.[287] In this first two seasons, on top of his Rookie of the Year award, he was named an All-Star during the 2018-19 season and was named to the 2017-18 NBA All-Rookie First Team. Simmons is the face of

Australia in the NBA and is expected to hold on to that honor for years to come. Other notable NBA players born in Australia include Andrew Bogut, Dante Exum, Joe Ingles, Matthew Dellavedova, Kyrie Irving, and Patty Mills.

Jakob Poeltl – Austria

Jakob Poeltl was born on October 15, 1995 in Vienna, Austria. [288] The 23-year old finished his third season in the NBA with the San Antonio Spurs. He played his first two years in the NBA with the Toronto Raptors, filling a bench role. Poeltl played in 136 games and averaged 15.8 minutes, 5.4 points, 4.1 rebounds, and 0.8 assists per game. With the Spurs, he came off the bench as well, playing in 77 games, averaging 16.5 minutes, 5.5 points, 5.3 rebounds, and 1.2 assists per game. [288]

Poeltl is currently the only player from Austria playing in the NBA and in fact is the only player in the history of the NBA to come from Austria.

Buddy Hield – Bahamas

Chavano Rainer "Buddy" Hield was born on December 17, 1992 in Freeport, Bahamas.[289] Hield moved to the United States before starting freshman year at Sunrise Christian Academy in Bel Aire, Kansas. He was not a highly recruited high school player but proved his worth with the Oklahoma Sooners. Hield spent four years at Oklahoma, playing in a total of 132 games.[289] He went on to win the Naismith Men's College Player of the Year Award in 2016. After establishing himself as one of the best college basketball shooters we have seen in a long time, Buddy Hield continues to shoot the lights out on the NBA hardwood.

In his three seasons in the NBA, Hield has split time with two teams. He was drafted by the New Orleans Pelicans with the sixth pick in the 2016 NBA Draft.[289] Hield played only one season with the Pelican and averaged 20.4 minutes, 8.6 points, 2.9 rebounds, and 1.4 assists per game. [289] His rookie season play earned in 2016-17 NBA All-Rookie First Team honors.

Hield was then traded to the Sacramento Kings in February of 2017.[289] He has played a total of three seasons with the Sacramento Kings and averaged 28.7 minutes, 16.9 points, 4.4 rebounds, and 2.2 assists per game.[289] As he was known in college, Hield is known for his three-point shooting in the NBA. He has shot the three-ball at .419 percent throughout his short NBA career, which is sixth best among active players in the league. [289]

The only other player in the NBA that is a native of the Bahamas is DeAndre Ayton of the Phoenix Suns, who is coming off a solid rookie season.

Both Ayton and Hield donated more than $100,000 in relief efforts for their native Bahamas due to the destruction of Hurricane Dorian.

> *"Buddy uses his basketball platform to help Bahamian people in many ways,"* Emmanuel Basulto said. *"The prime example is the way he raised money for the recent hurricane. Another example is how he hosts an Elite 24 camp for the top 24 basketball players in the Bahamas. The kid stayed at a hotel and practiced with Buddy's coaching team everyday for 5 days."*

Jusuf Nurkic – Bosnia and Herzegovina

Jusuf Nukic was born on August 23, 1994 in Tuzla, Bosnia and Herzegovina. [290] Nicknamed the Bosnian Beast and the Bosnian Bear, Nukic, like many international players, did not play college basketball. He played professional basketball overseas with Cedevita Zagreb for two years before declaring for the 2014 NBA Draft. [290]

He was drafted by the Chicago Bulls with the 16th overall pick but was traded on draft night to the Denver Nuggets. Following a successful rookie season, he was named to the 2014-15 NBA All-Rookie First Team.[290]

Nurkic went on to play three seasons with Denver. He averaged 17.7 minutes, 7.5 points, 5.9 rebounds, 1.1 assists per game.[290] Nurkic was dealt the Portland Trail Blazers in February of 2017. Following the completion of his first season in Portland, Nurkic signed a new deal to remain a Trail Blazer. In his three seasons with Portland, Nurkic has averaged 27.2 minutes, 15.0 points, 9.7 rebounds, and 2.6 assists per game.[290] In March of 2018, Nurkic suffered a leg fracture, which took the league by storm. The injury is likely to set him back till February of the upcoming 2019-20 season.

The only other player from Bosnia and Herzegovina currently playing in the NBA is Brooklyn Nets shooting guard/small forward Dzanan Musa. Mirza Teletovic played in the NBA from 2012-18 and is a native of Bosnia and Herzegovina.

Nene – Brazil

The country of Brazil has produced several NBA players over the past three decades but not many of their players lasted in the league for more than five years. Out of the active players in the league today, Nene is the face of Brazil.

Nene Hilario was born on September 13, 1982 in Sao Carlos, Brazil and has played a total of 17 seasons in the NBA.[291] In those 17 seasons, Nene has been a part of three different NBA teams. Prior to the 2019-20 NBA season, he has played in a total of 965 NBA games and has career averages of 26.2 minutes, 11.3 points, 6.0 rebounds, and 1.8 assists per game. [291]

Other than Nene, there are only two Brazilian natives playing in the NBA: Cristiano Felicio of the Chicago Bulls and Raul Neto of the Utah Jazz.

Joel Embiid – Cameroon

On the continent of Africa, there is one country that has produced some of the brightest NBA international talent in recent years. That country is Cameroon.

Cameroon was never viewed as a country notable for producing any NBA players but over the two decades, the nation has started to produce some of the best international talent. The most notable NBA player to come out of Cameroon is Philadelphia 76ers big man Joel Embiid.

Embiid was born on March 16, 1994 in Yaounde, Cameroon.[293] For the country of Cameroon, it started with Luc Mbah a Moute, who last played with the Los Angeles Clippers for the 2018-19 season. Born in the same town as Embiid, Mbah a Moute was a son of a tribal chief and quickly adapted the leadership skills of life. He was a prince growing up in the town of Yaounde and in his childhood basketball was rarely picked up upon young kids. [292]

Like many international players from countries in Africa, Mbah a Moute began his basketball journey with a bucket as a hoop.

> *"The first thing we did, we got a bucket and cut the bottom of it open and made a post and nailed it on the wall,"* Mbah a Moute said. *"That was our first hoop."* [292]

Mbah a Moute traveled to the United States and was granted a scholarship to play for the University of California Los Angeles (UCLA) for three years before getting drafted into the NBA by the Milwaukee Bucks with the 37th overall pick in the 2008 NBA Draft.[292] His journey to the NBA proved to the young kids in Cameroon that fulfilling a dream to the NBA is not just a dream but can be a reality.

Joel Embiid's father, Colonel Thomas Embiid, was the president of the handball federation in Cameroon. At the age of 16, Embiid was not focused on the game of basketball and was expected to become a professional volleyball player.

"When I was 16, I was supposed to go and become a professional volleyball player," Embiid said. *"My dad thought basketball was too physical for me, so he did not let me play."* [292]

When his father found out that Embiid started to gain an interest in basketball, he was not opposed to it. The only thing he worried was that, at his age, he was picking up the sport too late.

"If you want to play basketball, no problem," Colonel Thomas Embiid said. *"You can start playing basketball."* [292]

At the age of 16, Embiid was on the way to the United States to begin his journey to NBA stardom. With the help of Mbah a Moute, Embiid enrolled at Montverde Academy in Florida.[292] Montverde Academy is not only the alma mater to Mbah a Moute but is known to produce some of college basketball's brightest prospects.

Embiid thrived at Montverde Academy but not with the help of some road blocks along the way. He did not speak English well and had some trouble adjusting to life in a new country under the Montverde lights.

Following his tenure at Montverde Academy, Embiid was a highly recruited high school player and decided to declare to the University of Kansas and play under coach Bill Self. Embiid played only his freshman season at Kansas but suffered a back injury sidelining the big man for the college basketball postseason. He received surgery on his back in June of 2014 and less than a week later, was drafted by the Philadelphia 76ers with the 3rd overall pick in the 2014 NBA Draft.[293]

Embiid would miss both his rookie season, the 2014-15 season, and the 2015-16 season with injuries.[293] While missing 215 games in his first three seasons in the NBA, the question was raised whether Embiid is a draft bust. Despite missing a lot of games, Embiid proved, when on the court and healthy, he is a special NBA center.

When Embiid began to stay healthy and become one of the best centers on both sides of the ball, he wanted to change the outlook of his team.

"Before this year [2018], people were looking at the Sixers like losers," Embiid said. *"One thing I told myself was to really change the culture, then be a leader. It started with me. I had to dive into the stands, carry the offense, defensively be the best defensive player in the league. I really wanted to change the culture."* [292]

Embiid did not only change the culture of the Philadelphia 76ers but the culture of the NBA's global image. Entering his fourth season of play, sixth overall, Embiid is a two-time NBA All-Star, two-time All-NBA, and is a two-time All-Defensive NBA player. His career averages are 30.7 minutes, 24.3 points, 11.4 rebounds, 3.2 assists, and 2.0 blocks per game. [293]

The argument can be made that Embiid is the face of NBA globalization with his dominant play on the court and his story coming from Cameroon, a country not known for producing NBA talent, to become one of the league's best centers.

Some other notable players from Cameroon who are currently playing in the NBA are Pascal Siakam, who won the 2018-19 NBA Most Improved Player Award and an NBA Championship with the Toronto Raptors last season, and as mentioned before, Luc Mbah a Moute, the basketball trail blazer for the country of Cameroon.

Jamal Murray – Canada

As mentioned before, the country of Canada is a booming nation when it comes to producing NBA talent. Bob Hubregs and Hank Biasatti, two of the first international players to play in the NBA, resign from the country of Canada and were the original NBA trail blazers.

Prior to the 2019-20 NBA season, there are 15 NBA players from Canada. Out of those 15 players, some played in the NBA G League last season while others were drafted in the 2019 NBA Draft, Jamal Murray of the Denver Nuggets is the face of Canada in the NBA.

Murray was born in Kitchener, Ontario, Canada on February 23, 1997.[294] He spent his childhood in the province of Ontario, Canada and his dominant high school play landed him a scholarship at the prestigious University of Kentucky to play college basketball under John Calipari. Like many talented college basketball prospects, Murray played for Kentucky for only one year, the 2015-16 season. Following his freshman season, Murray declared for the 2016 NBA Draft, where he was selected by the Denver Nuggets with the 7th overall pick. [294]

In his rookie season, Murray played all 82 games for Denver but came off the bench. He started in only 10 games and averaged 21.5 minutes, 9.9 points, 2.6 rebounds, and 2.1 assists per game. [294] His rookie season play earned Murray 2016-17 All-Rookie honors. The following season, Murray missed only one game and started 80 of the 81 games he played.[294] The

Nuggets point guard is entering his fourth season and is showing consistent growth in his game play.

His career averages heading into the 2019-20 season are 28.5 minutes, 14.8 points, 3.5 rebounds, and 3.4 assists per game.[294] Murray is expected to have a breakout year for the Nuggets in the upcoming season and will be up for a new contract following the 2019-20 season.

Zhou Qi – China

The country of China has emerged as one of the blossoming nations of basketball around the world, despite the ongoing crisis between the NBA and the country. There is an argument that China has the craziest NBA fans in the world but their NBA talent from the country has been slow in recent years. Yao Ming blazed the trail for China when it comes to living an NBA dream and today is the President of the Chinese Basketball Association.

Since Ming, there has only been a handful of Chinese-born basketball players in the NBA. The most recent Chinese native to play in the NBA was Zhou Qi.

Zhou Qi was born in Xinxiang, Henan, China on January 16, 1996.[295] After thriving in the Chinese Basketball Association, Qi decided to declare for the 2016 NBA Draft, where he was selected 46th overall by Ming's former team, the Houston Rockets. [295]

Unlike Ming, Qi was not expected to play a lot of minutes with the Rockets. He did not begin playing with Houston until the 2017-18 season, where he split time with Houston and their NBA G League affiliate, the Rio Grande Valley Vipers.[295] He has played a combined 19 games with the Rockets in both the 2017-18 and the 2018-19 season, and averaged 6.6 minutes, 1.3 points, 1.2 rebounds, and 0.7 blocks per game.[295] With the Vipers, Qi played in a combined 30 games over the past two seasons and averaged 26.3 minutes, 11.2 points, 7.0 rebounds, 2.3 blocks, and 1.3 assists per game. [296] The NBA did not work out as expected for Qi and he returned to China, signing a deal with the Xinjiang Flying Tigers, his former club.[297] He was waived by the Rockets in December of 2018.

Dario Saric – Croatia

The country of Croatia has always been a nation well known for their rising NBA talent. The history goes back to when the country of Croatia was a part of Yugoslavia. It began with Drazen Petrovic, a crafty sharpshooter from Yugoslavia and today, there are several Croatians playing in the NBA.

The face of Croatia in the NBA today is Dario Saric, the Phoenix Suns' power forward. He was born on April 8, 1994 in Sibenik, Croatia, the same hometown as Petrovic.[298] Like Petrovic, Saric became a professional basketball player as a young teenager in 2009 and played for multiple European clubs.

In 2014, Saric declared for the NBA Draft and was projected to be a late lottery pick. When draft day came around, he was selected 12th overall by the Orlando Magic. On draft night, Saric was traded to the 76ers in a package deal for Elfrid Payton. The deal sent Saric, a 2015 second-round pick (Willy Hernangomez), and a 2018 first-round pick (Landry Shamet) to the 76ers for Elfrid Payton. [298]

Despite being drafted by the Magic then traded to Philadelphia, Saric did not play a single game for the NBA franchise and remained overseas until July of 2016, when he signed a multi-year contract. In November of 2018, he was again traded and was on his way to the Minnesota Timberwolves. The trade sent Saric, Jerryd Bayless, Robert Covington, and a 2022 second-round pick to Minnesota for Jimmy Bulter and Jarrett Culver. Following the 2018-19 season, he was traded to the Suns in a package deal to complete a draft day trade. [298]

It is safe to say Saric's NBA career has been a rollercoaster ride, but he has proved his worth in the NBA. In his three seasons in the league, splitting time with two teams, Saric has career averages of 26.9 minutes, 12.7 points, 6.2 rebounds, and 2.1 assists per game prior to starting the 2019-20 season with Phoenix. [298]

Along with Saric, there are six players from Croatia playing in the NBA. The six other players are Ante Zizic, Bojan Bogdanovic, Dragan Bender, Ivica Zubac, Mario Hezonja, and Luka Samanic.

Tomas Satoransky – Czech Republic

Tomas Satoransky was born on October 30, 1991 in Prague, Czechoslovakia. He began his professional basketball career in 2007 and played overseas, splitting time with three European clubs until 2014. [299]

Satoransky was drafted in the 2012 NBA Draft by the Washington Wizards with the 32nd overall pick.[299] Despite being selected, he did not begin playing with the Wizards until 2016 and remained with FC Barcelona Lassa and continued to show he was one of Liga ACB's best players.

Following his first three seasons in the NBA with the Wizards, Satoransky was traded to the Chicago Bulls on July 7, 2019. The deal sent

Satoransky to the Chicago Bulls in exchange for a 2020 second-round pick and a 2022 second-round pick. With the Wizards, Satoransky played in a total of 210 games and averaged 21.6 minutes, 6.6 points, 3.7 assists, and 2.8 rebounds per game. [299]

Satoransky is the only player from the Czech Republic in the NBA at the time of this writing.

Emmanuel Mudiay – Democratic Republic of Congo

Emmanuel Mudiay was born in Kinshasa, Zaire on March 5, 1996.[300] Early in his childhood, Mudiay and his family moved to the United States. They moved to Arlington, Texas and Mudiay attended high school. In high school, Mudiay thrived playing basketball and attended two high schools. His high school play earned him 2013-14 McDonald's All-American honors, which established him as a future NBA prospect.

Unlike most top high school prospects, Mudiay decided to take a unique route to get to the NBA. Instead of accepting any college basketball scholarship offers, Mudiay was on his way to China and play in the Chinese Basketball Association for the Guangdong Southern Tigers for one year.[300] The move gave Mudiay the chance to make a couple million dollars and play against professional basketball competition. Following one year with the Tigers, Mudiay declared for the 2015 NBA Draft.

In the 2015 NBA Draft, Mudiay was selected by the Denver Nuggets with the 7th overall pick. In his rookie year, Mudiay impressed and averaged 30.4 minutes, 12.8 points, 5.5 assists, and 3.4 rebounds per game, earning him 2015-16 All-Rookie NBA honors.[300] Mudiay went on to play three seasons with Denver before being traded at the trade deadline to the New York Knicks.

As part of a 3-team trade, traded by the Denver Nuggets to the New York Knicks, the Dallas Mavericks traded Devin Harris to the Denver Nuggets, and the Denver Nuggets traded a 2018 second-round pick (Shane Milton was later selected) to the Dallas Mavericks; the New York Knicks traded Doug McDermott to the Dallas Mavericks; and the New York Knicks traded a 2018 second-round pick (Justin Jackson was later selected) to the Denver Nuggets. [300]

Mudiay spent two seasons with the New York Knicks and averaged 25.9 minutes, 13.2 points, 3.9 assists, and 3.1 rebounds per game. In the summer of 2019, Mudiay became a free agent and signed with the Utah Jazz.[300]

Other than Mudiay, the only NBA player that represents the Democratic Republic of Congo is Bismack Biyombo. Serge Ibaka, who was born in Congo, but represents and plays for Spain.

Al Horford – Dominican Republic

Al Horford was born on June 3, 1986 in Puerto Plata, Dominican Republic.[301] His father, Tito Horford, played three seasons in the NBA but played most of his career overseas. Horford and his family moved to Michigan around the time of his freshman year of high school.

In high school, Horford quickly became the talk of the state when it came to high school basketball. He thrived on the court and dominated on both ends of the floor. His high school basketball dominance landed Horford an athletic scholarship to the University of Florida. At Florida, Horford was the main piece to a very talented Gators team filled with future NBA players like Corey Brewer, David Lee, Joakim Noah, and Taurean Green.

Horford spent three years at Florida and accomplished just about everything a college basketball player dreams of doing. He is a two-time NCAA Champion, earned NCAA All-Tourney honors, SEC Tournament MVP in 2007, and other individual honors. Horford played in a total of 109 games for the Gators and averaged 25.7 minutes, 10.3 points, 7.9 rebounds, 1.7 assists, and 1.7 blocks per game. [301]

Following his junior season, Horford declared for the 2007 NBA Draft and was drafted third overall by the Atlanta Hawks. In the NBA, Horford has played a total of 12 seasons, splitting time with two NBA teams. In those 12 seasons, Horford is a five-time NBA All-Star and earned 2007-08 NBA All-Rookie honors, 2010-11 All-NBA honors, and 2017-18 NBA All-Defensive honors. [302]

Prior to the start of his 13th season, the 2019-20 season, Horford has played in a total of 786 NBA games and has career averages of 32.8 minutes, 14.1 points, 8.4 rebounds, 3.2 assists, and 1.2 blocks per game. Following the 2018-19 season, Horford became an unrestricted free agent and signed a multi-year deal with the Philadelphia 76ers, joining international stars Ben Simmons and Joel Embiid in the chase for an NBA Championship. [302]

In addition to Horfords NBA career, he represented the Dominican Republic in international competition. As part of the Dominican Republic men's national team, Horford helped lead the team to one gold medal at the 2012 Centrobasket, held in Puerto Rico, and two bronze medals. [301]

Horford is the face of the Dominican Republic in the NBA. The other NBA player that is a native of the Dominican Republic is Angel Delgado.

OG Anunoby – England

OG Anunoby is the only player in the NBA currently from the country of England. He was born on July 17, 1997 in London, United Kingdom.[303] Despite being born in England, Anunoby was raised in Missouri and was well known for his skills on the hardwood. He was named Mr. Basketball in the state of Missouri for his senior high school season and earned an athletic scholarship to Indiana University. [304]

After spending two years at Indiana, Anunoby decided to declare for the 2017 NBA Draft. His play at Indiana was not highly looked upon but he was projected to go in the late first round. He was selected with the 23rd pick by the Toronto Raptors.[303]

Anunoby has played two seasons in the NBA, both with the Raptors, and coveted his first NBA Championship last season. In the two seasons he has played, he has career averages of 20.1 minutes, 6.4 points, 2.7 rebounds, and 0.7 assists per game.[303] He is expected by many to have a breakout season come the 2019-20 season, due to the departure of Kawhi Leonard to the Los Angeles Clippers, freeing up minutes for Anunoby.

Abdel Nader – Egypt

The country of Egypt has only produced two NBA players in their history. Abdel Nader is the only player playing now in the NBA from Egypt. Born on September 25, 1993, in Alexandria, Egypt, Nader had finished his second season in the NBA. [305]

Following three seasons at Iowa State, Nader was selected 58th overall by the Boston Celtics but never held steady ground on an NBA court. He split his rookie season with the Celtics and their NBA G League affiliate, the Maine Red Claw. Despite being sent down often, Nader was named the 2016-17 NBA Development League Rookie of the Year, becoming the first foreign-born player to win the honor. [305]

Prior to the 2018-19 season, he was traded to the Oklahoma City Thunder in exchange for Rodney Purvis. [305] Like his time in Boston, Nader split time with the Thunder and their NBA G League affiliate, the Oklahoma City Blue.

Nader is expected to see more time in the NBA as a member of the Thunder for the 2019-20 season.

Lauri Marrkanen – Finland

Lauri Marrkanen was born on May 22, 1997 in Vantaa, Finland.[306] Growing up, basketball was the main sport Marrkanen played and thrived at. He attended high school at Helsinki Academy in Helsinki, Finland, becoming the country's talked about basketball player with NBA. His name started to circulate around Finland due to his elite play with HBA-Marsky, a second-tier league basketball team in the Finnish league.[306] He spent two seasons with the team, from 2014-16, before enrolling at the University of Arizona to play college basketball in the United States.

At Arizona, Marrkanen only played his freshman season before declaring for the 2017 NBA Draft. It was expected Marrkanen would be a one-and-done player prior to the 2017-18 season due to his elite play with the Wildcats. His freshman year play earned him 2016-17 All-Pac 12 honors, 2017 All-Pac 12 honors, and Pac-12 All-Freshman honors. [306]

In the 2017 NBA Draft, he was selected by the Minnesota Timberwolves with the 7th overall pick but was dealt on draft night to the Chicago Bulls in a package deal involving Kris Dunn, Justin Patton, and Zach LaVine.[306]

Marrkanen has played two seasons in the NBA, both with the Bulls. In those two seasons, Marrkanen has played in a total of 120 games and has career averages of 30.9 minutes, 16.7 points, 8.2 rebounds, and 1.3 assists per game.[306] He is expected to have a breakout year in 2019-20 and there is no question he is the face of the country of Finland in the NBA.

Ruby Gobert – France

The country of France has established itself as a hot spot for producing NBA talent. Tony Parker was the face of France in the NBA held the throne for 19 years but following his retirement, Rudy Gobert has taken that throne.

Gobert was born on in Saint-Quentin, France on June 26, 1992.[307] He started to make a name for himself in France playing for Cholet Basket of the French League. Following three seasons with Cholet, Gobert declared for the 2013 NBA Draft and was selected with the 27th overall pick by the Utah Jazz.[307] Coming into the NBA, many thought the French big man was not ready to compete with other centers. He was viewed as physically under sized and was going to be bullied in the post.

Gobert spent his rookie season splitting time with the Jazz and their NBA G League affiliate, the Bakersfield Jam, to develop his game. He would only play 45 games with the Jazz and averaged 9.6 minutes, 2.3 points, and 3.4 rebounds per game.[307] His career began to blossom during the 2016-17 NBA season, where he played and started in 81 games for the Jazz and averaged 33.9 minutes, 14.0 points, 12.8 rebounds, and 2.6 blocks per game.[307] The French big man has played a total of six seasons in the NBA, all with Utah, and has career averages of 28.7 minutes, 11.1 points, 10.5 rebounds, and 2.2 blocks per game. [307]

Nicknamed the stifle tower, the French rejection and Gobzilla, Gobert was very close to being voted in as a first-time NBA-All Star last season, the 2018-19 season, but fell short in votes. Prior to the 2019-20 season, Gobert is a two-time NBA Defensive Player of the Year award winner, earned two All-NBA honors, is a three-time All-Defensive team honoree, and is expected to have a breakout year for the Jazz next season.[307] He is the glue for the Jazz and is one of the best centers currently playing in the NBA. As a member of the French national team, Gobert helped lead the team to two bronze medals. He played with France in the 2019 FIBA World Cup. [307]

The other current NBA players from France are Evan Fournier, Elie Okobo, Frank Ntilikina, Guerschon Yabusele, Ian Mahinmi, Joakim Noah, Nicolas Batum, and Timothe Luwawu-Cabarrott.

Zaza Pachulia – Georgia

Zaza Pachulia was born on February 10, 1984 in Tbilisi, Georgia.[308] At the time of his birth, the country of Georgia was a part of the Soviet Union.

Pachulia played with Ulkerspor from 1999-2003, a Turkish basketball club. He was a growing teenager when he started playing with the Turkish basketball club.[308] While with Ulkerspor, Pachulia became one of the Turkish league's best players and was viewed as an NBA prospect. Following the 2002-03 season, Pachulia declared for the 2003 NBA Draft.

He was selected 42nd overall by the Orlando Magic in the 2003 NBA Draft but was only a member of the team for one season. In the 2004 expansion draft, Pachulia was selected by the Charlotte Bobcats, a new NBA team at the time. One day later, he was on the move again, being dealt to the Milwaukee Bucks for a 2004 second-round pick, which ended up being Bernard Robinson.[308] Following just one season with the Bucks, Pachulia signed with the Atlanta Hawks as a free agent. He spent a total of seven years with the NBA franchise, his longest tenure with an NBA team in his career. [308]

After a seven-year stint with Atlanta, Pachulia has been a member of four other NBA teams and played overseas with Galatasaray in with 2011, another Turkish club.[308] At the time of this writing, he is a member of the Detroit Pistons.

His NBA career will always be shadowed by his dirty play. Pachulia has labeled himself as a dirty player following several hard-foul plays and dirty plays. His most infamous dirty play came in the game one of the 2017 Western Conference Finals against the San Antonio Spurs, where Pachulia landed dangerously close to Kawhi Leonard as he shot a three-point shot. The play resulted in Leonard suffering an ankle injury, sidelining him for the rest of the playoffs and arguably costing the Spurs another championship. The NBA, in response to Pachulia's play, now carefully calls those kinds of plays and the player at fault will receive a possible technical or flagrant foul.

Aside from Pachulia's harsh image and is two NBA Championships, he is a trail blazer for the country of Georgia in the NBA. He has the longest NBA tenure out of any player from the country of Georgia and is the only player from Georgia currently playing in the NBA.

Dennis Schroder – Germany

The face of Germany, when it comes to the NBA, is Dirk Nowitzki. Nowitzki helped pave the way for Germans who dream of playing in the NBA and helped the league globalize the game of basketball across the world.

Due to Nowitzki officially stepping away from the game of basketball, following a historic 21 year run in the NBA, the face of Germany playing in the NBA currently is Dennis Schroder.

Schroder was born on September 15, 1993 in Braunschweig, Germany.[310] He began his professional basketball career with Phantoms Braunschweig, a local basketball club in Germany. Like Nowitzki, Schroder made an international name for himself at the 2013 Nike Hoops Summit in Portland, Oregon and led his team to the win, attracting serious interest from multiple NBA scouts.[309] Following a three-year run with his local club, Schroder declared for the 2013 NBA Draft, where he was selected 17th overall by the Atlanta Hawks. [310]

Schroder will be entering his seventh season in the NBA come the 2019-20 season. In his six years in the league, the German guard has been a part of two NBA teams, the Hawks and the Oklahoma City Thunder, and has bounced around in the NBA G League in the early years of his career. He has played a total of 431 games and has career averages of 24.7 minutes, 13.4 points, 2.7 rebounds, and 4.6 assists per game.[310] Schroder, throughout his NBA career, has primarily came off the bench.

The other players from Germany who also play in the NBA are Daniel Theis, Isaiah Hartenstein, Issac Bonga, Maxi Kleber, and Mortiz Wagner.

Skal Labissiere – Haiti

The country of Haiti is not known for producing NBA talent. Skal Labissiere is only one of three players in the NBA's history to come from the country of Haiti.

Born on March 18, 1996, in Port-au-Prince, Haiti, Labissiere moved to the United States with his family at a young age.[311] He attended Lausanne Collegiate School in Memphis, Tenessee and thrived at the game of basketball. In fact, he attended the same high school as Marc Gasol, an NBA legend and trail blazer from the country of Spain. Following high school, Labissiere attended the University of Kentucky on an athletic scholarship to play under coach John Calipari.

In college, Labissiere was projected to be one of college basketball's best players for the 2015-16 season. After just one season at Kentucky, he declared for the 2016 NBA Draft, where he was selected 28th overall by the Phoenix Suns. On draft night, just less than an hour after his selection, he was dealt to the Sacramento Kings.[311]

Labissiere is entering his fifth season in the NBA, splitting time with the Sacramento Kings and the Portland Trail Blazers. In addition to being a part of two NBA teams, Labissiere bounced around in the NBA G League, as a member of the Reno Bighorns, the affiliate of the Kings. His NBA career averages are 17.6 minutes, 7.6 points, 4.3 rebounds, and 1,0 assists per game in 115 games. [311]

Omri Casspi – Israel

Omri Casspi was born on June 22, 1988 in Holon, Israel.[312] Casspi began his professional basketball career with Maccabi Tel Aviv, a powerhouse basketball club in the country of Israel before declaring for the 2009 NBA Draft, where he was selected by the Sacramento Kings, a franchise notorious for drafting international players. [312]

Casspi spent a total of 10 season in the NBA, splitting time with seven NBA franchises. He played in a total of 588 NBA games and has career averages of 20.3 minutes, 7.9 points, 4.0 rebounds, and 1.1 assists per game.[312] At the time of this writing, Casspi plays for Maccabi Tel Aviv, the club where it all began for the forward from Israel. He last played in the NBA during the

2018-19 season but was waived by the Memphis Grizzlies on February 7, 2019.
[312]

The only other active NBA player from Israel is TJ Leaf of the Indiana Pacers.

Danilo Gallinari – Italy

As mentioned earlier in this book, Mike D'Antoni was one of the first international trail blazers to take their talents and play in the NBA. Since his playing career, Italy has stayed consistent when it comes to producing NBA talent. Back in 2006, Italian forward Andrea Bargnani was selected with the 1st overall pick in the NBA Draft, making him the first European drafted number one. [313]

Today, Danilo Gallinari is the face of Italy in the NBA. Born on August 8, 1988 in Sant'Angelo, Lodigiano, Italy, Gallinari has played a total of 11 seasons in the NBA, splitting time with three NBA franchises.[313] He was drafted with the 6th overall pick in the 2008 NBA Draft by the New York Knicks, following a six-year run in the Italian League, splitting time with three clubs. Nicknamed Il Gallo, he has played in a total of 549 games and has career averages of 31.1 minutes, 15.9 points, 4.9 rebounds, and 2.0 assists per game. [313] Gallinari is currently a member of the Oklahoma City Thunder.

Aside from Gallinari, the only two other Italian born players in the league are Marco Bellinelli and Ryan Arcidiacono.

Kristaps Porzingis – Latvia

Nicknamed 'The Unicorn' by NBA All-Star and future Hall of Famer Kevin Durant, Kristaps Porzingis was born on August 2, 1995 in Liepaja, Latvia.[314]

Growing up, Porzingis began his basketball career training and practicing with his brother Janis, who played professionally in Europe, at a young age. At age 15, Porzingis joined his first basketball team, BK Liepajas Lauvas, a very well-known basketball club in his hometown of Liepajas.[315] His play at BK Liepajas Lauvas was above average compared to the leagues other star players. In 2011, following his agent posting and sending videos of Porzingis dunking and shooting from all areas of the court, Baloncesto Sevilla of Liga ACB in Spain, requested for him to come to work out for the team.[316] Sevilla, at the time, was looking for young talent to fill their junior squads and add final pieces to their actual club team.

> *"I came here with my brother for two or three days, but it was really hot and I couldn't play at my best because of that,"* Porzingis said. *"Still, I received a contract in summer 2010 and I signed it."* [315]

The reason for Porzingis' struggles to play in heat was due to anemia, a lack of red blood cells that causes someone to feel fatigue, shortness of breath, and makes them unable to exercise it. On top of his struggles with anemia, Porzingis, like any other person moving to a new country, struggled to learn the language of Spanish.

With a mixture of struggles lingering behind the play of Porzingis, he was very nervous but playing with other players his age helped boost his confidence.

> *"I was very nervous at the beginning: I wanted to do well and not pick up turnovers,"* Porzingis said. *"At the same time, I got a lot of confidence with players of my same age. That allowed me to play better with the first team and practice with more confidence."* [315]

Despite the concerns, Porzingis thrived with Sevilla, quickly jumping from youth squads to the senior team in 2013. Porzingis initially entered the 2014 NBA Draft but withdrew due to the recovering from the 2013-14 season with Sevilla.[315] The following year, 2015, Porzingis declared for the 2015 NBA Draft with four seasons at Sevilla under his belt. His most notable accomplishment during his four years with Sevilla was winning the EuroCup Rising Star award in 2015, becoming the youngest player to win the award (18). [315]

Prior to the 2015 NBA Draft, Porzingis was projected to be a lottery pick, who can surprisingly go in the top five. Due to him being from Europe, many draft experts compared him to other past European talent who played in the NBA like Dirk Nowitzki, which is not a bad player to be compared to.

Porzingis has always been a player that consistently works at his craft and wants to get better and better each day. This traces back to his European basketball days and now in America, he finds it great that there will always be a place to train and work no matter what time it is.

> *"The biggest thing for me – the thing that I think most about – is that you can get into the gym whenever you want here,"* Porzingis said. *"They give you a card, or a key, and in the middle of the night, if you want to work out, you just go to the gym and get your work in – and I think that's amazing."* [315]

"In Europe, you don't have that option," Porzingis said. *"You can't get your work in on a Sunday, because nobody is there. I think that's one of the coolest things. This year, I didn't have a place to play. I've got to talk to the GM, to talk one of the people who work in the arena to open the door for me. People don't want to do extra work at the arena."* [315]

Coming into the 2015 NBA Draft, Porzingis carried something most international players do not have, a good mindset. That is the way the American public sees a young European player, especially tall and skinny. In other words, the word bust did not faze him.

Porzingis has an innate awareness about the way the American public sees a young, long European teenager. He comes to the NBA with the full understanding that popular basketball culture declares him guilty until proven innocent of the basketball crimes of Darko Milicic and Nikoloz Tskitishvili and Andrea Bargnani. He's considered a stiff, a bust, a blown lottery pick until he doesn't become one – Adrian Wojnarowski of Yahoo Sports. [316]

"There are guys who have had incredible NBA careers – like Dirk [Nowitzki] and the Gasols [Pau and Marc] – and there are guys who haven't. They'll say, this guy is a bust. He'll be Tskitishvili, this Georgian guy. Bargnani, Darko ... That's why I am talking, because I want the fear to go away from me. I want people to get to know me. I don't want to be the mystery man from Europe." [316]

"Some fans – they don't want a European on their team," Porzingis said. *"People have opinions, but maybe they've never seen me play. There's nothing I can say, only I can go out and prove myself."* [316]

One call that Porzingis did not like back when he was scouted was being labeled as soft, a common term referenced with international players.

"I don't like being labeled soft," Porzingis said. *"I'm very hungry. I love the game. I've got to prove to coaches and GMs that I'm not soft just because I'm from Europe. They need to see that I'm not just some skinny white guy, that I'm going to be there fighting. They'll need to see that I'm a worker who's going to play hard, and play tough ..."* [315]

In the 2015 NBA Draft, Porzingis was selected by the New York Knicks with the 4th overall pick.[314] Following his selection, a series of boos and confused heads arose from the Barclays Center crowd, which was filled with

Knicks fans. The most memorable draft reaction was a young Knicks fan crying, thinking his team blew a great chance at choosing a franchise changing player.

Stefan Bondy, who covers the New York Knicks for the *New York Daily News*, saw the growth of the Latvian superstar from when he was drafted to where he is today. He compares the draft reaction of Porzingis to the drafting of Frederic Weis in 1999, an international bust.

> *"He opened certainly New York's eyes to a different kind of European player,"* Stefan Bondy of the *New York Daily News* said. *"When the Knicks drafted Frederic Weis, the moment Kristaps was drafted, everybody just thought back to that day. But obviously, he was anything but Frederick Weis so he certainly opened New York's eyes to the possibility of European players."*

Despite being booed, Porzingis was unfazed and absorbed the moment of finally making it to the NBA. It was clear, many NBA fans, especially Knick fans, have either never heard of Porzingis or never seen him play basketball before. Prior to his selection, Porzingis received quite the compliments from some of the NBA's greatest players in the recent years.

> *"I love his face-up game,"* Kevin Garnett said. *"He's got that mid-range shot. I've seen a lot of tape where he plays against guys like Shaq [O'Neal], a guy he can't bang inside with. So faces up, does his little step-back move ... amazing."*[316]

> *"That step-back he has, how he uses his body to get a little contact – he's a master,"* LaMarcus Aldridge said. *"He steps back to get the distance, to get his shot off."* [316]

> *"When he gets the ball, he's already making his move,"* Anthony Davis said. *"He's so aggressive going to the basket, getting fouled. And he's extending his range."* [316]

In his rookie year, Porzingis impressed, proving he was not going to be another European player added to the historic lottery pick bust conversation. He played and started 72 games and averaged 28.4 minutes, 14.3 points, 7.3 rebounds, 1.9 blocks, and 1.3 assists per game. His play earned him 2015-16 All-Rookie honors. [314]

Porzingis went on to spend three seasons with the Knicks, before demanding a trade. In those three seasons, the Latvian superstar averaged 31.0 minutes, 17.8 points, 7.1 rebounds, 2.0 blocks, and 1.3 assists per game. [314] His third season was cut short due to a devastating knee injury, which sidelined him for the rest of the 2017-18 season. He did not play one game for the Knicks or the Dallas Mavericks in 2018-19.

On January 31, 2019, Porzingis and the Knicks made NBA headlines. Porzingis went to the Knicks front office and demanded a trade out of New York. If the Knicks did not cooperate and get a deal done within the next few days, Porzingis threatened to go back and play in Europe. Just a couple hours later, the deal was done, he was a Dallas Maverick.

The trade sent Porzingis, Courtney Lee, Tim Hardaway Jr., and Trey Burke to the Mavericks in exchange for DeAndre Jordan, Dennis Smith Jr., Wesley Matthews, a 2021 first-round pick, and a 2023 first round pick. [314]

At the time of this writing, it is still unclear exactly why Porzingis, suddenly, wanted out of New York. Despite demanding a trade, Porzingis changed New York's views on drafting European players forever. From two past failures in Frederick Weis, who's most famously known for being jumped over on a dunk by Vince Carter in the Olympics, to selecting Andrea Bargnani with the 1st overall pick in 2006, Porzingis brought new light on international players in New York.

Despite being traded, Porzingis was entering his first summer as an unrestricted free agent. Following the trade to Dallas, it was clear Porzingis was very likely to remain a Maverick and play alongside Luka Doncic, another one of the league's brightest international talents. On July 12, 2019, Porzingis agreed to a multi-year deal to remain with his new team, the Dallas Mavericks. [314]

The NBA career of Kristaps Porzingis is unique compared to other recent international players. Today, the Latvian superstar has the potential to become an NBA MVP when he hits his prime years or even sooner. That will certainly be determined based on if he returns as the same player he was before his knee injury. To Stefan Bondy, Porzingis is different than some of the European players who came before him. In fact, Porzingis grew up loving the music genre of hip-hop. In addition, he had cornrows as a kid and idolized American NBA players.

> *"I think what he brought, obviously Dirk [Nowitzki] came before him and similar types of players but what Porzingis brought was a kind of swagger that you typically did not see with European players,"* Stefan Bondy said. *"His put back dunks were sometimes spectacular, his blocks, and he had a different persona than some of the European players that came before him."*

"He loved hip-hop," Stefan Bondy said. *"One of the pictures of him as a kid, he has cornrows. He had that different element to him. He grew up idolizing American players like Allen Iverson, so he was different from the previous Europeans."*

Kristaps Porzingis is the face of Latvia in the NBA. Other than Porzingis, Davis Bertans and Rodions Kurucs are the only two active NBA players from the small European country. Despite being from a small country, Kristaps Porzingis is one of the biggest faces of NBA Globalization playing in the NBA today.

Jonas Valanciunas – Lithuania

Jonas Valanciunas was born on May 6, 1992 in Utena, Lithunia. Prior to coming to the NBA, Valanciunas played for two professional European basketball clubs: Perlas Vilnius and Lietuvos Rytas Vilnius in his home country of Lithuania. [317]

Following his first season with Lietuvos Rytas Vilnius in 2011, he declared for the 2011 NBA Draft. Valanciunas was viewed as one of the top centers in all of Europe and was the best center available for selection. He was selected with the 5th overall pick by the Toronto Raptors, but did not come over to the NBA for another year.[317]

He played with Toronto for seven years, 2012-19, before being traded to the Memphis Grizzlies in a deal that involved Marc Gasol, another international center. The trade sent Valanciunas, C.J. Miles, Delon Wright, and a 2024 second-round pick to Memphis in exchange for Marc Gasol, who was the Raptors final piece to their 2018-19 NBA Championship team.[317] On July 11, 2019, Valanciunas signed a new deal with the Grizzlies to remain with the franchise. In seven seasons, the Lithuanian big man has played in 489 NBA games and has career averages of 25.2 minutes, 12.1 points, 8.5 rebounds, and 1.0 blocks per game. [317]

Jonas Valanciunas is the face of Lithuania in the NBA today. Domantis Sabonis, who is the son of Arvydas Sabonis, one of the greatest international bigs to play in the NBA, was born and raised in the United States. Other than Sabonis and Valanciunas, the only other player from Lithuania, currently playing in the NBA, is Donatas Motiejunas.

Cheick Diallo – Mali

Born on September 13, 1996 in Kayes, Mali, Cheick Diallo moved to the United States at a young age.[318] He played college basketball at the University of Kansas, under Bill Self, for only his freshman season before declaring for the 2016 NBA Draft, where he was selected by the Los Angeles Clippers with the 33rd overall pick.[318] Despite being drafted by the Clippers, he was traded on draft night to the New Orleans Pelicans. Diallo has played three seasons in the NBA and a total of 133 games. He has career averages of 12.6 minutes, 5.5 points, 4.6 rebounds, and 0.4 assist per game. [318]

Other than Diallo, Sagaba Konate is the only other active NBA player from the country of Mali.

Steven Adams – New Zealand

The country of New Zealand is a nation where basketball continues to grow. The National Basketball League, also known as the NBL, has one team from the country of New Zealand called the New Zealand Breakers. In the NBA, there is currently only one player from the country of New Zealand.

Steven Adams was born on July 20, 1993 in Rotorua, New Zealand.[319] Adams moved to the United States when he was in high school and attended Notre Dame Prep in Fitchburg, Massachusetts. Following high school basketball play and graduating, Adams returned home to and played for the Wellington Saints of the NBL, winning the league's championship in 2011. [319] Unlike most international players, Adams next journey was to play college basketball at the University of Pittsburgh for one year. Following his freshman season, Adams declared for the 2013 NBA Draft, where he was selected 12th overall by the Oklahoma City Thunder.[319]

The New Zealand big man has played a total of six seasons in the NBA, all with the Thunder. He had an impressive rookie season, playing in 81 games coming off the bench, and averaged 14.8 minutes, 3.3 points, 4.1 rebounds, and 0.7 blocks per game, earning 2013-14 All-Rookie honors. [319]

Steven Adams is the face of New Zealand in the NBA and is the only active player from the country in the league.

Josh Okogie – Nigeria

Josh Okogie was born on September 1, 1998 in Lagos, Nigeria.[320] He moved to the United States, along with his family, at a young age and attended Shiloh High School in Snellville, Georgia, where he thrived playing basketball. His play earned him a scholarship to Georgia Tech University, where he spent two years before declaring for the 2018 NBA Draft.

In the 2018 NBA Draft, Okogie was selected by the Minnesota Timberwolves with the 20th overall pick. He impressed in his rookie year, playing in 74 games, primarily coming off the bench, and averaged 23.7 minutes, 7.7 points, 2.9 rebounds, 1.2 steals, and 1.2 assists per game.[320]

Josh Okogie is the face and the future of Nigeria in the NBA. He is expected to have another good season with the Timberwolves in 2019-20. Other than Okogie, Al-Farouq Aminu is the only other active player from Nigeria playing in the league today.

Marcin Gortat – Poland

Born on February 17, 1984 in Lodz, Poland, Marcin Gortat is one of the greatest players in NBA history from the country of Poland.[321] Prior to coming to the NBA, Gortat played with two European basketball clubs before being selected in the 2005 NBA Draft with the 57th overall pick by the Phoenix Suns. Despite being selected in the 2005 NBA Draft, Gortat made his NBA debut in 2007 with the Orlando Magic.

Gortat has played 12 NBA seasons, splitting time with four teams. He has played in 806 NBA games and has career averages of 25.7 minutes, 9.9 points, 7.9 rebounds, 1.2 blocks, and 1.1 assists per game.[321] The Polish big man is currently the only active NBA player from Poland playing in the NBA.

J.J. Barea – Puerto Rico

Jose Juan Barea was born on June 26, 1984 in Mayaguez, Puerto Rico.[322] Barea and his family moved to the United States prior to Barea attending high school. He went to Miami Christian School in Miami, Florida. Following high school, Barea received a scholarship to play college basketball at Northeastern University, where he spent all four years. Barea went undrafted in the 2006 NBA Draft but signed with the Dallas Mavericks on August 11, 2006 to begin his NBA career. [322]

The Puerto Rican point guard has played in a total of 13 seasons in the NBA, splitting time with the Mavericks and the Minnesota Timberwolves.[322] Barea was a critical player in the 2011 NBA Finals as a member of the Dallas Mavericks team that took down 'The Big Three' and the Miami Heat, winning the 2011 NBA Championship. He currently plays for the Mavericks at the time of this writing.

In his 13 years in the NBA, Barea has played in 802 games, serving primarily as a bench player, and has career averages of 19.7 minutes, 9.0 points, 3.9 rebounds, and 2.1 rebounds per game. [322]

Barea is currently the face of Puerto Rico in the NBA and is the only active player from the country in the league. Bryan Fonseca, an on-air talent and journalist based in New York City, and co-hosts the *Ain't Hard to Tell Podcast*, believes what makes Barea unique is his fight, which is a common narrative for professional athletes native of Puerto Rico. To Fonseca, Puerto Rico is an island where you earn respect and Barea continues to follow that narrative.

> *"When thinking of the most revered athletes from Puerto Rico, they're typically fighters,"* Bryan Fonseca said. *"Not always in a literal sense – although, that would be the case with Felix Trinidad, Miguel Cotto, Wilfredo Gomez, and others. But in order to make it to a certain point as an undersized athlete, that requires a substantial amount of overcoming despite your diminutive stature, which the 6-foot JJ Barea has accomplished by merely being in the NBA since 2006 – out of Northeastern University, no less. That's before we get to his performances in the 2011 Finals opposite of LeBron James. None of that happens without fight. Neither does Carlos Arroyo's 24 points, seven assists and four steals against Team USA in the 2004 Olympics. Arroyo – like Barea – is listed around 6-feet tall and reached the NBA after dominating at a mid-major, which seldom produces high-level pros (Florida International University) and spent around a decade in the league. Puerto Rico is an island where respect means everything, and in order to earn said respect, you'll have to fight for it. On (and off) the hardwood, that's what Arroyo did, and that's what Barea continues to do."*

Timofey Mozgov – Russia

Timofey Mozgov was born on July 16, 1986 in St. Petersburg, Russia. [323] Prior to arriving in the NBA, Mozgov played a total of six years in Russia, splitting time with three basketball clubs. In 2008, Mozgov decided to declare for the 2006 NBA Draft but went undrafted. [323]

On July 13, 2010, Mozgov signed with the New York Knicks, beginning his NBA career. He has played in a total of eight seasons in the league, splitting time with five NBA teams. In those eight seasons, Mozgov played in a total of 454 games and has career averages of 18.0 minutes, 6.8 points, 4.9 rebounds, and 0.8 blocks per game. [323]

The Russian center has struggled not only to stay with one NBA team throughout his NBA career but was waived by the Orlando Magic on July 6, 2019.[323] The move may possibly be the last time Mozgov will play in the NBA. He currently plays for BC Khimki in his home country of Russia.

Despite his NBA struggles, Mozgov is the face of Russia when it comes to NBA basketball in recent years. There are currently zero players from Russia playing in the league prior to the start of the 2019-20 NBA season.

Gorgui Dieng – Senegal

Gorgui Dieng was born on January 18, 1990 in Kebemer, Senegal.[324] Along with his family, Dieng moved to the United States prior to his high school years. He attended Huntington Prep in Huntington, West Virginia. The high school is well-known for producing professional athletes in multiple professional leagues. Following high school, Dieng played three seasons at the University of Louisville, under coach Rick Pitino, before declaring for the 2013 NBA Draft, where he was selected 21st overall by the Utah Jazz. On draft night, he was traded to the Minnesota Timberwolves, along with Shabazz Mohammed, in exchange for Trey Burke. [324]

Dieng has played a total of six seasons in the NBA, all with the Timberwolves. He has played in 452 games, primarily serving as a bench player, with career averages of 22.7 minutes, 8.0 points, 6.2 rebounds, 1.0 blocks, and 0.8 steals per game. [324]

Aside from Dieng, Georges Niang and rookie Tacko Fall are the only other active NBA players from the country of Senegal. Dieng is the face of Senegal in the NBA today.

Nikola Jokic – Serbia

Nikola Jokic was born on February 19, 1995 in Sombor, Serbia.[325] Prior to being drafted into the NBA, Jokic played with Mega Basket, a local professional basketball club in Serbia. His play with Mega Basket was not highly scouted but he declared for the 2014 NBA Draft, where he was selected by the Denver Nuggets with the 41st overall pick. [325]

Jokic has risen from being a late second-round draft selection to a potential future NBA Most Valuable Player candidate. In his four seasons with the Nuggets, Jokic has played in 308 games and has career averages of 11.9 minutes, 16.9 points, 9.6 rebounds, 5.1 assists, 1.1 steals, and 0.7 blocks per game.[325] He is a one-time NBA All-Star and earned All-NBA First Team honors for the 2018-19 season. This past season, the 2018-19 season, Jokic has a career year and averaged 20.1 points, 10.8 rebounds, 7.3 assists, 1.4 steals, and 0.7 blocks per game. [325]

On top of his career year last season, Jokic became the third youngest player in NBA history to reach 20 triple doubles, joining Magic Johnson and Oscar Robertson.[325] He finished the season as one of two players in the league to lead their team in points, rebounds, and assists. The other player was LeBron James.[325] His play earned Jokic to be in the conversation for 2018-19 NBA Most Valuable Player. On Denver, he is the leader of the team.

> *"There's going to be much asked of him now that he's our franchise player,"* Denver Nuggets head coach Michael Malone said. *"He hasn't shied away from that ... All eyes are on him at all times, and he's embraced that, and I think he's doing a hell of a job with it."* [326]

Jokic, nicknamed 'The Joker' is the face of Serbia in the NBA and is one of the greatest international players the league has seen in a while. He is an all-around center who can shoot, pass, and dribble anywhere on the court.

Other than Jokic, Alen Smailagic, Boban Marjanovic, Marko Guduric, and Milos Teodosic represent the country of Serbia in the NBA today.

Luka Doncic – Slovenia

The country of Slovenia is starting to produce a good number of NBA talent over the past several years. Out of the several past NBA players from Slovenia, there is one player that has dominated and is the face of Slovenia in the NBA. His name is Luke Doncic

Doncic was born on February 28, 1999 in Ljubljana, Slovenia.[327] He began his professional basketball career with Liga ACB powerhouse Real Madrid in 2015 and has become a basketball global icon ever since. He spent a total of three years with Real Madrid, winning almost every award, individual and team, a player can dream of. [328]

On June 29, 2018, Luka Doncic said goodbye in a long letter to Real Madrid and hello to the Dallas Mavericks of the NBA.

> *Dear madridistas,*
>
> *Playing basketball means everything to me. My mum always says that she can never recall me doing anything but bouncing a basketball.*
>
> *I can't remember doing anything else either.*
>
> *I feel very fortunate. When I was 13, I came to Madrid, where I intended on making my dream of becoming a good basketball player come true. What I never imagined is that that journey would be the start of an adventure which would see not just one, but two of my dreams, which are the kind you only see in films, come true: I've played for the best club in the world and now, I'm going to play in the*

best league on the planet.

The special thing about basketball is that it's one of the sports in which you depend most heavily on your teammates. When I say that, I'm not just referring to the brilliant players that I've been lucky enough to share a court with and who have allowed me to learn with them, both as professionals and human beings. A team is made up of a lot of people: the president, the board of directors, the coaches, the doctors, the physios, the player liaison officers, the kitmen, the club staff... I want to thank you all very much. A special thanks goes to Alberto Angulo, Pablo Sañudo, Dani Sarto and Paco Redondo, who welcomed in a Slovenian kid who didn't know a word of Spanish and you looked after me as if I was a child of your own and have made me into a man. I love you lots.

Just in the same way that I really love Real Madrid, a club that has given me everything: the biggest sporting successes, values that will remain with me for a lifetime and that ability to fight that means you never give up, regardless of the challenge.

I also want to thank the media for treating me with respect when I was a youngster and for showing affection in their judgement of me when I grew up.

I'm writing this letter today to bid farewell in particular to you, the fans who have always backed me, forgiving my mistakes and revelling in my achievements. The same supporters who made the hairs on the back of my neck stand up with the ovation you gave me after I made my first trey as a 16 year old and from whom I felt tremendous support when I sunk my last basket (another triple, what a way for things to come full circle) some 350km away from the place I'll always call home. Many thanks for everything. You have a place in my heart.

From now on, there'll be another madridista in Dallas. However, as Terminator famously said: "I'll be back!" [328]

In the 2018 NBA Draft, Doncic was selected with the 3rd overall pick by the Atlanta Hawks but was on his way to Dallas via trade on draft night. He was traded to the Dallas Mavericks for Trae Young and a 2019 first-round draft pick, Cam Reddish. [327]

Doncic immediately made an impact in Dallas, becoming a fan favorite and playing alongside Dirk Nowitzki, an NBA Globalization icon in his rookie season, the 2018-19 season. He played and started 72 games for the Mavericks last season and averaged 32.2 minutes, 21.2 points, 7.8 rebounds, 6.0 assists, and 1.1 steals per game.[327] His rookie season play earned the Slovenian guard the 2018-19 NBA Rookie of the Year Award. In the voting for the award, Doncic received 98 out of a possible 100 place votes. [329] The other two votes went to Trae Young of the Atlanta Hawks. In addition to winning the Rookie of the Year Award for the 2018-19 season, Doncic earned 2018-19 All-Rookie honors.

Luka Doncic is one of the biggest global icons in the NBA today. He is the clear face of Slovenia in the NBA and with fellow European native, Dirk Nowitzki, calling it a career, Doncic is now the face of the Dallas Mavericks. The other player that represents Slovenia in the NBA today is Goran Dragic.

Bol Bol – Sudan

The country of Sudan is not known for producing NBA talent. In fact, there are two players in the history of the NBA to come from Sudan. Those two players are father and son: Manute Bol and Bol Bol.

As mentioned earlier in this book, Manute Bol played a huge role in globalizing the NBA, becoming one of the first seven-foot international centers in the league's history to come from overseas. His son, Bol Bol is beginning his NBA career.

Bol Bol was born on November 16, 1999 in Khartoum, Sudan.[330] At a young age, Bol Bol moved to the United States and played high school basketball at Mater Dei High School in Santa Ana, California, famously known for their basketball program. His elite high school basketball play earned Bol a scholarship to play at the University of Oregon, where he played one season but missed most of the season with a foot injury.

Due to his foot injury, which required surgery, Bol Bol fell into the mid second-round and was drafted by the Miami Heat with the 44th overall pick. [330] If Bol was not injured at the time of the draft and played most of his freshman year, he could have been a lottery pick in the 2019 NBA Draft. Just one day later, Bol Bol was traded to the Denver Nuggets for a 2022 second-round pick and cash considerations. [330]

Bol Bol is expected to play in the 2019-20 season as a member of the Denver Nuggets. He has spent time with the Chicago Bulls NBA G League affiliate, the Windy City Bulls, during the 2019-20 season to develop. His father, Manute Bol paved the way for the country of Sudan in the NBA and his son Bol Bol is now the second player from the country of Sudan to play in the NBA and is the face of Sudan in the NBA today.

Jonas Jerebko – Sweden

Jonas Jerebko was born on March 2, 1987 in Kinna, Sweden.[331] Jerebko, prior to playing in the NBA, played for three European basketball clubs before declaring for the 2009 NBA Draft, where he was drafted by the Detroit Pistons with the 39th overall pick. [331]

The Swedish power forward has played a total of 10 seasons in the NBA, splitting time with four NBA teams. He has played in a total of 635 games and has career averaged of 17.8 minutes, 6.2 points, 4.0 rebounds, and 0.8 assists per game. [331] Jerebko currently plays for Khimki in Russia.

The legacy of Jonas Jerebko will not be determined by his play. He became the first player to play in the NBA from the country of Sweden and remains the only player at the time of this writing.

Clint Capella – Switzerland

Clint Capella was born on May 18, 1994 in Geneva, Switzerland. [332] Prior to playing in the NBA, Capella played for Elan Chalon, a French basketball club for two years before declaring for the 2014 NBA Draft, where he was selected with the 25th pick by the Houston Rockets. [332]

Capella has played five years in the NBA, all with Houston. In those five seasons, Capella has played 295 games and has career averages of 25.1 minutes, 12.0 points, 9.2 rebounds, and 1.4 blocks per game.[332] He is one of the best all-around centers in the NBA and is known for his rim protection on defense.

The Swiss center is one of two players to play in the NBA. Thabo Sefolosha is the only other player from the country of Switzerland to play in the NBA. Today, Capella is the face of Switzerland in the league.

Salah Mejri – Tunisia

Salah Mejri was born on June 15, 1986 in Jendouba, Tunisa. [333] Prior to making his NBA debut, Mejri played with four European clubs. He declared for the 2008 NBA Draft but went undrafted and remained overseas until the Dallas Mavericks came knocking in 2015. [333]

On July 30, 2015, Mejri signed a multi-year contract with the Mavericks. He has played with Dallas for four seasons, playing in a total of 204 games and has career averages of 11.9 minutes, 3.4 points, 4.0 rebounds, and 0.9 blocks per game. [333]

Like Jerebko, Mejri's legacy will not be determined by his play more than the impact he has made on NBA globalization. He is the only player in the NBA's history to come from Tunisia and is the face of the country in the NBA.

Cedi Osman – Turkey

Cedi Osman was born on April 8, 1995 in Ohrid, Macedonia.[334] Prior to playing in the NBA, Osman played with two Turkish basketball clubs in Turkey before declaring for the 2015 NBA Draft, where he was selected with the 31st overall pick by the Minnesota Timberwolves. On draft night, Osman was traded to the Cleveland Cavaliers in a package deal. [334]

Despite being drafted in 2015, the Turkish small forward did not make his NBA debut until the 2017-18 NBA season. On July 18, 2017 Osman signed a multi-year contract with the Cleveland Cavaliers. In two seasons with Cleveland, Osman has played a total of 137 games and has career averages of 22.7 minutes, 9.0 points, 3.5 rebounds, and 1.7 assists per game. [334]

Osman is the face of Turkey in the NBA today. The debate can be made whether Boston Celtics center Enes Kanter is the face of Turkey in the NBA but due to his political conflicts with the country of Turkey, Osman is the face of Turkey in the league.

Other than Kanter and Osman, Ersan Ilyasova, and Furkan Korkmaz are the only other players that represent Turkey in the NBA prior to the 2019-20 season.

Alex Len – Ukraine

Alex Len was born on June 16, 1993 in Antratsit, Ukraine.[335] Prior to playing in the NBA, Len played high school and professional basketball in Ukraine. He played for Dnipro, a Ukrainian basketball team. Following one year with Dnipro, Len attended the University of Maryland and played two seasons of college basketball before declaring for the 2013 NBA Draft. In the draft, he was selected 5th overall by the Phoenix Suns. [335]

Len has played a total of six seasons in the NBA, splitting time with the Suns and the Atlanta Hawks. He has played in 412 NBA games and has career averages of 19.9 minutes, 7.9 points, 6.3 rebounds, and 1.0 blocks per game.[335] Despite not living up to expectations coming out of Maryland, Len is a solid center in the NBA and is the face of Ukraine in the league today.

The Story of Jeremy Lin and Linsanity

Jeremy Lin was born on August 23, 1998 in Torrance, California.[337] His parents, Lin Gie-Ming and Shirley Lin, raised Lin and his two brothers, Josh and Joseph, in the city of Palo Alto, which is in the San Francisco Bay Area. His parents moved to the United States from Taiwan to attend the prestigious Harvard University. His father's origin dates to the Fujian province in South China, and he was later raised and grew up in Beidou, Taiwan. His mother and her family were originally from Pinghu, which is located on the east coast of China, then moved to Taiwan in the late 1940s.[337] His parents both hold US and Taiwan citizenships.

Growing up, Jeremy Lin was introduced to the game of basketball by his father. Lin and his family were raised in a religious household and were very dedicated to education. He quickly gained an interest in the game and his talent with a basketball was quickly viewed as special. Despite having a special talent in basketball, his mother wanted Lin to have a good balance with education and the game.

Lin attended Palo Alto High School, where he was the editor of his high school newspaper and played basketball.[337] He achieved multiple individual and team honors playing for Palo Alto. Lin led his team to the California Interscholastic Federation (CIF), Division II state title championship. On his way to the championship, his team upset Mater Dei, which is one of the most talented high school basketball programs in the country. Lin was named All-State and Northern California Division II Player of the Year. He ended his high school career with averages of 15.1 points, 7.1 assists, 6.2 rebounds, and 5.0 steals per game. [337]

Before committing to his parent's alma mater, Harvard University, Lin applied to Stanford University, University of California Berkeley, and UCLA in hopes of obtaining a sports scholarship.[338] None of those schools, beside from Ivy League universities, Brown University and Harvard, awarded Lin with a sports scholarship, leading to the talented Asian American committing to Harvard.

Lin spent all four years at Harvard, playing in a total of 115 games, starting 87, and posted career averages of 29.2 minutes, 12.9 points, 4.3 rebounds, 3.5 assists, and 2.0 steals per game.[338] He was named to the All-Ivy League Second Team and finished as the first player in Ivy League to record 1,483 points, 487 rebounds, 406 assists, and 225 steals.[338] Lin graduated from Harvard with a degree in economics with a GPA of 3.1.

After four years at Harvard, Lin declared for the 2010 NBA Draft. He went undrafted but was signed by the Dallas Mavericks to play for their Summer League team, where he proved his NBA worth.

After proving his worth, Lin signed with his hometown NBA team, the Golden State Warriors, agreeing on a two-year deal.[336] On top of his new deal, Lin was awarded a three-year endorsement deal with Nike.[337] Lin bounced around with the Warriors and their NBA G League affiliate, the Reno Bighorns before being waived by Golden State in December of 2011. Three days later, he signed as a free agent with the Rockets, then released, and signed with the New York Knicks on December 27, 2011. [336]

On February 4, 2012, Jeremy Lin and the NBA changed forever. After receiving only 55 minutes in the first half of the season, Lin checked in, off the bench, to play against the New Jersey Nets, where he tallied 36 minutes.[339] Before the game, the Knicks lost 11 of their past 13 games and needed a spark to light up Madison Square Garden.

In that game, Lin, an unknown Asian-American player, dropped 25 points, seven assists, and five rebounds, leading the Knicks to a win over the Nets, 99-92, beginning the story of Linsanity.

"This night, it just hasn't really sunk in yet to be honest," Lin said. *"It's like I'm still kind of in shock about everything that happened but I'm just trying to soak it all in right now."* [339]

Five days later, Lin and the Knicks were riding a two-game winning streak were set to face the Washington Wizards. Lin showed out once again, proving he was not a one-hit-wonder on the NBA hardwood.

On February 10, 2012, Linsanity officially began. Madison Square Garden was sold out to watch a matchup between the Knicks and Kobe Bryant and the Los Angeles Lakers. The MSG crowd was filled with Asian-Americans, hoisting Chinese and Taiwan flags and other symbolic posters of the rising Jeremy Lin. He scored 38 points in the game. [336]

Then, four days later, came the poster moment of the Linsanity era. On February 14, 2012, the Knicks traveled to Toronto to face the Raptors. The game came down to the final seconds, tied at 87, and the ball was in Lin's hands. The Knicks point guard slowly walked from the halfcourt line to the three-point line and connected on a three to win the game with 0.5 seconds remaining. The crowd exploded with a mix of shocked reactions and cheers. Lin scored a total of 27 points, 12 of those 27 points came in the fourth quarter.[339] That game was the peak of Linsanity, taking the world by storm.

The Globalization of the NBA

The Linsanity era came to an end on March 31, 2012, when the Knicks announced Lin would undergo surgery to repair a torn meniscus. That season, Lin played 35 games for New York, posting averages of 14.6 points and 6.2 assists per game. [339]

In July of 2012, Lin and the Houston Rockets agreed on a three-year $25 million deal. [336] The Knicks had 48 hours to match Lin's new deal with the Rockets but could not afford the hefty tax bill in the contract's final year, which left Lin on his way to Houston.

Lin spent two years in Houston, playing in 153 games, starting 115, and averaged 30.7 minutes, 13.0 points, 5.2 assists, 2.4 rebounds, and 1.3 steals before being traded to the Los Angeles Lakers on July 15, 2014. [336] Following the trade, Linsanity was never the same. Lin struggled to find stability with an NBA team, playing with a total of five NBA teams from 2014 to 2019. He played with the Lakers, the Charlotte Hornets, Nets, the Atlanta Hawks, and the Toronto Raptors.

This past season, the 2018-19 season, Lin played 23 games for the Raptors, starting in three, and averaged 18.8 minutes, 7.0 points, 2.6 rebounds, and 2.2 assists per game.[336] As mentioned before, Lin and the Raptors won their first NBA Championship. Lin became the first Asian-American to win an NBA Championship.

In the 2019 offseason, Lin became a free agent and struggled to find a new home in the NBA. At the age of 30, Lin was devastated and believed the NBA had given up on him.

> *"Free agency has been tough because I feel like, in some ways, the NBA has given up on me,"* Lin said emotionally. *"In English there's a saying and it says once you hit rock bottom, the only way is up. But rock bottom just seems to keep getting more and more rock bottom for me."* [340]

On August 27, 2019, Jeremy Lin found a new home to play basketball. This time, it was not going to be an NBA team. Lin signed a deal to join the Beijing Ducks of the Chinese Basketball Association. [341]

> *"Jeremy joining the Beijing Ducks men's basketball shows his confidence in us and is an honour, we sincerely welcome him,"* Qin Xiaowen, the Ducks club chairman said. [341]

The story of Jeremy Lin is one of the greatest stories from an Asian-American athlete in the history of sports. From being an unknown Asian-American player, to achieving NBA stardom during Linsanity, winning an

NBA Championship in 2019, to now on his way to play in the CBA as a member of the Beijing Ducks, Lin has a story that only very few can relate to.

Jeremy Lin will always be the face of NBA globalization as he continues his legacy in China.

Chapter 33

A New Global Face of the NBA

Throughout the history of the National Basketball Association, there has only been a handful of players who can call themselves the face of the league. Usually, a player holds the unwritten honor for at least a decade. In the 1950s, George Mikan of the Minneapolis Lakers was the first face of the NBA followed by Bill Russell of the 1960s, Kareem Abdul-Jabbar in the 1970s, Magic Johnson in the 1980s, Michael Jordan in the 1990s, and Kobe Bryant from 2000-04.

LeBron James has been the face of the National Basketball Association since he was drafted by his hometown Cleveland Cavaliers with the 1st overall pick in the 2003 NBA Draft. James, best known as 'The King' has held the crown of being the face of the NBA for 16 years and has the chance to hold the throne till he officially steps away from the game of basketball.

There is only one player currently in the NBA that has a big chance of stripping King James and becoming the face of the NBA. His name is Giannis Antetokounmpo, also known as 'The Greek Freak.'

> *"What I also think Freak stands for is that the guy from nothing became everything,"* Antetokounmpo said. [342]

That quote describes the upbringing of a basketball legend in the making. Antetokounmpo was born on December 6, 1994 in Athens, Greece.[342] His parents Charles and Veronica emigrated from their native country of Nigeria in search of work. Giannis is one of five siblings in the Antetokounmpo family. Antetokounmpo, along with his brothers Alex, Thanasis and Kostas joined their parents selling goods on the streets of Athens to make money. The goods were anything from homemade bags to small products sold to make a couple Euros.

> *"From what I remember, it was always fun, it was always fun,"* said Giannis Antetokounmpo sitting next to his mother Veronica. *"I think I learned from the best. She [Veronica] used to be a great seller. A great smile."* [342]

For Giannis and his brothers, they were young children when they first began selling goods on the streets. Thanasis, the oldest brother in the

Antetokounmpo family, always felt a sense of pride coming home and giving their parents Euros made from their sales.

> *"It makes me feel very proud,"* Thanasis Antetokounmpo said. *"Sometimes I actually miss it. Do you know how much fun it is for kids to come back home and go 'mom I just sold like this bag and this bag and we made like 40 bucks' and you're twelve years old."*[342]

When the Antetokounmpo brothers were not on the streets selling goods or in school learning, they were playing the sport of basketball. Their father, Charles, grew up watching and playing soccer and before Giannis fell in love with the game of basketball, soccer was his dream sport. His interest in basketball grew because of his older brother Thanasis, who was talented and loved to play basketball.

The Antetokounmpo brothers growing up went to Sepolia, a neighborhood where Giannis and his brothers played basketball. After practicing with his older brother Thanasis, at the age of 12, Giannis joined Filathlitikos B.C. [342] All the Antetokounmpo brothers began their playing career with the basketball club.

> *"Giannis, the kid who left this place, that skinny kid, had already worked very hard to become what he was,"* Takis Zivas, the head coach of Filathlitikos B.C. said. *"He was at the gym every day, a skinny, sickly kid, probably with nutrition problems in his everyday life. Neverless, he was here every day."* [342]

> *"When we decided to put him on the men's team, he was 16 years old. We told him he had to get stronger to be able to compete with the other guys. The very next day, he started to work out. Before and after each practice, he was lifting weights."* [342]

When Giannis Antetokounmpo was 17 years old, his basketball career began to go in a very bright direction. During the 2011-12 season, Antetokounmpo played with the senior men's team of Filathlitikos B.C. and scouts from Europe and American began to look at the very tall Greek basketball player. At the time, Giannis' last name was spelt and pronounced differently. His last name was Adetokunbo, but Greek authorities changed his name to Antetokounmpo when he received his citizenship in 2013.

Due to Giannis' rise in popularity, the gym where he and Filathlitikos played needed to be renovated. The reason for the renovation was for scouts, general managers, and other team officials who wanted to come watch Antetokounmpo play in person. One of those people who watched him was John Hammond, who was the Milwaukee Bucks General Manager at the time.

> *"You see all these chairs right here? They never use to be here,"* Giannis said while showing off his old gym. *"You know, they start putting them there 2012, 2013, where people like the GMS [general managers] and scouts used to come here and watch me and my brothers play. John Hammond, the guy that drafted me, he was right here and he was sitting down, and the thing I always remember is that I was playing, so he was watching me play, but Alex was playing on the little rim. So, Alex was 10, and he was like, "Oh man, he's gonna be good, man." "But you know, they're not allowed to talk to you so, whenever I came here, because I used to go to the bathroom or to drink water, he would say "You look good, good, keep going" very fast. I knew him before he drafted me and he like – I had a really good impression about him before he drafted me and I went to Milwaukee."* [343]

Following his tenure with Filathlitikos, Antetokounmpo declared for the 2013 NBA Draft. He officially declared just two months prior to the draft and there were many lingering questions about the skinny and lengthy Greek star.

Draft Express, back in 2013, compared the Greek prospect to Nicolas Batum and Thabo Sefolosha.

> *"Adetokunbo stands out first and foremost thanks to the tremendous physical profile he brings to the table, reminding somewhat of a Nicolas Batum or Thabo Sefolosha on first glace. He has great size at 6-9, 196 pounds, to go along with a developed upper body and an overall terrific frame that should fill out considerably in time. His wingspan has reportedly been measured at 7-3, but perhaps most interesting is the size of his hands, as he's able to palm the ball like grapefruit which helps him out considerably as a passer, ball-handler, and finisher."* [347]

After declaring for the 2013 NBA Draft, Antetokounmpo's draft projections ranged from a late first round pick to possibly slipping to the second round.

> *"I remember, we got to New York, I was like "OK, tomorrow is draft night. Please let me just get drafted,"* Antetokounmpo recalled. *"That's what ... all I care about. Whoever takes me, I'm just gonna*

work as hard as I can and I am going to be a good player an I'm going to be able to provide for my family." [344]

The draft night story of Giannis Antetokounmpo is focused around the suits for him and his brothers. At the time of the draft, the night before, all the Antetokounmpo's did not have enough money to afford any expensive suits. One company came to help the Antetokounmpo brothers and provided them with suits.

> *"And then, the day before the draft, they're like, 'Oh, we're going to the draft, and you got to dress up and then you gotta buy a suit and everything,'"* Thanasis said. *"And I'm like 'This is a lot of money, this is 500-something, 600, 1,000, then I remember we had a company came, they gave us clothing and everything, and we finally waited.'"* [344]

Giannis, accompanied by his older brother Thanasis, watched the first 14 players get drafted into the league before it was his turn. Then, when Milwaukee was on the clock with the 15th overall pick, the wait was over. David Stern, the NBA's Commissioner walked to the podium and slowly announced that the Bucks selected Giannis Antetokounmpo from Greece. For Giannis, when he recalled the life changing moment, he refers to it as a blackout. He could not remember a lot and did not

> *"I was sitting there with my brother, it happened, I heard my name, after that it was a blackout,"* Antetokounmpo recalled. *"I don't remember much. The only thing I remember, I was on the stage, shaking his [David Stern's] hand, no I never looked up. I was so shy, I just walked down the stairs and I was just shaking."* [344]

Once a kid from Greece selling goods on the streets to help his parents' economic situation to being drafted into the NBA, Antetokounmpo's life changed forever at that moment.

For any international player, adjusting to not only your new team or a new league is tough but adapting to the culture of the United States and the simple things like shopping, living on your own, and getting sleep can be a difficult task. Antetokounmpo came to Milwaukee by himself. His family was in Greece and his older brother Thanasis was beginning a new chapter of his basketball career, joining the Delaware 87ers of the NBA Development League, in hopes of building a solid draft stock for next year's NBA Draft. The Bucks staff and front office accompanied Giannis and helped him adjust to his new life in Milwaukee.

"It was amazing," Antetokounmpo said. *"Maybe if I can turn the time back and just go back and relive those moments. I learnt how to drive by my GM. I learnt how to open a bank account by myself, I never had a bank account. I got into an apartment, rent apartment, with the help of my agent, but I found the apartment by myself. Like, I was 18, doing some adult, adult stuff, that I'd never, never done before."* [344]

Antetokounmpo's mentor for his first Bucks practice was OJ Mayo, a veteran point guard who had a great amount of NBA experience. At the time, Antetokounmpo did not know any of the players but he quickly became situated with his new team.

Antetokounmpo made his NBA debut at 18 years old and had a tremendous following from all around the world. In his rookie year, Antetokounmpo impressed, playing in a total of 77 games, starting 23 of them, and averaged 24.6 minutes, 6.8 points, 4.4 rebounds, 1.9 assists, 0.8 blocks. [350] His rookie season play earned the Greek Freak 2013-14 All-Rookie second-team honors.[350] He also participated in the Rising Stars Challenge at NBA All-Star Weekend.

At the time of this writing, Giannis Antetokounmpo will be entering seventh season in the league as a member of the Milwaukee Bucks. In those seven years, Antetokounmpo is a three-time All-NBA player, two-time All-Defensive player, a three-time NBA All-Star, and won the 2016-17 NBA Most Improved Player award, which is given to the player that made the biggest jump from the previous season. Giannis has played in a total of 465 games, starting 400, and has career averages of 32.7 minutes, 18.8 points, 8.3 rebounds, 4.1 assists, 1.3 blocks, and 1.3 steals per game. [350]

The 2018-19 NBA season was a historic season for not just Giannis Antetokounmpo but for the game of basketball. Antetokounmpo has a career year, posting averages of 32.8 minutes, 27.7 points, 12.5 rebounds, 5.9 assists, 1.5 blocks, and 1.3 steals per game in 72 games of play.[350]

His impressive breakout play earned Antetokounmpo the 2018-19 NBA Most Valuable Player Award. Antetokounmpo became just the 12th player to win MVP before turning 25 and is the youngest MVP since Derrick Rose, who was 22, winning the award in 2010-11.[346] He joined Kareem Abdul-Jabbar as the only players in Milwaukee Bucks history to earn MVP honors.

"While leading the Bucks to their best record since the 1980-81 season and the top mark in the NBA at 60-22, Antetokounmpo averaged 27.7 points (3rd in the NBA), 12.5 rebounds (6th in the NBA)

and 5.9 assists (T-20th in the NBA) per game – all career-highs. He also shot a franchise record 57.8% from the field (11th in the NBA), blocked 1.5 shots (10th in the NBA) and swiped 1.3 steals per contest. Antetokounmpo became just the ninth player in NBA history to average at least 25.0 points, 10.0 rebounds and 5.0 assists per game over the course of a season and did so with the highest shooting percentage." [346]

"We are beyond proud of Giannis for earning his first MVP award," John Horst, the Milwaukee Bucs general manager said. *"This well-deserved honor is due to his relentless hard work and dedication in becoming the most impactful player in the NBA. Giannis propelled the Bucks to great heights last season with his leadership, drive and unselfish play. His grace on and off the court has made him one of the most admired players in the world. On behalf of ownership, the entire Bucks organization and Bucks fans everywhere, we congratulate Giannis for being named MVP."* [346]

In his seven years in the NBA, Antetokounmpo is viewed as one of the most hardworking players in the whole league. From coming into the league as a well-known global basketball player to becoming an NBA MVP, Giannis Antetokounmpo continues to grow his game and is becoming one of the NBA greats.

Nike, which is the top endorsement company in the NBA, has signed Giannis Antetokounmpo to an endorsement deal. During his breakout MVP season, Nike decided to award Antetokounmpo with a signature shoe, which is a limited honor to only some of the NBA's best talents that are signed with the company. The shoe is named *Zoom Freak 1*. The shoe exemplifies Antetokounmpo's journey from Greece to the person he is today, and all his family members names are engraved on the shoe. As mentioned before, from borrowing his older brother Thanasis' shoes growing up to having his own Nike shoe is monumental.

On top of Antetokounmpo's excellent play on the NBA hardwood, he is one of the most followed NBA athletes on social media and is a global superstar. His play has helped the Milwaukee Bucks, a small-market NBA team, reach heights the franchise would have never reached in such a short amount of time. The Bucks, heading into the 2018-19 NBA season, are considered favorites to come out of Eastern Conference and make a run at the 2019-20 NBA Championship.

His older brother, Thanasis, who was a huge mentor for Giannis growing up and learning the game of basketball, signed a free agent deal to join the Milwaukee Bucks in July of 2019. [351] Thanasis played a total of two games for the New York Knicks during the 2015-16 season and has bounced around in the NBA G League as well as playing overseas. [351] For their younger brother Kostas Antetokounmpo, he was drafted by the Philadelphia 76ers with the 60th pick in the 2018 NBA Draft. [345] In July of 2019, he was claimed off waivers by the Los Angeles Lakers and signed a two-way deal. Kostas, as well, has only played in two NBA games back in the 2018-19 season as a member of the Dallas Mavericks. [345]

In addition to his domination in the NBA, Giannis Antetokounmpo played for the Greek men's national team in the 2019 FIBA World Cup. (More to Add when tournament is over)

On a global platform, Giannis Antetokounmpo has become the new face of the NBA. After winning the 2018-19 NBA Most Valuable Player award, Antetokounmpo is poised to lead the Milwaukee Bucks to an NBA Championship. Every game he plays, Antetokounmpo has a global following like no other player in the NBA today.

> *"Every time, let's say, Giannis goes to play in New York, he has 4, 5, 6, 10,000 [fans],"* Thanasis said. *"Do you understand, to go to any city, you go and play, you have 10,000 Greek or Nigerian people overnight? People to come and see you play. You have 10,000 people come to watch you play from the places you are. It's unbelievable. Anywhere you go in the world, you find somebody that's from where you are, and loves you like crazy and supports you, that you've never met, that you've never, like, shaken their hands or you've never done something for them, and they support you, so, so you do this for them. You represent them, and you show them that love comes unconditionally. You don't need love to give somebody love. You just give it and that's it."* [344]

Giannis Antetokounmpo is the face of Greece in the NBA and has a global following at almost every NBA game he plays in. In addition to being the face of Greece, Antetokounmpo is paving a new trail for international players not just with aspirations of making the league but the international players in the league today.

The Globalization of the NBA

Conclusion

The sports industry has concentrated around globalization as a successful marketing strategy for the past couple of decades. The National Basketball Association, the NBA, has established itself as one of the fastest and successful sports leagues in the world to globalize.

At the time of this writing, the NBA offers programming for their games to over 200 countries in several different languages. On top of their offered programming and television deals across the world to hundreds of countries, the NBA, over the past decade, has aggressively brought their fame overseas, giving fans outside the borders of the United States the ability to watch their games in person. A great majority of those games have been preseason games, in other words, games that do not count towards a team's record. In addition to the NBA bringing its action across borders, the league has 12 international regional offices outside the United States borders: NBA Asia (Hong Kong, Manila), NBA Canada (Toronto), NBA China, (Beijing, Shanghai, Taipei), NBA Europe (London, Madrid), NBA India (Mumbai), NBA Latin America (Mexico City, Rio de Janeiro), and NBA South Africa (Johannesburg). Each of its international offices help grow the league and spread the popularity of the NBA and the game of basketball across the world.

Due to the power of technology, fans across the world do not need to watch games either in person or all the time to gain interest in the NBA. The power of social media offers fans free access to keep up to date on everything and anything that happens in the league daily.

Overall, the NBA would not have reached the heights of its global success if it was not for the players who paved the way. The game of basketball has always contained international roots since its establishment in 1891 by Dr. James Naismith, a Canadian.

In the last three decades, two of the biggest factors in the success of the NBA globalizing their league has been the 1992 United States men's national team, famously known as the "Dream Team," and the rising global superstar, Giannis Antetokounmpo, who is currently one of the global faces of the NBA.

"The NBA game, we see it just sort of here in the states in its popularity, but the growth of the game is enormous, it is amazing," Grant Hill told me at the 2019 Sports PR Summit in New York City. *"You look back to the 1992 Dream Team that won in Barcelona and the impact it has had. Having players from international countries*

coming in and having a big impact and now, I think, last year, the [2018-19 season], 45 percent of the platers were born outside the United States. So we have players from all over the world and when you go to China, go to Africa, go to India. You see basketball is gaining popularity, so it is great for business. They are some of the best players in the world. If you can play basketball and you have talent, you have a chance. The league is trending. It's on a global stage now and I think that will continue to happen and grow, which is great for marketing and PR for the NBA."

Although the NBA is rising and taking tremendous steps globalizing their league, the lingering question remains … How far can the NBA and the game of basketball go globally?

"The game itself, has been internationalized," Ric Bucher said. "It is a drive-and-kick game, it has a global reach obviously with the players and the percentage of international players. I believe it is going to end up being right there with soccer because everyone is just playing it around the world. It is a game that translates easy to TV. You can play it and there is no such thing as a language barrier in basketball. In the NFL, [National Football League], there is a language barrier. You can communicate by saying anything or speaking the same language so I feel like there are a number of things that the game of basketball can tap into that allows it to be globally influential that other sports just do not have and that soccer does have. It is just right there and it's just a matter of expansion when it comes down to that."

"As someone who has covered a fair amount of both [Basketball and Soccer], I think soccer is in the DNA of the sports fans worldwide," Brian Lewis of the New York Post said. *"Over the last so decade, the NBA has made astounding strides. I am not saying the NBA will or won't pass soccer I think that is extreme because right now they are behind the NFL just in this country but I do think they have more growth potential than the NFL has because there are certain problems inherently in growing your product in countries like Argentina, Spain, or in China while the NBA is a worldwide league. Whether it catches soccer or not I am not sure but there is a lot of growth potential."*

Dzanan Musa, the Brooklyn Nets shooting guard/small forward and a foreign player himself, believes the NBA has the chance to continue growing more and more when it comes to globalizing. In terms of attracting more players to the NBA, he believes if the NBA presents more opportunities for younger international players, the number of international players will most certainly grow.

"It is increasing," Dzanan Musa said. "The NBA league is growing. I believe players don't want to stay here too long when they don't play.

When they do not have enough minutes, they are trying to find themselves in China and Europe, but I think that if the NBA starts to give opportunities to younger guys, guys who are hungry for success, I think the NBA will increase more."

The game of basketball has the potential to keep rising as one of the world's most popular sports while the NBA has the potential to become one of the world's most popular sport leagues as long as the international talent and the global business continues to rise.

The Globalization of the NBA

Postscript

The NBA – China Controversy

The globalization of the NBA took a major hit, tarnishing relationships with China, who are their biggest market outside the United States of America.

It began on Oct. 6 with Houston Rockets general manager, Daryl Morey, who's tweet focused around supporting Hong Kong protesters. His tweet stated: "Fight for Freedom. Stand with Hong Kong." Morey's remarks were viewed by as criticism and was opposed to China's political strategy.

In less than 12 hours after the tweet was posted, Morey faced over 16,000 tweets in backlash. Morey then responded, via Twitter, to the previous remark, in a series of tweets, stating he did not mean any harm. It could not have been worse timing for the NBA, with their 2019-20 season starting only a couple weeks prior to the Morey tweet.

The NBA, as a league, in addition with Morey's team, the Rockets, faced immediate backlash was well. Sponsors immediately cut their ties with the NBA and the Rockets as well.

Two days after Morey's tweet, on Oct. 8, the NBA released an official statement on the controversy stating:

> *"We recognize that the views expressed by Houston Rockets general manager Daryl Morey have deeply offended many of our friends and fans in China, which is regrettable. While Daryl has made it clear that his tweet does not represent the Rockets or the NBA, the values of the league support individuals' educating themselves and sharing their views on matters important to them. We have great respect for the history and culture of China and hope that sports and the NBA can be used as a unifying force to bridge cultural divides and bring people together."*[352]

Adam Silver, the Commissioner of the NBA, quickly responded to the backlash the league has faced in a series of interviews and statement releases. He clarified the league's stance on the rising tensions and issue.

> *"It is inevitable that people around the world – including from America to China – will have different viewpoints over different issues. It is not the role of the NBA to adjudicate those differences. However, the NBA will not put itself in a position of regulating what players, employees, and team owners, say and will not say on these issues. We simply could not operate that way."* [352]

Since the initial tweet, the NBA has already faced some of the consequences. The economic impact is evident while, over in China, a good number of fans are burning jerseys and no longer supporting the NBA.

The Brooklyn Nets and the Los Angeles Lakers played two preseason games in China on Oct. 10 and Oct. 12. Silver attended the games despite the ongoing crisis. Brooklyn and Los Angeles split the series, winning one game each, but the games were not ordinary games. Instead, the crisis hovered over the heads of both teams.

From the Morey tweet to the United States' trade dispute with China, the scenery in China was gloomy. Due to the circumstances and the magnitude of the problems at hand, media access was limited. Either the NBA or the Chinese government cancelled media access from reporters interviewing players and coaches to fan interactions with Brooklyn Nets and Los Angeles Lakers players and coaches, the trip was nowhere near as familiar to past experiences.

Silver, at the time of this writing, is planning to meet with Yao Ming, who is a global ambassador, based out of China, for the NBA and the President of the Chinese Basketball Association.

> *"I'm hoping together that Yao Ming and I can find accommodation,"*
> *Silver said. "But he is extremely hot at the moment, and I understand*
> *it. There's no question that Daryl Morey's tweet has hit what I would*
> *describe as a third-rail issue in China. I think Yao is extremely*
> *unsettled. I'm not quite sure he accepts how the how we are*
> *operating our business right now."* [352]

Acknowledgements

I want to thank the following people who have contributed to the writing of *Basketball Beyond Borders: The Globalization of the NBA.*

Harvey Araton is a journalist and author.

Isaiah Batkay is a graphic designer.

Emmanuel Basulto is a photo editor for *Cowbell Kingdom.*

Filip Bondy is a long-time New York sports columnist and author.

Stefan Bondy is a sportswriter covering the Brooklyn Nets and the New York Knicks for the *New York Daily News.*

Ric Bucher is an NBA analyst for *FOX Sports*, NBA senior writer for *Bleacher Report*, and the podcast host of *Bucher & Friends.*

Alton Byrd is the vice president of business operations for the Long Island Nets, a 5x Scottish League champion, and one of the most revered British pro basketball players ever.

Bryan Fonseca is an on-air talent and journalist based in New York City, and co-hosts the *Ain't Hard to Tell Podcast.*

Grant Hill is a *Naismith Basketball Hall of Famer* and the vice chair of the board for the Atlanta Hawks.

Diamond Leung is a managing editor at *The Athletic.*

Brian Lewis is staff writer at *The New York Post* covering the Brooklyn Nets and the NBA.

Robin Lundberg is a host for *Sports Illustrated*, *CBS Sports Radio*, and *Sirius XM.*

Leo McKenzie was the editor of *Basketball Beyond Borders: The Globalization of the NBA.*

Dzanan Musa is a Brooklyn Nets shooting guard/ small forward.

Dzennis Musa is a public relations manager.

Eric Oberman is the executive director of *The Atlanta Tip Off Club/ Naismith Awards.*

Will Thomas is a freelance photographer (onewaywill.com).

Kelly Whiteside is a contributor for *The New York Times, USA Today, Newsday,* and *Sports Illustrated* alum.

About the Author

(Photo by Will Thomas)

Chris Milholen is a sportswriter and reporter, covering the Brooklyn Nets and the Long Island Nets for *SBNations*' NetsDaily. Milholen has written bylines for *USA TODAY's* NetsWire. He is a social media intern for *The Atlanta Tipoff Club/Naismith Trophy*. Milholen is currently a senior at Montclair State University majoring in Television and Digital Media with a concentration in Sports Media and Journalism, minoring in Sociology, and will graduate in May of 2020.

Milholen resides in Emerson, New Jersey.

Endnotes

1. "International Timeline." *NBA Encyclopedia Playoff Edition*. n.d. https://www.nba.com/history/International_Timeline.html

2. Riddick, John F. *The History of British India: A Chronology*. Greenwood Publishing Group 2006.

3. Naismith, James. *Basketball Its Origins And Development*. Bison Books 2006.

4. "The Globalization of the NBA." *United Language Group*. 2019 https://unitedlanguagegroup.com/blog/globalization-of-the-nba/

5. "Dr. James Naismith's Original 13 Rules of Basketball." *USA Basketball*. n.d. https://www.usab.com/history/dr-james-naismiths-original-13-rules-of-basketball.aspx.

6. Philips. Curtis J. "Search for Top 100 [Canadian] Players of All Times." *Frozen Hoops – Tripod*. n.d. http://curtisjphilips.tripod.com/frozenhoops/index.html

7. "1898-1899." *A Complete History of Pro Basketball: The Early Years*. 2019.https://probasketballencyclopedia.com/seasons/1898-1899/.

8. "National Basketball League (1898-1904)." *Mwal Wiki*. n.d. https://mwal.fandom.com/wiki/National_Basketball_League_(1898%E2%80%931904).

9. "World of Basketball: Your Guide to the Most Popular Sport." n.d. https://www.worldofbasketball.org/basketball-rules.htm.

10. "All About Basketball." *Online Basketball Magazine*. 2019 https://www.allaboutbasketball.us/basketball-leagues/national-basketball-league-nbl-phase-i.html.

11. Kirschman, Lauren. "First on the Court." *The Beaver Times*. November 29, 2014. https://www.ncaa.com/news/basketball-men/article/2014-11-29/vanderbilt-lays-claim-true-birthplace-college-basketball.

12. Organ, Mike. "Historian: Vandy Is Birthplace of College Basketball." *Tennessean*. March 7, 2015. https://www.tennessean.com/story/sports/2015/03/07/vanderbilt-birthplace-college-basketball-according-historian/24549765/.

13. "Basketball Origins, Growth and History of the Game." *The People History*. n.d. https://www.thepeoplehistory.com/basketballhistory.html.

14. "NBA Hoops Online." n.d. https://nbahoopsonline.com/History/Leagues/BAA/.

15. "College Basketball." *Wiki*. n.d. https://en.wikipedia.org/wiki/College_basketball

16. "Basketball at the 1904 Summer Olympics." *Wiki*. n.d. https://en.wikipedia.org/wiki/Basketball_at_the_1904_Summer_Olympics

17. "New York Knicks at Toronto Huskies Box Score, November 1, 1941. *Basketball Reference*. November 1. 1946. https://www.basketball-reference.com/boxscores/194611010TRH.html

18. "Basketball Leagues." *All About Basketball*. 2019. https://www.allaboutbasketball.us/basketball-leagues/basketball-association-of-america-baa.html

19. Shwartz, Larry. "Basketball Association of America is born." *ESPN Classic*. November 19, 2003. http://www.espn.com/classic/s/moment010606BAAopens.html

20. Zarum, Dave. "Toronto Huskies." *The Canadian Encyclopedia*. October 29, 2018. https://www.thecanadianencyclopedia.ca/en/article/toronto-huskies

21. "NBA Merges with ABA." History: *This Day in History*. August 05, 1976. November 16, 2009. www.history.com/this-day-in-history/nba-merges-with-aba.

22. "The History of the NBA-ABA Merger." *History Locker*. n.d. https://historylocker.com/the-nbaaba-merger/.

23. "The History of the American Basketball Association." *ABALiveAction.Com*. n.d.

https://abaliveactio.com/about-the-aba/.

24. Flannery, Paul. "Remembering the ABA, the Upstart League that Challenged Pro Basketball and Won." *SBNation.* August 24, 2005. https://www.sbnation.com/2015/8/24/9066375/aba-legacy-julius-erving-basketball-history

25. "Hank Biasatti." *Basketball Reference.* n.d. https://www.basketball-reference.com/players/b/biasaha01.html

26. "Hank Biasatti G Toronto Raptors." *basketball.realgm.com.* Advanced Stats. 2019. https://basketball.realgm.com/player/Hank-Biasatti/Summary/101314

27. Philips, Curtis J. "Frozen Hoops: A History A to B." *Tripod.* December 2012, Issue 1. https://www.lulu.com/shop/curtis-j-philips/frozen-hoops-a-history-a-to-b-/ebook/product20539000.html.

28. "Hank Biasatti." *Retrosheet.* n.d. https://www.retrosheet.org/boxesetc/B/Pbiash101.htm.

29. "Gino Sovran." *Revolvy.* n.d. https://www.revolvy.com/page/Gino-Sovran

30. "Gino Sovran." *Basketball Reference.* n.d. https://www.basketball-reference.com/players/s/sovragi01.html

31. "Bob Houbregs." *Basketball References.* 2000-2019. www.basketball-reference.com/players/h/houbrbo01.html.

32. "#17 Bob Houbregs." *NBA Advanced Stats.* 2019. https://stats.nba.com/player/77062/career.

33. "Hall of Famer, ex-No-2 Overall Pick Houbregs Dies at 82." *NBA.* May 29, 2014. www.nba.com/2014/news/05/29/bob-houbregs-dies-at-82.ap/.

34. "Robert J. 'Bobby' Houbregs." *Basketball Hall of Fame.* n.d. http://www.hoophall.com/hall-of-famers/bobby-houbregs/

35. "Bob Houbregs / FC." *The Atlantic: Insider NBA Pass. Real GM.*

2000-2019.
https://basketball.realgm.com/player/Bob-
Houbregs/Summary/70704

36. "Bob Houbregs, Basketball Hall of Fame Member, Dies at 82." *The New York Times*. May 29, 2014.
https://www.nytimes.com/2014/05/30/sports/bob-houbregs-
basketball-hall-of-fame-member-dies-at-82.html

37. Wood, Mark. "NBA's Original Brit Still in Play." *MVP Original Basketball*. March 3, 2011.
http://www.mvp247.com/2011/03/chris-harris-original-brit/

38. "#3 Chris Harris G / Rochester Royals." *NBA Advanced Stats*. 2019.
https://stats.nba.com/player/76958/career/

39. "Chris Harris." *The Atlantic: Insider NBA Pass. Real GM*. 2000-2019.
https://basketball.realgm.com/player/Chris-
Harris/Summary/71019

40. "Chris Harris." *Wiki*. September 25, 2013.
https://en.wikipedia.org/wiki/Chris_Harris_(basketball)

41. Archdeacon, Tom. "UD Great Harris Finally Getting His Due." *Dayton Daily News*. March 1, 2013.
https://www.daytondailynews.com/sports/college-
basketball/great-harris-finally-getting-his-
due/GN6Cj7FH9qUvTpMoptoNEI/

42. Hazeltine, Rick. "Looking Up to Him Swen Nater Is a Lifetime Rebounder with Valuable Lessons to Pass On." *Los Angeles Times*. December 17, 1988. http://articles.latimes.com/1988-12-17/sports/sp-
105_1_swen-nater/2

43. "Swen Nater." Basketball Reference. n.d.
https://www.basketball-
reference.com/players/n/natersw01.html

44. Broussard, Chris. "Then and Now - Swen Nater, Big Man Loved the Game, Then Learned to Play It." *The New York Times*. January 11, 2004.
https://www.nytimes.com/2004/01/11/sports/then-and-now-
swen-nater-big-man-loved-the-game-then-learned-to-play-
it.html

45. "Mike D'Antoni." *Basketball Reference*. n.d.

https://www.basketball-reference.com/players/d/dantomi01.html

46. "Mike D'Antoni." *NBA Coach File*. n.d. https://www.nba.com/coachfile/mike_dantoni/

47. "Mike D'Antoni." *Wiki*. n.d. https://en.wikipedia.org/wiki/Mike_D%27Antoni

48. "Mike D'Antoni." *Olimpia Milano*. n.d. http://www.olimpiamilano.com/en/hall-of-fame-22-mike-dantoni-2/

49. Thompson, Teri and Frank Isola. "Mike D'Antoni a Legend in Italy." *New York Daily News*. May 11, 2018. https://www.nydailynews.com/sports/basketball/knicks/mike-antoni-legend-italy-article-1.329975

50. Davis, Scott. "The Coach Who Designed the Offense that Changed the NBA Nearly Failed before He Started." *Business Insider*. December 3, 2017. https://www.businessinsider.com/mike-dantoni-offense-shaped-nba-2017-11

51. Feigen, Jonathan. "From West Virginia to Italy, the Making of Mike D'Antoni." *Houston Chronicle*. June 4, 2016. https://www.houstonchronicle.com/sports/rockets/article/From-West-Virginia-to-Italy-the-making-of-Mike-7962758.php

52. Cohen, Ben. "The Coach Who Changed the NBA from Italy." *The Wall Street Journal*. November 14, 2018. https://www.wsj.com/articles/dan-peterson-the-coach-who-changed-the-nba-from-italy-1542204603

53. "Swen Nater." *Wiki*. n.d. https://en.wikipedia.org/wiki/Swen_Nater

54. "Swen Nater." *Sports Reference*. n.d. https://www.sports-reference.com/cbb/players/swen-nater-1.html

55. "Kiki VanDeWeghe." *Basketball Reference*. n.d. https://www.sports-reference.com/cbb/players/kiki-vandeweghe-1.html

56. "Denver Nuggets Acquire Kiki VanDeWeghe." *NBA Trades*. n.d. http://nbatrades.tumblr.com/post/37087257935/denver-nuggets-acquire-kiki-vandeweghe

57. "Kiki Signs Big Pact with Denver Nuggets." *The Spokesman Review*. December 11, 1980. https://news.google.com/newspapers?nid=1314&dat=1980 1211&id=NsopAAAAIBAJ&sjid=W-4DAAAAIBAJ&pg=6084,5166165

58. "Kiki VanDeWeghe." *Wiki*. n.d https://en.wikipedia.org/wiki/Kiki_VanDeWeghe

59. "1982-83 Denver Nuggets Roster and Stats." *Basketball Reference*. n.d. https://www.basketball-reference.com/teams/DEN/1983_games.html

60. "1984-85 Portland Trail Blazers Roster and Stats." *Basketball Reference*. n.d. https://www.basketball-reference.com/teams/POR/1985.html

61. "Kiki VanDeWeghe." *NBA Career Opportunities*. n.d. https://careers.nba.com/leadership/#kiki-vandeweghe

62. "Kiki VanDeWeghe." *Sports Reference*. n.d. https://www.sports-reference.com/cbb/players/kiki-vandeweghe-1.html

63. "Basketball at the 1904 Summer Olympics." *Wikipedia*. June 23, 2019. https://en.wikipedia.org/wiki/Basketball_at_the_1904_Summer_Olympics#Amateur_championships

64. "1904 Olympic Gold." *Hiram College Terriers*. n.d. http://www.hiramterriers.com/athletics/olympicgold

65. McCallum, Jack. "Could Be the Start of Something Big." *Hiram College Terriers*. November 29, 1999. http://www.hiramterriers.com/athletics/siaccount

66. "Basketball Demonstrations at the Olympics." *topendsports.com*. n.d. https://www.topendsports.com/events/demonstration/basketball.htm

67. Harmon, W. H. "What Happened at St. Louis." *Hiram College Terriers*. n.d. https://www.hiramterriers.com/athletics/harmonaccount

68. "Basketball at the 1936 Summer Olympics." *Wikipedia*. September 13, 2019. https://en.wikipedia.org/wiki/Basketball_at_the_1936_Summer_Olympics

69. "1972 Olympic Men's Basketball Final." *Wikipedia*. October 13, 2019. https://en.wikipedia.org/wiki/1972_Olympic_Men%27s_Ba sketball_Final

70. Amdur, Neil. "The Three Seconds That Never Seem to Run Out." *The New York Times*. July 28, 2012. https://www.nytimes.com/2012/07/29/sports/olympics/three-seconds-of-the-munich-olympics-that-never-seem-to-run-out.html

71. Saraceno, Frank. "Classic 1972 USA vs. USSR Basketball game." *ESPN Classic*. August 6, 2004. http://www.espn.com/classic/s/Classic_1972_usa_ussr_gold _medal_hoop.html

72. "Basketball at the 1976 Summer Olympics." *Wikipedia*. August 15, 2019. https://en.wikipedia.org/wiki/Basketball_at_the_1976_Sum mer_Olympics

73. Claiborne, William. "Jerusalem a Humbling Experience for the Bullets." *Washington Post*. September 7, 1978. https://www.washingtonpost.com/archive/sports/1978/09/0 7/jerusalem-a-humbling-experience-for-the-bullets/38a846c8-538f-44ab-89d7-321cb95725e7/

74. Parker, Josh. "This Day in History: First NBA Team Plays in China." *thatsmags.com*. August 24, 2018. http://www.thatsmags.com/beijing/post/20352/this-day-in-history-washington- bullets-visit-china

75. "1977-78 Washington Bullets Roster and Stats." *Basketball Reference*. n.d. https://www.basketball-reference.com/teams/WSB/1978.html

76. "Maccabi Tel Aviv B.C. *Wikipedia*. November 1, 2019. https://en.wikipedia.org/wiki/Maccabi_Tel_Aviv_B.C.

77. Buckner, Candace. "The Wizards' ties to China stretch back nearly 40 years, to the days of the Bullets." *Washington Post*. October 1, 2017. https://www.washingtonpost.com/news/wizards-insider/wp/2017/10/01/the-wizards-ties-to-china-stretch-back-nearly-40-years-to-the-days-of-the-bullets/

78. "Virtus Pallacanestro Bologna." *Wikipedia*. October 26, 2019. https://en.wikipedia.org/wiki/Virtus_Pallacanestro_Bologn a#Through_1980s

79. Scheitrum, Kevin. "History of the NBA Global Games." *NBA.com.* n.d. https://www.nba.com/global/games2013/all-time-international-game-list.html

80. Fall, Steve. "Recalling the Hawks' Trip to Russia in 1988." *NBA.com.* September 25, 2013. https://www.nba.com/hawks/recalling-hawks-trip-russia-1988

81. "Wilkins Honored as One of 35 Greatest McDonald's All Americans." *NBA.com.* n.d. https://www.nba.com/hawks/news/wilkins-honored-one-35-greatest-mcdonalds-all-americans

82. Walker, Jason. "Dominique Wilkins ESPN Documentary shows what was behind all the   highlights." *peachtreehoops.com.* April 15, 2016. https://www.peachtreehoops.com/2015/4/15/8419137/dominique-wilkins-espn-documentary-atlanta-hawks

83. "Dominique Wilkins." *sports.jrank.org.* n.d. https://sports.jrank.org/pages/5290/Wilkins-Dominique-Born-in-Paris-France.html

84. Bilic, Linda & George. "Dominique Wilkins." *The HistoryMakers.* October 5, 2016. https://www.thehistorymakers.org/biography/dominique-wilkins

85. "Dominique Wilkins." *Sports Reference.* n.d. https://www.sports-reference.com/cbb/players/dominique-wilkins-1.html

86. "Legends profile: Dominique Wilkins." *NBA.com.* n.d. https://www.nba.com/history/legends/profiles/dominique-wilkins

87. Dover, Sandy. "1985: AN NBA SLAM DUNK CONTEST RETROSPECTIVE." *SLAM.* February 16, 2010. https://www.slamonline.com/archives/1985-an-nba-slam-dunk-contest- retrospective/

88. Greer, Jordan. "Dominique Wilkins still thinks he beat Michael Jordan in 1988 Slam Dunk Contest." *SportingNews.* February 18, 2017. https://www.sportingnews.com/us/nba/news/dominique-

wilkins-nba-slam-dunk-contest-michael-jordan-
1988/yhkk5zfmqh151s0gwlsyo2ytr

89. Thomsen, Ian International Herald Tribune. "'Easy Money' Opens
Door to Hard Times in Greece for a Former NBA Star/
Vantage Point." *The New York Times*. March 12, 1996.
https://www.nytimes.com/1996/03/12/sports/IHT-easy-
money-opens-door-to-hard-times-in-greece-for-a-former-
nba.html

90. Spears, Marc J. "Dominique Wilkins: 'Father Time don't wait for no
one, man'." *The Undefeated*. November 13, 2018.
https://theundefeated.com/features/dominique-wilkins-
carmelo-anthony-father-time-dont-wait-for-no-one-man/

91. Bernstein, Joshua D. "Dominique Wilkins (b. 1960)." *New Georgia
Encyclopedia*. January 14, 2005.
https://www.georgiaencyclopedia.org/articles/sports-
outdoor-recreation/dominique-wilkins-b-1960

92. "Dominique Wilkins." *Basketball Reference*. n.d.
https://www.basketball-
reference.com/players/w/wilkido01.html

93. "Hakeem Olajuwon." *Sports Reference*. n.d.
https://www.sports-reference.com/cbb/players/hakeem-
olajuwon-1.html

94. "Hakeem Olajuwon: Living The Dream." *Houston Alumni
Association*. n.d.
https://houstonalumni.com/notable-alumni/hakeem-
olajuwon/

95. "Legends profile: Hakeem Olajuwon." *NBA.com*. n.d.
https://www.nba.com/history/legends/profiles/hakeem-
olajuwon

96. Evans, Thayer. "Long Arms Groom Nigeria's Long Shot." *The New
York Times*. August 14, 2006.
https://www.nytimes.com/2006/08/14/sports/basketball/14o
lajuwon.html

97. "Hakeem Olajuwon Quotes." *Brainy Quote*. n.d.
https://www.brainyquote.com/authors/hakeem-olajuwon-
quotes

98. "Hakeem Olajuwon." *Basketball Reference*. n.d.

https://www.basketball-reference.com/players/o/olajuha01.html

99. "Hakeem Olajuwon." *Wikipedia*. October 4, 2019.
    https://en.wikipedia.org/wiki/Hakeem_Olajuwon

100. "Your Gifts at Work Living the Dream." *University of Houston Giving*. n.d.
    http://development.uh.edu/blog/living-the-dream/

101. Case, Jeff. "Legendary Moments In NBA History: Hakeem Olajuwon powers Houston Rockets to 1994 title." *NBA.com*. June 21, 2018.
    https://www.nba.com/article/2018/06/21/legendary-moments-history-hakeem-olajuwon-dominates-game-7-1994-finals

102. "Patrick Ewing Basketball's "most Important Figure"." *sports.jrank.org*. n.d.
    https://sports.jrank.org/pages/1395/Ewing-Patrick-Basketball-s-Most-Important-Figure.html

103. "Patrick Ewing "something I'd Have To Work At"." *sports.jrank.org*. n.d.
    https://sports.jrank.org/pages/1394/Ewing-Patrick--Something-I-d-Have-Work-At.html

104. Ballard, Chris. "The Ewing Conspiracy." *SI.com*. May 12, 1985.
    https://www.si.com/longform/2015/1985/ewing/index.html

105. "Patrick Ewing." *Wikipedia*. October 27, 2019.
    https://en.wikipedia.org/wiki/Patrick_Ewing

106. "Patrick Ewing." *Sports Reference*. n.d.
    https://www.sports-reference.com/cbb/players/patrick-ewing-1.html

107. "Patrick Ewing." *Basketball Reference*. n.d.
    https://www.basketball-reference.com/players/e/ewingpa01.html

108. Augustyn, Adam. "Patrick Ewing." *Britannica*. n.d.
    https://www.britannica.com/biography/Patrick-Ewing

109. "Manute Bol." *Famous African Americans*. n.d.
    https://www.famousafricanamericans.org/manute-bol.

110. "Manute Bol." *Basketball Reference*. n.d.
https://www.basketballreference.com/players/b/bolma01.html.

111. Harden, Blaine. "The Long Lonely Journey of Manute Bol: You Can Take the Basketball Player Out of Africa, but You Can't Take the African Out of the Basketball Player." *Washington Post*. March 22, 1987.
https://www.washingtonpost.com/archive/lifestyle/magazine/1987/03/22/the-long-lonely-journey-of-manute-bol-you-can-take-the-basketball-player-out-of-africa-but-you-cant-take-the-africa-out-of-the-basketball-player/957c6862-1292-42e1-9c57-d043882e2c9a/

112. "Manute Bol." *Wikipedia*. September 21, 2019.
https://en.wikipedia.org/wiki/Manute_Bol

113. Cox, Tony. "Former NBA Star Manute Bol Remembered for Height, Charity." June 21, 2010. *National Public Radio*.
https://www.npr.org/templates/story/story.php?storyId=127985053

114. "In Honor of Drazen Petrovic." *NBA.com*. n.d.
http://www.nba.com/nets/history/drazenpetrovic.html

115. The Editors of Britannica. "Drazen Petrovic Croatian Basketball Player." *Britannica*. n.d.
https://www.britannica.com/biography/Drazen-Petrovic

116. Blazeski, Goran. "Drazen Petrovic: The story of a star that didn't get to shine." *The Vintage News*. October 16, 2016.
https://www.thevintagenews.com/2016/10/16/drazen-petrovic-the-story-of-a-star-that-didnt-get-to-shine/

117. "Drazen Petrovic." *Wikipedia*. October 26, 2019.
https://en.wikipedia.org/wiki/Dražen_Petrović

118. "Drazen Petrovic." *Basketball Reference*. n.d.
https://www.basketball-reference.com/players/p/petrodr01.html

119. Spehr, Todd. "The tragic death of Drazen Petrovic." *Sports Illustrated*. March 29, 2015.
https://www.si.com/nba/2015/03/30/drazen-petrovic-nets-book-excerpt-car-accident-death

120. Nizinski, John. "Drazen Petrovic: Remembering the Star That Didn't

Get to Shine." *Bleacher Report*. January 17, 2002. https://bleacherreport.com/articles/1020997-drazen-petrovic-remembering-the-star-that-didnt-get-to-shine

121. "Dikembe Mutombo Growing Up In Africa." *Sports.jrank.org*. n.d. https://sports.jrank.org/pages/3382/Mutombo-Dikembe-Growing-Up-in-Africa.html

122. Augustyn, Adam. "Dikembe Mutombo Congolese-American Basketball Player."*Britannica*. n.d. https://www.britannica.com/biography/Dikembe-Mutombo

123. "Dikembe Mutombo." *Basketball Reference*. n.d. https://www.sports-reference.com/cbb/players/dikembe-mutombo-1.html

124. "1990-91 Denver Nuggets Roster and Stats." *Basketball Reference*. n.d. https://www.basketball-reference.com/teams/DEN/1991.html

125. "Dikembe Mutombo Develops Basketball Skills." *Sports.jrank.org*. https://sports.jrank.org/pages/3383/Mutombo-Dikembe-Develops-Basketball-Skills.html

126. "Dikembe Mutombo." *Sports Reference*. n.d. https://www.sports-reference.com/cbb/players/dikembe-mutombo-1.html

127. Augustyn, Adam. "Dikembe Mutombo." *Britannica*. n.d. https://www.britannica.com/biography/Dikembe-Mutombo

128. "2001-02 Philadelphia 76ers Roster and Stats." *Basketball Reference*. n.d. https://www.basketball-reference.com/teams/PHI/2002.html

129. "2002-03 New Jersey Nets Roster and Stats." *Basketball Reference*. n.d. https://www.basketball-reference.com/teams/NJN/2003.html

130. "2003-04 New York Knicks Roster and Stats." *Basketball Reference*. n.d. https://www.basketball-reference.com/teams/NYK/2004.html

131. "Dikembe Mutombo." Wikipedia. October 24, 2019. https://en.wikipedia.org/wiki/Dikembe_Mutombo

132. "2004-05 Houston Rockets Roster and Stats." *Basketball Reference*.

n.d. https://www.basketball-reference.com/teams/HOU/2005.html

133. Whitley, Heather. "Big Hands and a big heart saves tiny lives in The Congo." *CNN World*. February 16, 2014. https://www.cnn.com/2014/02/10/world/africa/iyw-dikembe-mutombo/index.html?no-st=9999999999

134. "1981-82 Washington Huskies Roster and Stats." *Sports Reference*. n.d. https://www.sports-reference.com/cbb/schools/washington/1982.html

135. "1983-84 Washington Huskies Schedule and Roster." *Sports Reference*. n.d. https://www.sports-reference.com/cbb/schools/washington/1984-schedule.html

136. "1984-85 Washington Huskies Schedule and Results." *Sports Reference*. n.d. https://www.sports-reference.com/cbb/schools/washington/1985-schedule.html

137. "Detlef Schrempf." *Wikipedia*. September 21, 2019. https://en.wikipedia.org/wiki/Detlef_Schrempf

138. "Detlef Schrempf." *Sports Reference*. n.d. https://www.sports-reference.com/cbb/players/detlef-schrempf-1.html

139. Green, Tom. "Two West Germans Play for Huskies." *UPI*. January 28, 1984.https://www.upi.com/Archives/1984/01/28/Two-West-Germans-Play-for-Huskies/2339444114000/

140. Engel, Mac. "As we say goodbye to Dirk, thank the German Mavs who made him possible: Uwe and Detlef." *Fort Worth Star-Telegram*. April 9, 2016. https://www.startelegram.com/sports/sptcolumnsblogs/mac engel/article228895099.html

141. Webeck, Evan. "Catching Up With … Detlef Schrempf." *Sports Illustrated*. August 11, 2014. https://www.si.com/nba/2014/08/12/detlef-schrempf-nba-sonics-pacers-parks-and-recreation

142. Brunner, Conrad. "Where are They Now? Detlef Schrempf. *NBA.com*. September 10, 2002. https://www.nba.com/pacers/news/detlefschrempfhtml

143. "Detlef Schrempf." *Basketball Reference*. n.d.

https://www.basketball-reference.com/players/s/schrede01.html

144. Lisk, Jason. "The Dallas Mavericks Once Passes on Drafting Karl Malone and Their GM Called Him "Half a Man."." *The Big Lead*. June 13, 2016. https://www.thebiglead.com/2016/06/13/the-dallas-mavericks-once-passed-on-drafting-karl-malone-and-their-gm-called-him-half-a-man/

145. "Arvydas Sabonis' Career Retrospective." *YouTube*. August 31, 2011. https://www.youtube.com/watch?v=18tnToDLHV4&t=126s.

146. "Arvydas Sabonis." *Wikipedia*. November 2, 2019. https://en.wikipedia.org/wiki/Arvydas_Sabonis

147. Abrams, Jonathan. "Arvydas Sabonis' Long, Strange Trip." *Grantland*. August 29, 2011. https://grantland.com/features/arvydas-sabonis-long-strange-trip/.

148. "InterBasket>Profiles>Sabonis." *Interbasket.net*. n.d. https://www.interbasket.net/players/sabonis.htm.

149. "The Legend, Zalgiris Kaunas: Arvydas Sabonis." *Euroleague.net*. May 8, 2018. https://www.euroleague.net/news/i/8q43bf557tqcqkg5/the-legend-zalgiris-kaunas-arvydas-sabonis.

150. "Arvydas Sabonis." *Basketball Reference*. n.d. https://www.basketball-reference.com/players/s/sabonar01.html.

151. "Portland Trail Blazers." *Basketball Reference*. n.d. https://www.basketball-reference.com/teams/POR/.

152. Smith, Keith. "Arvydas Sabonis: The Original Unicorn." *Medium.com*. n.d. https://medium.com/@keithpsmith78/arvydas-sabonis-the-original-unicorn-a10ab6c3738e.

153. "Rik Smits." *Basketball Reference*. n.d. https://www.basketball-reference.com/players/s/smitsri01.html

154. "1988 NBA Draft." *Basketball Reference*. n.d. https://www.basketball-reference.com/draft/NBA_1988.html

155. "1984-85 Marist Red Foxes Roster and Stats." *Sports Reference*. n.d. https://www.sports-reference.com/cbb/schools/marist/1985.html

156. "Rik Smits." *Sports Reference*. n.d. https://www.sports-reference.com/cbb/players/rik-smits-1.html

157. Benbow, Dana Hunsinger. "30 years ago, Rik Smits became the improbable superstar of the Indiana Pacers." *Indianapolis Star*. October 31, 2018. https://www.indystar.com/story/sports/2018/10/31/30-years-ago-rik-smits-became-unlikely-superstar-indiana-pacers/1814783002/

158. Webb, Tyler. "The Oral History of the Rik Smits Era at Marist College. *Centerfield Marist*. January 31, 2019. https://centerfieldmarist.com/2019/01/31/the-oral-history-of-the-rik-smits-era-at-marist- college/

159. Ryan, Shannon. "Rik Smits battled the Bulls with the 1990s Pacers. Now his son is playing a big role for Valparaiso." *Chicago Tribune*. January 19, 2019. https://www.chicagotribune.com/sports/college/ct-spt-valparaiso-derrik-smits-rik-son-20190119-story.html

160. "Rik Smits." Wikipedia. September 24, 2019. https://en.wikipedia.org/wiki/Rik_Smits

161. "Rik Smits [1966] Professional Sports Figure." *New Netherland Institute*. n.d. https://www.newnetherlandinstitute.org/history-and-heritage/dutch_americans/rik-smits/

162. Ryan, Bob. "ADVICE FOR THE DRAFT: GET IN EARLY." *Chicago Tribune*. June 20, 1988. https://www.chicagotribune.com/news/ct-xpm-1988-06-20-8801090212-story.html

163. "Catching up with Rik and Derrik Smits." *Zionville Monthly Magazine*. n.d. https://zionsvillemonthlymagazine.com/catching-up-with-rik-and-derrik-smits/

164. "Vlade Divac Retires." *ESPN.com*. July 15, 2005. https://www.espn.com/blog/truehoop/post/_/id/303/vlade-divac-retires

165. Jones, Jason. "Vlade Divac was a bridge-builder for European players, a leader and now Hall of Famer." *The Athletic*. April 7, 2019. https://theathletic.com/911409/2019/04/08/vlade-divac-was-a- bridge-builder-for-european-players-a-leader-and-now-a-hall-of-famer/?redirected=1

166. "General Manager Vlade Divac." *NBA.com*. n.d. https://www.nba.com/kings/roster/vlade_divac

167. "Vlade Divac." *Wikipedia*. November 5, 2019. https://en.wikipedia.org/wiki/Vlade_Divac

168. "Vlade Divac." *LA Times All Things Lakers*. n.d. http://projects.latimes.com/lakers/player/vlade-divac/

169. "Year-by-year NBA All-Rookie Teams." *NBA History*. March 23, 2019. https://www.nba.com/history/awards/all-rookie-team

170. "Vlade Divac." *Basketball Reference*. n.d. https://www.basketball-reference.com/players/d/divacvl01.html

171. "1989-90 Los Angeles Lakers Roster and Stats." *Basketball Reference*. n.d. https://www.basketball-reference.com/teams/LAL/1990.html

172. "1998-99 Sacramento Kings Roster and Stats." *Basketball Reference*. n.d.https://www.basketball-reference.com/teams/SAC/1999.html

173. Associated Press. "Divac will scout for the Lakers." *Deseret News*. October 19, 2005. https://www.deseret.com/platform/amp/2005/10/19/19918080/divac-will-scout-for-the-lakers

174. "SER – Divac chosen as new president of Serbian Olympic Committee." *FIBA.basketball*. February 2, 2009. http://www.fiba.basketball/news/SER---Divac-chosen-as-new-president-of-Serbian-	Olympic-Committee

175. Golianopoulous, Thomas. "It Was All About Money.": An Oral History of the 1998-99 NBA Lockout." *The Ringer*. February 14, 2019. https://www.theringer.com/nba/2019/2/14/18222040/lockout - 1998-99-season-david-stern-david-falk-billy-hunter-patrick-ewing-michael-jordan-oral-history

176. Levitt, Zak. "The Dream Team." *IMDb.com*. June 13, 2012.
https://www.imdb.com/title/tt2292576/

177. Emerick, Peter. "Legends of the NBA: 25 Best Players of the 80s."
Bleacher Report. September 20, 2012.
https://bleacherreport.com/articles/1338152-legends-of-the-nba-25-best-players-of-the-80s#slide19

178. NBA.com Staff. "Top Moments: Dream Team takes world by storm
in 1992." *NBA History*. n.d.
https://www.nba.com/history/top-moments/1992-dream-team-usa-basketball

179. AP. "Dream Team, Barcelona Games continue to impact NBA." *USA
Today*. September 15, 2014.
https://www.usatoday.com/story/sports/nba/2014/09/15/dream-team-barcelona-games-continue-to-impact-nba/15654271/

180. Walsh, Peter. "The Relentless Drive of Toni Kukoc." *Narratively*.
February 8, 2015.
https://narratively.com/the-relentless-drive-of-toni-kukoc/

181. "Toni Kukoc. *Wikipedia*. September 25, 2019.
https://en.wikipedia.org/wiki/Toni_Kuko%C4%8D

182. "Toni Kukoc." *Basketball Reference*. n.d.
https://www.basketball-reference.com/players/k/kukocto01.html

183. Zucker, Joseph. "Toni Kukoc Named Special Advisor to Chicago
Bulls COO Michael Reinsdorf." *Bleacher Report*. August
17, 2015. https://bleacherreport.com/articles/2549647-toni-kukoc-named-special-advisor-to-bulls-coo-

184. "Toni Kukoc In FIMBA." *FIMBA MAXIBASKETBALL*. n.d.
http://www.fimba.net/en/fullnews.php?id=249

185. Farnsworth, Clyde H. "Path Is Cleared for Toronto to Rejoin N.B.A.
The New York Times. February 11, 1994.
https://www.nytimes.com/1994/02/11/sports/path-is-cleared-for-toronto-to-rejoin-nba.html

186. Dodge, Sam. "Raptors NBA Finals: How Long has Toronto Been in
League? *Heavy.com*. May 30, 2019.
https://heavy.com/sports/2019/05/toronto-raptors-how-long-in-nba/

187. "Laying the Groundwork for the NBA in Toronto." *NBA.com*. n.d. https://www.nba.com/raptors/history/raptors_history.html

188. "Toronto Raptors Team History." *Sports Team History*. n.d. https://sportsteamhistory.com/toronto-raptors

189. "NBA Settles North Of The Border." *NBA.com*. n.d. https://www.nba.com/grizzlies/history/00400478.html

190. Francis, Steve. "I Got a Story to Tell." *The Players' Tribune*. March 8, 2018. https://www.theplayerstribune.com/en-us/articles/steve-francis-i-got-a-story-to-tell

191. Schwartz, Peter. "NBA: a Case Study of the Vancouver Grizzlies." *Bleacher Report*. January 19, 2011. https://bleacherreport.com/articles/578763-the-vancouver-grizzlies-a-case-study

192. Unterberger, Andrew. "Draft Flashback: Did drafting Steve Francis kill the Vancouver Grizzlies?" *The Score*. n.d. https://www.thescore.com/nba/news/525985

193. "1995 NBA Draft." *Basketball Reference*. n.d. https://www.basketball-reference.com/draft/NBA_1995.html

194. "Looking Back 90 Years: The NBA Comes Back to Canada." *Canada Basketball*. n.d. http://www.basketball.ca/f/news-article/looking-back-90-years-the-nba-comes-back-to-canada-p154197

195. "1995 NBA Draft." *nbadraft.net*. n.d. https://www.nbadraft.net/nba_draft_history/1995.html

196. Gaines, Cork and Davis, Scott. "WHERE ARE THEY NOW? The players from Kevin Garnett's 1995 NBA Draft class." *Business Insider*. September 24, 2016. https://www.businessinsider.com/where-are-they-now-1995-nba-draft-2016-9

197. Thomas, Vincent. "Dream Team II: The U.S. Team That Time Forgot." *Bleacher Report*. September 11, 2014. https://bleacherreport.com/articles/2186790-dream-team-ii-the-us-team-that-time-forgot

198. "A Look Back At The USA Men's 1994 World Championship Gold Medal." *USA Basketball*. July 20, 2014. https://www.usab.com/news-events/news/2014/07/a-look-

back-at-the-usa-mens-1994-world-championship-gold-medal.aspx

199. Maisonet, Eddie. "Dream Team II: the cocky champions history forgot." *SBNation*. August 29, 2014. https://www.sbnation.com/2014/8/29/6006257/dream-team-ii-fiba-world-cup-1994

200. Moll, Allen. "Remembering Dream Teams II and III." *The Hoops Doctors*. October 13, 2009. http://thehoopdoctors.com/2009/10/remembering-dream-teams-ii-and-iii/

201. "1994 World Championship For Men." *FIBA ARCHIVE*. August 14, 1994. https://archive.fiba.com/pages/eng/fa/team/p/sid/2913/tid/379/_/1994_World_Championship_for_Men/index.html

202. "Steve Nash." *Sports Reference*. n.d. https://www.sports-reference.com/cbb/players/steve-nash-1.html

203. "Steve Nash." *Basketball Reference*. n.d. https://www.basketball-reference.com/players/n/nashst01.html

204. McPeek, Jeramie. "The Canadian Kid." *NBA.com*. July 12, 2004. https://www.nba.com/suns/news/fastbreak_nash_cover.html

205. Zarum, Dave. "Steve Nash." *The Canadian Encyclopedia*. May 27, 2008.https://www.thecanadianencyclopedia.ca/en/article/steve-nash

206. Wahl, Grant. "Inside Steve Nash's Futbol Fascination." *Sports Illustrated*. 28 October 2016. https://www.si.com/nba/2016/10/28/steve-nash-soccer-tottenham-whitecaps-mallorca-warriors.

207. "Stephen J. "Steve" Nash '96." *Bronco Bench Foundation*. n.d. https://www.scu.edu/athletics/broncobench/hall-of-fame/hall-of-fame-inductees/nash-steven-j-steve/.

208. Cunningham, Cody. "Steve Nash: The Unlikely Journey of a Two-Time MVP." 6 September 2018. *NBA*. https://www.nba.com/suns/features/steve-nash-unlikely-journey-two-time-mvp#.

209. Zawistowski, Richie. "Steve Nash Proves He and the Phoenix Suns Are Still Amongst NBA Elite. *Bleacher Report*. May 4, 2010. https://bleacherreport.com/articles/387765-steve-nash-proves-he-and-the-suns-are-still-amongst-nba-elite.

210. "2005-06 NBA Award Voting." *Basketball Reference*. n.d. https://www.basketball-reference.com/awards/awards_2006.html.

211. McPeek, Jeramie. "Steve Nash 2004-05 NBA Most Valuable Player Award." *NBA.com*. May 8, 2005. https://www.nba.com/suns/news/nash_mvp_050508.html#

212. "Nash Officially Named MVP For 2nd Straight Season." SportsTwo. May 7, 2006. http://www.sportstwo.com/threads/nash-officially-named-mvp-for-2nd-straight-season.11411/

213. "Steve Nash Out for the Season." *Los Angeles Lakers*. 23 Oct. 2014. https://www.nba.com/lakers/news/141023_steveNash.

214. "Point Guards Steve Nash, Jason Kidd and Maurice Cheeks among Hall Inductees."*Associated Press*. September 8, 2018. https://www.espn.com/nba/story/_/id/24611047/steve-nash-jason-kidd-maurice-cheeks-basketball-hall-fame-inductees.

215. Peterson, Matt. "Prodigal Sun: Steve Nash shines through it all to reach hoops immortality." *NBA.com*. September 1, 2018. https://www.nba.com/article/2018/09/01/steve-nash-prodigal-sun-hall-fame

216. "Barkley Dishes on Night He Discovered Nowitzki." *FOXSPORTS*. July 1, 2012. https://www.foxsports.com/arizona/story/barkley-dishes-on-night-he-discovered-nowitzki-070112.

217. Doyle, Rader. "Dirk Nowitzki Plays His Final NBA Game, Ending an Historic Career. *Forbes*. April 11, 2019. https://www.forbes.com/sites/doylerader/2019/04/11/dirk-nowitzki-final-nba-game-historic-career-dallas-mavericks/#7b9cface685f.

218. "Dallas Mavericks." *Basketball Reference*. n.d. https://www.basketball-reference.com/teams/DAL/.

219. Augustyn, Adam. "Dirk Nowitzki German Basketball Player. *Britannica*. June 15, 2019. https://www.britannica.com/biography/Dirk-Nowitzki

220. Eisenberg, Jeff. "Charles Barkley once tried to bribe Dirk Nowitzki to come to Auburn." *Yahoo Sports*. July 2, 2012. https://sports.yahoo.com/blogs/ncaab-the-dagger/charles-barkley-once-tried-bribe-dirk-nowitzki-come-153031318--ncaab.html

221. "Dirk Nowitzki." *Basketball Reference*. n.d. https://www.basketball-reference.com/players/n/nowitdi01.html.

222. "#56 Dirk Nowitzki." *Forbes*. June 7, 2017. https://www.forbes.com/profile/dirk-nowitzki/#29df7ef20603.

223. "NBA History - Points Leaders." *ESPN*. n.d. http://www.espn.com/nba/history/leaders.

224. Chang, Ailsa. "A Look At The Legacy Dirk Nowitzki Is Leaving In Dallas After His 21-Year NBA Career." *NPR*. April 10, 2019. https://www.npr.org/2019/04/10/711951976/a-look-at-the-legacy-dirk-nowitzki-is-leaving-in-dallas-after-his-21-year-nba-ca

225. Stein, Mark. "Dirk Nowitzki Knew LeBron Would Pass Him, but He's Still Gunning for Wilt." *The New York Times*. November 7, 2018. https://www.nytimes.com/2018/11/07/sports/dirk-nowitzki-lebron-james.html

226. Associated Press. "Mavericks Thump Knicks as Dirk Nowitzki Comes Alive at The Garden." *The New York Times*. January 30, 2019 https://www.nytimes.com/2019/01/30/sports/basketball/knicks-mavericks-dirk-nowitzki.html

227. Wise, Mike. "PRO BASKETBALL; The Americanization of Dirk Nowitzki." *The New York Times*. February 7, 2001. https://www.nytimes.com/2001/02/07/sports/pro-basketball-the-americanization-of-dirk-nowitzki.html

228. Dominguez, Raul, The Associated Press. "Dirk Nowitzki brought to tears during tribute video, thanks Spurs and fans." *KSAT*. April 10, 2019. https://www.ksat.com/sports/nba/spurs/dirk-nowitzki-brought-to-tears-during-tribute-video-thanks-spurs-and-fans

229. "Schrempf discusses Nowitzki and his legacy on Kevin Garnett's

"Area 21". *Eurohoops.net*. February 20, 2017.
https://www.eurohoops.net/en/nba-news/404681/schrempf-
discusses-nowitzki-legacy-kevin-garnetts-area-21/

230. Stein, Marc. "With a Flurry of Shots, Dirk Nowitzki Wraps Up His
Time in Dallas." *The New York Times*. April 10, 2019.
https://www.nytimes.com/2019/04/10/sports/dirk-nowitzki-
retirement.html

231. "Peja Stojakovic." *Wikipedia*. November 7, 2019.
https://en.wikipedia.org/wiki/Peja_Stojakovi%C4%87

232. "Peja Stojakovic." *Basketball Reference*." n.d.
https://www.basketball-
reference.com/players/s/stojape01.html

233. "Assistant General Manager Peja Stojakovic." *NBA.com*. n.d.
https://www.nba.com/kings/roster/peja_stojakovic

234. Stein, Marc. "Peja Stojakovic to retire after 13 years." *ESPN.com*.
December 19, 2011.
https://www.espn.com/nba/story/_/id/7370035/peja-
stojakovic-decides-retirement-dallas-mavericks-
championship-run

235. Jones, Jason. "Kings make a change to Peja Stojakovic's job title. How
his role will be affected." *The Sacramento Bee*. May 9,
2018. https://www.sacbee.com/sports/nba/sacramento-
kings/kings-blog/article210750459.html

236. "Sacramento Kings to Retire Jersey of Peja Stojakovic." *NBA.com*.
September 16, 2014.
https://www.nba.com/kings/news/kings-to-retire-jersey-of-
peja-stojakovic

237. "Diamantidis named mister Europe 2007." *FIBA Europe*. December
10, 2007.
http://www.fibaeurope.com/nfID_291.coid_9FRlHDPsIj2X
5N4sgG43m0.articleMode_on.html

238. Weitzman, Yaron. "Peta Stojakovic Helped Save the Way for
European Players." *Slam*. February 14, 2018.
https://www.slamonline.com/nba/peja-stojakovic-feature/.

239. Brown, Clifton. "The Foundation of a Dynasty." *NBA Encyclopedia
Playoff Edition*. n.d.
http://archive.nba.com/encyclopedia/celtics_1957.html.

240. Saleh, Tariq. "The San Antonio Spurs A Dynasty that Began on This Day 23 Years Ago." *Givemesport.* March 26, 2016. https://www.givemesport.com/737840-the-san-antonio-spurs-a-dynasty-that-began-on-this-day-23-years-ago.

241. "2018-19 San Antonio Spurs: Roster and Stats." *Basketball Reference.* n.d. https://www.basketball-reference.com/teams/SAS/2019.html.San

242. "1998 San Antonio Spurs Roster and Stats." *Basketball Reference.* n.d. https://www.basketball-reference.com/teams/SAS/1998.html.

243. "1999 NBA Playoffs Summary." *Basketball Reference.* n.d. https://www.basketball-reference.com/playoffs/NBA_1999.html.

244. Broussard, Chris. "N.B.A. Finals; For Spurs, One Title Just Is Not Enough." *The New York Times.* June 27, 1999. https://www.nytimes.com/1999/06/27/sports/nba-finals-for-spurs-one-title-just-is-not-enough.html.

245. "Tim Duncan Remembers Not Knowing Who Manu Ginobili Was When Spurs Drafted Him." *YouTube.* March 28, 2019. https://www.youtube.com/watch?v=JXSSE8KUp6s.

246. "Tony Parker." *Basketball Reference.* n.d. https://www.basketball-reference.com/players/p/parketo01.html.

247. "2003 NBA Playoff Summary." *Basketball Reference.* n.d. https://www.basketball-reference.com/playoffs/NBA_2003.html.

248. "NBA: Spurs' Big Three's Legacy Defined by Championships." *GMA News Online.* June 17, 2014. https://www.gmanetwork.com/news/sports/basketball/366032/nba-spurs-big-three-s-legacy-defined-by-championships/story/.

249. Loverro, Thom. "Tim Duncan Changed the NBA in a Greater Way Than Kobe or LeBron." *The Washington Times.* July 12, 2016. https://www.washingtontimes.com/news/2016/jul/12/tim-duncan-changed-nba-greater-way-kobe-and-lebron/.

250. Rollins, Khadrice. "Spurs Legend Tim Duncan to Join Gregg

Popovich's Staff as Assistant Coach." *Sports Illustrated.* July 22, 2019. https://www.si.com/nba/2019/07/22/tim-duncan-spurs-assistant-coach-gregg-popovich.

251. "Manu Ginobili." *Basketball Reference.* n.d. https://www.basketball-reference.com/players/g/ginobma01.html

252. Curtis, Charles. "Tony Parker Retires as the Greatest European Guard Ever to Play in the NBA." *USA Today.* June 10, 2019. https://ftw.usatoday.com/2019/06/tony-parker-retires-nba-greatest-european.

253. Amack, Sam. "Manu Ginobili Leaves Legacy of Selfless, Passionate Play with Spurs." *USA Today.* August 27, 2018. https://www.usatoday.com/story/sports/nba/columnist/sam-amick/2018/08/27/manu-ginobili-spurs-retirement-legacy-passionate-selfless-play/1116280002/.

254. "Tim Duncan." *Basketball Reference.* n.d. https://www.basketball-reference.com/players/d/duncati01.html

255. Spears, Marc J. 'I can't be Tony Parker anymore.' *The Undefeated.* June 10, 2019. https://theundefeated.com/features/tony-parker-retire-from-nba/

256. The Editors of Encyclopedia Britannica. "Yao Ming Chinese Basketball Player." *Britannica.* n.d. https://www.britannica.com/biography/Yao-Ming

257. Feigen, Jonathan. "Rockets' Yao Makes It Official, Retires from Basketball." *Chron.* July 20, 2011. https://www.chron.com/sports/rockets/article/Rockets-Yao-makes-it-official-retires-from-2081184.php.

258. Pan, Jeff. "Yao Ming the Philosopher." *China Daily.* March 1, 2007. http://www.chinadaily.com.cn/sports/2007-03/01/content_817152.htm.

259. "Statistics from Yao Ming in CBA (China). *World Hoopsstats.* n.d. http://english.worldhoopstats.com/stats/cba-cn/yao-ming-101628.html.

260. Case, Jeff. "legendary Moments in NBA History: Houston Rockets

Draft Yao Ming with No. 1 Pick." *NBA History.* June 28, 2018. https://www.nba.com/article/2018/06/25/legendary-moments-history-houston-rockets-draft-yao-ming-2002.

261. Lago, Joe. "Rockets Make Yao Ming First Overall Pick." *ESPN.* June 26, 2002.
https://www.espn.com/nbadraft/story?id=1399417.

262. "2018-19 Houston Rockets Roster and Stats." *Basketball Reference.* n.d. https://www.basketball-reference.com/teams/HOU/2019.html.

263. "Yao Ming." *Basketball Reference.* n.d.
https://www.basketball-reference.com/players/m/mingya01.html.

264. Ming, Yao. "My Rookie Year." *The Players Tribune.* July 19, 2016. https://www.theplayerstribune.com/en-us/articles/yao-ming-my-rookie-year-rockets-china.

265. "Yao Ming Biography." *The Famous People.* n.d. https://www.theplayerstribune.com/en-us/articles/yao-ming-my-rookie-year-rockets-china.

266. "Former Houston Rockets Star Yao Ming Named President of Chinese Basketball Association." *Associated Press.* February 23, 2017. https://www.nba.com/article/2017/02/23/yao-ming-named-president-chinese-basketball-association.

267. Abrams, Jonathan. "The Legacy of Yao." *Grantland.* July 20, 2011. https://grantland.com/features/the-legacy-yao/.

268. "McGrundy: Bringing Basketball to China Was Yao Ming's Legacy." *The Score.* September 6, 2016. https://www.thescore.com/news/1094823-mcgrady-bringing-basketball-to-china-was-yao-ming-s-legacy?fb_comment_id=1070039646426360_10718816329 08828/amp.

269. Conn, Jordan Ritter. "The (Big) Man Skilled in All Ways of Contending." *Grantland.* February 15, 2013. https://grantland.com/features/memphis-grizzlies-center-marc-gasol-most-overlooked-big-man-nba-maybe-best/.

270. "Pau Gasol Biography." *The Famous People.* n.d. https://www.thefamouspeople.com/profiles/pau-gasol-9027.php.

271. "Marc Gasol." *ESPN*. n.d.
https://www.espn.com/nba/player/_/id/3206/marc-gasol.

272. "#98 Marc Gasol: Athlete NBA." *Forbes*. June 10, 2019.
https://www.forbes.com/profile/marc-gasol/#5b2963536add.

273. "Lakers Acquire Gasol from Grizzlies." *Los Angeles Lakers*. February 1, 2008.
https://www.nba.com/lakers/news/080201gasol_trade.html.

274. "Pau Gasol." Basketball Reference. n.d.
https://www.basketball-reference.com/players/g/gasolpa01.html

275. "Marc Gasol." *Basketball Reference*. n.d.
https://www.basketball-reference.com/players/g/gasolma01.html.

276. "Marc Gasol." *Wikipedia*. November 11, 2019.
https://en.wikipedia.org/wiki/Marc_Gasol

277. Toussaint, Jensen. "Brothers from Spain Become First Sibling Pair Crowned NBA Champions." *Al Dia*. June 17, 2019.
https://aldianews.com/articles/culture/sports/brothers-spain-become-first-sibling-pair-crowned-nba-champions/55847.

278. "Marc Gasol." *Land of Basketball*. n.d.
https://www.landofbasketball.com/nba_players/g/marc_gasol.htm.

279. "Memphis Grizzlies Career Leaders." *Basketball Reference*. n.d.
https://www.landofbasketball.com/nba_players/g/marc_gasol.htm.

280. "NBA Jersey Sponsors Are Seeing Their Investment Pay Off." *Prowl Public Relations*. November 17, 2018.
https://prowlpr.com/2018/11/17/nba-jersey-sponsors-are-seeing-their-investment-pay-off/.

281. Hancock, Benjamin. "The Globalization of the NBA." *Forbes*. June 17, 2013. https://www.forbes.com/sites/sap/2013/06/17/the-globalization-of-the-nba/#fd3c62e71354

282. "List of Team Owners." *Checkli*. n.d.
https://www.checkli.com/checklists/viewro/5b8ccb1b3ed10

283. "Ben Simmons Biography." *The Famous People.* n.d.
https://www.thefamouspeople.com/profiles/ben-simmons-41703.php.

284. Wassink, Zac. "Best Active NBA Player from Every Country."
Yardbarker. December 12, 2018.
https://www.yardbarker.com/nba/articles/best_active_nba_player_from_every_country/s1__27992852.

285. Zucker, Joseph. "2016 NBA Draft Sets Record for Most International
Players Selected in 1st Round." *Bleacher Report.* June 23,
2016. https://bleacherreport.com/articles/2648221-2016-nba-draft-sets-record-for-most-international-players-selected-in-1st-round

286. Zagoria, Adam. "Canada Makes History With Six Players Chosen In
NBA Draft; Knicks Land Two. Forbes. June 21, 2019.
https://www.forbes.com/sites/adamzagoria/2019/06/21/canada-makes-history-with-six-players-chosen-in-nba-draft/#42e6b397fa40

287. "Ben Simmons." *Basketball Reference.* n.d.
https://www.basketball-reference.com/players/s/simmobe01.html.

288. "Jakob Poltl." *Basketball Reference.* n.d.
https://www.basketball-reference.com/players/p/poeltja01.html.

289. "Buddy Hield." *Basketball Reference.* n.d.
https://www.basketball-reference.com/players/h/hieldbu01.html.

290. "Jusuf Nurkic." *Basketball Reference.* n.d.
https://www.basketball-reference.com/players/n/nurkiju01.html.

291. "Nene." *Basketball Reference.* n.d.
https://www.basketball-reference.com/players/h/hilarne01.html.

292. "Joel Embiid's Rise to NBA Stardom." *YouTube.* September 25, 2018.
https://www.youtube.com/watch?v=vlwtwUnwzqg.

293. "Joel Embiid" *Basketball Reference.* n.d.
https://www.basketball-reference.com/players/e/embiijo01.html.

294. "Jamal Murray." *Basketball Reference.* n.d. https://www.basketball-reference.com/players/m/murraja01.html.

295. "Zhou Qi." *Basketball Reference.* n.d. https://www.basketball-reference.com/players/q/qizh01.html.

296. "Zhou Qi G-League Stats." *Basketball Reference.* n.d. https://www.basketball-reference.com/gleague/players/q/qizh01d.html.

297. Kent, Austin. "Former Rockets Center Zhou Qi Sign Contract in China." *Slam.* August 15, 2019. https://www.slamonline.com/nba/former-rockets-center-zhou-qi-signs-contract-in-china/.

298. "Dario Saric." *Basketball Reference.* n.d. https://www.basketball-reference.com/players/s/saricda01.html.

299. "Tomas Satoransky." *Basketball Reference.* n.d. https://www.basketball-reference.com/players/s/satorto01.html.

300. "Emmanuel Mudiay." *Basketball Reference.* n.d. https://www.basketball-reference.com/players/m/mudiaem01.html.

301. "Al Horford." *SRCBB.* n.d. https://www.sports- reference.com/cbb/players/al-horford-1.html.

302. "Al Horford." *Basketball Reference.* n.d. https://www.mobca.org/news_article/show/501906referenc e.com/players/h/horfoal01.html.

303. "OG Anunoby." *Basketball Reference.* n.d. https://www.basketball-reference.com/players/a/anunoog01.html.

304. "MBCA Hall of Fame Weekend Schedule Is Set." *Missouri Basketball Coaches Association.* April 10, 2015. https://www.mobca.org/news_article/show/501906referenc e.com/players/h/horfoal01.html.

305. "Abdel Nader." *Basketball Reference.* n.d.

https://www.basketball-reference.com/players/n/naderab01.html.

306. "Lauri Markkanen." *Basketball Reference.* n.d. https://www.basketball-reference.com/players/m/markkla01.html.

307. "Rudy Gobert." *Basketball Reference.* n.d. https://www.basketball-reference.com/players/g/goberru01.html.

308. "Zaza Pachulia." *Basketball Reference.* n.d. https://www.basketball-reference.com/players/p/pachuza01.html.

309. Myron, Chuck. "Dennis Schroeder to Enter Draft." *Hoop Rumors.* April 19, 2013. https://www.basketball-reference.com/players/p/pachuza01.html.

310. "Dennis Schroder." *Basketball Reference.* n.d. https://www.basketball-reference.com/players/s/schrode01.html.

311. "Skal Labissiere." *Basketball Reference.* n.d. https://www.basketball-reference.com/players/l/labissk01.html.

312. "Omri Casspi." *Basketball Reference.* n.d. https://www.basketball-reference.com/players/c/casspom01.html.

313. "Danilo Gallinari." *Basketball Reference.* n.d. https://www.basketball-reference.com/players/g/gallida01.html.

314. "Kristaps Porzingis." *Basketball Reference.* n.d. https://www.basketball-reference.com/players/p/porzikr01.html.

315. Amann, Ryan. "Kristaps Porzingis' Rise to Fame Was Sudden and Anemic Like He Is." *Sports Journal.* March 11, 2016. http://sportsjournal.ca/2016/03/11/kristaps-porzingis-rise-to-fame-was-sudden-and-anemic-like-he-is/.

316. Wojnarowski, Adrian. "Meet the Euro Prodigy Who Seems Unlike the Flops Who Came before Him." *Yahoo! Sports.* June 15, 2016. https://sports.yahoo.com/news/meet-the-euro-

prodigy-who-seems-unlike-the-flops-who-came-before-him-193427860.html.

317. "Jonas Valanciunas." *Basketball Reference.* n.d. https://www.basketball-reference.com/players/v/valanjo01.html.

318. "Cheick Diallo." *Basketball Reference.* n.d. https://www.basketball-reference.com/players/d/diallch01.html.

319. "Steven Adams." *Basketball Reference.* n.d. https://www.basketball-reference.com/players/a/adamsst01.html.

320. "Josh Okogie." *Basketball Reference.* n.d. https://www.basketball-reference.com/players/o/okogijo01.html.

321. "Marcin Gortat." *Basketball Reference.* n.d. https://www.basketball-reference.com/players/g/gortama01.html.

322. "J. J. Barea." *Basketball Reference.* n.d. https://www.basketball-reference.com/players/b/bareajo01.html.

323. "Timofey Mozgov." *Basketball Reference.* n.d. https://www.basketball-reference.com/players/m/mozgoti01.html.

324. "Gorgui Dieng." *Basketball Reference.* n.d. https://www.basketball-reference.com/players/d/dienggo01.html

325. "Nikola Jokic." *Basketball Reference.* n.d. https://www.basketball-reference.com/players/j/jokicni01.html.

326. Labidou, Alex. "Denver Nuggets' Nikola Jokic for NBA MVP." *NBA.* April 8, 2019. https://www.nba.com/nuggets/news/nuggets-nikola-jokic-for-mvp.

327. "Luca Doncic." *Basketball Reference.* n.d. https://www.basketball-reference.com/players/d/doncilu01.html

328. "Luca Doncic's Farewell Letter: Two Dreams." *Real Madrid.* June 29, 2018. https://www.realmadrid.com/en/news/2018/06/luka-doncics-farewell-letter-two-dreams.

329. Daniels, Tim. "Luca Doncic Wins Rookie of the Year over Trae Young, DeAndre Ayton." *Bleacher Report.* June 24, 2019. https://bleacherreport.com/articles/2832020-luka-doncic-wins-2019-nba-rookie-of-the-year-over-trae-young-deandre-ayton.

330. "Bol Bol." *Basketball Reference.* n.d. https://www.basketball-reference.com/players/b/bolbo01.html.

331. "Jonas Jerebko." *Basketball Reference.* n.d. https://www.basketball-reference.com/players/j/jerebjo01.html.

332. "Clint Capela." *Basketball Reference.* n.d. https://www.basketball-reference.com/players/c/capelca01.html.

333. "Salah Mejri." *Basketball Reference.* n.d. https://www.basketball-reference.com/players/m/mejrisa01.html.

334. "Cedi Osman." *Basketball Reference.* n.d. https://www.basketball-reference.com/players/o/osmande01.html.

335. "Alex Len." *Basketball Reference.* n.d. https://www.basketball-reference.com/players/l/lenal01.html.

336. "Jeremy Lin." *Basketball Reference.* n.d. https://www.basketball-reference.com/players/l/linje01.html.

337. "Jeremy Lin Biography." *The Famous People.* n.d. https://www.thefamouspeople.com/profiles/jeremy-lin-15644.php.Lin."

338. "Jeremy Lin." *SRCBB.* n.d. https://www.sports-reference.com/cbb/players/jeremy-lin-1.html.

339. Hughes, Grant. "Timeline of Jeremy Lin's Rise to Linsanity and

Journey to Where He Is Today." *Bleacher Report.* August 23, 2013. https://bleacherreport.com/articles/1747434-timeline-of-jeremy-lins-rise-to-linsanity-and-journey-to-where-he-is-today.

340. Schilken, Chuck. "Jeremy Lin Struggles as a Free Agent: 'The NBA Has Kind of Given Up on Me.'" *Los Angeles Times.* July 28, 2019. https://www.latimes.com/sports/story/2019-07-28/jeremy-lin-nba-free-agent-rock-bottom.

341. Terranova, Justin. "Jeremy Lin's NBA Fears Realized with Beijing Ducks Signing." *New York Post.* August 27, 2017. https://nypost.com/2019/08/27/jeremy-lins-nba-fears-realized-with-beijing-ducks-signing/.

342. "Nike – I Am Giannis Episode 1: Self Made." *YouTube.* July 1, 2019. https://www.youtube.com/watch?v=XyxLKFDwwU4.

343. "Nike – I Am Giannis Episode 2: Angels." *YouTube.* July 1, 2019. https://www.youtube.com/watch?v=aOFcC6nT3EY.

344. "Nike – I Am Giannis Episode 3: Coming to America." *YouTube.* July 1, 2019. https://www.youtube.com/watch?v=qE13bfZvOOI.

345. "Kostas Antetokounmpo." *Basketball Reference.* n.d. https://www.basketball-reference.com/players/a/antetko01.html.

346. "Giannis Antetokounmpo Named NBA's Most Valuable Player." *NBA.* June 24, 2019. https://www.nba.com/bucks/release/giannis-antetokounmpo-named-nbas-most-valuable-player.

347. Bauman, Jeremy. "The Pro-perspective of Giannis Antetokounmpo." *Draft Express.* December 6, 2016. http://www.draftexpress.com/profile/giannis-antetokounmpo-7223/.

348. "Giannis' Former Team Gym to Be Named 'AntetokounBros." *Eurohoops.* June 19, 2019. https://www.eurohoops.net/en/nba-news/899888/giannis-former-team-gym-to-be-named-antetokounbros/.

349. "Giannis Antetokounmpo Biography." *The Famous People.* n.d. https://www.thefamouspeople.com/profiles/giannis-antetokounmpo-16115.php.

350. "Giannis Antetokounmpo." *Basketball Reference*. n.d.
https://www.basketball-
reference.com/players/a/antetgi01.html.

351. "Thanasis Antetokounmpo." *Basketball Reference*. n.d.
https://www.basketball-
reference.com/players/a/antetth01.html

352. Wimbush, Jasmyn & Ward-Henninger, Colin. "NBA-China issue:
Latest news resulting from Hong-Kong tweet, what it
means for the league. *CBS Sports*. October 14, 2019.
https://www.cbssports.com/nba/news/nba-china-issue-
latest-news-resulting-from-daryl-moreys-hong-kong-tweet-
what-it-means-for-the-league/

Made in USA - North Chelmsford, MA
1036344_9781670469816
12.16.2019 0936